Liz Wells writes and lectures on photographic practices. She edited *The Photography Reader* (2003), and *Photography: A Critical Introduction* (2009, 4th edn) and is also co-editor of *Photographies*, the Routledge journals.

Exhibitions as curator include *Uneasy Spaces* (New York, 2006), *Facing East: Contemporary Landscape Photography from Baltic Areas* (UK tour, 2004–2007), *Chrystel Lebas and Sofija Silvia: Conversations on Nature* (Rijeka, Croatia, 2011) and *Landscapes of Exploration*, recent British art from Antarctica (forthcoming, 2012). Publications on landscape include Liz Wells, Kate Newton and Catherine Fehily, eds, *Shifting Horizons: Women's Landscape Photography Now* (2000). Essays on photographers exploring people and place include 'Silent Landscape', *EXIT* 38 (Spring 2010); 'Figures in a Landscape' in Trine Søndergaard and Nicolai Howalt, *How to Hunt* (2010); 'The Extraordinary Everyday', *Marte Aas* (2010) and 'Poetics and Silence', Jorma Puranen, *Icy Prospects* (2009).

She is Professor in Photographic Culture, Faculty of Arts, University of Plymouth, UK, and convenes the research group for Land/Water and the Visual Arts. www.landwater-research.co.uk

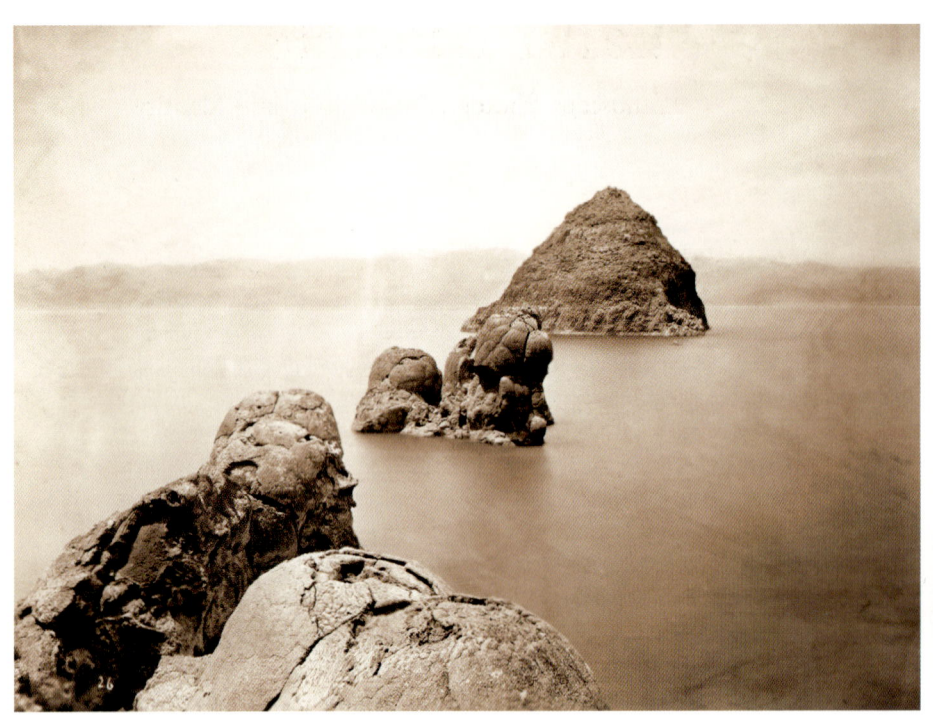

Timothy O'Sullivan, 'Tufa Domes, Pyramid Lake', Nevada, 1868.

Land Matters
Landscape Photography, Culture and Identity

Liz Wells

I.B. TAURIS
LONDON · NEW YORK

TR
660
.W 455
2011

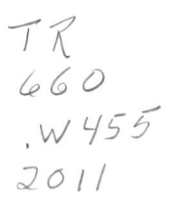

Published in 2011 by I.B.Tauris & Co Ltd
6 Salem Road, London W2 4BU
175 Fifth Avenue, New York NY 10010
www.ibtauris.com

Distributed in the United States and Canada Exclusively by Palgrave Macmillan
175 Fifth Avenue, New York NY 10010

Copyright © 2011 Liz Wells

The right of Liz Wells to be identified as the author of this work has been asserted by her in accordance with the Copyright, Designs and Patent Act 1988.

All rights reserved. Except for brief quotations in a review, this book, or any part thereof, may not be reproduced, stored in or introduced into a retrieval system, or transmitted, in any form or by any means, electronic, mechanical, photocopying, recording or otherwise, without the prior written permission of the publisher.

International Library of Cultural Studies 6

ISBN: 978 1 84511 864 8 (pb)
        978 1 84511 865 5 (hb)

A full CIP record for this book is available from the British Library
A full CIP record is available from the Library of Congress

Library of Congress Catalog Card Number: available

Typeset in Adobe Garamond Pro by Free Range Book Design & Production Limited
Printed and bound in Spain

CONTENTS

List of Illustrations   vii
Preface   xv
Acknowledgements   xvii

Introduction   1

1. Landscape: Time, Space, Place, Aesthetics   19

2. A North American Place: Land and Settlement   59

3. After the Frontier: Environment and the West   107

4. Pastoral Heritage: Britain Viewed through a Critical Lens   161

5. Views from the North: Landscape, Photography and National Identity   211

6. Sense of Location: Topography, Journey, Memory   261

Notes   303
Bibliography   313
General Index   323
Index of Illustrations   331

You can't depend on your eyes when your imagination is out of focus.

Mark Twain, 1889

Sometimes Alice felt tall, able to see the things around her, confident in occupying her space – except occasionally when she bumped her head on the ceiling and remembered not to take anything for granted. Sometimes she felt small, insignificant and imperceptible relative to the place and circumstances around her. That was the nature of Wonderland.

Lewis Carroll, *Alice in Wonderland*, 1865

ILLUSTRATIONS

Frontispiece: Timothy O'Sullivan, 'Tufa Domes, Pyramid Lake', Nevada, 1868. Credit: Courtesy George Eastman House, International Museum of Photography and Film.   ii

CHAPTER 1

Peter Kennard, 'Hay Wain with Cruise Missiles', 1980. Published in *Camerawork*, London, July 1980 to illustrate an essay by E.P. Thompson on 'The State of the Nation'. Credit: Peter Kennard.   18

Roger Fenton, 'The Long Walk', Windsor, 1860. Credit: The Royal Collection © 2008, Her Majesty Queen Elizabeth II.   29

Lynn Silverman, 'Horizon No. 9', Outside Packsaddle, New South Wales, from the series *Horizons*, 1981. Credit: Lynn Silverman.   42

Wright Morris, 'Haystack', near Norfolk, Nebraska, 1947. Credit: Collection Center for Creative Photography, University of Arizona © 2003 Arizona Board of Regents.   52

CHAPTER 2

John Pfahl, 'Great Falls of the Passaic', Paterson, New Jersey, 1988, from the series *Waterfalls*. Credit: Janet Borden Gallery, NYC.   58

Deborah Bright, 'Lucky Pennies', from the series *Glacial Erratic*, 2003. Credit: Deborah Bright.   70

'Turner Ashby, of Fauquier City, Virginia, age 33, was photographed after being killed here', 6 June 1862, Harrisonburg, Virginia. Credit: Chicago Historical Society.   76

LAND MATTERS

John Huddleston, 'The Center of the Battlefield', 130 American
Casualties, Harrisonburg, Virginia. From the series *Killing Ground*,
2000. Credit: John Huddleston. 77

William Earle Williams, '5th Infantry New Hampshire Monument',
1986, from the series *Gettysburg*, 1997. Credit: William Earle Williams. 78

Sally Mann, 'No. 6', from the series *Deep South*, 1998. Credit: Sally Mann. 80

Marlene Creates, 'Rosie Webb, Labrador, 1988', from the series
The Distance Between Two Points is Measured in Memories. Credit:
Collection: MacKenzie Art Gallery, Regina, Canada. 83

Janet Pritchard, 'Abandoned Field with Glacial Stone', from the series
Dwelling: Expressions of Time, 2003. Credit: Janet Pritchard. 85

Kilburn Brothers, 'R R Trains on Mt. Washington'. Credit: Courtesy
George Eastman House, International Museum of Photography and Film. 88

Kilburn Brothers, 'Echo Lake, Francona Notch'. Credit: Courtesy George
Eastman House, International Museum of Photography and Film. 92

John Pfahl, 'Music 1, Elliotsville, New York', May 1974, from the series
Altered Landscapes. Credit: Janet Borden Gallery, NYC. 94

MANUAL, 'Et in Arcadia Ego: Observer and Tomb, 1998', from the
series *Arcadia Project*. Credit: Ed Hill and Suzanne Bloom. 98

Joann Brennan, 'Electro-shocking for Apache Trout on the West Fork of
the Black River, Apache Trout Project', Arizona, September 2003, from
the series *Managing Eden*. Credit: Joann Brennan. 100

Ron Jude, 'Plain St., Ithaca, NY', from the series *Landscapes (for Antoine)*,
2000. Credit: Jackson Fine Art, Atlanta. 101

Jeff Wall, 'Steves Farm, Steveston', 1980. Credit: Jeff Wall. Courtesy
Marian Goodman Gallery, New York. 104

CHAPTER 3

Richard Misrach, 'The Santa Fe', from the series *Desert Canto I: The
Terrain*, 1982. Credit: Fraenkel Gallery, San Francisco; Pace/MacGill,
New York; Marc Selwyn Fine Arts, Los Angeles. 106

LIST OF ILLUSTRATIONS

Evelyn Cameron, 'Sheep Crossing on Scott's Ferry', Yellowstone River, 1905. Credit: The Montana Historical Society. 116

Richard Prince, from the series *Untitled (cowboys)* 1980–86. Credit: © Richard Prince. Courtesy Gladstone Gallery, New York. 118

Arthur Renwick, 'MO-TA-VAH-TO (Black Kettle)', from the series *Delegates: Chiefs of the Earth and Sky*, 2004. Credit: Arthur Renwick. Courtesy Leo Kamen Gallery, Toronto, Canada. 120

Joel Sternfeld, 'Mount Rushmore National Monument', Black Hills National Forest, South Dakota, August 1994. Credit: Joel Sternfeld and Luhring Augustine, New York. 123

Kilburn Brothers, 'Cloud's Rest', Yosemite, Cal. Credit: Courtesy George Eastman House, International Museum of Photography and Film. 127

Mark Klett for the Rephotographic Survey Project, 1978. Six views of Monument Rock, Canyon de Chelly, AZ. Credit: Mark Klett. 131

Rick Dingus, 'Tertiary Conglomerates (Witches Rocks No. 5)', 1978. Credit: Rick Dingus for the Rephotographic Survey Project. Collection of Rick Dingus. 133

Ansel Adams, 'Half Dome and Moon', Yosemite, 1960. Credit: Collection Center for Creative Photography, University of Arizona © Trustees of The Ansel Adams Publishing Rights Trust. 139

John Ganis, 'Earthmover', Texarkana, Texas, 1984, from the series *Consuming the American Landscape*. Credit: John Ganis. 141

Robert Adams, 'Fort Collins', Colorado, 1976, from the series *Summer Nights*. Credit: © Robert Adams. Courtesy Fraenkel Gallery, San Francisco and Matthew Marks Gallery, New York. 144

Frank Gohlke, *Grain Elevators*, Series 1, No. 26 – Minneapolis 1973. Credit: Frank Gohlke and Howard Greenberg Gallery. 145

Terry Evans, 'Field Museum, Echinaccea, 1899', 2001, from the series *Prairie Specimens*. Credit: Terry Evans. 148

Terry Evans, 'Field Museum, Spartina, 1857', 2000, from the series *Prairie Specimens*. Credit: Terry Evans. 148

Peter Goin, 'Artificial Boulders', from the series *Humanature*, 1996.
Credit: Peter Goin. 149

Wanda Hammerbeck, 'Confluence of Arroyo Calabasas & Bell Creek Canyon', 1991, The Headwaters of the Los Angeles River. Credit: Wanda Hammerbeck. 151

Robert Dawson, 'Party with Rainbow at Hot Springs', the Needles, Pyramid Lake, Nevada, 1989, from *A Doubtful River*. Credit: Aperture Images. 154

Karen Halverson, 'Valley Oak Tree, Cosumnes River Preserve', California, 2000, from the series *Trees*. Credit: Karen Halverson. 156

CHAPTER 4

Karen Knorr, 'Frontiers of Utopia', from the series *The Virtues and the Delights*, 1992. Credit: Karen Knorr. 160

Paul Hill, 'Paths and Mineshafts', No. 1, Bradbourne, from the series *On Land*, 1979. Credit: Paul Hill. 169

John Davies, 'Bargoed Viaduct', Rhymney Valley, Mid Glamorgan, 1984, from the series *A Green and Pleasant Land*. Credit: John Davies. 171

James Ravilious, From the series *An English Eye*, 1974–1986.
Credit: James Ravilious for the Beaford Archive © Beaford Arts. 173

Chris Wainwright, 'Teesside', from the series *Futureland*, 1989. Credit: Chris Wainwright, work in the collection of Middlesbrough City Council. 177

John Kippin, 'The Visit', 2000, from the series *Compton Verney*. Credit: John Kippin. 179

John Darwell, 'Hadrian's Wall', from the series *Dark Days*, 2001. Credit: John Darwell. 180

Anthony Haughey, 'Shotgun Cartridges', Armagh/Louth Border, 2006, from the series *Disputed Border*. Credit: Anthony Haughey. 182

Jo Spence and Terry Dennett, 'Industrialisation', from the series *Re-Modelling Photo-History*, 1982. Credit: Jo Spence Memorial Archive, London. 187

LIST OF ILLUSTRATIONS

Fay Godwin, *Land*, publication, 1985. Credit: Courtesy British Library Board, FG3137-4-16.   190

Ingrid Hesling, 'Creek', 1994, from the series *Anarchy in Arcady*. Credit: Ingrid Hesling.   191

Su Grierson, 'Torness', 2001, from the Exhibition, *Eyeshine*. Credit: Su Grierson.   192

Sian Bonnell, 'Scrub', No. 1, 1999, from the series *when the domestic meets the wild*. Credit: Sian Bonnell.   194

Gina Glover, 'Pram', 1998, from the series *Pathways to Memory*. Credit: Gina Glover.   195

Andrea Liggins, Untitled, from the series *Uncertain Terrain*, 2003. Credit: Andrea Liggins.   198

Helen Sear, 'No. 13', from the series *Inside the View*, 2005–07. Credit: Helen Sear.   199

Susan Trangmar, 'Constellation IV', from the series *Suspended States*, 1992. Credit: Susan Trangmar.   201

Roshini Kempadoo, video still from *Ghosting*, 2004. Installation shot, Susanne Ramsenthaler, New York, 2006. Credits: Roshini Kempadoo; Susanne Ramsenthaler.   207

CHAPTER 5

Jorma Puranen; No. 18, 2005, from the series *Icy Prospects*. Credit: Jorma Puranen and Galerie Anhava.   210

Knud Knudsen, 'Parti fra Odda I Hardanger' (An area of Odda, Hardanger), 4 June 1863. Credit: Photographer: Knud Knudsen, University of Bergen Library, the Picture Collection.   219

Petter Magnusson, 'Explosion', No. 1, 2002, from the series *1/3*. Credit: Petter Magnusson.   222

Ane Hjort Guttu, 'Untitled' (Romsas, Oslo), from the series *Modernistic Journey*, 2002. Credit: Ane Hjort Guttu.   224

Mikkel McAlinden, 'The Evil Cottage', 2000. Credit: Mikkel
McAlinden. 226

Lars Tunbjörk, 'Öland', 1991, from the series *Landet utom sig* (Country
Beside Itself). Credit: Galerie Vu, Paris. 228

Margareta Klingberg, 'Åtjärnlider', 2001, from the series *On the Move*.
Credit: Margareta Klingberg. 230

Joakim Eskildsen, 'The Road', 2001, from the series *Requiem*. Credit:
Joakim Eskildsen. 231

Kirsten Klein, 'Raincloud above Draaby Dove', Winter, 1994. Credit:
Kirsten Klein. 232

Per Bak Jensen, 'Seamark', 2006, from the series *Greenland*. Credit:
© Per Bak Jensen, Galleri Bo Bjerggaard. 234

Remigijus Treigys, 'Signs 2', 2001. Credit: Remigijus Treigys. 239

Herkki-Erich Merila, 'Lunaatika II', 2000, from the series *Lunaatika*.
Credit: Herkki-Erich Merila. 241

Juha Suonpää, 'The photographer standing on the hut', Kuhmo
Finland, 1994, from the series *The Beastly Image of the Beast*. Credit:
Juha Suonpää. 244

Ritva Kovalainen and Sanni Seppo, 'Memorial trees in Pyhakangas', 1997,
from the series *Tree People*. Credit: Ritva Kovalainen and Sanni Seppo. 245

(Martti) Kapa (Kapanen), 'Kaustinen', from the series *After Ski*,
1998–2002. Credit: Kapa. 247

Ilkha Halso, 'Untitled 6', from the series *Restoration*, 2001. Credit:
Ilkha Halso. 248

Marja Pirelä, 'Sarianna', Tampere, 1996, from the series *Interior/
Exterior*. Credit: Marja Pirelä. 249

Martti Jämsä, *Summertime*, 2002. Credit: Martti Jämsä. 251

Jari Silomäki, 'Untitled', from the series *My Weather Diary*, 2001–07.
Credit: Jari Silomäki. 256

LIST OF ILLUSTRATIONS

Riitta Päiväläinen, 'Relation', from the series *Vestige – Ice*, 2001. Credit: Riitta Päiväläinen.   258

CHAPTER 6

Jem Southam, 'River Hayle January 2000', from the series *Rockfalls, Rivermouths and Ponds*. Credit: Jem Southam.   260

Lewis Baltz, 'Prospector Village, Lot 65, Looking Northwest', Salt Lake City, 1978–79. Credit: © Lewis Baltz/V&A Images, London [Museum No: PH.277-1983].   269

Hilla and Bernd Becher, 'Water Towers', 1980. Credit: Courtesy Sonnabend Gallery.   270

Kate Mellor, from the series *Island: Sea Front*, 1989–94. Credit: Kate Mellor.   272

Mark Power, four pictures from *26 Different Endings*, 2003–05. Credit: Mark Power.   274

Jem Southam, 'Red Mudstone, Sidmouth', 1995–97, from the series *Rockfalls, Rivermouths and Ponds*. Credit: Jem Southam.   276

Ingrid Pollard, from *Hidden Histories, Heritage Stories*, 1994. Credit: Ingrid Pollard and Lea Valley Park Authority.   277

Olafur Eliasson, *The Green River Series*, 1998. Credit: Olafur Eliasson; Tanya Bonakdar Gallery, New York; Neugerriemschneider, Berlin. Photo: Oren Slor.   278–9

Doris Frohnapfel, *Border Horizons – Photographs from Europe*. Credit: Krings-Ernst Gallery, Cologne.   283

Richard Long, 'All Ireland Walk', 1995. Credit: Courtesy Haunch of Venison © Richard Long.   287

Thomas Joshua Cooper, 'Unexpected Nightfall, The Mid North Atlantic Ocean', Porto Moniz, The Isle of Madeira (near the north-most point of the Island), Portugal, 2002. Credit: Courtesy Haunch of Venison.   293

xiii

Susan Derges, 'Larch', from the series *The Streens*, 2003. Credit:
Susan Derges. 295

Ori Gersht, 'In Line', from the series *Liquidation*, 2005. Credit:
Ori Gersht. 298

Ann Chwatsky, 'WHEN I WAS A GIRL, I Kept Separate', 2006,
from the series *WHEN I WAS A GIRL*. Credit: Ann Chwatsky. 300

PREFACE

In 1992 I visited Rotterdam to see *Wasteland*, a major international exhibition of photography relating to land and environment. Seven British photographers were included, none of whom were women. This led to various animated discussions about women and landscape photography, which became the start of a longer investigation into landscape traditions in Britain and elsewhere. This book thus results from many years of interest in landscape photography, provoked initially from questioning why there seemed to be relatively few women landscape photographers working in Britain in the 1980s and 90s. This questioning led to curatorial involvement in two exhibitions on British-based women landscape photographers, namely, *Viewfindings: Women Photographers, 'Landscape' and Environment* (1994) and *Shifting Horizons: Women's Landscape Photography Now* (2000); it also led to *Facing East: Contemporary Landscape Photography from Baltic Areas* (2004). Some of my happiest times have been spent in studio visits, exhibitions and archives, viewing and discussing photographic imagery (including video) that variously reflects upon land and environment.

Why should this be of interest? In the 1990s landscape, as a genre, was generally not fore-grounded within debates which, at that time, were very preoccupied with the import and impact of digital modes of photography. Yet photographers persist in exploring place in terms of histories, geographies and geologies, focusing on the interaction of people and environment and on shifting ecologies. In the 2000s, with widespread concerns relating to environmental change, imagery relating to land and place has re-emerged with renewed socio-political orientation. Related to this is a developing body of critical literature within which this book is intended to contribute. It brings together ideas and research pursued between 1993 and 2006. The manuscript was completed in December 2007; it does not take into account several interesting papers and bodies of work that have come into the public domain since then.

Why is land and environment of particular interest to me? I have come to acknowledge quite deep-seated motivations and curiosities. I was born and spent my childhood in inner west London. My familiarity with 'landscape' was largely restricted to London parks, summer drives to 'countryside', occasional holidays by car to France, Switzerland or North Italy, and seaside holidays in Sussex and, later, Normandy, where I stayed with a French family who had a home on the coast. I loved being there, enjoying the beach and exploring the lanes, even though my English was not up to naming most of the vegetation, let alone my French. The woods were sometimes scary, the weather could be awesome, the cliff paths steep and challenging, and I never did manage the water-skiing. Yet I can still hear the echoes of the cicadas as we walked down to the beach of an evening. My pen-friend's father ran the orchard; her mother picked mushrooms, and fresh shellfish from rock pools; at night her older brother and friends used to go off *à la chasse* (not strictly legal!). Products of their enterprise would be consumed the next day – a rather different approach to food gathering than doing the shopping in London. There was also an amalgam of local histories and social mores that was difficult to grasp, especially as memories of wartime occupation were not far from the surface. In short, I discovered that rural areas were very much more complex and interesting than the romanticisation of animals and countryside that informed Shell posters, 'Uncle Mac' and children's books – although Grimm's fairytales do pick up this undertow. My interest in landscape imagery thus has root in curiosity about the 'otherness' of countryside that interacted with a fascination with Frenchness as 'difference', for which the evidence was derived from my annual month in the country on the Normandy coast.

I now live in Southeast Devon, an area characterised by craggy red cliffs. Echoes, perhaps, of the Normandy *falaises*.

ACKNOWLEDGEMENTS

I should acknowledge many discussions about landscape photography with all those, nationally and internationally, whose work has been included in books I have edited and exhibitions that I have curated. I must stress that this book is not an overview; there are many photographers/artists whose ideas have influenced my thinking, whose company I have enjoyed, but whose work is not specifically referenced – the range of examples of critical practices is simply too extensive to be encompassed in one book. There are also areas of the world that I have not touched upon but that I know include photographers whose work is interesting and challenging in terms of engagement with land and environment.

I should also thank staff and students involved with the Land/Water and the Visual Arts research group at the University of Plymouth, a source of many interesting events and discussions. I am very grateful for the support of colleagues, particularly Liz Nicol and Jem Southam and also to the many friends with whom, over the years, I've had interesting and lively discussions about place, land and landscape. Naming names is invidious – there is always a sense of having failed to mention someone crucial – but I am particularly grateful to David Bate, Deborah Bright, Ann Chwatsky, Ingrid Pollard, Derrick Price, Jorma Puranen, Shirley Read and Elizabeth Williams for various conversations since the mid-1990s. Several chapter sections were first explored through various conference papers; I am grateful for the comments, feedback and references that participants generously shared.

The book would not have happened without the help and support of staff at I.B.Tauris, especially my editors, Philippa Brewster and Susan Lawson ,and production team, Paul Tompsett and Cecile Rault. I am specifically grateful to the University of Plymouth for funding the extra costs incurred in colour reproduction. Particular thanks are due to the many photographers whose work is illustrated. I am also hugely indebted to Claire Carter and to Kate Isherwood, who between them undertook the massive job of sorting out permissions and collating images for reproduction.

The University of Plymouth supported study leave in 2003, and an AHRC small grant in that year facilitated travel in Scandinavia and the Baltic States to research my exhibition, *Facing East*, thereby enabling engagement with materials later used in Chapter 5. I should also thank all the curators and archivists – too many to name – who have given me so much time and help on various research trips; these include staff at George Eastman House, Rochester; Center for Creative Photography, Tucson; Knud Knudsen collection, Bergen; the Photography Museum, Helsinki; Hasselblad Foundation, Gothenburg.

Finally, none of this could have been thought through, let alone written, without the formative and provocative context of feminist, post-structuralist and post-colonial debates that fostered my thinking about visual practices.

Liz Wells

INTRODUCTION

> The camera eye is the one in the middle of our forehead, combining how we see with what there is to be seen.
>
> (Wright Morris, 1999: 11)

> … to supply a production apparatus without trying, within the limits of the possible, to change it, is a highly disputable activity even when the material supplied appears to be of a revolutionary nature. For we are confronted with the fact … that the bourgeois apparatus of production and publication is capable of assimilating, indeed of propagating, an astonishing amount of revolutionary themes without ever seriously putting into question its own continued existence or that of the class which owns it.
>
> (Benjamin, 1977: 94)

'Land Matters' is a play on words: taken rhetorically, it means that land is important; taken literally, the phrase references business relating to land. It also refers to the 'matter' or substance of land, to soil chemistry. This book is concerned with ways in which photographers engage issues about land, its representation and idealisation. Representation of land as landscape, whether in romantic or in more topographic modes, reflects and reinforces contemporary political, social and environmental attitudes. This is seated within and influences cultural identity, which can be defined as a complex and fluid articulation of the subjective and the collective that draws into play a range of factors such as class, gender, ethnicity, nationality, but is by no means limited to these social formations.

Landscape is a social product; particular landscapes tell us something about cultural histories and attitudes. Landscape results from human intervention to shape or transform natural phenomena, of which we are simultaneously a part. A basic useful definition of landscape thus would be *vistas encompassing both nature and the changes that humans have effected on the natural world*. But, in considering human agency in relation to land and landscape we also need to bear in mind that, biologically, we are an integral element within the ecosystem. Such considerations, whether framed in terms, for instance, of bio-forensics, or of Buddhist epistemologies, cannot be addressed here. Suffice it to note that our relation to the environment in which we find ourselves, and of which we form a part, is multiply constituted: the real, perceptions of the real, the imaginary, the symbolic, memory and experience, form a complex tapestry at the heart of our response to our environment, and, by extension, to landscape imagery.

SPACE AND PLACE

Discussing *Landscape and Power* W.J.T. Mitchell argued that landscape is best used not as a noun, but as a verb, 'to landscape' (Mitchell, 1994). This acts as a useful reminder that landscape results from human action, whether from direct intervention to make changes on the land (town planning, landscape architecture, gardening …), or from exploring how land might be represented (in writing, art, film, photography, or everyday journalism and casual conversation). To 'landscape' is to impose a certain order. Landscaping involves working with natural phenomena. Environmental interventions anticipate natural change and development: growth of trees and plants; weathering of buildings, furniture, statues; animal behaviour; erosion of the earth by rain, river or sea; and so on. Assumptions may also be made about social uses of designed places (parks, gardens, picnic spots …). Plans are predicated on imagining types of land use, landscape and social environment that might be constructed. Whether industrial, agricultural or domestic, urban, suburban or rural, space is (trans-)formed into place through such interventions.

'Space' is conceptually complex and etymologically slippery (sometimes apparently contradictory). It may refer to that which is not known, and thus cannot be precisely categorised (for instance, 'outer space'). It may reference expanses of land, or of time, with potential – as in 'space' for development, 'space' to play, 'space' to think … 'Living space' or 'play space' indicate determinate areas within which function is specified (but precise use – lifestyle, or games played – may be fluid). Excursions into mountains, desert, across seas, to remote islands or regions, to 'wilderness', may be seen as offering 'space' for self-replenishment.[1]

Space also refers to that which exists between the determinate; for instance, distance between identifiable geographical points, or the interval between words or lines on a page, or gaps left open for specific functions. This in-betweenness may be categorical (measurable), or, following French philosopher and linguist Jacques Derrida, it may be taken as an arena of slippages testifying to the fluidity of meaning. 'Space' flows around the determinant, the quantifiable, inducing metaphysical unboundedness, the poetic, indeterminacy, voidness. To be void is to be meaningless, to lack designation. In semiotic terms, a void functions relationally through lending meaning to that which surrounds it – for example, space beyond the edge of a mountain peak or cliff transforms the land edge into precipice (and lends urgency to holding that ground). Voidness involves existential incomprehensibility; to 'touch the void' is to risk the trauma of uncertainty.

The act of naming is an act of taming. In Western culture, describing space as desert, or wilderness, or planet, represents potential comprehensibility and cues scientific and philosophical enquiry. By naming I mean both the terming of a space as, for example, wilderness, and the naming of such space, for example, Antarctica. Naming turns space into place. Once named we no longer view somewhere as unknowable – although as yet relatively little may be known. Likewise, of course, *familiar* places are those that have come to seem 'known'. There is a political dimension: for instance, 'wilderness' or 'outer space' may also be seen as that which has not yet been territorialised economically, geographically or astronomically.

Geography, through naming and investigation, crucially contributes to defining place. Geo means earth, so geo-graphy literally means earth 'drawing', encompassing diagrams, maps, graphs, writings and photographs. Geography is concerned with knowledge about place, communicable in various modes, including the pictorial. Landscape as a genre within visual art shares investigative concerns with geography and feeds into geographic imagination. As has been acknowledged in recent developments in cultural geography, space is rendered into place through representation, the domain of the cartographers and artists, as well as writers and storytellers; through their maps and charts draughtsmen and women contributed to developing pictorial semiotics. From its inception photography has been involved in investigating and detailing environments, helping culture to appropriate nature. Just as it is the responsibility of philosophers to think about how we think, artists, including photographers, along with art theorists, have responsibility to consider how we picture, to reflect upon the implications of thinking through the visual.

SPACE AND REPRESENTATION

The pictorial offers more than graphic representation. It articulates subjective memory and cultural currencies not only in relation to literal readings of images but also in terms of emotive affects. We may look at a picture, which is essentially mute, yet respond to sounds associated with the type of scene depicted. A form of sensory memory resonates, enhancing our pleasure in reverie; the geographic imaginary conjured up is complex. In discussing *The Poetics of Space*, Gaston Bachelard emphasised the relation between the experiential, the real, and the imaginary (Bachelard, 1994). In this series of essays he distances himself from French (structuralist) philosophy, which he critiques for its lack of interest in the distinction between mind and what he terms 'soul' that is evident in the German tradition. Bachelard's enquiry into human response to space sits alongside discussions of beauty and the sublime that have been central to art theory. He explores what he terms 'topophilia' in relation to human desire for the comfort of familiar spaces, wondering at the subjective processes whereby certain spaces – or images of such spaces – come to reassure. His starting point is the human imaginary, and that which cannot be cast in terms of logic, words or explanation, but which induces depth of sensory response to the extent that an image or feeling resonates and haunts. Such experience is essentially subjective, and, since such a poetic imaginary resists definitive communication, it is difficult to know to what extent sensory affects echo similarly or differently for each of us. He explores the phenomenological import of poetic imagery, resisting reductionist containment in terms of the scientific, semiotic or psychoanalytic. This poses problems for relevant, academic explanatory systems, more at ease within the systematic, the logical. At the same time he is concerned to explore emotional ramifications of sensory responses which elide precise definition. He explores ways in which art enhances experience, viewing art as significantly more than mere representation. He suggests that to read poetry is to daydream. Likewise, perhaps, contemplating photographs. Bachelard locates himself slightly apart from contemporary French philosophy although, epistemologically, his position in some respects parallels the distinction that French feminist philosopher, Julia Kristeva, makes between the systematic and the poetic, suggesting that the latter disrupts the former. Where they differ, of course, is in her concern with gender traits; for Kristeva it is the 'feminine' operations of poetics that interfere with patriarchal social order (see Chapter 4).

In Western philosophy, culture and nature have been posited as a binary with culture viewed as superseding, and thereby repressing, nature. There has also been an association of the masculine with culture, and the feminine with nature. But culture and nature are complexly inter-related, as, indeed, are masculinity and femininity. Nature is both 'internal', fundamental to what constitutes us as human, and 'out there' in that we experience the external world through the senses, including sight. Writing on reason, in the mid-seventeenth century, the philosopher, René Descartes, posited an ontological separation of mind and body, which in turn supported the notion that the human subject is existentially separate from phenomena perceivable through the senses. Cartesian thinking emphasises ego-centrality as each individually encounters and attempts to make sense of experience. In this formulation 'nature' becomes a source of pleasure and bewilderment experienced through touch, taste, smell, hearing and sight. Implicit within this approach is the suggestion that whilst we experience sensation bodily our rational mind retains an observational and analytic stance.

The representation of nature, in still life or in landscape, offers opportunities for extended contemplation of scenes and scenarios. But landscape pictures, composed in accordance with the rules of perspective, offer a single, central viewing position; this draws upon and contributes to reaffirming the Cartesian – and Catholic – emphasis on unique subjectivity. Spectatorship becomes, in effect, a symbolic exercise of control – of mind over matter – articulated via the pleasures of contemplation. But the pleasure of looking carries inherent risk as images of less benign aspects of nature may invoke more sublime insecurities. Desire, awe of natural phenomena, drive to subdue nature, fear of loss of control, all variously play within the contradictory delights of looking at images that disturb. Imagery feeds our desire for a clear sense of identity and of cultural belonging; critical imagery may question that previously accepted. This is a continuous process of apprehension and reassurance, especially since identity is neither uniform, nor fixed, and is constantly subject to challenge and shift. In other words, any sense of self-location through the contemplation of the photographic image is temporary. Indeed, desire for reassurance may be one of the factors propelling us to keep on making and looking at images. In addition, in terms of a politics of representation, imagery offers us ways of comprehending phenomena and experiences; photographic perceptions influence ways of seeing. For this reason *what* is represented, *how* it is represented, and *who* has the power to represent constitute contested terrain.

The content of images may seem natural. But representational and interpretative processes are cultural in that they are anchored in aesthetic conventions. Photographs substitute for direct encounter; they act as surrogates, mediating that which was seen through the camera viewfinder. Visuality, that is, systems of seeing, operates through codes and conventionalised meanings. Conventions are not entirely arbitrary. Pictorial constructs echo human vision. On a clear day, viewed from sea level, the horizon is just under five kilometers away; this is a function of the curve of the earth. It appears linear, *horizontal*; the etymology is not coincidence! Leonardo da Vinci posited human desire for order, and considered ways in which this is reflected in aesthetic modes. Mediaeval draughtsman, Leon Alberti, drawing on the architectural principles explored by Filippo Brunelleschi, achieved a geometric method of simulating perspective; it became the means of representational construction central to landscape aesthetics. Again, this is not an arbitrary conceit. The camera obscura, and, indeed, the reflection on the wall in Plato's cave caused by light entering through a hole, both suggest that perspective as a basis for visual organisation is founded in a natural effect – it is what light does if siphoned through a gap. The golden mean (or golden rule) central to the representation of land as landscape since the Renaissance is likewise founded in natural phenomena. Imagine being at sea; in calm conditions the horizon appears about one-third of the way up in our line of vision. The sky dominates within the pictorial plane. On land, mountains, trees and other phenomena may protrude into the space of the sky, but the rule of thirds may still form the primary representational structure. Three is a primary number – it cannot be sub-divided. The conventional division of the picture plane into horizontal thirds and vertical halves articulates mathematical fundamentals. The pictorial system is premised upon order and harmony.

Landscape as a cultural concept thus reflects both perception (how we have come to 'see' and relate to our surroundings) and practical interventions in terms of land usage (agrarian, industrial, architectural, and so on). Artists are variously positioned in relation to this. Sculptors and land artists, for instance, may employ natural materials or intervene physically within a particular place. This study is concerned with photography, specifically with contemporary critical landscape practices. This begs the question, 'why photography?', especially as painting, sculpture, land art and domestic design all play their part in representation, in questioning aesthetic conventions and in exploring politics of land. Photography is the field that I know best. Besides which, the stakes are especially high in terms of photographic intervention for a number of reasons. Most particularly, photographs are afforded an authority, founded in the authenticity that has been ascribed to the photographic since its inception (not accorded to painterly or sculptural practices – although, of course, also accorded to film and video when they purport to be documentary). In French the lens is an *objectif*. Despite the advent of the digital a sense of authenticity remains implicated. This sense of authority adheres and supports photographic imagery across a range of spheres, from the everyday snapshot to photojournalism or pictures and projects seriously researched for gallery and book publication. As I shall argue (Chapter 6), this is founded in the professional authority of the photographer, rather than in the medium. The topographic dimension of landscape photography strongly supports documentary testimony, but there is a general fascination with photographs that draws on indexicality, that is, the apparently unmediated relation with scenarios and phenomena. The spectator, even if highly tutored in the effects of aesthetic and photographic coding and of the judgements that must have been exercised by the photographer, still at one level looks 'through' the representation at that depicted. Photography is thus powerful in contributing to specifying spaces as particular sorts of places. It constructs a point of view, a way of seeing which is underpinned by the authority of the literal. Through re-deploying this constructed sense of authenticity photography can be equally powerful as a means of interrogating environment through experimentation and critical exposures.

In his essay on 'Truth and Landscape' Robert Adams remarks that,

> Landscape pictures can offer us … three verities – geography, autobiography, and metaphor. Geography is, if taken alone, sometimes boring, autobiography is frequently trivial, and metaphor can be

dubious. But taken together, as in the best work of people like Alfred Stieglitz and Edward Weston, the three kings of information strengthen each other and reinforce what we all work to keep intact – an affection for life.

(Adams, 1996: 14)

Rereading Adams' essay as I came towards the end of writing *Land Matters* I was struck by the extent to which his linkage of geography, autobiography and metaphor fits with the examples that I have chosen to explore in this book. The subtitle of his collection, *Beauty in Photography*, in which this essay appears, is 'Essays in Defense of Traditional Values'. The collection was published by Aperture which, whilst a central player in the production of photography books – critical writings as well as work by photographers – would not immediately be associated with more edgy theoretical speculations or with avant-garde practices. Does this mean then, after about fifteen years of thinking about land and landscape photography, I have ended up subscribing to traditional values? Perhaps yes; but for the humanist reasons that probably initially impelled my interest in land and landscape, namely, curiosity about ways in which we, as transient individuals, relate to our environment which, although changing seasonally and adjusting over time, is ultimately longer-standing than us. Such reflections, however, are not disassociated from the socio-political. We impact on our environment, constraining natural phenomena, managing social and environmental change, causing physical, botanical, chemical and meteorological shifts of varying import. From small acts such as re-routing local village paths (with implications for hedgerow habitation) to larger decisions such as developing industrial 'parks' with, as we now acknowledge, troublesome legacies in terms of fuel consumption, emissions and global warming, we impact on the holistic integrity of localities.

Photography works very directly in terms of geography, autobiography and metaphor, but mapped over this are questions of theme, form and politics that anchor image-making in relation to contemporary issues, and in terms of aesthetics. For the most part, photographers belong to the stream of visual arts wherein the primary drive has been observation rather than intervention (although land artists, such as Andy Goldsworthy or Richard Long, use photography as an outcome of intervention). Photographers look at and note what they see, and in so doing comment on what there is to be viewed and – by extension – offer a response to external phenomena. As Edward Weston remarked:

> Photography as a creative expression – or what you will – must be seeing plus. Seeing alone means factual recording. Photography is not at all seeing in the sense that the eyes see. Our vision is binocular, it is in a continuous state of flux, while the camera captures but a single isolated condition of the moment. Besides, we use lenses of various focal lengths to purposely exaggerate actual seeing; we 'overcorrect' color for the same reason. In printing we carry our willful distortion of fact – 'seeing' – by using papers to intensify the contrast of the original scene or object. This is all legitimate procedure; but it is not seeing literally, it is seeing with intention, with reason.[2]
>
> (Weston, 1932)

'Seeing plus' as thus described, reminds us that photography is rhetorical and that photographers use a range of tactics in order to add emphasis to their observations. Photographs may seem more-or-less critical in condoning or questioning histories of place and notions associated with landscape but, as Weston indicates, it is never neutral as the deployment of aesthetic and photographic codes reflects decisions taken by the photographer.

RESEARCH MODELS AND METHODS

My discussion develops through critical appraisal of examples of work by selected contemporary photographers. The book is not a survey of the book is not a survey of contemporary landscape photography. Rather, it is a set of questions, and speculations are explored through critical appraisal of specific series or bodies of work. Many of the photographers whose work is discussed have twin careers as artists and as university professors. But my interest is not in their formal status; it is in the ways in which their approach may be characterised as interventionist. They variously engage or question hegemonic notions and processes relating to space, place, land and environment. I am interested in aesthetic and practical strategies whereby artists bring critical perspectives to bear on what may be quite well-worn subjects or traditions. It follows that I am interested in approaches to researching and clarifying projects; also in ways in which contexts influence, facilitate or limit work both as it is being produced and in relation to sites and processes of reception and interpretation. Several of the artists whose work most captures my attention are notable for their emphasis not only on research and pre-visualisation, but also on *listening* to what people have to say about familiar environments. Artists collect, log and sift through a diversity of information about places in order to deepen the insights that will inform photographic method and processes. They are not journalists going in and getting the shot; rather they are storytellers whose depth of research and analysis is reflected in the philosophic perceptions and visual rhetorical strategies which characterise their picture-making. Most of the examples discussed are intended for gallery, book and/or web publication. They are generally reflective in mode; landscape photographs rarely 'shout', rather, they are quietly assertive.

In order to evaluate the import of contemporary work we need to locate it in historical context both in respect of landscape and aesthetics, and in terms of cultural characteristics, concerns and priorities. This is, of course, vast. All that can be done here is to indicate some of the issues that have resonated historically and that contribute to the currencies reinflected through a particular imagery. Work is discussed with some reference to broader historical and (popular) cultural contexts – I am interested in stories told and how these intersect and resonate with the multiplicities of other stories and perspectives in play.

In analysing photographs and assessing photographic projects we are primarily interested in ways in which content, metaphor and form come together to provoke questions of history, representation and identity. Key examples considered include work from North America, Britain and Ireland, Scandinavia and Baltic areas, dating from the final decades of the twentieth century and early years of the twenty-first. I want to suggest that there is a critical tendency within landscape photography that has irrevocably changed our understanding of the genre. First, the extent to which landscape imagery relates, and has always related, to questions of class, nationhood, heritage and identity has been clearly exposed through questioning more established ways of seeing and representing land. Second, developments in landscape aesthetics in parts of the Western world indicate a widespread critical evaluation of the relation between land, landscape and photography. Indeed, the politics of place increasingly features as an artistic and curatorial concern. In this respect, we can think of post-modern landscape photography as a *grounded aesthetics*; formal and thematic perceptions are situated within socio-historical contexts. In contrast to the over-arching philosophical concerns informing Romanticism and Modernism, such situating is understood as conditioned in terms of place and particular histories.

Vision – with all the weight of the *double entendre* associated with the notion – constitutes a form of knowledge. Furthermore, the act of observation brings into being what is being observed. As cultural historian, Simon Schama, has noted, 'it is our shaping perception that makes the difference between raw matter and landscape' (Schama, 1996: 10). If photographs are documents with particular topographic authority, we have to ask questions about the motivations underpinning specific projects and ways in which photographers shape what they see. We also want to consider the subject matter of the image and to examine the picture as a semiotic system, organised in terms of particular formal and aesthetic conventions. As a modern development camera technology synthesised established representational modes of vision; the photo-image is predominantly monocular. In addition, we have to take into account a number of questions of reception and interpretation. What does the viewer, as observer of the image, bring into play in terms of reading the image? How does context inflect reading? In what ways does the *objectness* of a photograph, its size, surface qualities and tonal or colour intensity, influence our response? Photographic vision thus entangles knowledge discourses, the technical and the aesthetic within both processes of production of images and those of viewing and interpretation.

Photographs demonstrate something! They can seem incontrovertible. Despite all hesitation, we have little option but to take them as indicators of something that, we presume, once obtained – the shape of a field, a type of forestation, the conjunction of buildings around the mouth of a harbour. One purpose of this book is to discuss strategies through which photographers have opened up and questioned the relation between image and representation. As Walter Benjamin noted – in the comment that I have taken as a keynote for this introduction (p. 1) – the hegemonic power of the establishment is extensive and difficult to breach. Photography is limited in what it can achieve. Elsewhere he reminded us of realist dramatist, Bertholt Brecht, who remarked that a picture of the outside of a building, such as the Krupp factory in Germany in the 1930s, tells one nothing about the institution and the socio-economic relations that obtain (Benjamin, 1931). The point was forceful as the Krupp family were supporters of National Socialism (the Nazi party). Finding ways of transcending the limitations of the literal characteristics of photography has challenged many contemporary photographers investigating land and landscape. What seems radical in one situation may appear passé in another. Critical questioning, through exploring ways of seeing and experimenting in alternative aesthetics, is complex rhetorically, especially as in terms of tactics the refusal of conventional pictorial structures risks alienating audiences with whom photographers want to engage but whose familiarity with contemporary art language and references may be limited.

Such investigations sit within a broader context whereby notions of history and geography, that is, time and space, are under interrogation. Doreen Massey has pointed to a Western tendency for history to supersede geography in accounting for social change, and for singular accounts of progress towards, for instance, democracy or globalisation to be offered unquestioningly, as if somehow beyond ideology. She conceptualises 'space' as produced through intersections of stories, attitudes, power struggles that fundamentally reflect particular ideological paradigms (which may be in tension with one another). Space then becomes a site of the inter-relational. Places, and how they are named or represented, tell us something about relations that obtain.[3] Following Massey, my interest is in photographers and *oeuvres* that, variously, take space as constituted inter-relationally, as multiplicitous and heterogeneous, as always provisional, under construction, in process of change (Massey, 2005: 9). It follows that my concern is more with attitudes and the ideological than with natural or cultural effects and interventions (soil erosion, property development …) although, of course, it is impossible to analyse photographs without some concern with literal content.

As a discursive system photography also integrally works with the symbolic and the mythological. For many artists land is a space of symbol and myth. Rocks stand for eternity; thus, for example, a community or church can – metaphorically – be built on a rock. Water represents human survival, cleansing, renewal, flow, fluidity. In Christianity, baptism by water symbolises purification and renewal. Expressing the affects of water and of its movement has been a challenge engaged by many photographers; this was particularly typical of formalist preoccupations within modernist movements. Likewise, seasonal change, whereby the environment literally shifts in shapes and colours, also reminds us of regeneration and mortality – from dust to dust. The ebb and flow of the tide responds to the axis of movement of the moon. For some artists such effects relate to notions of the timelessness of nature, but for others they symbolise fluidity, shift and change, and, in various respects, may be seen as consequences of human interaction (for example, global warming) rather than homologous entity. As humans we simultaneously form a part of and perceive ourselves as standing outside of the natural.

Deborah Bright has remarked that

> Landscape art is the last preserve of American myths about Nature, Culture, and Beauty. It is no accident that its resurgence in popular and highbrow art is taking place during a right-wing political period in which big business has virtually free rein over the social and physical environment. Photographs of the strong forms of a Chicago or Pittsburgh blast furnace say nothing about the tragedy of massive unemployment in the Rust Belt or the profit motive of a corporation that rends the social fabric of a company town …
>
> Landscape has been appropriated by our cultural establishment as 'proof' of the timeless virtues of a Nature that transcends history – which is to say, collective human action. For most photographer-artists, landscape has been reduced to a locus for the experience of the isolated individual.
>
> (Bright, 1989: 140)

She is referring in particular to North America, but the echoing of Brecht via Benjamin underlines the broader applicability. Her critique also reminds us of strands within landscape practices that avoid grounding through emphasis on the formal, the expressive, and the metaphoric at the expense of engagement with particularities of place. This is not to resist or refute symbolic dimensions of imagery; indeed, the symbolic can be deployed strategically (for instance, as a tactic within feminist critiques of myth). But formalist renderings seek to extract the elemental from broader sets of observations about human presence.

WHAT FOLLOWS

This book thus articulates a range of concerns in order to situate analysis and critical discussion of specific work and projects within broader art historical, political and social contexts. As already noted, the book is not and was never intended to offer a survey or encyclopaedia of landscape photography, historically and now. Indeed, several projects or bodies of work that interest me are not discussed due to limitations of space, and because I had to make choices that were in part geared by particular chapter themes. For instance, since examples of British work are related to the chapter's thematic exploration of class, region, gender and race, the work of several key photographers based in the UK is not discussed because they have not happened to engage these themes or related issues. The investigation was fuelled by my interest in aesthetic modes in relation to cultural issues. The historical mapping is not an overview of the field, and the selection of examples for discussion, whilst acknowledging the significance of specific themes and the contribution of particular photographers, is not intended to prioritise or indicate a hierarchy of practices and practitioners. As such, the focus is upon photography within visual culture and the politics of place, rather than on definitional discussion of landscape as a genre within photography.

Research for each chapter was initiated through extensive literature search. But the book draws upon materials developed over many years. I have no doubt that there is now new material which I could – and perhaps should – have drawn into play. For instance, primary research for Chapter 3 was conducted in 2002, and much has been published on photography and the American West since then. Again, my concern has not been to review all that has been written on the subject so much as to critically appraise the effects and affects of interventionist practices in what I hope is an interesting manner, and one that could equally be applied to other examples in different contexts.

The argument is developed thematically. The first chapter offers a summary overview of the historical and discursive parameters that inform landscape practices and, arguably, operate to limit experimentation. Its primary tasks are philosophical and art historical; it directly engages the inter-relation of aesthetics and politics. The final chapter is also thematic in the broader sense of exploring the making and the effects of imagery ranging from that which presents itself as literal-topographic to that evidently constructed. This chapter most explicitly engages the inter-relation of geography, autobiography and metaphor. The other four chapters each centre on particular sets of ideas and concerns, exploring them through critical discussion of examples from a particular region of the world.

The American landscape has particularly dominated Western photographic modes and perceptions, and there is an extensive body of contemporary work that variously is more-or-less explicitly critical. Chapter 2 considers photography in relation to land settlement, focusing on North American work mostly – but not entirely – from Eastern regions. This is the first of two chapters in which the development of a landscape tradition in North America, and its critical succession, are discussed.[4] Whilst the chapters are clearly inter-linked, this chapter takes 'settlement' as its anchoring theme whilst the following chapter is centred on quests for territorial expansion. Both include reference to nineteenth-century American landscape photography in order to offer historical context for the work of contemporary practitioners in Canada and the United States.

If, as the popular saying has it, the USA is 'God's Own Country' and the West is extolled as a remaining Wilderness, then the East Coast is surely Eden. Chapter 2 opens through focusing on settlement, the Civil War, European influences and legacies, tourism and East Coast picturesque. This extended introduction sketches a framework for more detailed examination of contemporary practices relating to settlement and identity. Uses of (popular) photography to celebrate place in the nineteenth century have given way to more critical views of histories, cultural identity, and the impact of people on place. How such critical practices sit within the gallery and art market is questioned. The chapter also focuses on ways in which contemporary practitioners have deployed photography to interrogate legacies of the early settlers and of the Civil War, critically discussing the import of work in terms of an inter-relation of theme, aesthetics and context. Discussion of the implication of photography in picturing the White Mountains as a tourist destination offers an example of early popular photography and the emergence of the photographic souvenir in the second half of the nineteenth century.

Chapter 3 particularly considers the legacy and influence of nineteenth- and early twentieth-century photography on landscape and notions of wilderness in photography of the West. Attention is paid to the long shadow cast by the work of Ansel Adams. Contemporary critical engagement is then discussed through examples of work by photo-artists mostly based in the West and the Midwest, including group projects such as *Third View*, *Water in the West* and *In Response to Place* (commissioned to mark the fiftieth anniversary of the Nature Conservancy). Taken together, the two chapters explore landscape and ideology in contrasting areas of the North American continent. The distinction between the two chapters is partly thematic and partly geographic. It is a 'soft' division since many concerns, both aesthetic and political, cut across the divide.[5]

Chapter 4 considers questions of class, region, gender and ethnicity through critical discussion both of the pastoral landscape tradition of

Britain and Ireland and, more particularly, of the thematic concerns and aesthetic strategies which have variously been deployed by contemporary practitioners. Britain is an old country, with many layers of histories often marked on the land and certainly deeply woven within British culture. It thus lends itself to critical exploration relating to land ownership and control, regionalism, colonialism and (still persistent) patriarchal attitudes. But Britain might equally have formed the focus of the case study of nation and identity that follows, although on this occasion this has been explored through reference to Nordic and Baltic areas within which tensions have been rife for many centuries. Chapter 5 thus focuses on nationhood and visual rhetoric, noting shifting inter-relations of States within the Baltic region. Examples of work from Estonia, Latvia and Lithuania, former Soviet areas, as well as from Scandinavia and Finland are considered in order to evaluate aesthetic strategies and thematic engagements that characterise contemporary landscape practices.

The book thus tackles some of the questions concisely summarised by Deborah Bright:

> Whatever the aesthetic merits, every representation of landscape is also a record of human values and actions imposed on the land over time. What stake do landscape photographers have in constructing such representations? A large one, I believe. Whatever the photographer's claims, landscapes as subject matter in photography can be analyzed as documents extending beyond the formally aesthetic or personally expressive. Even formal and personal choices do not emerge *sui generis*, but instead reflect collective interests and influences, whether philosophical, political, economic, or otherwise … The sorts of questions we might ask concern what ideologies landscape photographs perpetuate; in whose interests they were conceived; why we still desire to make and consume them; and why the art of landscape photography remains so singularly identified with a masculine eye.
>
> (Bright, 1989: 126)

My interest is in exploring ways in which photographers investigating land and landscape have addressed some of these issues through practices which are variously philosophically, theoretically and critically informed. In thinking through practice they ground engagement with ideological and political issues on the actual terrain that is the focus of debate.

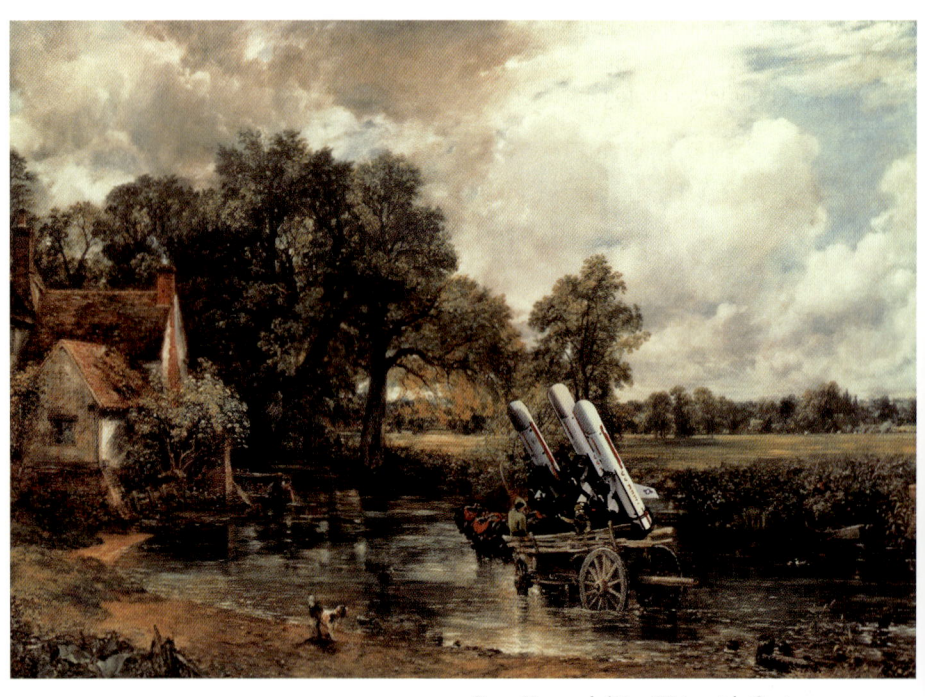

Peter Kennard, 'Hay Wain with Cruise Missiles', 1980. Published in *Camerawork*, London, July 1980 to illustrate an essay by E.P. Thompson on 'The State of the Nation'.

1

LANDSCAPE

TIME, SPACE, PLACE, AESTHETICS

The point of art has never been to make something synonymous with life … but to make something of reduced complexity that is nonetheless analogous to life and that can thereby clarify it.
(Robert Adams, 1996: 68)[1]

Stories are the perfect skin of time.
(Victor Masayesva, 2002)[2]

History turns space into place. This simple statement masks a complexity of ideological processes associated with the relation of humankind and our environment. For a start, we need to take into account the symbiotic inter-relation of nature and culture. Where nature might once have been viewed as 'timeless', self-regenerating, and somehow 'outside' of culture, we are now increasingly aware of the ecological implications of techno-cultural change. Furthermore, our perception of nature is filtered through cultural understandings.

There are few regions in the world that remain untouched by human presence. Indeed, most people live in regions with long histories of human habitation – even if, in some cases, sparsely populated. Traces of previous human tenancy mark the lands we inhabit. As Doreen Massey has argued, space becomes meaningful through histories told (Massey, 2005). This is a fluid definitional process with new stories – those yet to come – further adding to or shifting our sense of the character of particular places. Histories articulate differing discourses and material forces, often forming terrains of contestation as stories may be recounted from different points of view. The purpose of historical investigation may be to find new materials that enhance – or unseat – previous understandings of place and circumstances. Human action contours the landscape, and stories told give meaning to it.

In order to explore the processes involved in the specification of place, we need to consider a range of formative influences articulated through landscape practices – both the *making* of the landscape and its representation. Any such exploration draws upon diverse epistemological fields including: aesthetics, geography and political economy, gender and ethnicity, nationalism and territorialism, settlement and social planning, and psychology (individual and collective). Naming involves the objectification of that which is being designated. Designation of places inserts a sense of distance; in order to describe and categorise we position ourselves conceptually as somehow outside of our environment. Thus we can look on, and give it a name (whilst simultaneously *being* a part of it experientially). Whether this distinction is ontologically a binary – people versus environment, culture versus nature – has been a matter of dispute since eighteenth-century so-called 'Enlightenment' debates. We may take the distinction as partial, suggesting there is not a complete rupture between humans as species and other natural orders, perhaps following Darwin in viewing the inter-relations in terms of hierarchy of species. But we still encounter moral issues to do with relative position, power and responsibility within any such hierarchy. Our sense of our location in relation to space and place is not uniform; it plays out differently, informed by a combination of philosophic principles and understandings (religious, or otherwise), and the physical particularities of environments. The purpose of this chapter is to map and explore some of the discursive currencies that contribute to the formation of ideas about landscape. Given that this is a book about photographic practices, it also relates these to my primary concern with photography. The intention of the book is to investigate landscape photography as a critical practice. This chapter aims to ground the evaluative discussions of aesthetics and critical strategies that are central to ensuing chapters through situating analysis of contemporary representational practices in relation to broader cultural currencies and debates.

THE EMERGENCE OF LANDSCAPE

Whether noble, picturesque, sublime or mundane, the landscape image bears the imprint of its cultural pedigree. It is a selected and constructed text, and while the formal choices of what has been included and excluded have been the focus of most art-historical criticism to date, the historical and social significance of those choices has rarely been addressed and even intentionally avoided.

(Bright, 1989: 127)

Peter Kennard's photomontage of Constable's 'The Hay Wain' (1821), the farm cart replete with cruise missiles, references a well-known representation of landscape and human activity in order to draw attention to the contemporary threat of annihilation of a particular place – in this case England and Englishness. Several discourses are in play. First, of course, Constable's painting, which at the time that he painted it was intended to describe ordinary rural circumstances but later became taken up as an icon of the English pastoral. The scene has come to connote Englishness. Second, hay-making is an annual event, the harvest is brought in, year after year; there is continuity. The insertion of the missiles in the space of such patterned seasonal activity emphasises the threat to the nation and to everyday ways of life. Evaluating the critique offered by the artist, something of a paradox emerges; the image could be taken to support a traditional view of Britain, one more akin to Thomas Hardy's depiction of the complexities of class and subsistence than the industrial and post-colonial scenarios that obtained and became the focus of socio-political debates in the 1980s.[3] But as political rhetoric the composite effectively draws attention to the dangers of annihilation through suggesting what might happen if a nuclear war was played out on British land. Photomontage may not be subtle but it is effective as a tactic when the aim is to make a point quickly and directly. We grasp immediately that Britain is under threat.

In introducing a collection of essays on *Landscapes and Politics*, Mark Dorrian and Gillian Rose acknowledge two distinct current clusters of (academic) use of the term 'landscape' (Dorrian and Rose, 2003). On the one hand, in geographical, sociological or anthropological terms, landscape refers primarily to everyday experience and practices as situated within and mediated in relation to the social and the topographic (the latter formed in part through histories of relations between people and land – reclamation, cultivation, urbanisation, etc.). On the other hand, landscape refers to a set of representational practices, the picturing of place (through words, sounds, visual images). Although within different academic disciplines – sciences, agriculture, social sciences, geography, architecture and design on the one hand, the arts and humanities on the other – the domains are inextricably inter-related;

scientific understanding and strategic intervention are fuelled by the poetic imaginary whilst in formulating projects artists and writers research environmental issues as defined through scientific lenses. It follows that discourses relating to land and environment transcend the concerns of historically specific academic disciplines, research questions and methodologies.

Dorrian and Rose also remind us that historical separation from land, and its constitution as *landscape*, was concomitant with early modernity and the emergence of Capitalism. In alternative economic systems, such as feudal systems (typical of Western Europe in the mediaeval era) or hunter/gatherer nomadism, people live directly off the land; they are not estranged from basic sources of sustenance. In such circumstances there is no need to represent land pictorially as it can be seen and experienced every day; although, of course, land may be the canvas for track signs, and related information, as in aboriginal bark painting. Visual idioms also became used for storytelling – as in cave paintings, or, later, mediaeval church frescoes. Here, again, the concern was not with the representation of land itself, but the retelling of tales which variously celebrate the natural environment and natural resources as well as offering existential reassurances in the form of biblical myth. Land is also the backdrop against which the classic Greek tales, revived in Renaissance Europe, were replayed through paintings.

Urbanisation induced a gradual distancing from land (over many centuries). This surely contributed to the development of desire to represent land *in itself* in pictures or words.[4] The term 'landscape' dates from the Flemish 'landschap'. It developed as a generic term for picturing 'out of doors'. (Conventions regarding composition meant it also came to designate picture format – landscape, as opposed to portrait.) Landscape can be taken to encompass riverscape and seascape. Indeed, land and water are not inherently separate and should not be considered discrete. In geological terms, they interact: water both erodes and replenishes land (without water there is drought or desert). Sea covers seven-tenths of the earth, and has figured variously in human imagination from threat and punishment (The Flood) to the sublime (great waves – for instance, Turner's depiction of Herculean struggle). That noted, there is a slippage between the generic use of the concept and use of 'landscape' specifically to refer to inland scenes, by contrast with, on the one hand, 'seascape' or, on the other hand, 'cityscape' or urban landscape. That adjectives are added for further precision, as in 'urban landscape' or 'industrial landscape', indicates the central association of 'landscape' with an idealised rural; in the industrial rural (mining, mills, nuclear power stations, coastal ship-building regions), the additional descriptor clearly indicates the otherness of that which is not pastoral.

Coastal dwellers and seafarers (naval, fishing, marine transport …) have a continuing interest in the sea, and the littoral space of beaches or cliffs. For others, interest in 'seaside' dates only from the early Modern era, although the sea as backdrop within marine painting was, of course, a currency within history painting. 'Pure' seascape – sea painted as a theme in itself – did not appear until later, but was certainly accepted as a subject in its own right by the time of Turner or Courbet. Landscape includes water: rain, river, coast, canal, stream or waterfall, but seascape as a genre has remained slightly apart, perhaps because the ocean is less fully charted than the land. In a catalogue essay for the exhibition *Sea Change* (1998), James Hamilton-Paterson notes a series of developments which, he suggests, came together to shift attitudes to the coast (Hamilton-Paterson, 1998). These included the ascendance of modern sciences such as geology and, later, oceanography, with associated challenges to the dominance of myth and superstition. Romanticism, with its metaphoric interest in nature, and the medical advocacy of the health-giving properties of sea-water, together led to the coast being redefined as 'seaside', and a burgeoning of coastal resorts in Europe. This in turn enhanced taxonomic interest in natural phenomena that included shoreline items (seagrasses, shellfish …) (ibid.: 10). The sea, which had once been viewed as that which lay beyond the land, became incorporated pictorially, along with the rivers and streams feeding into it.

LANDSCAPE AS GENRE IN ART

Constable remarked that 'By a close observation of nature [the artist] discovers qualities … which have never been portrayed before' (Pevsner, 1997: 58). This indicates an empirical model within which the emphasis is on detailed looking in order to *see*. By contrast, William Blake commented, 'No man of sense can think that an Imitation of the Objects of Nature is the Art of Painting, or that such Imitation … is worthy of Notice' (ibid.). For Blake art was above all a work of imagination. Clearly their attitudes to representation differ fundamentally, a difference that begs exploration.

The late mediaeval period had offered something of a turning point in the emergence of painting as a representational form. The Florentine artist and architect, Filippo Brunelleschi (1377–1446) drew upon mathematical rules which dictated that objects appear smaller in size as they recede into the distance in order to incorporate a sense of depth within church paintings. Leon Battista Alberti (1404–72) subsequently developed this into the principles of perspective that continue to inform two-dimensional art. His postulation of rules of image construction was intended as a means of instilling accuracy of depiction. However, as a number of recent critics have noted, pictorial composition constructed in relation to a single central viewing position also emphasised (ego-)centrality as the pictorial world appears organised in relation to the viewer. Perspective, as a system organised around a vanishing point thereby replicating the actual experience of looking into the distance, also lent itself to the emphasis on harmony of composition which emerged within topographic modes. Arguably this sense of order and harmony is pleasurable in part because the centrality of the spectator is reaffirmed perspectivally.

The late mediaeval period also witnessed developments in the material means of representation. Ernst Gombrich cites Jan Van Eyck (*c.* 1389–1441) as an artist whose paintings were – and remain – remarkable for attention to detail, whether such famous portraits as the Arnolfini wedding couple, or the landscape settings within which he depicted people, stories and events (Gombrich, 1978 [1950]). He credits Van Eyck with the invention of oil painting. As a medium, oil allows for slower, more precise, work that (unlike its predecessor, tempera, based on egg white) facilitated the shading of one colour into another; this was particularly appropriate for rendering the subtleties of the hues of land and sky. John Berger has commented that such effects of the use of oil as method of visual rendering have come to define what we mean by 'pictorial likeness'. He argues that oil centrally contributed to the construction of ways of seeing as the detail that it can provide crucially fuelled the analogous relation between seeing and possession: 'To have a thing painted and put on a canvas is not unlike buying it and putting it in your house. If you buy a painting you buy also the look of the thing it represents' (Berger, 1972: 83). He might have added that oil as a medium also operates evocatively through density, tone, light and shade, thereby enhancing desire for ownership and the metonymic effects of painterly depiction. In this respect, oil remains influential – even though its technical detailing characteristics later seemed superseded by photography.

Landscape as a genre thus began to emerge towards the end of the fifteenth century. Kenneth Clark offers a useful overview of changing ideals in landscape painting (albeit based on a binary notion of nature and the 'natural' as somehow other to culture) (Clark, 1976). Significantly, he remarks that a precondition for a painted landscape was a renewed sense of space, suggesting that there was a 'curiosity about the precise character of a particular spot, which was a part of the general curiosity of the fifteenth century' (ibid.: 41). He specifically cites topographical watercolours, for instance, in the work of the German painter, Albrecht Durer (1471–1528). In Italy the early Renaissance period was particularly characterised by interest in classical Greek ideals of art, science and scholarship. Gombrich identifies a number of key developments. He notes an Albertian emphasis upon compositional construction in Italian Renaissance art, reflecting Grecian notions of harmony as beauty (particularly related to sculpture and architecture – Michelangelo; Brunelleschi). He also contrasts Italian emphasis on classical construction with the work of Northern European artists of the period, for instance, the work of the Flemish painter, Breughel the Elder (*c.* 1520–69) who painted many scenes from peasant life, described by Gombrich as 'human comedies' (Gombrich, 1983: 298). Two parallel, increasingly inter-linked, traditions developed. On the one hand there was Italianate emphasis on classical harmony; on the other hand, there was *description*, which developed not only in terms of paintings and sketches – for example, the pictorial depiction or 'mapping' of rural vistas – but also included diarist accounts and 'nature poetry' (Williams, 1975).

Landscape pictures thus centrally contribute to the representation of space as place and, crucially, imply responses to particular places. For many centuries landscape had been viewed as a minor genre within art, largely descriptive in function, secondary to the storytelling and myth-sustaining operations of Christian symbolism, history painting or, later, allegorical modes such as still life. In fifteenth-century painting, landscape appears primarily as backdrop, for instance, in biblical or mythical stories (such as the landscape iconography in Botticelli's 'The Birth of Venus', *c.* 1485). The exception was 'prospect' paintings; their overt purpose was 'straight' or topographic description, rather than fantasy, allegory or metaphor. Such paintings were relatively small, commissioned by early Renaissance landowners to depict their estates, for instance, Medici holdings on the Tuscan Hills. (There are several examples in the collection at the Uffizi Gallery, Florence.) The representations are not simply cartographic, but detail fertile fields, sturdy livestock, lush orchards and vines laden with grapes. In other words, the pictures reflect agricultural ideals. The visual geometry is non-perspectival, somewhat akin to a mediaeval fresco, but the twin purposes of topography and reassurance of agricultural plenitude were clearly satisfied. Here we find the seeds of the pictorial imaginary. Prospect paintings also reaffirmed the social and economic status of powerful families as successful landowners. Although at one level reflecting agrarian ideals, the detailing of content (which may or may not have been accurately 'stencilled' from actuality) gives them a place within topographic histories.

Stephen Daniels acknowledges the influence of both Dutch and Italian prospect art on developments in England (Daniels, 1990). He notes that English prospect paintings of the late seventeenth century were normally no less than four by six feet, often constructed from a 'bird's-eye' overview, and included any urban or industrial features within the estate, and immediately beyond. They were intended to make an impression of landed property, in England a primary determinate of class, status and political authority – particularly significant in the period immediately following the civil war in Britain (1642–60). As he suggests, estates were areas of conspicuous production, as well as conspicuous consumption; property represented investment and prospect art emphasised economically effective land management. He remarks that the term 'prospect' relates not only to vista but also to future economic endeavour. The inter-relation of economic wealth – actual or potential – and pictorial representation was marked in the social usage of such imagery. Such pictures (along with family portraits) were commonly hung in public areas such as reception rooms, hallways, or over a mantelpiece, both at the place depicted and also in the owner's other properties, perhaps a London home. This supports John Berger's famous comment that seeing is a form of reaffirmation of possession, through which he made the associated point that display also functions to affirm the (social) standing of the possessor (Berger, 1972). Paintings from overseas estates, as colonies became established, thus enhanced rhetoric of status and entrepreneurial success. Unlike earlier Italian examples, pictures were constructed in accordance with the principles of perspective. The scale allowed for detailed views, and, as such, might be seen as a precursor of contemporary topographic photography. It is no accident that the camera was greeted for its ability to depict precisely that within the viewfinder; the desire for topographic representation was long established.

Levi-Strauss likewise comments on later uses of painting and the intellectual context of commissions:

> For Renaissance artists, painting was perhaps an instrument of knowledge but it was also an instrument of possession, and we must not forget, when we are dealing with Renaissance painting, that it was only possible because of the immense fortunes which were being amassed in Florence and elsewhere, and that rich Italian merchants looked upon painters as agents, who allowed them to confirm their possession of all that was beautiful and desirable in the world. The pictures in a Florentine palace represented a kind of microcosm in which the proprietor, thanks to his artists, had recreated within easy reach and in as real a form as possible, all those features of the world to which he was attached.
>
> (Levi-Strauss, 1969)[5]

Such comments also apply to the broader Renaissance context of overseas exploration wherein painters operated, in effect, as recorders of an expanding world. Expeditions by explorers date as far back as the late thirteenth century, but became increasingly significant in the sixteenth century.[6] Explorations were financed by the European aristocracy who were intent not only on (geographic) discovery, but also on trade and colonisation. A sense of expanded space must have underpinned such investment. The ships of British, Dutch, Italian, Portuguese and Spanish explorers carried artists as additional crew, their role being akin to that of a diarist. We can assume that these painters, who, after all, risked their lives at sea on such commissions, were genuinely interested in the task of elaborating images of distant lands previously unseen by Europeans. Levi-Strauss's comments also remind us that painters were dependent upon patronage; the cost of materials, especially certain colour pigments, was high and some income guarantee was necessary.[7]

The shift from landscape as setting to landscape as subject in its own right is a more modern phenomenon; landscape did not become established until the seventeenth and eighteenth centuries, and even then remained viewed by art academicians as a minor genre. Here, there emerged a contrast between Northern and Southern Europe that might be summed up through comparing the work of Poussin or Lorrain, both of whom were concerned with questions of Arcadian beauty, and the more topographic mode which characterised Dutch painting from the seventeenth century on.[8] Poussin, Lorrain and, later, Friedrich were preoccupied with the inter-relation of humankind and nature and explicitly operated through visual metaphor. By contrast, Dutch pictures typically took an apparently natural landscape as context for the depiction of windmills, ships, fields and estates, in effect celebrating the emblems of property ownership and mercantile success. Deborah Bright, although primarily concerned with the American landscape, was among the first to point to some of the ways in which specificity of subject matter and iconography reflect particular cultural histories (Bright, 1989). She comments that English landscape painting in the eighteenth century did not simply echo the Dutch model with its flat lands, windmills and canals, but re-articulated the genre so that particular characteristics of the English countryside feature.

In Europe the eighteenth-century fashion for landscaping gardens clearly reflected desire for vistas from the house (the family 'seat') as well as romantic preoccupations with classical culture. As already indicated, landscape as a set of interests, and as a genre in painting, had begun to emerge prior to this so-called Age of Enlightenment. But this era witnessed a consolidation of European landscape styles in painting, architecture and, most particularly, landscape gardening as aristocracy and wealthy bourgeois families variously commissioned new villas and formally laid-out parks and gardens. In Britain, as in most of Western Europe, land is managed; it follows that vistas or landscapes are constructed, which means that a sense of aesthetic principles, as well as social mores, are in play. As can be seen from visiting estates now managed by the National Trust or English Heritage, the eighteenth-century English country house became a place from which to look out, to contemplate 'views', as well as one within which to live and entertain. The key architectural influence stemmed from Italy, especially the work of Palladio.[9] This was not restricted to Britain; French châteaux offer a parallel example, as do estates situated apart from cities throughout Europe, from Versailles to the Summer Palace of the Czars outside St Petersburg. Country houses adopted grand style. In England, houses previously had been located in valleys, taking advantage of shelter and running water (streams); now they were built on hills with views which might be re-shaped in accordance with preconceived idealised landscapes (hence the status and reputation of eighteenth-century landscape gardeners such as Capability Brown and Humphrey Repton). As John Brewer remarks, country houses were built away from villages, with increasingly large, walled parks, and the actual construction of idyllic views sometimes involved shifting hills and rivers, or demolishing entire villages (Brewer, 1997: 627ff). The construction of a 'natural' landscape involved an imperious disregard for that which previously obtained. The cult of the picturesque encouraged landscaping which appeared spontaneous, in contrast with the formal garden which characterised French or Dutch taste of the period. Increasingly, the emphasis was less upon land as a working environment (although it continued to be so) and more upon landscape as a prospect for contemplation. Later, for the newly wealthy nineteenth-century industrialists, acquisition of land symbolised entrepreneurial success. The commanding view from the house on the hill over its own park reinforced the symbolic status of the owner for whom this (expansive) space was 'my' place. A photograph such as Roger Fenton's picture of the driveway leading up to Windsor Castle, wherein the long carriageway leads up to the house which dominates the land from the distance, is a key example. The family within look out, and down, on us as visitors, estate workers or, indeed, viewers of the representation of this particular place.

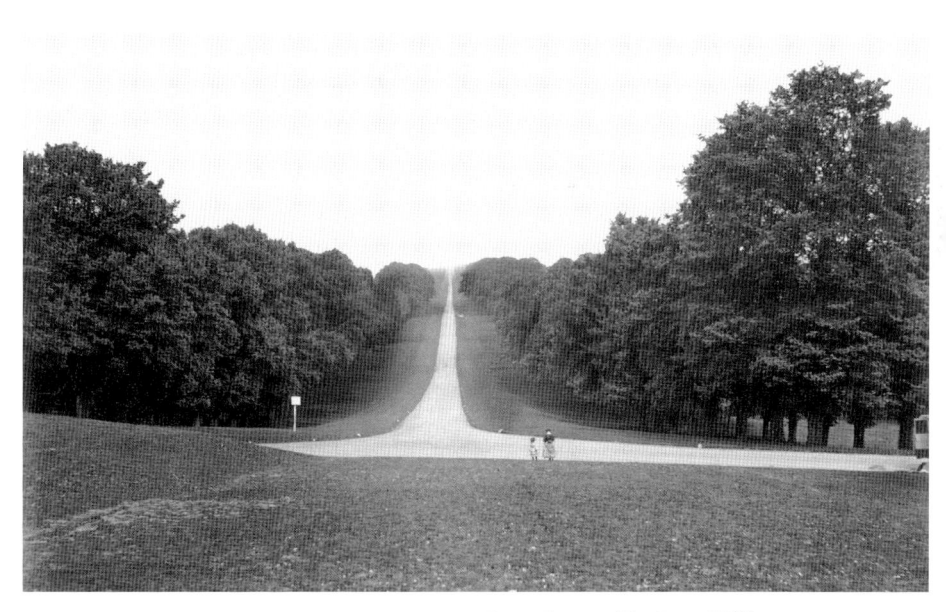

Roger Fenton, 'The Long Walk', Windsor, 1860.

PAINTING AND PHOTOGRAPHY

Photography, announced in France and Britain in 1839, was initially heralded for its technical recording abilities. With few exceptions, the emphasis was upon *picture-taking* rather than *picture-making* (Harker, 1979). As I shall suggest, the aesthetic echo was more in the line of Constable, with his emphasis upon empirical observation, than, for instance, Claude Lorrain or, indeed, Turner.

The nineteenth century, which was an era of massive industrial change in Britain, Northern Europe and some parts of the USA, witnessed shifts in landscape subject matter and style. In Britain, Constable (in the late eighteenth century) and Turner shifted landscape towards a more research-based mode of painting, repeatedly exploring the same themes (Salisbury Cathedral; cloud formations; history as myth). The two artists represent very different philosophies of art. As Gombrich suggests:

> The break with tradition had left artists with the two possibilities which were embodied in Turner and Constable. They could become poets in painting, and seek moving and dramatic effects, or they could decide to keep to the motif in front of them, and explore it with all the insistence and honesty at their command.
>
> (Gombrich, 1978 [1950]: 393–4)

As already noted, Constable emphasised 'close observation of nature'. He dismissed picturesque set pieces that accorded with aesthetic codes of colour and composition. As the story goes, a friend once told him off for not giving his foreground the requisite brown of an old violin; Constable put a violin on the grass to demonstrate the difference between the fresh green of English grass and the warm tones expected by convention. Such conventions had been influenced by French and Italian artists drawing upon Mediterranean hues. In terms of British art, Constable's radicalism lay in his insistence on looking at the actual landscape; he argued that 'the great vice of the present day is *bravura*, an attempt to do something beyond the truth' (ibid.: 393). Dazzling pageantry such as Turner's 'Snow Storm – Steam-Boat off a Harbour's Mouth' (1842) would for Constable be anathema. As Gombrich remarks, 'In Turner, nature always reflects and expresses man's emotions. We feel small and over-whelmed in the face of the powers we cannot control' (ibid.). Constable and Turner represent two very different approaches to painting, one of which emphasises calm and beauty in a picturesque manner and one that is generally more sublime, engaging allegorically with history and myth. Both models influenced nineteenth-century developments in photography, in North America as well as in Britain.

For Europeans now travelling in the US or Canada (or in other continental regions such as Australia) the scale remains almost incomprehensible. Natural phenomena such as Niagara Falls must have appeared particularly breathtaking to early East Coast Anglo-Celtic settlers, accustomed to the smaller scale of Britain and Ireland. Some of this feeling is conveyed in the pictures of Thomas Cole, Frederick Church and other painters associated with what was retrospectively termed the Hudson River School. For instance, Church's 1856 depiction of 'Niagara Falls' from a viewpoint below Horseshoe Falls (on the American side) is surprisingly small (*c*. 30 x 45 cm) but the power and density of the water and the luminosity are nonetheless striking. In his larger-scale 1857 painting, 'Niagara' (*c*. 168 x 303 cm), intensity of movement, light and shade enhance a sense of wonder; he places the viewer precariously looking out, across and down over the Falls. Niagara was already a well-established tourist destination, subject of many paintings and diary descriptions, and had come to stand in the popular imaginary as a manifest symbol of the natural sublime which, reflecting Puritan influences, was also perceived as a religious sublime (Hughes, 1997: 169). These paintings were not merely mimetic; they represented moral principles. Church's picture reinforces such wilderness ideologies; as Hughes remarks, in the 1850s, Niagara was a popular tourist destination, crowded with people, hotels and factories, all of which are edited out of the painting in order to enhance the sublime significance of the Falls:

> At Niagara, the painting insists, you do not communicate with other tourists; you are confronted by God's creation, and through that with His mind. The rainbow suggests a pristine America rising from the cataract, a promise of ongoing American renewal. Niagara's equivalence with the Deluge indicated a wiping-out of failure, a sort of cosmic baptism – strong and resonant themes for Americans in the mid-nineteenth century.
>
> (Hughes, 1997: 161)

Such landscape paintings functioned topographically, but, in line with earlier European themes, were also preoccupied with the allegorical and the spiritual.

Meanwhile, French painters, pre-eminently Courbet and Manet – later viewed as founders of Realism – sought to distance landscape from the metaphoric, to depict that which was observed in a detail that lent authenticity to the status of the painting as social commentary. Critically commenting on Realism as a movement, Linda Nochlin emphasises the socio-political context, noting collective interest in better understanding a changing, industrialising, world within which debates about relations between labour and wealth, class and power had acquired currency.[10] One reason for the impact of Realism as an art movement in mid-nineteenth-century France was its challenge to ways in which landscape imagery previously obscured class relations. Realist landscapes depicted events, people and their relationship to place: a rural funeral, or stonebreakers (Courbet) or agricultural labourers (Millais) – or, indeed, urban environments (Manet), exploring continuities along with effects of modernity. It is no accident that Realism coincided with enhanced urbanisation, including the re-forming of Paris, and with industrialisation (especially in the northeast of France).

Curiosity about other cultures along with fashions for that seen as exotic were further currencies within this era of modernity and change. The development of the steam train had led to an increase in people travelling to places new to them, and European colonialism was at its height, with overseas lands a source of stories as well as commodities. Such relative mobility enhanced cultural appetite for information about distant places which both painting, and, very soon, photography, contributed to feeding. Expositions such as the Great Exhibitions in London, 1851, and Paris, 1855, offered venues for photographers' 'views', and many storytellers toured the country with glass slides bringing the distant and the exotic close to home. In other words, landscape became a component within the travel photography that became popular as a form of contemporary spectacle. The aesthetic was generally conservative and the mode uncritical. Such pictures also increasingly featured in publications, initially as reproductions of wood engravings based on photographs and later, with the introduction of lithography around the turn of the twentieth century, direct use of photographs themselves within newspapers, books and magazines. Walter Benjamin particularly welcomed the mass reproduction and circulation of imagery, proposing that it democratically undermined the aura of the uniqueness of the work of art (Benjamin, 1936). This expansion of contexts of seeing extended the rhetorical influence of photography. Benjamin was associated with the Frankfurt School, a cluster of academics (including Theodore Adorno and Herbert Marcuse) originally based in Frankfurt who became centrally concerned with (Marxist) critical theory, ideological processes, and the analysis of the operations of mass culture, for example, in the support of fascism. Photography had become a tool of reportage, its authority underpinned by notions of authenticity and objectivity that had become associated with the idea of the camera eye. The press and publishing thus had become – and remain – sites of tensions over visual discourses and the politics of representation.

Photography also developed as a medium of artistic expression as a result partly of the involvement of artists using photographs as substitutes for sketches, eliminating the need to work *en plein air*. The use of photography allowed artists to extend their range of references, returning from urban and rural public or 'open' spaces with photographic notes to support paintings made in the studio. For example, Aaron Scharf notes a riverscape and a seascape, by Courbet, which seem to be based directly upon contemporary photographs (Scharf, 1974: 127). Indeed, initially photographers had difficulty with the landscape, as it was not possible to expose for land and sky simultaneously (since the different light intensities required differing lengths of exposure). Mark Haworth-Booth has examined the construction of 'River Scene, France' (1858) by Camille Silvy, which was made through combination printing and involved staging people within the rural setting, requiring them not to move as exposures were necessarily relatively long (Haworth-Booth, 1992). Established pictorial conventions remained in play: the picturesque composition echoes traditional aesthetics, and the content romanticises the pastoral (although the photographers' interest was probably to do with developing a technique which would cope with the diversity of light intensity of the natural environment). The classical references resonate! In effect, the picturesque is a conventional 'beauty spot', landscaped as such, and painted/photographed as such. This statement is, of course, not neutral; 'beauty' is a cultural construct. In Britain, tourism (for the affluent) to places considered picturesque became popular in the eighteenth century, reinforcing underpinning ideological discourses. This was not only the Grand Tour (of classical Europe – considered central to the education of young gentlemen, and some ladies), but also a reverence for beauty spots in Britain, for instance, Tintern Abbey in the Wye Valley or Salisbury Plain, from which there is view of the cathedral. These tourist haunts became the subject of landscape paintings (and a source of income for painters).

The conceptual lineage as well as the compositional lineage is clear; there are many examples of mid-Victorian photographers staging picturesque and mythical images (for example, Julia Margaret Cameron) that deploy landscape as symbolic setting. Yet it was only towards the end of the nineteenth century that pictorial 'secessionist' movements, within which photography was defined in terms of aesthetics (rather than 'fact'), developed internationally.[11] The welcoming of photography into major arts institutions did not emerge until later; in 1940 the Museum of Modern Art (MoMA), New York, established the first ever department of photography within an art museum. In the nineteenth century photography had occupied a space within the exhibition gallery as a technological development and for its visual storytelling capabilities. By the end of the twentieth century the photographer claimed status as artist and, indeed, imagery by named nineteenth-century photographers had been acclaimed for aesthetic sensibilities and had taken pride of place within collections.

The hailing of earlier landscape photographers as artists, and of photography as a modernist art form, has been challenged on a number of counts, not the least of which is that this claim is premised on a romantic view of the artist as a special sort of seer. It also tells us very little about actual working practices, or about meaning-production processes. Questions of context are particularly salient. Taking Timothy O'Sullivan's picture of 'Tufa Domes, Pyramid Lake', Rosalind Krauss contrasts two versions, O'Sullivan's own print, later acclaimed by the art museum, and a lithograph made for publication in Clarence King's *Systematic Geology* in 1878[12] (see Frontispiece). Krauss observes that, for the latter version to function as information, topographic elements had to be restored to the picture. The difference between the two versions is not to do with the brilliance of the photographer and the dullness of lithography; rather it stems from the needs and expectations of different cultural domains: scientific utility versus aesthetic sensibility. Furthermore, she suggests that the image, acclaimed by Szarkowski as – what he would surely have termed – a masterpiece of composition, was more likely to have been determined by an intention to sell it for stereoscopes than by an aesthetic economy of the photographer's eye.[13] Stereographic views require strong central features to provide focal points and heighten the illusion of the three-dimensional. The context within which O'Sullivan was working was commercial, not artistic; he worked as an 'operator' selling views to photographic businesses who became the copyright holders. The work of these early jobbing photographers became acclaimed as 'art' retrospectively, at a point when it suited those within the arts institution to argue a case for photography. The argument brought into play a claim for photographers as artists that would not have been how they saw themselves. Landscape photography thus secured a place within the art archive. Whilst not necessarily subscribing to the modernist claims about artistic perception, it has to be conceded that this has probably contributed to the preservation of a range of imagery that might otherwise be lost, or less known. Historical work is conserved and exhibited both in the art museum and in national or regional historical collections. In the former it is framed in terms of the photographer as artist, in the latter more in terms of social history.

AESTHETICS: PERSPECTIVE AND THE ORGANISATION OF VISION

Two early nineteenth-century landscapes are displayed side by side in the tiny municipal picture collection at Abano Terme, a small town in northeast Italy near Padua. One, by Giuseppe Canella, depicts 'The Bridge at Torino' ('Il po a Torino', n.d.); it is oil on canvas, 24 x 42.5 cm, in a gold-coloured frame. The other, by Pietro Ronzoni, depicts the 'Journey on the Flight to Egypt' ('Paesaggio con Fuga in Egitto', n.d.); also oil on canvas, 37 x 48 cm, but unframed.[14] They are very ordinary. What is remarkable is not the quality of the individual works, but compositional similarities, despite difference in theme and style – the former is topographic (proto-Realist), whereas the latter offers a scene from biblical myth. Both include a river. In the Canella it runs from foreground left into the distant horizon; in the Ronzoni it runs up from the right of the frame disappearing behind a rockface. Both use vertical height to move the eye within the frame: Canella includes buildings to the left of the river, and also high up on a hill in the far right. Ronzoni includes trees to the right of the canvas, and also high up on the cliffs in the middle left. Both include figures in the foreground, not posed, ostensibly engaged in activity, but functioning to lend a sense of scale to the land and river around them. Both include an inverted triangle of sky with some cloud, off-centre, and occupying about a third of the picture. They remind us of the extent of the influence of Albertian perspective, with its central viewing position and vanishing point around which the geometry of the image triangulates.

Along with use of light and shade for emphasis and mood enhancement, perspective came to characterise European landscape painting. Gombrich suggests that visual ideas spread, courtesy of the introduction of woodcut engravings in Germany (Gutenberg) in the late fifteenth century, fostering a degree of synthesis between developing styles in various regions of Europe (Gombrich, 1978).

Art theory has paid central attention to the organisation of space within the frame and also that of implied space beyond it. Drawing on the work of the German Enlightenment philosopher Gotthold Lessing, Erwin Panofsky proposed that:

> For us perspective is, quite precisely, the capacity to represent a number of objects together with a part of the space around them in such a way that the conception of the material picture support is completely supplanted by the conception of a transparent plane through which we believe we are looking into an imaginary space. This space comprises the entirety of the objects in apparent recession into depth, and is not bounded by the edges of the picture, but rather only cut off.
>
> (Panofsky, 1991: 77)

Writing in the 1920s Panofsky famously characterised perspective as a set of visual conventions that transform what he terms 'psycho-physiological space' into mathematical space, in effect, symbolising that which has been seen rather than directly representing it (Panofsky, 1991: 30–1). But, by contrast with Lessing, he argued that pictorial conventions were not founded in actual ocular sight. This can be tested through looking over flatlands or looking out to sea where the horizon is wide, relatively unvaried, and requires scanning panoramically. A sail or a buoy might momentarily anchor vision, offering a point of focus, but the overall scene is not subject to the system of triangles proposed by Alberti – although, of course, this system could be used to represent it. Perhaps the nearest equivalence between the actual landscape and the painted landscape can be found in the line of a river (or road, path, canal) leading into the distance. In such a view we *do* experience a vanishing point (provided it does not culminate in a lake or the sea, which forms a 'T' junction rather than an illusory inverted 'V'). Human sight is nearly replicated through the perspectival system, except that, by contrast with pictorial representation, natural sight does not have fixed focal arrangements; our eyes (two of them) scan from foreground to background adjusting focus accordingly, in turn bringing different elements of the landscape up for specific attention. Panofsky's most trenchant criticism was that perspective transforms investigation of ideas of form into emphasis on appearance; the ordering of visual phenomena reduces them to 'mere seen things' (Panofsky, 1991: 72).

As is well documented, technological developments were central to the Renaissance, although in some respects founded on older knowledge – for instance, Plato commented on shadow-play consequent on the reflection of light through a hole in the wall of a cave. A number of instruments of observation, including the camera obscura (eleventh century) and telescopes (using lenses with prisms or mirrors) were developed and refined in the mediaeval and Renaissance eras as means of more detailed interrogation of the physical and astronomical world. The movement of light as it funnels through a hole echoes (and perhaps influenced) the development of the perspectival system of triangles. Philosophically the foundations of perspective were complex, reflecting the religious ideologies of the era. Martin Jay summarises shifts in critical understanding of what he terms Cartesian perspectivalism, from the mediaeval to the modern:

> a rough consensus seems to have emerged around the following points. Growing out of the late medieval fascination with the metaphysical implication of light – light as divine *lux* rather than perceived *lumen* – linear perspective came to symbolize a harmony between the mathematical regularities in optics and God's will. Even after the religious underpinnings of the equation were eroded, the favorable connotations surrounding the allegedly objective optical order remained powerfully in place. These positive associations had been displaced from the objects, often religious in content, depicted in earlier painting to the spatial relations of the perspectival canvas itself. This new concept of space was geometrically isotropic, rectilinear, abstract, and uniform. The *velo* or veil of threads Alberti used to depict it conventionalized that space in a way that anticipated the grids so characteristic of twentieth-century art, although, as Rosalind Krauss has reminded us, Alberti's veil was assumed to correspond to external reality in a way that its modernist successor did not.
>
> (Jay, 1998: 67–8)

Indeed, photography stands as the inheritor of the Albertian system, always in some respect linked to actuality – however abstract the rendering. Standard cameras retain perspective; the technique operates through the monocular construction of lenses and the centrality of organisation of focal depth of field. The veil is echoed in evenness of chemical (silver) treatment of the paper and developing processes. (Of course, more recent digital technologies in principle render perspective obsolete – although a screen of pixels might be seen as corresponding to the Albertian veil in that it is equally mathematical in its constitution – but the underpinning mathematics differ.)

Helmut Gernsheim defines the development of the camera obscura as a key precursor of photography as it established the foundations of photographic seeing (Gernsheim, 1955). But desire to invent such a device stands as evidence of interest in space. This also laid the foundations for landscape photography which synthesises perspective (built into lens design and mechanisms), light, tonal density and the documentation of detail – one of the central objectives of the idea of *photo-graphy*, Fox Talbot's 'pencil of nature'. A number of specific devices had long since been developed as aids for painters. David Hockney has drawn particular attention to geometric devices, able to measure objects for representation, including views, and translate them proportionally and perspectivally to the canvas (Hockney, 2011). One of the most curious devices was the Claude mirror, used to isolate and frame a view, whilst the viewer appears to look in the opposite direction – perhaps an apt metaphor for concealment of exercise of power of spectatorship! Indeed, any history of the camera as an instrument needs to also ask questions about purpose, instrumentality and social use, and about the epistemological context of its development and use. Panofsky's distinction between formal ideas and explorations, on the one hand, and 'mere' appearances, on the other, recalls debates in which photography, as a new medium, was either extolled for its detailed depiction facilities (Eastlake, 1857) or dismissed as a *minor* art fit only for reportage (Baudelaire, 1859), lacking in metaphysical properties. It was not accidental that camera technology, although dating from the mediaeval, was significantly developed in the nineteenth century. Empirical methodologies were central to the interest in and development of scientific and technological capabilities, and photography was seen as a useful fact-based tool. Imperialist expansion of territories in 'new worlds' was a further factor in the increasing demand for images of places and phenomena about which stories were being told, but which lay beyond the immediate experience of most people.

Use of mirrors and lenses thus was not new; camera technology incorporated previous systems of vision. The key nineteenth-century innovation was in discovering how to 'fix' an image, initially in the form of so-called daguerreotypes, tintypes or silver prints. The making of landscape imagery at first involved combination printing, as differing lengths of exposure were needed for land and sky, but nonetheless photography incorporated perspective, and settled into rectilinear mode. Teleological versions of history tend to suggest a direct lineage from camera obscura technology, Albertian perspective and, even, Plato's cave. But the implications of the new 'photo-eye' cannot be comprehended just through reference to histories of technologies; shifting political circumstances and social uses of images also have to be taken into account. The realist properties associated with photography at the time of its development suited nineteenth-century principles of empiricism. Photography is not only quicker than sketching; it is comprehensive, allowing access to detail which might not otherwise be observed. Walter Benjamin defined this as the 'optical unconscious', that which is more than the human eye absorbs (Benjamin, 1931). It is in this respect that photography has *revelatory* capacity; it remarks more than that which might at first be perceived and facilitates detailed analysis and contemplation. Explorations of human or animal movement (Marey, Muybridge) offer well-known illustrations of the deliberate use of this facility, although Benjamin was referring more to unanticipated (visual) information. Benjamin's proposition has a number of implications. It reminds us that we do not perceive, let alone engage with, all that is experientially available to us. It also implies that we might desire to see more. Following this line, a number of theorists have related photography to cryogenics, suggesting that photographs 'freeze' moments in time, rendering scenes available for scrutiny.[15] Since time moves on, this is not entirely helpful; the image may not be changed, but the viewer and the context are. The photograph is perhaps best understood as transcending simple *aide-mémoire*, acting as a mnemonic which generates not a precise return so much as a means of revisiting specific histories, unfolding and refolding narratives.

The Cartesian model places the spectator outside of that viewed, thereby reflecting rationalist philosophic models wherein a central distinction is made between subject (human) and object under scrutiny (nature). For landscape to develop as a genre, painters had to see themselves as observers depicting – rather than forming a part of – environments pictured. French theorist Michel Foucault famously analysed panopticon architectural systems in terms of the exercise of power. Paul Virilio's phrase 'vision machine' evokes Orwellian fears, reminding us that techno-cultural systems are not neutral, but have developed in correspondence with particular economic and political arrangements (Virilio, 1994). One effect of Cartesian perspectivalism is that 'man' becomes centred as spectator of a scene organised around a single point of view (Crary, 1990). The *double entendre* of the phrase 'point of view' reminds us once again of the inter-relation of looking, ways of seeing, knowledge and vision as empowerment. Discussing the import of digital technologies, Crary argues that images, and image-production technologies, are mutable; and, indeed, currently changing, as new imaging possibilities and digital technologies are further explored. But he also insists that, to comprehend systems of representation, historically and now, we have to take into account socio-economic relations. He specifically focuses on ways in which power relations are literally and metaphorically made manifest through cultural phenomena such as the single viewing position of (most) camera technologies and, in particular, the Cartesian ego-centrality of the position from which we *see*. Fenton's view of 'The Long Walk, Windsor' offers one example (p. 29). The avenue leads uphill, acting as a central line and conduit for the 'camera eye' and, by extension, the eye of the spectator. The landscape ordered around the drive thus acts not only as vista down from the house, but also, photographically, to position the spectator looking up from the bottom of the drive.

Indeed, nineteenth-century landscape photography generally echoed Albertian conventions. Francis Frith's photograph of 'Hastings from the beach low water' (1864) offers an unusual scene looking towards the line of houses from beyond the littoral of the beach (rather than, as in many images, looking out to sea). In terms of composition it obeys the golden rule of thirds, which contributes to the harmony of image. The rule is essentially a horizontal geometry whereby the sky, or the land, occupies two-thirds of the image, and the other element (land or sky) occupies the remaining third. Frith became a photo-industry; he commissioned photographers nationwide to record local scenes. The work together now constitutes an interesting archive of rural and urban environs in the second half of the nineteenth century. The mode was empirical, but emphasis upon composition and concern with vista is nonetheless evident. That imagery appeared harmonious no doubt contributed to the popularity of the many thousand views that were made into postcards for mass circulation. A further – and slightly later

– English example is the work of Peter Henry Emerson, who became known for picturesque renderings of life in East Anglia. In *Naturalistic Photography for Students of the Art* he in fact argued for 'naturalistic photography' advocating 'truth-to-nature', as opposed to the impressionistic or the idealistic (Emerson, 1889). He photographed rural workers as well as places, but often used soft focus for pictorial effect. We are reminded of aesthetic relativities; his work appears naturalistic by contrast with the pictorialism that characterised secessionist movements of the same era.[16]

In a series made in Australia in the late 1970s, Lynn Silverman directly explored the effects of perspective through a series of pairs of photographs within which the centre ground is absent. In the upper photograph we see the horizon line, almost at the bottom of the image; there are no landmarks and little to suggest scale or distance from the viewing point. We are in the 'outback', the 'interior', the 'desert'. Rather than being drawn into the image and towards a vanishing point, we have an overwhelming sense of the sky towering over us. The lower photographs are of the ground below the photographer's feet. They intimately detail textures of earth, stones and shrubby plants. The toes of her walking boots appear in a couple of the series, whilst her shadow hovers in others. We are forced to acknowledge the presence of the photographer; the landscape is not simply 'there', it is being viewed from somewhere specific, although not somewhere specified as anywhere in particular. But there is nothing to link the lower shot to the shot above except that, in exhibition or publication, the photographer places them vertically above and below one another. This implies the absence of the middle ground that so often contains features around which a pictorial has been constructed. It also implies a spatial link between the two images, which in fact may or may not have been composed at the same time in the same place. Of course the Australian outback – like the US Midwest – lends itself to exploration of landscape form through being less congested by signifiers of place and history than, say, European environments. It enabled Silverman to explore form minus the 'distraction' of conventional content. It also enabled a questioning of landscape conventions and our positioning, as spectators, within Albertian systems. Writing about this series, Meaghan Morris suggested:

> The work then confronts us, not with objective and subjective interpretations of the same space, but with two different ways of

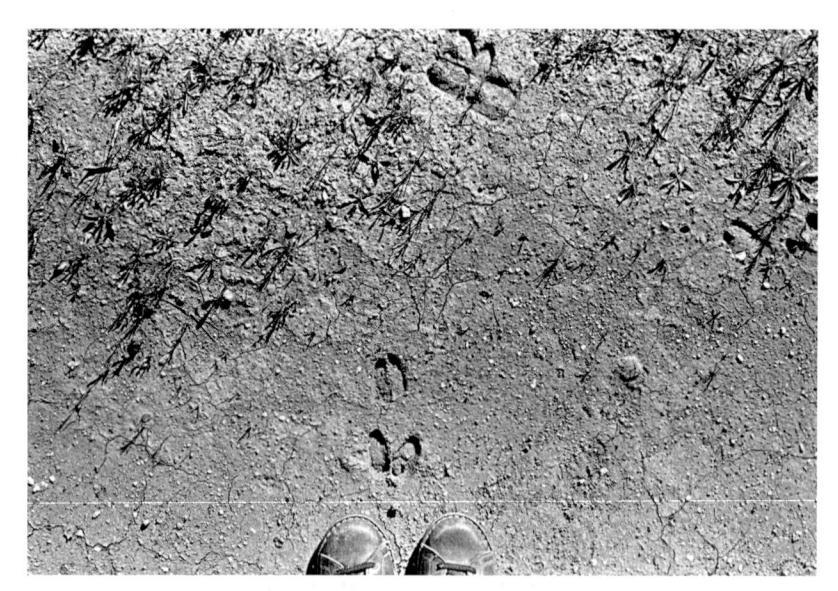

Lynn Silverman, 'Horizon No. 9',
Outside Packsaddle, New South Wales,
from the series *Horizons*, 1981.

manipulating subject–object relationships. One makes myth, the other makes personal statement; one includes us, the other addresses.

The images of landstrip, horizon and sky seem anonymous, impersonal; all trace of the photographer's presence is effaced. Yet for that reason subjectivity dominates here; anyone of I/you/all of us can take her place and assume that vision. This is the timeless land, 'our' land, laid out ahead alluringly for acts of possession to come – the product of an imperial way of seeing and proceeding.

The ground shots, in contrast, are personal in a way which does not absorb us into a universal vision of inviting emptiness, and which fills the frame with the clarity of a particular place and time. There has been an event.

(Morris, 1988: 143–6)

The example included here was particularly disorienting when reprinted in conjunction with Morris's essay, as the picture of the ground was mistakenly printed upside down – the boots appeared in the top of the lower image, suggesting the presence of someone (the photographer?) immediately in front of the camera, although no shadow testified to this or, indeed, to the tripod probably also in play. The unorthodox juxtaposition, between the close-ups and the broad horizon lines underpinning an anonymous geometry of skies and clouds, also draws attention to framing and focal distance as key constitutive decisions within picture-making.

Use of the frame as a device in landscape photography begs interrogation. In effect, a rectilinear scene is abstracted and presented as if it represents the actual experience of looking at – or being within – an environment. Since photographs are paper or film or pixelated composites, rather than earth, air or vegetation, interpretative processes are metonymic in that the image stands in for the object (or scene) referencing it metaphorically. The edges of the image constitute a 'slice' of the environment as 'landscape', using the geometry of perspective to determine focal emphasis (usually central). On the (gallery) wall, edges particularly emphasise composition. Derrida, discussing *The Truth in Painting*, questioned the effects of the use of physical frames, noting a slippage whereby it is not clear rhetorically whether the frame relates primarily to the picture, enhancing its delineation, or primarily to the wall, isolating a space which becomes the place of the picture (Derrida, 1987). Arguably it does both, in which case the logic of framing, focal arrangements and composition operate as spatial architecture within this viewing context.

Victor Burgin comments that framing, along with single viewpoint composition, structures representation and emphasises subject matter, thereby distracting from the condition of the photograph as a particular sort of text which contributes to reproducing ideological discourses. Photographs implicate multiple systems of codification, but they can appear uncoded (Burgin, 1982: 46; Lister and Wells, 2001). For Burgin the inability to actually enter the space of the image and the limitations of the edge/frame and point of view contribute to a dis-ease if a photograph is considered for over-long (Burgin, 1982: 152). Maybe. But this fails to account, first, for the intellectual pleasures of de-construction and interrogation of the means by which 'the monocular perspective system of representation' operates as 'systematic deception' which he himself so clearly enjoys (ibid.). Second, it does not account for the operation of the imagery in relation to memory. Perhaps particularly with landscape imagery, as Bachelard suggests, images invoke reverie, which, in turn, may avert the discomfort of discovering the limits of the image in itself (Bachelard, 1994). Experiencing a photograph cannot be the same as experiencing actual place. Environmental photography conveys something of how places look, and, through attention to texture, how things might feel. They do not convey the haptic (sensory) affects of sound, smell and taste; but memory brings such sensations into associative play. Photographs cannot replicate the multi-sensual actuality of the out of doors, but they do offer some form of imaginary substitute, albeit one within which memories of actual physical experience and mediated experience are complexly and inextricably entwined.

PLEASURES OF THE IMAGINATION

Welsh cultural and literary historian Raymond Williams located 'landscape' in terms of an emergent binary between 'city' and 'country' (Williams, 1975). Taking examples from literature and other arts (although not photography), he argued that the idea of countryside acquired extra significance in Britain in the nineteenth century as industrial revolution heralded the expansion of cities. He drew attention to the increasing romanticisation of the 'pastoral' as space of retreat, noting a shift, from the late 1400s onwards, from designation of pasture areas (for sheep or cattle) to a more complex set of Arcadian myths relating to beauty and rural ideals.[17] The idealised rustic as literary motif dates from the work of classical Greek poet, Virgil. Given a revived interest in classical (Greek) culture in the Renaissance period, it is not surprising to find the rustic once more eulogised. Williams' primary reference was to English literature, including examples from drama (wherein shepherds and nymphs figured in aristocratic entertainment, for instance, in the works of Shakespeare). But the Arcadian idyll was equally manifest in landscape gardening, for example, the gardens at Versailles where Queen Marie-Antoinette famously amused herself in her 'petit trianon' farm garden, or the peaceful glades incorporated within English estates landscaped by Humphrey Repton or Capability Brown. There is a parallel lineage in the visual arts, for instance in the work of Claude Lorrain (1600–82) or the late nineteenth-century Pre-Raphaelite painters. Similar themes emerged in photography, for example, in the pastoral scenes staged by Julia Margaret Cameron in the mid-nineteenth century, or in some aspects of late nineteenth-century pictorialism which, as a movement, has been defined by photography historian, Mike Weaver, in terms of the aim:

> To make a picture in which the sensuous beauty of the fine print is consonant with the moral beauty of the fine image, without particular reference to documentary or design values, and without specific regard to personal or topographical identity.
>
> (Weaver, 1986: Preface)

In secessionist movements at the end of the nineteenth century it was allegory and myth, rather than the observational, that preoccupied photographers as artists.

A number of factors contributed to the idealisation of the pastoral in Britain and its particular manifestation through art. Most particularly, limitations of land space in Britain as an island enhance the valuation of land not only economically, but also culturally. But urban expansion and increased population density was also manifest elsewhere, albeit later in the nineteenth century, to similar effect in terms of alienation from the rural and related idealisation. For instance, in Nordic regions, the woods, mountains, lakes, islands and fjords, not to mention the midnight sun of summer, play within a pastoral imaginary, and in North America, forests, lakes and mountain ranges came to be seen as special places to visit for physical and spiritual replenishment. Actual environments, political economies and related cultural histories differ from region to region, nation to nation, but it seems that the rural feeds both the geographic and the collective imaginary.

Arcadian ideals thread through Western modern philosophy. Enlightenment thinking was concerned with critique of the status quo power structures and with conceptualising a socially influential role for the intelligentsia. Emphasis was upon knowledge, experience, scientific revolution and intellectual freedom. The Arcadian vision was one of order and harmony. Law, administration, education, aesthetics and technological progress were taken as axiomatic for 'modernisation' and the improvement of social conditions. Precise emphasis differed: for instance, Jeremy Bentham (1748–1832) paid particular attention to the role of education, whereas Immanuel Kant (1724–1804) investigated notions of beauty. Resistance to modernity was also manifest, taking various forms, especially as the pace of change developed through the nineteenth century. Luddites resisted what they saw as the threat of mechanisation; the impact was both in terms of individual economic loss as machinery took over jobs and on traditional social modes of organisation. Later in the century, Pre-Raphaelites and Primitivists looked to the mediaeval, or to other cultures, for inspiration, rather than engaging with immediate phenomena. Such resistance might be viewed as response to a (human-made) sublime that was ontological, as well as economic, in import. There was a not unjustified fear that machines, time and commerce might come to dominate human rhythms and lifestyles. The related idealisation of the pastoral indicated an alienation from the rural that allowed the pastoral to be re-conceptualised and mythologised.

Edmund Burke (1729–97) distinguished philosophically between the *beautiful* and the *sublime*, discussing beauty in terms of that which inspires tenderness and affection (Burke, 1757). For Burke, as for Kant, questions of beauty are intimately linked to issues of taste. Burke related taste to the societal, considering conceptual distinctions in terms of consensus – a general agreement, for instance, that vinegar is sour and honey is sweet. Within this model the picturesque is, perhaps, a diluted sweetness – beauty that is psychologically manageable as scale, topographic content and lyrical responses are framed and contained. The cult of the picturesque attracted contemporary critique; many novelists satirised it. John Brewer reminds us of a scene in *Northanger Abbey* wherein Jane Austen's apparently uncultured heroine is baffled by a discussion between two new friends as they walk near Bath. But she quickly learns to perceive views in terms of foreground and distance, light and shade, and so on, to the extent that, within minutes, she dismisses the city of Bath as an entirely unworthy part of a landscape (Brewer, 1997: 615). Margaret Harker defines the picturesque (literally, possession of picture qualities) as 'emphasis on acute observations and appreciation of scenery; an understanding of proportion and perspective in landscape; and the conception of architecture at one with its natural environment (not to be considered in isolation)' (Harker, 1979: 27). As suggested, the picturesque influenced notions of landscape composition and 'point of view'. It continues to do so – manifest now, for example, in signposted 'photo-opportunities', encouraging tourists to take pictures from spots that facilitate conventional Cartesian aesthetics. In terms of pleasures of the imagination, the picturesque as a constructed visual mode within broader concepts of beauty feeds a sense of order and harmony which, by extension, contributes to a reassuring sense of security. Nothing untoward is likely to happen here. If the landscape viewed, or pictured, is typically British – or Norwegian, or Californian – then metonymically our sense of national or regional identity is also reassured.

The American landscape photographer, Robert Adams, relates questions of aesthetic beauty to form, suggesting that beauty is:

> a synonym for the coherence and structure underlying life … the overriding demonstration of pattern that one observes, for example, in the plays of Sophocles and Shakespeare, the fiction of Joyce, the films of Ozu, the paintings of Cézanne and Matisse and Hopper, and the photographs of Timothy O'Sullivan, Alfred Stieglitz, Edward Weston, and Dorothea Lange.
>
> (Adams, 1996: 24–5)

Representation – in words or imagery – celebrates that which is outstanding, striking or intense by singling it out, bringing it into focus. In this respect art reveals something about our environment through abstracting specific phenomena for contemplation. Adams asks, rhetorically, 'Why is Form beautiful?' He adds, 'Because … it helps us to meet our worst fear, the suspicion that life may be chaos and that therefore our suffering is without meaning' (ibid.). He also distinguishes between *beautiful* photographs and *significant* ones, suggesting, in effect, that significance emerges from content whereas beauty is an effect of conventions and composition. Of course the latter does not preclude the former – a photograph that is about something significant may also be harmonious in its geometry. Indeed, Cartier-Bresson's notion of 'decisive moment' specifically references this as a factor within social documentary. Beauty in landscape is, however, of a slightly different order in that it rests on a doubling of aesthetic and photographic coding, and topographic seeing.

Formalism in landscape arts, including photography, can thus be related to explorations of the beautiful; artists bring natural form under scrutiny. For instance, Edward Weston's detailed renderings of clouds or his series of pictures of the sand dunes in Oceano represent a poetics of the phenomenological. Phenomenology, as a form of knowledge, is concerned with the description and classification of materials (phenomena) in terms that acknowledge the intuitive and accept that meaning and significance rest, at least in part, on subjective experiential apprehension. Within this, 'beauty', as a concept, is not easily dismissed. Whilst conventions of the picturesque have allowed for construction of imagery that appears orderly and harmonious, easy on the eye, beauty can be more challenging. Shape, colour, texture, pattern may be crucial elements, and harmony again may be in play. Exploration of natural form has been central to the practice of many artists (from Breughel then Constable onwards, although most particularly in the Modern period of the early twentieth century). In some respects formalist concerns fall somewhere between still life and landscape as genres, as the central objective is detailed depiction of flora, fauna, forestry or vegetation in order to extol the extraordinary characteristics of natural phenomena in some cases portrayed as elementally symbolic. Very many pretty images have been painted or photographed under the guise of looking at our environment; there is little here to disturb us. Occasionally, however, explorations of beauty transcend 'nature portrait', inviting more critically reflective, existential responses to that pictured.

By contrast with the beautiful and the picturesque, the sublime is associated with awe, danger and pain, with places where accidents happen, where things run beyond human control, where nature is untamable. In his essay, Burke places discussion of the sublime ahead of that of the beautiful, suggesting that pain is a stronger emotional force than pleasure. Burke wanted to explore human fascination with the sublime, noting that, if pain or danger are too imminent they are simply terrible, but if held at some distance they are pleasurable. This apparent paradox has excited much subsequent debate, not the least within psychoanalysis. In relation to land and landscape, very roughly speaking mountains are associated with the sublime, hills with the picturesque; sea with the sublime, rivers and canals with the picturesque. At one level this is a matter of what cannot be brought under control: spring tides at equinox crash against cliffs, demolish ships and harbour walls, and drown people. It does not follow from this that mountains or sea are always sublime; it is not the physical presence in itself so much as the mood induced in the onlooker, who is also subject to a range of other personal mood-forming factors. Relative scale may be the key factor; the majesty of a lake, or a fjord with mountains rising around it, is sublime not in the sense of actual danger so much as in the reminder of our relative insignificance and of the transience of self. Natural phenomena are not sublime *per se*; the sublime is an attitude of mind related to existential insecurities. High emotion is triggered through experience, or spectacle, of scale, grandeur or wilderness. Although we may accept Plato's dictum that pain and pleasure have to be understood in relation to one another, Burke's assertion that pain is the stronger emotion perhaps relates to the sheer force of natural elements when experienced directly. Real danger is, of course, exactly that. But representation holds the sublime at bay, allowing imaginary indulgence.

Women are complexly positioned within such formulations. Within the Western patriarchal order 'woman' has been seen as somehow closer to nature. The moon, with its 28-day cycle of rise and wane, not only rules the tides but is also associated with the feminine. Within patriarchy, this association might enhance a sublime sense of the sea as a space of threat. Conversely the association has been a strand of influence within feminist art practices, with a number of women artists taking water and the symbolism of fluidity, ebb and flow as metaphorical themes. By extension 'woman' has been determined as undermining masculine mastery – Eve took the first bite of the apple of temptation and Pandora became an unwitting agent of destruction, opening her box and letting sublime whirlwinds loose. Myth reveals cultural attitudes, which, of course, variously shift over time.

For Freud the sublime relates to repressed desire and the uncanny, that which is strange and frightening because it leads back to or stirs up something deep-seated or primordial concealed beneath the veneer of human culture. Irit Rogoff interprets this in terms of Freud's Austro-Germanic routes as linked to a sense of *unheimlich*, 'not home' (Rogoff, 2000: 7). The German term *heimlich* refers not only to 'home' in terms of location, and ways in which personal and national identity may stem from this, but also in terms of the sense of roots and security associated with this. To be 'unhomed' thus has very fundamental implications within Germanic cultures and this currency no doubt influenced Freud's definitional interpretation. The sublime, in dealing with that which is awesome or unsettling, is uncanny in a double sense of stirring up elemental responses and activating threat of undermining of social order; risking loss of a security of identity that is founded in belonging to something established and knowable. There is a direct link between the sublime in aesthetics and processes of sublimation in psychoanalysis. The latter may refer to the elevation of something to make it sublime, but may also refer to the bringing of instinctual drives, particularly sexual impulses, under control so that they become manifest in socially acceptable ways. Thus for Freud the subliminal relates to the unconscious influence of messages transmitted just below the surface of awareness, yet, significantly, contained below the conscious. Such containment arguably parallels the containment processes implicated in representation – especially of aspects of our environment that feel unsafe, uneasy, beyond control and difficult to comprehend. One of the perverse pleasures of engagement with our actual environment is that it is always threatened with disruption as storms break and weeds grow through.

The sublime was central to eighteenth-century Romanticism, producing, amongst other effects, the cult of wilderness that became reflected in paintings, poetry and landscaped gardens. Taken literally, wilderness is unknowable; the very presence of those, such as scientists, anthropologists, geographers, and, indeed, photographers, who would investigate uncharted regions initiates the violation of wilderness.[18] The sea retains particular sublime symbolism, deployed variously by writers and artists. The idea of 'The Flood' as a form of cultural cleansing remains powerful in Christian myth and 'Ancient Mariners' recount stories of heightened emotional intensity as they experience the wildness, endlessness and unfathomability of the ocean. Following Burke, in visual terms, the sublime comes to refer to that which cannot be contained within the picture – literally not picture-esque. It may be that a particular place or scenario *literally* defies pictorial containment on the grounds of scale or viewpoints (some scenes are simply beyond the 'reach' of sight, or of camera technologies). More significantly, such scenes resist submitting to the 'mastery' of the viewer/painter/photographer. It thus inspires awe, or fear, seeming grand or sinister. For Casper Friedrich this included the craggy mountain beyond the misty clouds, or dense woods, within which the figure of man seems small and vulnerable. Such a figure, whether perched halfway up a mountain, below an immense waterfall, or in the shadows at the edge of the forest, is an 'everyman': humankind daunted by circumstances and environment.[19]

LANDSCAPE AND TIME

Photographs are trans-historical. The image may fade or otherwise deteriorate, but in principle the photo persists as an *afterimage*. Each represents that which was seen at a point in time. Photographs do not in themselves locate the place pictured or the historical moment of picturing. The time between exposure and viewing varies, but is experienced more as an ellipsis than as chronological time. As viewers we attempt to position photographs through reading the content as a set of clues of various orders. We also draw upon photographs as evidence of environmental change. Time and place are of particular relevance to 'straight' observational photography. The literal appearance of the image, along with its implicit 'I was there/it was there' statement of witness to scenarios or events, lends historic and topographic authority. Despite awareness that photographs are complexly constructed texts, the facticity with which photography as a medium was originally greeted still adheres.[20] Perhaps the desire to see what we might not otherwise be able to see, or to re-view that which we might otherwise forget, overcomes ontological hesitations.

Landscape does not lend itself to historical precision. We might be able to interpret time of day or season from the quality, angle and sharpness of sunlight, that is, from natural phenomena. But clues may be few. For instance, in *Time Pieces*, writer-photographer Wright Morris discusses the experience of travelling, noting and photographing across the American Midwest, his homeland, in the late 1940s. He argued that the camera exposes the inner eye of the photographer and discussed photography in terms of a long-standing human desire (from cave paintings onwards) to make images as fictions through which experience is explored (Morris, 1999: 11, 82). In considering the pictures, we would have difficulty placing them, were it not for titles giving place and year. The 'Haystack' near Norfolk, Nebraska, or the 'Landscape, Rolling County', Eastern Nebraska, both made in 1947, appear on pages opposite one another. Pictorially they might better be described not as 'time pieces' but as 'timeless pieces'; which is indeed part of the point Morris is making about time and about ways in which photographs mirror not the world so much as our way of seeing it. The haystack is by definition autumnal, but seemingly it could have been photographed any year since time immemorial. Of course, this representation could not have been recorded in the very early days of photography; there are intense whites not only in the clouds but also as the sun strikes the walls of farm buildings in the foreground and in the distance which would have defied Victorian combination printing. No modern elements – such as a car or agricultural vehicle – are included so we lack additional clues. No doubt a similar scene could be photographed today. Whilst landscape paintings and photographs may offer evidence of social historical interest and significance, the picture content may also seem apart from history, more as environmental archetype, contributing to our sense of character of specific regions or places.

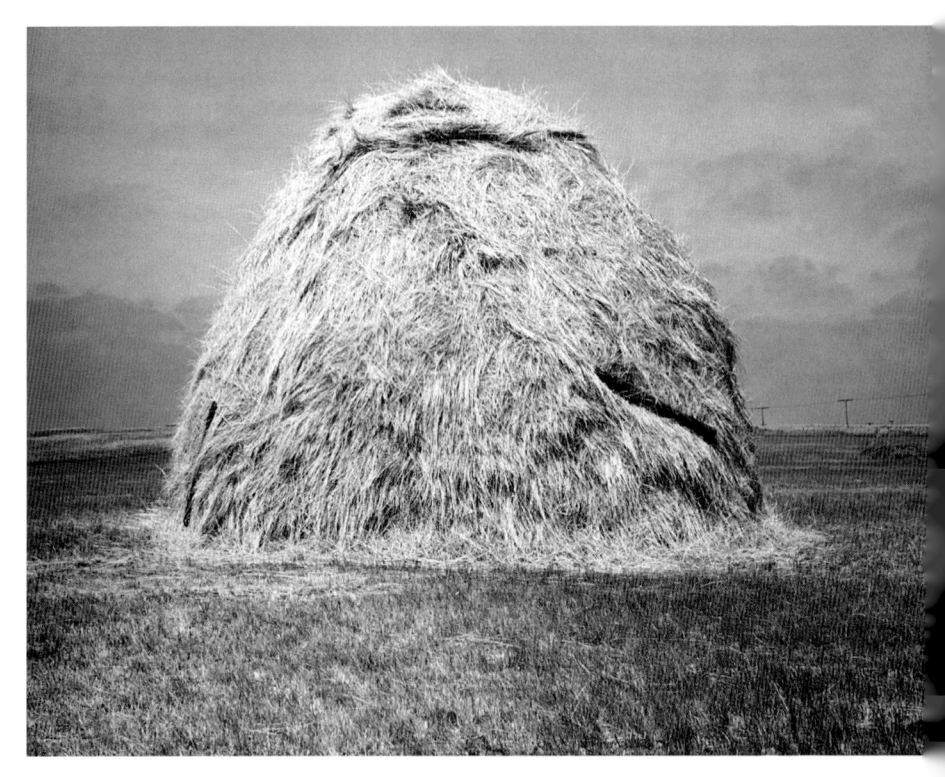

Wright Morris, 'Haystack', near Norfolk, Nebraska, 1947.

'Time' is not straightforward. Since the foundation of international time zones, it has become relatively un-interrogated, taken for granted as a simple narrative progression of seconds, minutes, hours, days, weeks and years. In the Western industrial world concepts such as time of day, or time taken for a particular task, or fear of 'time wasted', assume prominence – 'time is money'. This model does not characterise all cultures; it is a Western trope to prioritise chronological time over the cyclical time of climate, tidal movement, season, and other elemental phenomena. In Western culture, time 'lost' cannot be regained, except, perhaps, through Proustian musings. But, the photograph, in simulating moments from the past, can seem to help us unfold the layers of history. As such it feeds our sense of heritage, which in turn contributes formatively to identity and subjectivity and to collective consciousness.

PLACE, TERRITORY, IDENTITY

The above discussion at various points relates our engagement with land and landscape to our sense of identity. Questions of identity have been extensively debated, especially very recently. As Madan Sarup remarks, 'Identity' was not included in Raymond Williams' 1983 edition of *Keywords* (Sarup, 1996). A range of factors may explain current interest; they include older post-colonial issues, the end of the Soviet era and the subsequent expansion of the European Union, Western perceptions of developments in Islamic culture, and concerns over the implications of economic migration. Little of this is new, but political developments have brought identity, belonging, rights of habitation and questions of homeland into immediate focus. As a number of theorists have argued, identity is neither singular nor fixed (Hall, 1997a; Sarup, 1996). It is better conceptualised as a site of interacting influences and discourses. The debate is commonly pursued in terms of our identities as individuals with reference to family roles, profession or work status, and categories such as gender, ethnicity, size, region/nation, and so on. Debates as to the effects of (media) representation and stereotyping on individuals and social groups have been central, and psychoanalytic and sociological understandings have offered epistemological foundations. Identities are formed through social interaction and processes of identification – generally in the first instance with the (m)other. Identity implicates a sense of belonging within varying groups or social institutions – family, professional, and so on. As Sarup remarks, boundaries are also important as a point of reference and delineation; these 'may refer to, or consist of, geographical areas, political or religious viewpoints, occupational categories, or linguistic and cultural traditions' (Sarup, 1996: 11). Of course, these points of reference are not mutually exclusive. Rather, they interact multiply. For instance, religious viewpoints are reflected in everyday linguistic idioms and social behaviour; mosques, churches and temples foster a sense of congregation within specific communities organised in relation to belief. Geographically based occupations, such as farming, mining or shipping, have contributed centrally within historically constructed regional profiles, and have fostered particular cultural modes and traditions, some of which – such as annual galas and union banners, or harvest festivals – persist, this despite mine closures and the economic dominance of supermarkets. Typical features may also become incorporated as local iconography, for instance, the tourism kitsch of the miniature lighthouse.

Place plays a key role within identity, both actual place and imagined place. I tend to describe myself as a Londoner who has lived in the southwest of England for over 25 years. Holding on to my understanding of myself as from London, the capital city, remains important. Besides, I couldn't pass myself off as Devonian; my accent gives me away! The 'green, green grass of home' may be sung about wistfully, or with pride; landscapes – actual, remembered or idealised – feed our sense of belonging to whatever place, region or nation that we view as homeland. To belong – be/long – has existential implications; 'knowing where we stand' contributes to our sense of security. Reaffirmation of identity also works through difference. Jacques Derrida argued that discourse consists of slippage, and that meaning is relational, provisional and subject to ongoing shift (Derrida, 1978). He proposed that language operates not only in terms of what is stated and amended through continuing processes of deferral of meaning, but also through erasure, through what is other or opposite. Thus a concept is comprehended through reference to that which it is not: male is not female, light contrasts with dark, and so on. This is not a simple set of binaries so much as a clustering of oppositions and associations. Otherness involves individuals or groups distinguishing themselves, or being distinguished as 'different' in some respect or another, not a part of 'us'. To define people or places as different is simultaneously to acknowledge different histories and allegiances and, ego-centrically, to reaffirm subjective or collective identities.

Identity thus directly articulates the geographic. It also references place through notions of Diaspora – dispersal of peoples who, under different historical circumstance, might have been expected to be more closely clustered. Paul Gilroy explores effects of transcontinental links between descendants of those moved from Africa in the slave trade, who later emigrated or migrated from the Caribbean region and the Southern States of the USA to northern USA or, more particularly, re-crossed the Atlantic (some several generations later) to Britain (Gilroy, 1993). Taking examples from painting, literature and music, he argues that the Atlantic as actual and as conceptual space fundamentally influenced modern consciousness, not only for those for whom historical roots were African. Modernity, as realised economically through industrial revolution, exploited raw materials imported cheaply from plantations using slave labour. That is a part of the history of Western entrepreneurialism. Industrial wealth rested on the backs of slavery. This, he argues, had deep-seated psychological ramifications in terms of the collective consciousness of Imperialist Nations which remain marked in the character and identity of such nation states post-colonially. Discussing Turner's painting of a slave ship, he suggests that it represented a form of sublime – Black people contained and controlled (ibid.). Ethnicity, along with gender and nature, unsettles patriarchal and imperialist discourses.

This double consciousness – which Gilroy discusses in relation to Britain but which can be extended and tested as a more general post-colonial phenomenon affecting many European nations – articulates land and environment in a number of respects. First, the idea of 'homeland' or 'motherland' was complexly in play. For many Asian, African or Caribbean people the 'motherland' or '*la patrie*' must have seemed a place of promises (ones often unfulfilled). For those born in the colonies, as children of European families based abroad, it was a 'home' mediated via stories and images standing in for direct experience of the land and environment depicted. Paintings and photographs had an inverse role here, introducing Europe to Asia or Africa (as opposed to travel imagery or social anthropological enquiry). There were also more physical manifestations of European modes, for example, the introduction of lawns to the gardens of houses in India (a region where drought makes lawns somewhat oxymoronic). Second, and more obviously, the landscaped gardens which so succinctly represented the imposition of order in the Enlightenment era (in England, France and elsewhere), were generally financed through wealth in some respect linked to overseas investment (venture capital, plantations, import/export trading). Colonialism moulded the histories of coloniser and colonised in tandem. As Gilroy suggests, along with the socio-economic and political, the arts are inevitably imbued with sociological and psychological ramifications of the various histories. To have – or not have – a clear sense of place or territory crucially informs identity. For many contemporary artists, questioning roots and lineages contributes centrally to unlocking the histories through which we position ourselves now.

PHOTOGRAPHY, SITE, SPACE AND PLACE

Photographs slice space into place; land is framed as landscape. Representation envelops reality; it becomes an act of colonisation. Photography contributes to characterising sites as particular types of places within the order of things. The photographic image, in its precision and detail, operates topographically and metaphorically. The image itself evokes mood, a sense of what it might be to actually experience this place. The viewer of the image responds in terms of a nexus of aesthetic judgement, emotional recognition, identification, empirical appreciation. Unlike the relatively unbounded experience of looking, the photograph defines and frames, suggesting particular ways of seeing.

Representation is, of course, ideological, but so is looking, since our engagement with what we perceive is subject to cultural currencies and preconceptions. The image is a statement of what was *seen*.[21] We know that photographic vision is highly constructed. Nonetheless, photography significantly contributes to our sense of knowledge, perception and experience, and to (trans)forming our feelings about our relation to history and geography and, by extension, to our sense of ourselves.

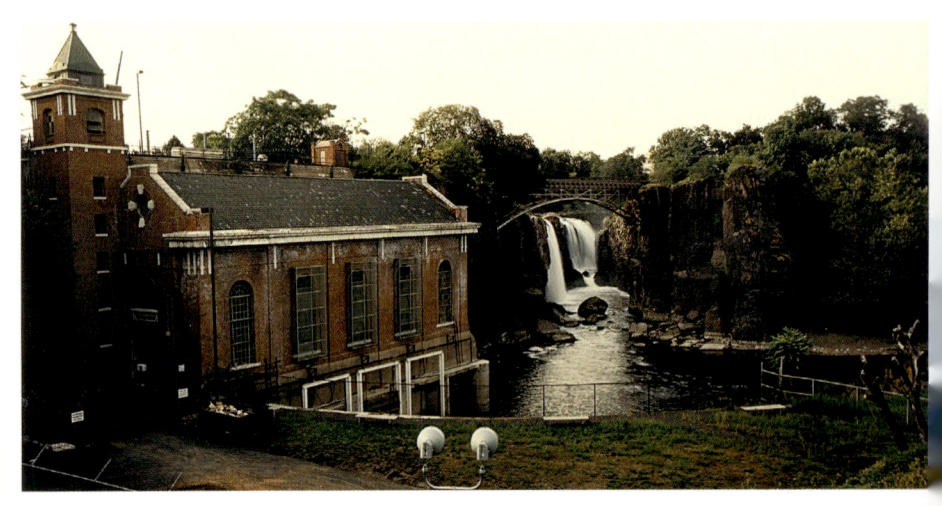

John Pfahl, 'Great Falls of the Passaic', Paterson, New Jersey, 1988, from the series *Waterfalls*.

2

A NORTH AMERICAN PLACE

LAND AND SETTLEMENT

Let us begin by briefly suggesting what North America would have looked like to a late fifteenth-century European who, through some feat of wizardry, could have soared like an eagle across the continent.

He would fly from the east over millions of acres of dark forest, a long line of densely wooded mountains behind the coastal plain, a thousand miles of lush, green prairie. He would see long, wide rivers that made their European counterparts look like modest creeks and vast inland seas empty of traffic save for a few solitary canoes. He would pass over a chain of soaring, snowcapped mountains, deserts punctuated by dreamlike pinnacles and deep canyons, a final chain of high mountains, and then a last narrow coastal area, filled with trees in the north and sere in the south. Beyond would be a wide blue ocean, stretching to who knew what fabled lands. Every detail of the landscape below would be vividly etched through the sparkling air.

(Shabecoff, 2003: 1)

This photographically evocative description opens a discussion of the American green movement. It reminds us how young Canada and the USA are as nations and, also, how strange North America must have seemed to the first explorers and settlers. Even now, with relatively speedy train travel, the journey from Toronto to Vancouver takes three whole days and nights. There is a seemingly interminable sameness of view, as the relatively populated East gives way to prairies for over a day, then the spectacular Rocky Mountains for a further twenty-four hours. This immensity is, of course, what greeted the early European travellers gradually hacking their way inland through forests, across mountains and valleys, through snows and storms in winter or the intense heat of summer. For Europeans, North America was, literally, a new-found-land, new territory for colonisation, celebration and exploitation, yet the sheer scale of the continent must have occasionally daunted even the sturdiest of travellers.

John Pfahl, in his series on waterfalls, draws attention to the harnessing of such striking natural forces for industrial purposes. The viewpoint emphasises the scale of falls as natural phenomena, used as power sources in the industrial era. Pfahl is one of a number of contemporary photographers to have questioned ways in which land is pictured as landscape. Titles of his various series and books are indicative; they include, *Altered Landscapes* (1981); *Picture Windows* (1987), landscape framed through windows; *Arcadia Revisited* (1988); *Tainted Prospects* (1991); *Extreme Horticulture* (2000), on human intervention, such as highway planting or formal gardens, explicitly shaping landscape; *Permutations on the Picturesque* (1997). His work, which stems from his enjoyment of nineteenth-century painting, is critically investigative. He wants to explore whether ideas of the picturesque and the sublime have continuing validity.[1] He comments on the effects of photography of place.

> Some people think that the camera steals their soul. Places, I am convinced, are affected in the opposite way. The more they are photographed (or drawn and painted) the more soul they seem to accumulate.
>
> (Pfahl, 1997: n.p.)

That certain places are photographed repeatedly would seem to testify to this; the more often they are imaged the more their aura is enhanced. Niagara is an obvious example; repeated representation in painting, photography and film has contributed to underpinning its iconic status.

For *Waterfalls* (first exhibited, 1992) Pfahl used a wide-angle lens to extend the range of the image to include that which is of interest around the waterfall itself, thus bringing in early industrial legacy. As he noted, in the West, water being scarce, waterfalls were protected in national parks, but in the East – Niagara aside – they were available for industrial use. His *Waterfalls* shows disused mills and warehouses, perhaps rehabilitated as picnic sites overlooking the falls, as well as waterpower-dammed, re-routed or otherwise harnessed for current hydroelectrical plants. In these pictures the sublimity of the power of the water is juxtaposed with the history of its utilisation; whilst not exactly tamed, it was drawn into industrial service. There are four types of image in the series: the first group consists of relatively close-up, pictorially composed, pictures of natural waterfalls. The second shows old industrial buildings, such as mills, by natural waterfalls with some sort of bridge across the fall for moving materials, now evidently disused. In other words, they speak of industrial legacy and also of the inter-dependence of technology and nature in terms of industrial fuel, in this case, hydro-power turning waterwheels. In addition, there is some indication of continuing human presence; for instance, benches and spotlights to look out over the fall, now re-positioned as 'view' (p. 58). The third type of image depicts current industrial plant with manmade 'races', water diverted from otherwise flat river, flowing over concrete walls to becoming a power source, nowadays hydroelectric. Finally, he pictures waterfalls in urban areas, for example, on the edge of town or, in the only example in the series of actual human presence within the picture, men and boys fishing at the base of one of the falls in Rochester City. This group also includes the Frank Lloyd Wright House built on the rocks above the waterfall at Bear Run Falls, Mill Run, Penn, again reminding us of the cultural centrality of vistas – we look up at this architectural wonder, and those in the house look out over the waters.

In some respects, composition is traditional; he uses gentle daylight as highlight. But, rather than being organised around a central point of interest, many of the pictures are formed in two sections. For example, the Lloyd Wright house and falls are in the left part of the image and woodlands are to the right. In this respect his concern with the organisation of the picture filters into his work. Although I have categorised types of image, the series is not organised in groups and the overall import is subtle. Exhibition prints are 14" x 28", no larger than an ordinary watercolour. We note tensions between the industrial plants and the otherwise natural elements, for example, billowing smoke in otherwise clear blue skies or stark buildings reflected on the water surface. Deceptive beauty: the aesthetic form is picturesque but the waterfall may be concrete and the factory or mill may have polluted the local atmosphere – indeed, it may continue to do so, invisibly. Within the series overall, tension emerges between the natural waterfalls in creeks or woodlands, and their colonisation for industrial use.

This tension between content and aesthetics is not new within Pfahl's *oeuvre*; it also characterises his earlier series, *Powerplaces* (1981–83). Here, through choice of viewpoint, he drew attention to geometric continuities, for example in the 'Niagara Power Project, Niagara Falls, NY' (September 1981) where the shape and textures of the metal pylons above echo the marks on the brown cliff-face below. Likewise, in 'Three Mile Island', a natural earth promontory out into calm water in the lower right-hand-side counterbalances the nuclear plant in the distant top left corner. Some *Powerplaces* were made in the West. The landscape becomes more craggy and the viewpoint more distant, for instance, in 'The Geysers Power Plane, Mayacamos Mts. California' (June 1983) trains on the rail track in the middle distance look tiny, like toy trains, and the industrial plant, which must be immense, sits like a small castle on top of a hill. Perspective is disoriented: a tall tree in the foreground seems so much larger than the industrial artifacts (train, power station) in the distance. This series has been criticised for preoccupation with form. Deborah Bright located it squarely within the art museum canon, suggesting that,

> If setting up a 'dissonance' between the romantic pastoralism of the landscapes and the potentially dangerous power plants within them was Pfahl's intended strategy, it is not carried through consistently, for he photographs nonhazardous *power places* such as hydro-electric facilities and dams with identical concerns for beauty and formal control ... By combining conventionally beautiful photographs of socially-loaded subjects with a fashionably ambiguous high-tech/political/ecological theme, the work was highly marketable without offending any potential buyer – a corporate client in the energy industry, for example.
>
> (Bright, 1989: 135–6)

Her critique is valid; the series articulates modernist concerns with aesthetics and photographic ways of seeing. But an alternative reading might focus more on monstrous beauty, trusting the spectator to discern the paradoxical tension between formal harmony and fears about nuclear energy to which the depiction of power stations surely points, or, to wryly observe the presence of concrete functionalist hydro-plants within pastoral spaces. Pfahl's power station series is one of the precursors of a now familiar sub-genre, 'industrial sublime'. Edifices, which may in themselves be formally striking, are photographed in order to draw attention to their presence, but composition enhances a sense of form and beauty which, arguably, distracts from the implications of the site or buildings in terms of purpose and use. That which should horrify is lent credence through the pictorial – hence the possible appeal to corporate clients.

The issue may not be a question of form so much as one of viewing context and shifts in the market for art. The established gallery as a socially valued (and commercially exclusive) site of engagement veneered by *politesse* in effect dilutes socio-political critique. Photographers who elect to show and sell work with critical edge in commercial galleries, and to produce books with publishers for whom the bottom line is, likewise, profitability, have sometimes been thought to be 'selling out'. Yet photography aims to communicate; this involves reaching out to audiences (self-publishing or exhibition in personal studios does not engage those with whom the artist is not already in contact). Besides which, artists need to sell work not only to gain recognition for themselves and for the issues with which they engage, but also to finance new projects. In this respect, exhibition and publishing may be regarded as sites of hegemonic tension; the gallery as institution may operate to contain aspects of the critical import of imagery, yet ideas may transcend such limitations, thereby in some respect challenging consensus. If critical photographic practices are to contribute rhetorically to questioning ideological orthodoxies, including histories and mythologies, then for many artists the mainstream is a valid site of engagement.

NORTH AMERICAN SETTLEMENT

New England, Newfoundland, Virginia, New Hampshire, Cheshire County, New York ... the names are redolent of the British heritage that is deep-seated in the east and northeast of the United States and in the southeast of Canada. Other place name references are French: Montreal, New Orleans. Along with Midwest names such as Indiana or Sioux City, we are reminded that the cultural hybridity that is North America is marked by an extraordinary diversity of ethnic lineages and cultural histories.

In his discussion of the early settlement of North America Robert Hughes argued that, whilst the English were not the first European colonisers on the continent, they had the most significant cultural impact (Hughes, 1997). The history of the US has predominately been recorded from an Anglo-Protestant perspective within which accounts date from the landing of the Pilgrim Fathers at what became Plymouth, Massachusetts in 1620 (although the Spanish had first arrived in 1513).

The majority of immigrants were, then as now, (self-)exiled from their country of origin, seeking a life with better economic prospects and with freedom of belief. Hughes argues that, for the Puritans, whose emigration from Europe dates from the 1630s, America was emphatically a new Eden. He suggests that the Protestant work ethic, emphasis on new possibilities, and the centrality of God are key Puritan legacies. His analysis highlights ideological currencies fostering the ideals of individual freedom and opportunity that characterised Protestant Anglo-Saxon attitudes historically, and remain centrally inscribed within North American culture. In relation to land and landscape, this accounts for the complex mix which developed over the centuries of, on the one hand, prospecting with the objective of rendering land productive (mining, logging, farming ...) and, on the other hand, a view of land as sacred, God-given. The latter was particularly marked in Henry David Thoreau's *Walden*, his account of two years (1845–47) spent living in a self-built cabin, in relative seclusion, by Walden Pond in Massachusetts (Thoreau, 1910 [1854]). Thoreau eulogised Walden, linking this American landscape to Eden:

> Perhaps on that Spring morning when Adam and Eve were driven out of Eden, Walden Pond was already in existence, and even then breaking up in a gentle spring rain accompanied with mist and a southerly wind, and covered with myriads of ducks and geese, which had not heard of the fall.
>
> (Thoreau, 1910: 158–9)

For Thoreau the future for humankind lay in the West; to look East was to look back towards Europe, but to look West was to look to the future, to forested lands stretching towards the horizon, offering ample possibilities for sustenance and spiritual replenishment. For those remaining in Europe, North American territory and attitudes became – and remain – matters of curiosity. Examples are myriad, from Thomas Paine's concerns with the rights of man and Alexis de Tocqueville's interest in exploring models of democracy to more recent semiotic interrogation by Umberto Eco and Jean Baudrillard.

Nineteenth-century French writer Alexis de Tocqueville visited North America after the French Revolution, at a time when political structures in Europe were under question. Considering *Democracy in America*, his primary interest was in socio-political organisation. Travelling just before the advent of photography he gives an account that includes details that later might have been documented photographically. The potential for a new sort of society excited him. He commented that much of the central valley, between the mountain ranges in the east and the west, is arid, describing the prairies to the east of the Mississippi as 'immense deserts' (de Tocqueville, 1946 [1835]: 24) and the forests of the West as gloomily overgrown. This was not the untrodden Eden that Thoreau was to describe a couple of decades later. But for de Tocqueville, North America offered potential for experiment in the creation of a new sort of nation. This depended upon agricultural endeavour: he noted that Native Americans, as nomadic hunters, occupied land 'without possessing it' (ibid.: 27) and suggested that, 'It is by agricultural labour that man appropriates the soil' (ibid.). His observations implicitly support the founding fathers' notion of Manifest Destiny (the will of God), which was already serving to justify colonisation. The religiosity is echoed in his comment that for immigrant Europeans 'Their ancestors gave them the love of equality and of freedom, but God himself gave them the means of remaining equal and free, by placing them upon a boundless continent, which is open to their exertions' (ibid.: 218). He clearly had no doubts about the rectitude of this:

> At this very time thirteen millions of civilized Europeans are peaceably spreading over those fertile plains, with whose resources and whose extent they are not yet themselves accurately acquainted. Three or four thousand soldiers drive the wandering races of the aborigines before them; these are followed by the pioneers, who pierce the woods, scare off the beasts of prey, explore the courses of the inland streams, and make ready the triumphal procession of civilization across the waste.
>
> (Ibid.: 219)

In other words, open lands were to be tamed.

For nineteenth-century North Americans of Anglo-European heritage, Europe had become a past, a place of histories and legacies of particular societies (earlier 'civilisations') to be explored and reflected upon, in particular, by writers (Henry James, Ernest Hemingway) or, earlier, painters such as Thomas Cole (1801–48). Cole was born in Bolton, Lancashire; in 1819 his family emigrated to Catskill, New York State, so the mountains became an immediate environment for exploration, although he made several study trips back to Western Europe (England,

France and Italy). The Hudson River School is commonly dated from 1825 when Cole arrived in New York. As an art movement it drew upon European interest in landscape art and architecture, particularly the Palladian. It also reflected the more general engagement in the philosophy and culture of Western Europe, marked, for instance, by the Grand Tour for young aristocrats, an educational *rite de passage* that later became taken up by wealthy East Coast Americans. Elizabeth Mankin Kornhauser notes that English writings on landscape aesthetics, defining notions of beauty, the picturesque and the sublime, were widely available in the USA (Kornhauser and Ellis, 2003: Introduction). Cultural links with Europe remained strong in New England, if only because it was the point of entry for many new European emigrants. Hudson River artists were unique in drawing upon European painterly aesthetics, yet responding to the scale and characteristics of the American landscape. They travelled, and made study sketches, not only in New England, especially at Niagara, and across to the Catskill Mountains (New York State), and the White Mountains (New Hampshire) but also, in many cases, completed what might be regarded as classical study tours in Europe. Some also voyaged to (what we now know as) Central America and the Caribbean. Second-generation artists also travelled west, following the frontier. Albert Bierstadt's 1866 painting 'In the Yosemite Valley' will have been among the earliest pictures brought back to New York, no doubt contributing to firing the frontier imaginary.

Thomas Cole's 1834–36 series of five paintings, *The Course of Empire*, questions American ideals via analogy with the rise and decline of classical civilisations. The same setting, initially pictured as 'savage' or natural, then as an Arcadian pastoral scenario, is transformed into an urban wealthy city, which is later destroyed, leading to desolation. It was painted following travels in Western Europe; its allegorical subject matter reflects an established tradition of landscape as setting for history painting, but it does more than this, as attitudes to land and environment are a part of the prophetic theme. Landscape painting was readily taken to be narrative with mythological references. This is partly because of work processes; the works were not painted *en plein air* and would not have been expected to be strictly topographical.[2] Commenting on Cole's 1827 painting, 'View of the White Mountains', Kornhauser and Ellis note anecdotally that, on being asked the precise location, Cole refers to a range of locations which he had drawn upon, in effect, compositing elements from a number of his sketches. He also added figures, for instance, a man with basket and axe towards the foreground; this functions to lend scale to the picture and also to suggest the taming of the wilderness (Kornhauser and Ellis, 2003: 74–5). Robert Hughes likewise comments on the symbolic dimensions of his work. For instance, he notes that Cole included a solitary Native American in 'Falls of Kaaterskill' (1826), synthesising him within the scene so that he becomes an emblem of the conquest of wilderness (especially so, as by that time Native peoples in New England were more-or-less vanquished). Such paintings, by contrast with photography, were understood as articulating detail from nature via artistic imagination and licence; in other words, the narrative function was acknowledged. As critic Adrian Searle comments in his review of *American Sublime* (Tate Modern, 2002), many of the Hudson River pictures remain significant not so much for their quality as paintings but as records not only of place but also of 'moral values and religious aspirations' (Searle, 2002: 11). He distinguishes between some of the larger-scale celebrations of nature and smaller, more topographic, studies of coves and flat lands, which he finds more ominous, despite a homeliness of scale and subject, as details of cultural phenomena such as haystacks or ships emerge through mists and storms. This was the everyday environment that challenged settlers and their descendants.

In his critical overview of the history of American environmentalism referenced at the beginning of this chapter, Philip Shabecoff reminds us that immigrants brought in not only European histories and attitudes but also crops and animals. They sought to subdue nature in order to acquire land for commercial purposes, especially agricultural, mining and logging, as well as claiming land for the building of towns and cities. A culture/nature binary was generally implicit, and 'frontier' was seen as civilisation advancing on nature, primarily for economic purposes. However, as Shabecoff remarks, religiosity was drawn into legitimising such reclamations: Manifest Destiny supported not only the conquest of nature but also the 'civilising' (or extermination) of peoples seen as 'savages'. This was not a matter of proclamation so much as a matter of mundane beliefs and actions:

> Translated into the everyday acts and habits of the pioneers and settlers, farmers and townspeople, workers and entrepreneurs, Manifest Destiny became an irresistible force for altering nature. By clearing a patch in the forest, building a home, plowing a field, driving cattle, constructing a road, using and throwing away farm implements, diverting a stream, building a mill, laying track, digging

a mine, the Americans who spread across the continent changed the natural environment, and they did it with breathtaking speed.

(Shabecoff, 2003: 11)

Furthermore, he adds, mechanical and technological progress, and industrialisation, especially in the nineteenth century, enhanced both possibilities for colonising land and the speed of change. This is not the 'oneness' with nature advocated by Thoreau. Rather, the history suggests a hierarchical notion of species, and a view of land as a resource to be used to satisfy human needs.

Indeed, faith in technology as a means of economic development characterised nineteenth-century North America (as, indeed, elsewhere, pre-eminently Britain). Railroads, hydroelectric dams, factories, and industrial-scale farming were symptomatic of the Industrial Revolution, which, of course, impacted on rural areas, as plains were bisected by the railroad and open lands enclosed for agri-business. Technology becomes incorporated within the landscape. Take, for instance, the comment from a speech by Jacob Bigelow, physician and botanist, at the opening of the Massachusetts Institute of Technology (MIT):

> I know nothing in nature or art more beautiful than a railroad train, when it shoots by us with a swiftness that renders its inmates invisible and winds off its sinuous way among mountain and forest, spanning abysses, cleaving hills asunder, and traveling onward to its destination, steadily smoothly, unerringly, as a migratory bird advances to the polar regions.
>
> (Bigelow, 1865; quoted in MANUAL, 2002: 9)

This comment is significant for a number of reasons. First, the description is highly pictorial. It could refer to any number of photographs of trains snaking across open spaces. Second, the new technology is rhetorically incorporated within the natural environment. This synthesis operates both through the description of trains moving through the landscape and through the analogy with birds in flight. Third, this image figured on the occasion of the opening of MIT, a centre for technological research. The harmonious integration of new technology within the natural environment presaged a vision of America wherein invention is harnessed and, in effect, naturalised. Within this vision, any nature/culture binary dissolves. Of course the vision was rhetorical. New industrial and economic aspirations were in conflict with earlier agrarian ideals. There was political tension between perceptions of land as a source of raw material for industrial exploitation, and land as nature's garden (see Chapter 3). Religiosity underpinned both, through a Puritan work ethic, on the one hand, and more romantic views of nature defined as God's handicraft (now more commonly described in terms of 'intelligent design') on the other.

Thus, attitudes to land and landscape simultaneously encompassed pastoral myth and economic demand. If settlers, as they spread out from the East, were initially functionalist in their colonising impulses, they also become imbued with romantic sensibilities fundamentally derived from European Romantic movements (Rousseau, Wordsworth, Friedrich) and also from the homegrown vision of American-born philosophers (particularly Thoreau). American arcadia was not a utopian pastoral community living within and preserving a natural environment; rather it was a facet of Manifest Destiny and a natural environment out of which a living could be wrought.

HISTORIES AND HERITAGE

Boston-based photographer and critic Deborah Bright has investigated sites of patriotic memory and histories of East Coast settlement. Her series of nine pictures, *Glacial Erratic* (2000–03), focuses on Plymouth Rock in Massachusetts. The Rock is now enshrined as a heritage site on the shore of Plymouth Bay. It is promoted as a tourist attraction along with a reconstructed Pilgrim village nearby and a model (two-thirds scale) of the *Mayflower*, the ship that first brought the Pilgrims from the Netherlands and England to North America. The artist describes the tourism experience:

> Visitors usually look down on the rock from above its sunken pit, but from shore level, the rock may be viewed from the side through a steel grate that protects it from storms and vandalism. As the tides wash in and out of Plymouth Bay, they leave their residue behind: seaweed, exposed sandbags and shifted rocks. Layers of copper pennies, tossed into the pit by generations of visitors, are exposed by winter erosion. Changing weather and seasons create their own sensuous play of color and light on the immobilized rock, restoring the grace of nature to this most unnatural and ambiguously symbolic scene.
>
> (Artist's statement, 2003)

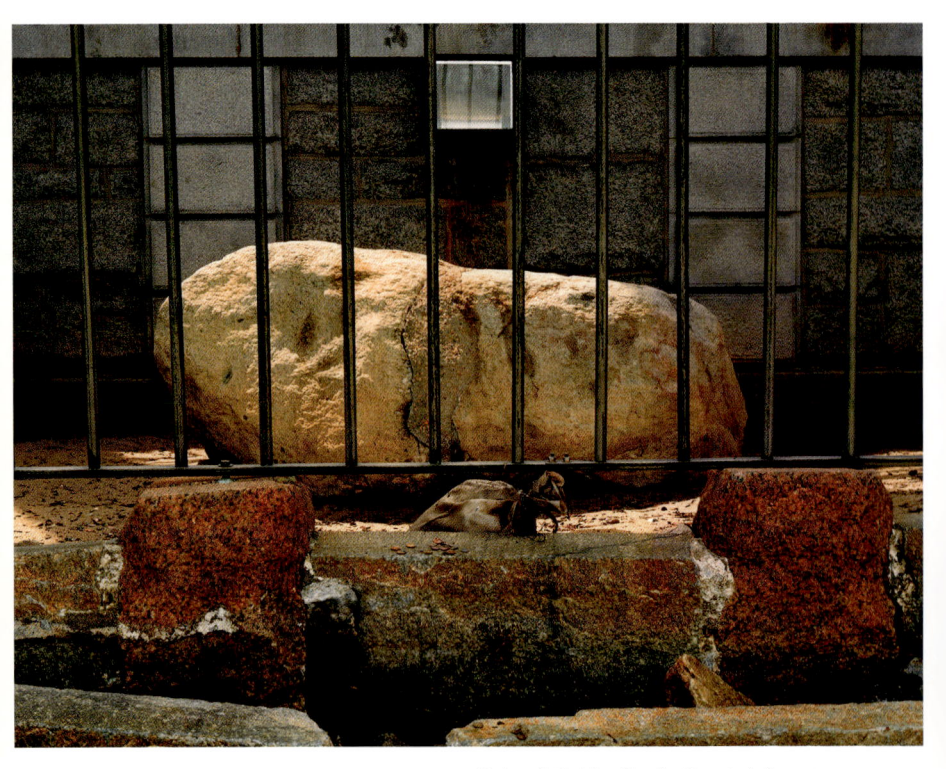

Deborah Bright, 'Lucky Pennies', from the series *Glacial Erratic*, 2003

At first glance this is simply a rock, behind bars, which can be viewed from more than one angle, and which changes according to light, weather and tidal conditions. But it symbolises much more than this. Geologically, the Rock is a 'glacial erratic'; it dates from the last Ice Age (over 10,000 years ago) and was deposited as glaciers retreated. Its geological heritage lies elsewhere; it thus differs from surrounding rocks, marked out by particularities of mineral composition, shape and colour. Bright's photographs are closely framed, echoing the containment of the Rock, behind bars, now sitting on a flat ledge, fronted by brick and stone. The close framing limits possibilities for comparison with surrounding rock facia; but for those with relevant scientific knowledge, that the Rock was 'immigrant' is immediately apparent.

The Pilgrim Fathers first landed at 'Plymouth', then an apparently vacant shore, presumably sufficiently sheltered for the creation of a harbour. (The notion that they landed precisely at the Rock is probably mythical – they are more likely to have rowed ashore towards the beach rather than risking anchoring by rocks.) The name, Plymouth, reflects the fact that the *Mayflower*'s final departure port was Plymouth in Devon, UK (a city where 'Mayflower Steps' still lead down to a harbour). Naming functions as a claim on territory. This east coast area was soon designated 'New England', even though places already had Native American names and functions (as sources of food or sites for seasonal camps). Although the Pilgrim Fathers and the settlers who immediately followed had set out to seek new prospects, it seems that, through naming, they were glancing back at a Europe that they had not quite left behind. The Rock was only designated as a memorial to the European immigrants after the American Revolution and the founding of the United States of America, with George Washington elected in 1789 as the first President.[3] As the artist comments, 'this shoreline rock was selected by town fathers to commemorate the Pilgrim settlement in 1620 and create a national myth of freedom-seeking self-determination for the new country' (Bright, 2003). But it was not named 'Independence' Rock, or 'Washington' Rock. The landing clearly acquired enhanced significance in the mid-nineteenth century immediately following the colonial period, but the literal cartographic naming emphasises historical lineage rather than new prospects; symbolic links to England were not entirely severed. Resonances are multiple: the Rock links to England, not France or Spain; and to Europe, not to Native American histories. This is New England asserting its White Anglo-Saxon Protestant lineage.

Bright's series of nine pictures portray the Rock in varying lights, at different points in the year. All but one appear 'natural' in the sense that climate and weather are conditioning the actions of light and water on the Rock – a point reinforced through specific picture titles such as 'Glacial Erratic – Snow' or 'Glacial Erratic – Nor'easter'. Each image shows the Rock in a different light, its surface varying from greys to russet browns, from smooth to rough-textured, the fracture across the centre of the rock attracting more or less emphasis as the elements variously illuminate perception. Bright explains that 'There is a small beach that slopes down to the bay that is exposed at lower tides. I timed my excursions at low tide except for the "storm surge" photograph when I was up to my chest in choppy surf, camera enshrouded in plastic bags' (email, Deborah Bright, 3 October 2005). Sun caresses, wind erodes, and waves break over the rocks rather as the Pilgrim Fathers might have first spotted the shore. In 'Lucky Pennies', an old leather purse sits under the railings encasing the rock. For incomers, then as now, economic prospects formed a part of the potential – and myth – of the Americas. Manifest Destiny, as a notional justification for territorialisation, articulated religiosity, the Protestant work ethic, and economic ambitions; this combination came to characterise American Capitalism. Plymouth Rock is one of the foundations upon which this particular Holy See was built. That changing seasons and weather shift our sense of the hues and aspects of the Rock perhaps symbolises broader shifts, changes and ruptures if we scrutinise the notion of 'united' states.

Production values reinforce the status accorded to the Rock as a mythical initiation point for the 'New World'. Each image is produced in limited editions of five as Iris prints, 22" x 29", on gallery high-quality paper. The work is intended for display in the public, and somewhat hallowed, space of the art gallery and for private acquisition as a work of art. The aura attributed to the Rock is reflected in the specificity of the limited edition. As landscape art the strategy is ambiguous. By photographing the paraphernalia of the metal bars enclosing the Rock, Bright enhances discourses within which the Rock stands for continuity and timelessness. But this is not a symbolist celebration of nature (or biblical reference); rather, it is a comment on the deliberate construction of nationalist myth.

In a previous series, *Manifest*, 2000–01, Deborah Bright explored early agricultural enclosures and family heritage in New England, particularly in Cheshire county, New Hampshire. Early settlers established small farms; they dug up glacial boulders sedimented in the earth and used them to wall off fields. As Bright comments, this marked 'the original footprint of generations of farmers of English ancestry whose economy, self-definition and political enfranchisement centered on individual male property ownership' (Artist's statement, 2001). Settlement had moved inland. The series title testifies to the belief in Manifest Destiny that fuelled the determination involved in transforming open space into farmland. The farms have fallen into disuse, woodlands have re-grown, and the area is now used for logging, some residential accommodation, and holiday homes. But the walls remain, historical reminders both of struggle for survival through settlement and of enclosures which functioned to keep animals in and to exclude others, including Native groups. Image titles are factual: 'Harvey to Goodrich, 1799' or 'Pierce to Draper, 1837'. Researched through records of inheritance and conveyance deeds, they describe the passing on of land from one man to another at a certain date, and, in effect, testify to the legacy of Anglo (in one case, Welsh) surnames, families and culture in the area. Exhibition prints are standard size: 20" x 24" chromogenic photographs printed from black and white negatives. Place and history are not fetishised through expanded imagery or saturated colour; rather, through according with conventional documentary scale and idiom, attention is drawn to residues of a particular era. This may be 'new' England but, as in 'old' England, patriarchal lines of inheritance are centrally woven within the destiny manifest. The historical research and precision of photo-method render Bright's work scholarly; as such, both *Glacial Erratic* and *Manifest* should contribute to socio-historical debate. But with the art museum and private collector as likely destination – especially for work produced in a limited edition – the pictures will probably reside on walls in contexts which detract from any intended critical reading and, perhaps especially post-9/11, operate to enhance nationalism. The artist is, of course, aware of this Catch-22; it is the point that she herself made in relation to the work of Pfahl.

MONUMENT AND MEMORIAL

The East Coast has been settled for many generations, and histories of settlement – let alone preceding Native American histories – are often hidden or multi-layered. Monuments claim the significance of particular characters or stories, often contributing to sidelining complexities. War memorials are especially remarkable: they celebrate that which is actually horrendous, and canonise the deaths of individuals without reminders of the effects of such losses on community and family. The realities of war cannot be fully acknowledged, if only for fear of deterring future support, so heroism becomes idealised. Gettysburg offers one such example. Now a national monument, with paths and signposts directing visitors to statues of particular military leaders or regiments, the bloodiness of the battleground has been sanitised, and heroes created. Gettysburg stands for the ideal that all 'men' are created equal, which in principle is central to the US constitution (although in practice some men seem more equal than others, and women still face struggles for inclusion).

The American Civil War played a key role in the establishment of democratic principles of freedom; it is one of a number of defining moments in the constitution of the United States, then still largely rural.[4] The war focused on slavery and was triggered by the 1860 election of abolitionist Abraham Lincoln as President. Questions of self-determination were thus key to this struggle, both for plantation workers as individuals, and for the Southern States which together had formed the secessionist Confederacy. Underpinning the conflict for the South was the economic question of how to maintain the profitability of estates without slave labour; for plantation owners and those involved in related economic activities (transportation, shops and commerce) the war concerned defence of territory, culture and lifestyle.

The American Civil War was also among the first wars to be photographed. We might now take the presence of photojournalists for granted, and be cynical about the types of image shown. But photographers then, including Matthew Brady (1823–96) and Timothy O'Sullivan (1840–82), were contributing to founding a genre, taking their darkroom carts into danger zones and confronting the pain and death of others. The war was also the first occasion of military conscription (on both sides); most soldiers were farmers with no professional army training and no previous experience of battlefield-scale combat. As photographer, John Huddleston, suggests,

> The experience of the Civil War shaped the self-reliant nature of the American into a character more amenable to serving in large, hierarchic institutions. Total war spawned powerful, national systems of government, transportation, and industry that operated under centralized control, replacing former localized and individual power bases. When the war began, states issued their own paper currency: citizens and militias owed their allegiance to states. By war's end both North and South had a national paper currency, a national definition of citizenship, and national conscription. The national military organisations served as models for large corporate structures of the future. Primary resistance to this capitalist growth had come from Southern agrarianism. The South was destroyed, and the Northern ideal of the independent craftsman, businessman, or farmer was eroded in the process of trying to assert it. Hierarchy, subordination, and obedience to political and economic institutions became the new American way.
>
> The steamboat, the railway, newspapers, and the telegraph enabled the United States to maintain an evolving unity.
>
> (Huddleston, 2002: 5)

Huddleston also comments that, for Black people, the war was about slavery right from the start, but that few others would have noted this as a motive for fighting. Racist attitudes were as endemic in the North as in the South, and it was only in the second year of the war that emancipation was formally incorporated into Union objectives.

Huddleston's concern is with the legacy of the Civil War for the American landscape; specifically, ways in which it is irrevocably marked in the land. He notes physical changes to vistas where trenches were dug, earthwork fortifications were built, or scorched-earth tactics left a permanent mark. He also asks whether the muted reds of the soil incorporate body parts, blood and minerals (lead from cannon balls and iron from bullets). Huddleston is concerned with what he terms 'spiritual traces', by which he means ways in which 'tensions and sufferings of the soldiers involved in the riotous circumstance of these locations 140 years ago may come to us through written descriptions, the color of the soil, or collective memory' (ibid.: 7). He suggests that,

> The battlefield is a talisman, a physical focus of violent acts. The land sparks personal memory of wartime accounts. It triggers a shared, deeper memory of human conflict and suffering, and it evokes a way of perceiving that sees in a leaf falling a man falling, a fallen man seeing a leaf falling. In the amphitheater of death many visions may have been the final sight of closing eyes.
>
> (Ibid.: 7–8)

I quote this at length because Huddleston's writing indicates something of his approach to photography. He emphasises content, metaphor and form as key facets of imagery in itself. In his publication, *Killing Ground* (2002), contemporary colour photographs made at battle sites are juxtaposed with archive materials, thereby paying attention to historical context. Archive images include studio portraits of those newly enlisted, no doubt intended as mementos for family and friends that testify to the fear of never returning. This was a war in which 30 per cent of Southern white men under age 40 and 10 per cent of all Northern men under 45 died – two out of five men were killed or wounded (also many civilians in the South) (Huddleston, 2002: 3). Along with maps and early photographs of campsites and battlefields, the portraits are juxtaposed with Huddleston's pictures detailing contemporary uses of the land. Captions state location, comment on the old photographs, and

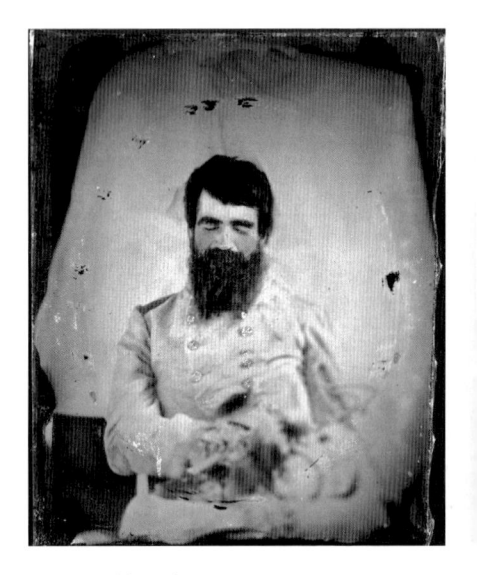

'Turner Ashby, of Fauquier City, Virginia, age 33, was photographed after being killed here', 6 June 1862, Harrisonburg, Virginia.

note casualty statistics. The diarist montage tactic is effective poetically as well as for historical detail. For example, a portrait of a Virginian who died in battle at Harrisonburg, Virginia in June 1862 is juxtaposed with a close-up of the red earth of the battlefield; a disintegrating piece of material in the form of a cross is held on the surface of the ground by boulders. The symbolism is perhaps over-stated, but the effect is nonetheless poignant.

As William Earle Williams indicates in his extensive photographic studies of battlefields, there is something ominously ordinary about these hills and woodlands where so many soldiers fought and died. Williams,

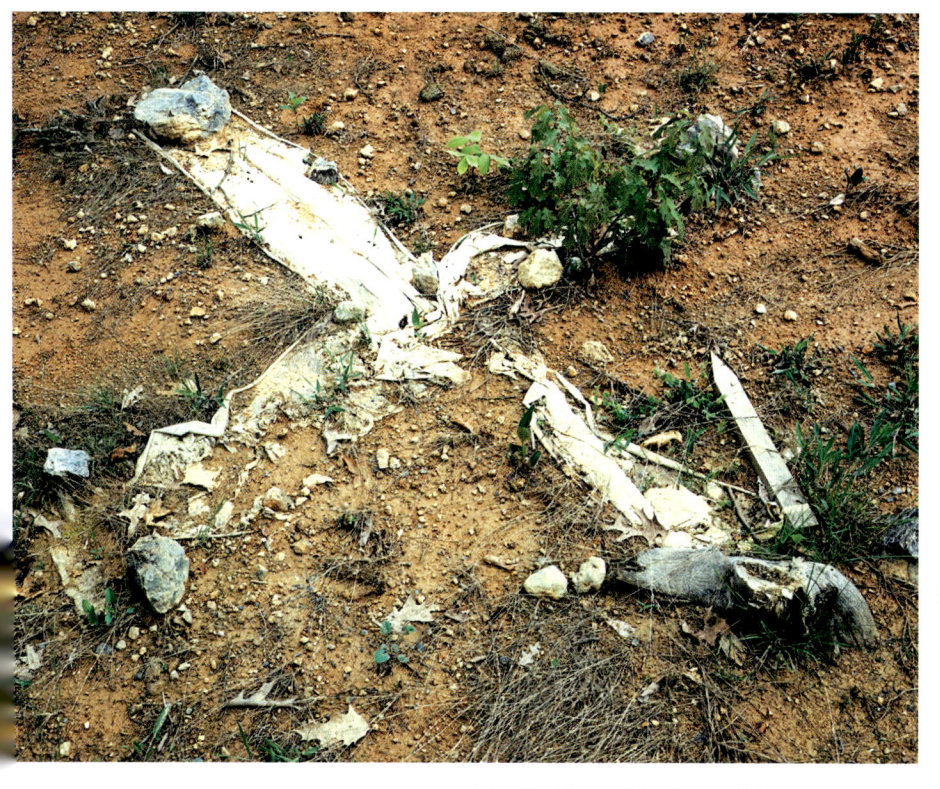

John Huddleston, 'The Center of the Battlefield', 130 American Casualties, Harrisonburg, Virginia. From the series *Killing Ground*, 2000.

like Huddleston, takes the Civil War as a key historical juncture. In *Gettysburg* (1997) he avoids the tourists and photographs the monuments, offering detail – the name of a State regiment or of a field where we presume parts of the battle were fought. These may mean little now, except to military historians, but the site's symbolic function of articulating moral principle and national pride persists. The corpses lined up in pictures by Brady or O'Sullivan have given way to well-organised memorial parklands. Cracked boulders may or may not testify to cannon damage; but little else other than well-maintained monuments and position posts remark the event, and it takes a leap of imagination to grasp the full horrors of what must have occurred. Williams' monochrome prints are small, in keeping with the size of the glass plates used by the earlier photographers. That the contemporary site is depicted through scale that references 'then' enhances a sense of temporality, although there is also a sense of *timelessness* as monuments look into the past. His next study, *The Vicksburg Campaign: Photographs of The Civil War Battlefields*, photographed 1997–99, is more specifically focused on the participation of African American regiments, remarking a history often overlooked. The battle ranged over extensive areas of Louisiana, Arkansas and Mississippi in 1863. The blandness of the sites pictured reminds us that photographs of the surface of the land tell us little about the events that have contributed to shaping those lands, literally and symbolically. Discussing 'Sacred Ground', Williams states

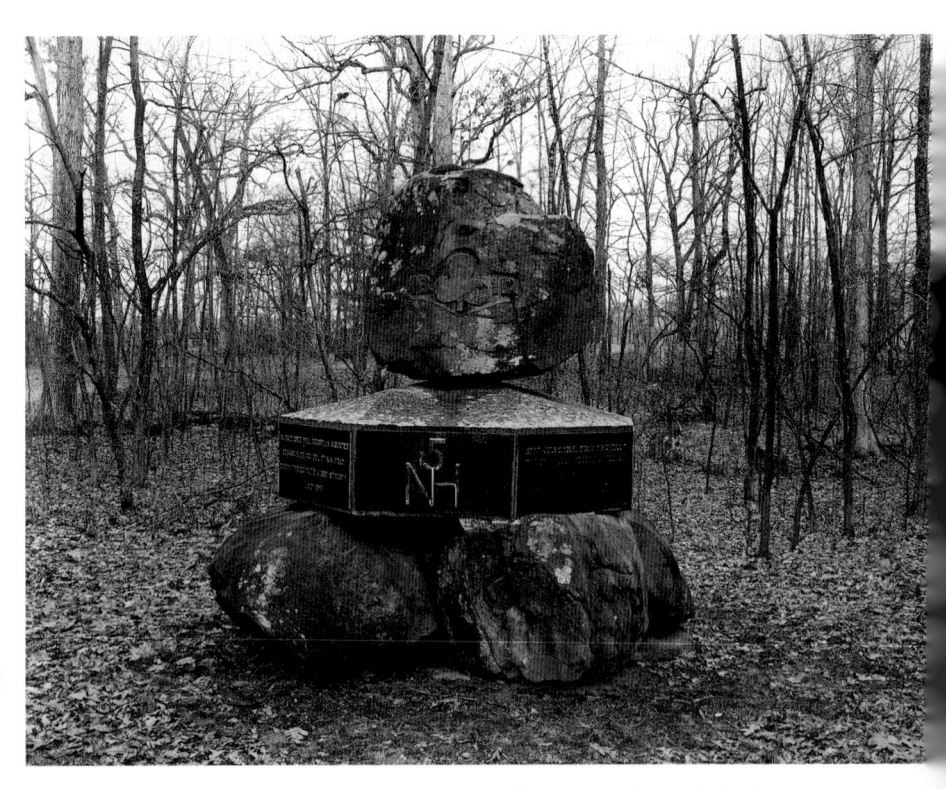

William Earle Williams, '5th Infantry New Hampshire Monument', 1986, from the series *Gettysburg*, 1997.

that his photographs 'strive to emphasise the social history of American life as determined on the Gettysburg battlefield and on the battlefields where Black soldiers fought. The images are interpretations which capture certain concerns about the Civil War history and its ramifications for our present and future.'[5] Williams himself is steeped in Civil War history, which, as a Black American, is a history of struggle for emancipation; he collects Civil War documentation, so for him these are hallowed sites. One challenge for contemporary photographers is finding means of relating the historical through the visual. The affect of this work depends on the degree of familiarity with this particular history.

Sally Mann is among the many photographers from the South for whom the legacy of civil war resonates. *Deep South* (2005) includes several series, all of which reflect her ambiguity towards the history of the land that for her is home – she still lives in Lexington, Virginia. Like Williams, she notes the ordinariness of the landscape. But for Southern white families reference to the civil war is a reminder of defeat; a loss of a heritage which in States such as Virginia dates back to the very first settlers. *Mother Land* (1997 – reprinted in *Deep South*) twins landscapes from Georgia with landscapes from her home state. In keeping with nineteenth-century processes, the picture edges are definitively marked, thereby implying 'authenticity' and historical reference; indeed, Mann makes wet-plate negatives (and refers to her 'rolling darkroom').[6] Processing marks are sometimes evident, perhaps symbolising the photographer's emotional as well as physical involvement in image-making. The pictures retain slight haze, an aesthetic effect that she attributes to the seepage of damp-laden air; for her this implies the many layers of histories never spoken but still inscribed within the soil on which so many died. As she comments:

> Flannery O'Connor said the South is Christ-haunted, but I say it's death-haunted. The pictures I took on those awestruck, heartbreaking trips down south were pegged to the familiar corner posts of my conscious being: memory, loss, time, and love. The repertoire of the Southern artist has long included place, the past, family, death, and dosages of romance that would be fatal to most contemporary artists. But the stage on which these are played out is always the Southern landscape, terrible in its beauty, in its indifference.
>
> (Mann, 2005: 52)

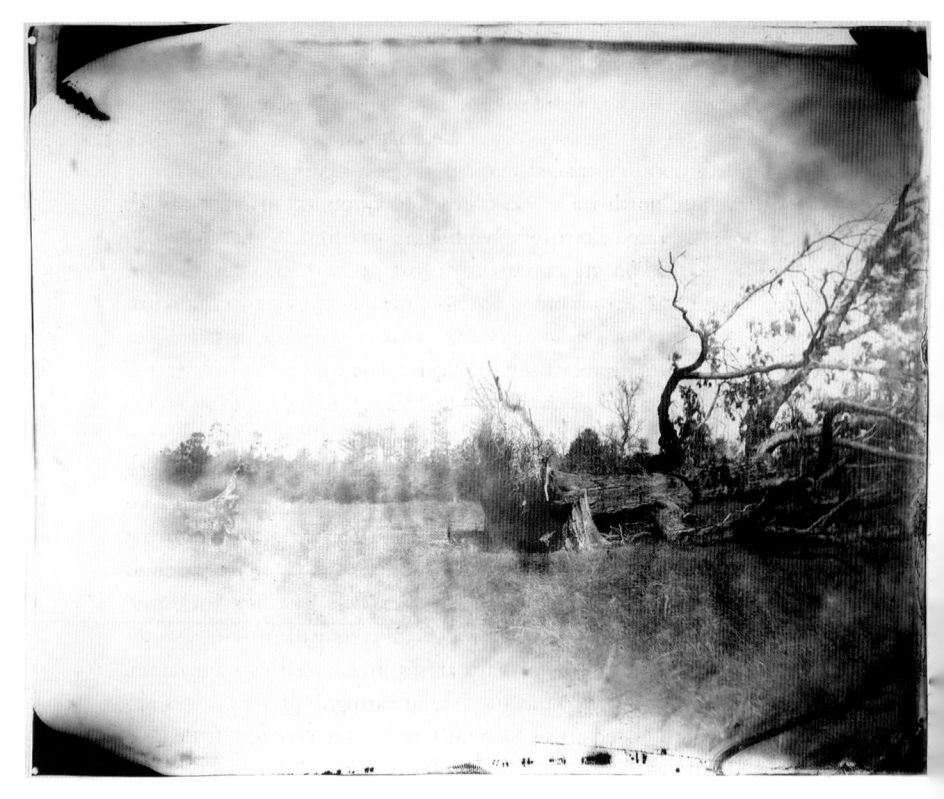

Sally Mann, 'No. 6', from the series *Deep South*, 1998.

The contextualisation is precise. Mann's primary interest is existential, hence her photographic involvement with her own children in *Immediate Family* (1992), for which she is well known, and also a series *What Remains* (2003) in which she explored her responses to the deaths of her father, her dog, and also to that of various strangers. Her familiarity with the landscape of the South, and the lingering wounds of history, is clearly of import; whilst at first glance the images might seem unduly pictorial, on fuller contemplation they come to reference a certain sadness of the South.

MAPPING SETTLEMENT

Borders – for instance, between 'South' or 'West' and the rest of the USA – are historical constructs; they are imaginary as much as they are physical. This does not make them any the less significant. For former slaves, travelling north via the so-called underground railway (network of safe houses), Yankee territory symbolised freedom. Sometimes such borders are marked on the land itself, for instance, the Rio Grande (with barbed wire fences reinforcing the frontier between the US and Mexico) or shifts in vegetation marking different farm or ranch ownership. But the natural is no respecter of the political; rivers wend their way to the sea regardless of State boundaries and the water flowing over Horseshoe Falls at Niagara (Canadian side) blends seamlessly with that flowing over the American Falls (US side). Indeed, borders and histories may be relatively invisible unless we know where to look and are prepared to look closely; they relate to cultural knowledge, which may not be obviously marked on the land itself. Furthermore, away from the cities and immediate coastal areas, the geographic scale is so immense that boundaries may be known regionally, but not systematically marked. As such, borders, boundaries and maps are as much matters of everyday knowledge, local or regional, as they are of cartography.

Newfoundland-based artist, Marlene Creates, has explored settlement in the Northeast Territories of Canada. The area is remote, wild, but not the 'wilderness' of the American sublime that has become associated with the mountain ranges of the West. In this region wildness is related more to climate, distances and relative isolation. In these respects it has more in common with the prairies than with the mountains, although it lacks the relentlessness of agri-industrial contouring effected by crops, cornfields and cattle ranches in the US and Canadian Midwest. Working through oral history, photography, and site-specific installation, Creates documents and investigates coastal communities. She comments:

> My work is about places and paths: absence and presence, leaving and arriving, identification and dislocation.
>
> In the remote places where I have gone to work, my projects are a kind of overlaying of a fragile moment on an enormous natural and historical past. The land is important to me, but even more important is the idea that it becomes a 'place' because someone has been there.
> (Creates, 1993b: 18)

Thus she explicitly acknowledges the function of presence, perception, memory, and the visual recording of having-been-present, in the processes of transformation of space into place. Her interest is in marginal territories. Projects have taken her to remoter Celtic areas in Britain, as well as to island and coastal regions of Newfoundland and Labrador, Baffin Island and Vancouver Island (and, exceptionally, to Alberta in the Midwest, which is remote but land-locked). She collects and re-assembles materials (rocks, stones, pebbles), or uses paper to make delicate imprints from natural phenomena. Her work, installed in the gallery or collated into books, commemorates these personal acts of appropriation alongside the recounted experiences of those in the community whose recollections are drawn into play. The performative dimension of the work bears relation to that of British artists such as Hamish Fulton or Richard Long (see Chapter 6). Interventions are subtle, operating suggestively to trace something of the interaction of humankind and nature. For instance, *Sleeping Places*, made in Newfoundland in 1982, records the visible outline of Creates' body where she slept on the ground. She acknowledges the limits of what the photograph can imply about actual process and experience. Apparently, on one such occasion, the landowner remarked that she wasn't going to *see* the wind which had kept her awake through the night.

For Creates, land has memory, marked by imprints and evolution. If she leaves a pile of rocks on the ground, eventually the ground will envelop them with grasses or flora. The artist herself does not particularly assert a feminist position, but the relative understatement has attracted comment on gender and relation with land (Garvey, 1992 in Creates, 1993b; Lippard, 1997). Initially her work concerned her own experience of being in, and journeying through, relatively isolated environments. More recent work explicitly engages the relation between social groups, memory and place, as others have been drawn into her projects. For instance, *The Distance Between Two Points is Measured in Memories*, made in Labrador in 1988, is based on interviews with older people, now relocated to small urban settlements, about memories of living in remoter parts. A portrait of each person in their current domestic surroundings is accompanied by a memory map of where they once lived and their comments on that place, which the artist has also photographed as it is now. In some cases, remnants of that remembered still remain. For example, one photograph shows the bow end of a broken boat upturned to form a smokehouse out on rough grasslands, even though many of the settlers (Northern Labrador

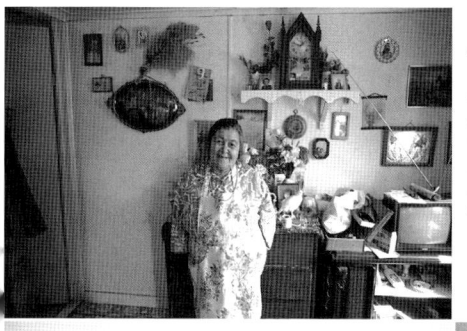

I had ten boys and one girl. I had fifteen altogether. Some of them is dead. I don't know how many grandchildren. I never counted. I stayed up there in Webb's Bay ever since I got married. When we got married there was only one house, his father's house. That old house is still up. Log house. Smokehouse and everything up there. Smokes char. Use what they call blackberry leaves. Cuts out square pieces of sod. It was a boat, half a boat. Just the top of a boat put on the ground. Old man's house here. Path up to our house. And Jim's house up here. Our house. And Ronald's. And Henry's little old house there. It's old that smokehouse. Way over a hundred years it must be now. Still uses it. Still good.

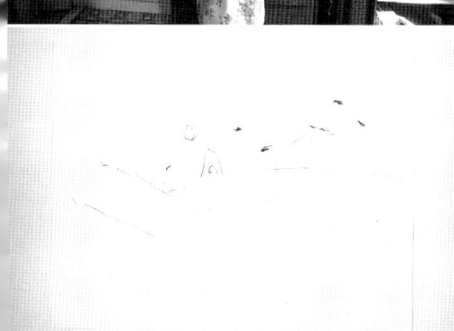

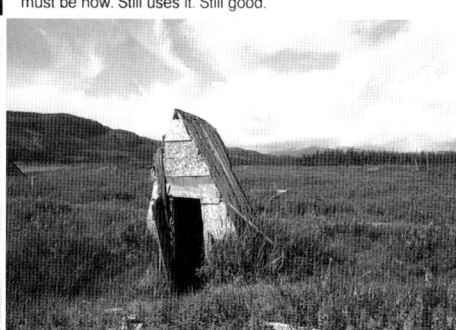

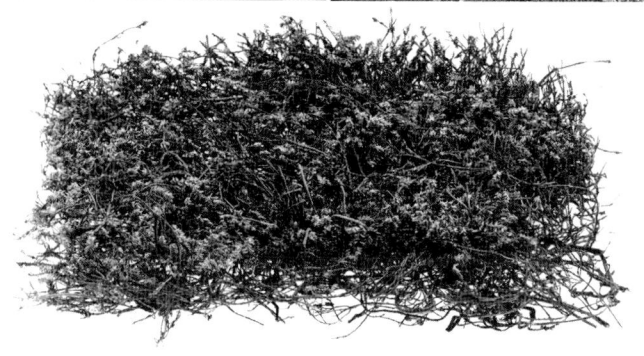

Marlene Creates, 'Rosie Webb, Labrador, 1988', from the series *The Distance Between Two Points is Measured in Memories*.

Inuit, Naskapi Innu, as well as those of Euro-Canadian heritage) have moved away. Lucy R. Lippard comments that documentation, personal memory and 'sensuous evidence' – materials gathered on site for inclusion/installation – articulate a complex portrait of places remembered. That the artist herself has made a particular journey of exploration adds further resonance. Lippard also remarks on the poignancy of maps:

> The beauty of maps, and the reason they aesthetically approach, even surpass, many intentional works of art is their unintentional subjectivity. This is why they have been so important to the cultural construction of landscape. A map is a composite of places, and like a place, it hides as much as it reveals. It is also a composite of times, blandly laying out on a single surface the results of billions of years of activity by nature and humanity.
> (Lippard, 1997: 82)

Three points are worth remarking. First, memory maps inscribe the personal use and experience of place. This has some relation to uses of snapshots to record a journey or a *séjour*; the 'shape' or emphasis is subjective. Two visitors, or two inhabitants of a particular place, may recount similar memories but they are never identical. Second, mapping is undertaken through exploration and measurement. Maps, and conventions as to what are remarked (churches, rivers, contours of hills ...), are social constructs reflecting particular cultural priorities. Creates' work incorporates interest in different cognitive approaches to mapping: she observes, for example, that in directions relating to tundra Euro-Canadians typically described landmarks, whereas the Inuit characterised contours (ibid.). Attention to landmarks reflects a mode of cartography wherein land is represented geometrically through reference to observable phenomena; environment becomes conceptualised as *object* of navigation. This contrasts with more sensual approaches in which the *experience* of journeying through hills, valleys, and so on is prioritised. Third, as Creates herself commented, in the memory maps drawn by former rural dwellers, the principal observable distinction between what was remarked was not between Euro-Canadian and Inuit groups, but in terms of gender; men tended to note hunting and fishing grounds whereas women's maps were closer to the domestic. The strategy of combining her experience with material generated locally effectively points to the complexity of responses to space and place. The work has been shown in galleries, but she pays particular attention to the book as a form of dissemination. Given distances between places in Canada, and the consequent relative inaccessibility of galleries, this seems appropriate. The scale of the books, and the act of turning pages, also function to retain a sense of the intimacy of individual memory.

In her series *Dwelling: Expressions of Time*, Janet Pritchard is likewise concerned with memory, but the formal strategies that she deploys are very different. She likens layers of memory to geologic stratification, like Deborah Bright, reminding us that New England lands are formed from glacial remnants. Her pictures note ways in which the social history of appropriation of land is registered through stone walls and other marking devices, especially in winter when the mask of vegetation dies away.

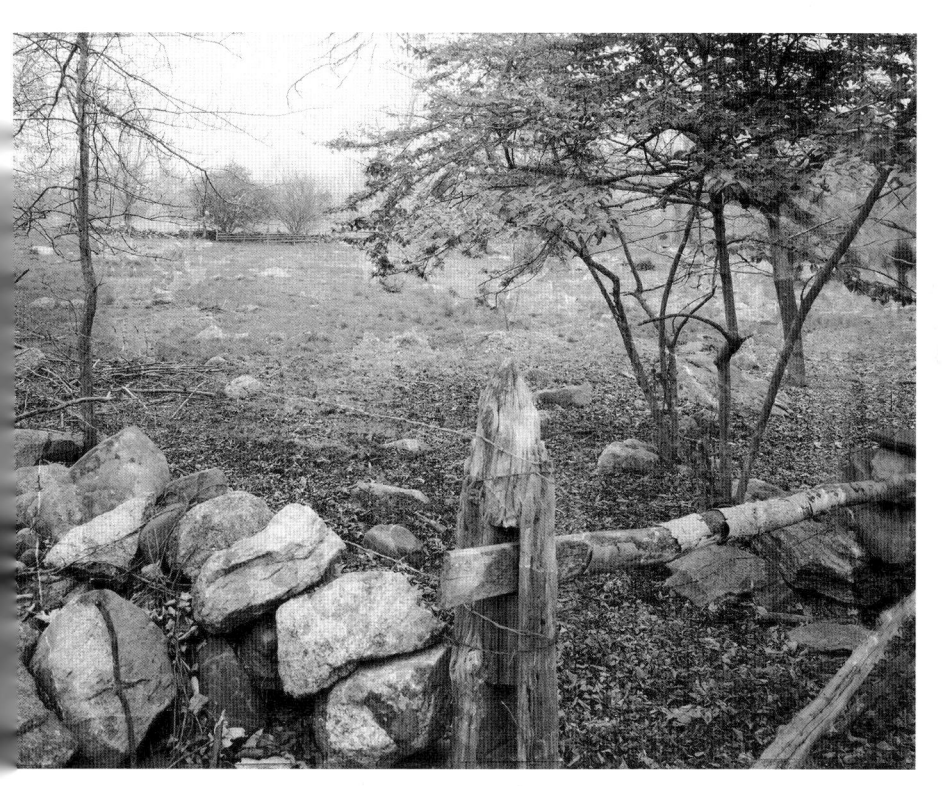

Janet Pritchard, 'Abandoned Field with Glacial Stone', from the series *Dwelling: Expressions of Time*, 2003.

At first glance the pictures look old and damaged. Rhetorically the images work through a distressed aesthetic whereby they acquire a pictorial illusion of age.[7] But chemical stains and digital manipulation are intended to refuse links with a romantic poetics or with formalist preoccupations with shape, texture and symbolism. Just as Sally Mann re-deploys visual tropes more often associated with late nineteenth-century pictorialism to reference discomforting histories associated with the South, so Pritchard distresses the picture surface in order to point to processes of image construction. Thus a doubling comes into play whereby early aesthetic modes are referenced yet undermined as specific composition invites us to reflect on ways in which legacies of the past are landscaped within the present. Whereas the pictorial is concerned with the geometry of the image, here the material layering of the image invites us to explore beyond most immediate surface appearances.

NINETEENTH-CENTURY PICTORIAL PHOTOGRAPHY: THE EXAMPLE OF THE WHITE MOUNTAINS

Marlene Creates and Deborah Bright are among many contemporary photographers investigating histories of settlement. Historically, 'settlement' particularly involved agriculture, although, as R. Stuart Wallace points out in a discussion of the social history of the White Mountains, land use changes (Wallace, 1980). According to his account, in the late eighteenth century in the White Mountain area spanning the north of New England, there was tension between logging, and prospecting for mineral wealth, on the one hand, and farming, on the other. Writing on *Views in the White Mountains* in 1879, Moses Foster Sweetser refers to the mountains as 'highlands' (reminding us of extensive Scottish immigration). He comments that, although the Pilgrims who landed at Plymouth thought they had found an 'empty continent', it was not until 1760, with the conquest of Canada, that people ventured much into wilderness. Thomas Starr King likewise notes that, although ranger parties had travelled into the region since the early eighteenth century, attempts to map and describe the White Mountains only date from 1812 onwards, along with the beginnings of botanical, zoological and mineralogical interests (King, 1869: 43). By the end of the Civil War, several farms had been established, some of which prospered, and some of which failed in this environment which posed many challenges.

The White Mountain region is over 1200 square miles; it includes Mt Washington (1916 metres), the highest mountain on the East Coast, which has been used by explorers to simulate Arctic conditions. The range is bounded by Connecticut valley in the north and west, and the lake-country of New Hampshire in the south; the eastern limit is less clear – some have seen the range not as separate but as linked with the Alleghanies in Maine. The latitude matches Bordeaux, Genoa, Bologna, but, Sweetser commented, the climate was more severe than Switzerland. The reason for the name, White Mountains, is also unclear. Samuel Bemis (a Boston dentist) made several daguerrotypes during visits to the mountains, 1840–41.[8] The resulting images are fascinating as examples of very early photography and for some of the detail shown, but they are blotchy, and do not cast any light on 'whiteness'. There is little sense of composition, but they heralded the incorporation of this new medium, photography, as a tourist interest. By the mid-nineteenth century, settlement in New England and in the South (Virginia, North and South Carolina) was well established; lands east and west of the White Mountains were largely agricultural. Having been of interest for some time to geologists and botanists, the mountains became the first site of US nature tourism, and prospered as such since it was accessible by railroad.[9] Sweetser comments that:

> The majority of travelers prefer to come into the immediate presence of the highest mountains, to face their frowning cliffs, be overshadowed by their immense ridges, and hear the music of their white cascades.
>
> (Sweetser, 1879: n.p.)

The pleasures were evidently in part transcendental, offering moments of sublimity given the wildness by contrast with towns on the coastal strip; such comments also remind us of Thoreau's writings on oneness with nature. An American pictorial had emerged and many artists and photographers visited, including Hudson River artists such as Cole and, later, Bierstadt.[10] Sweetser distinguishes between the Franconia Mountains and the White Mountains (east of the Franconia range), which, he suggests, are more majestic, although less beautiful in terms of vegetation.

The White Mountains offer an interesting case study in the history of popular landscape photography. Although established as a national forest area in 1911, the scale is muted relative to the west and the natural drama less stunning. But in the mid-nineteenth century, with the 'West' still relatively unknown, this area was advocated as a holiday resort for nature, fresh air, spiritual and physical self-replenishment, and 'views'. Christian myth adds strength to this infusion. For instance, the much-stereoscoped railway up Mt Washington, first proposed in the 1850s, is called 'Jacob's Ladder'. The title was adopted for this railroad on trestles, which, by the time of Sweetser's writing, apparently carried from six to eight thousand visitors each year. He describes 'the path over which the tourists of forty years ago slowly toiled, while the horn of Fabyan sounded in the clouds above … still tinctured with the Puritanism of the morning era, ere yet (as Lowell saith) New England had become New Ireland, named this skyward ascent *Jacob's Ladder*, as if, per chance, the angels of God might have been seen by the eye of faith ascending and descending thereon' (Sweetser, 1879: n.p.). Biblical legacies are variously inscribed, for instance, as response to engagement with natural phenomena (or, indeed, in the author's 'Christian' name, Moses!).

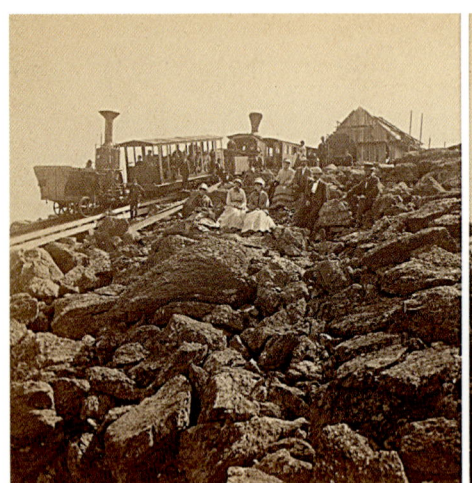

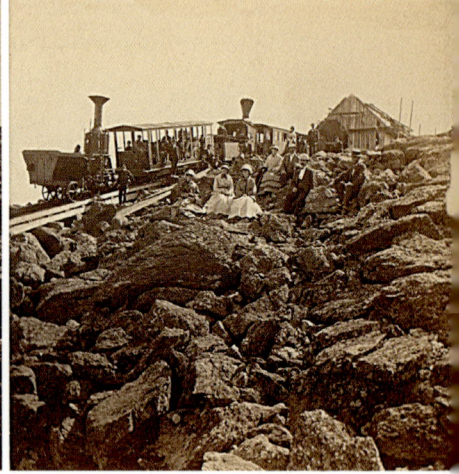

Kilburn Brothers, 'R R Trains on Mt. Washington', n.d.

Thomas Starr King likewise introduced *The White Hills; their legends, landscape and poetry* for tourists, bringing together pictures, selected poems, and a history of the region in a single volume, the purpose being that travellers need carry only one book (King, 1869). He tells us how to look at mountains:

> Going close to a great mountain is like going close to a powerfully painted picture; you see only the roughnesses, the blotches of paint, the coarsely contrasted hues, which at the proper distance alone are grouped into grandeur and mellowed into beauty … Even the height of a great mountain is not usually appreciated by looking up from its base. If it rose in one wall, and tapered regularly with a smooth surface, like a pyramid, or Bunker Hill monument, the expectations of many who rush to the foot of Mount Washington, and suppose that they are to receive an overpowering ocular impression of a mile of vertical height, would be satisfied. But a great mountain is protected by outworks and braced by spurs; its dome retreats modestly by plateaus; and it is only at a distance of some miles that the effect of foreshortening is corrected, and it stands out in full royalty. And from such a point of view alone, by the added effect of atmosphere and shadows, is its real sublimity discerned. The majesty of a mountain is determined by the outlines of its bulk; its expression depends on the distance and the states of the air through which it is seen.
>
> (King, 1869: 6)

In effect, he proposes that distance lends awe to the experience. Describing a view (near the Alpine House, Gorham), he also advises on time of day for best light:

> A perfectly finished picture is shown from a small hill about four miles from the hotel, just at the turn of the road that leads to 'The Lead-mine Bridge.' Mount Madison sits on a plateau over the Androscoggin meadows … He towers clear, symmetrical, and proud, against the vivid blue of the western sky. And as if the bright foreground of the meadows golden in the afternoon light and the velvety softness of the vague blue shadows that dim the desolation of the mountain, and the hues that flame on the peaks of its lower ridges, and the vigor of its sweep upwards to a sharp crest, are not enough to perfect the artistic finish of the picture, a *frame* is gracefully carved out of two nearer hills, to seclude it from any neighboring roughness around the Peabody valley, and to narrow into the most shapely proportions the plateau from which it soars …

This view, during the long midsummer days, can be enjoyed after tea and before sunset, when the light is most propitious, on the same day that the traveler leaves Boston.

(King, 1869: 9–10)

The traveller is clearly directed towards the picturesque, and, indeed, advised to seek out this spot as an initial (spiritual) experience to be enjoyed at the end of the journey out from Boston. This was clearly a forerunner of the 'viewpoints' signed along roadsides today or beauty spots, such as might be noted in Baedekker. The poems and poets quoted are generally not credited – perhaps the educated traveller was supposed to know them – but the references are to the English Romantic poets as well as to Emerson or Thoreau. The influence of English culture resonates not only through Christian references but also, and inter-related to this, through European aesthetics, in particular, notions of beauty.

This association of the Edenic with Manifest Destiny was refracted and reinforced through popular imagery. By the mid-nineteenth century, photo exchange clubs had been established, and, from the mid-1860s onwards, there was inordinate growth in the commercial sale of stereoscopic views produced by family firms such as Kilburn Brothers of Littleton, New Hampshire.[11] Kilburn Brothers functioned from 1865 to 1909 (when the business was sold to Keystone – also a stereographic publisher) and printed an average of 3,000 finished prints, mounted, *per day*, that is, a million cards a year (Darrah, 1977). Stereoscopes pair identical photographs that are looked at through a binocular (stereoscopic) viewer which causes them to appear as if three-dimensional. To create the effect there had to be a central element – typically a rock or a person – so that when the pair was seen through the viewer the element appeared to acquire depth as each eye perceives the object positioned slightly differently. Stereoscopes encompassed the kitsch as well as the extraordinary.[12] But landscape was a central theme. The initial emphasis was on White Mountain views (several examples are dated 1879), although there are some more vernacular scenes, for example, women gossiping at the garden gate. The company later diversified, commissioning photographers in the West and also internationally. In the early 1880s a trade list of about a thousand reference numbers (images) was available, including around 300 White Mountain pictures. The commercial value of the images undoubtedly emanated from curiosity about places; it was the water, boats, reflections of trees on water, and similar idyllic scenes, which were of interest to the buying public. We can assume that, rather like postcards and travel brochures today, they operated both as mementos of places visited and to lure tourists to places new to them. The Kilburn Brothers' White Mountain stereoscopes are pictorially constructed, with emphasis on foreground and middle ground, and soft tonal contrast. Often a stream, or waterfall, or gorge – or even the railroad – leads towards the vanishing point. Sometimes the water curves round a bend or flows across the image. A rowing boat may be moored. Typically mountain peaks appear in soft focus in the distance. By contrast with, for example, the paintings of the Hudson River School, there is little emphasis on sky, which is sometimes absent and never fills more than 20–25 per cent of the image, often as a triangle across a corner (the golden rule is not in operation). Difficulties posed by the different exposure times needed for ground and sky may account for this in part. But this was photography, not 'art'; latitude of interpretation was the province of painters.

Stereoscopes and postcards stereotype landscape. We see idealised space. For instance, in 'Echo Lake, Franconia Notch', two men, on a wooden pier leading out into the lake with a boat moored towards the middle, stare diagonally across the water, their left shoulders and backs turned to us; one sits with his legs dangling over – we can't see if his ankles are in the water – the other sits on something which raises him up, and holds some sort of pipe or musical instrument. We look at them, and beyond them, across the space of the lake towards the tree-lined incline over the other side of the lake. They are apparently at one with nature which, here, is relatively accessible. Rowing boats, paths and bridges allow walkers to access streams and inlets, calm waters, slopes, woodlands and gentle waterfalls. This is not the sublime of the West or of Niagara. In 'Cloud View from Mt. Washington' we look across at billowy white but thick clouds, suggesting a more awesome experience, and in 'Summit of Mt. Washington' we are on top of the world – literally! Low reference numbers in the Kilburn Brothers series indicate that these are early photographs; they have not been made under the influence of more sublime imagery later popularised as photographers sent pictures from the Rockies in the west. Rather, the White Mountain terrain itself must have dictated composition. But these pictures are atypical; generally the images are more domestic in scale. For instance, 'Valley of the Connecticut' depicts farmlands of triangular haystacks, roadway, fences and a wooden pylon, with the river

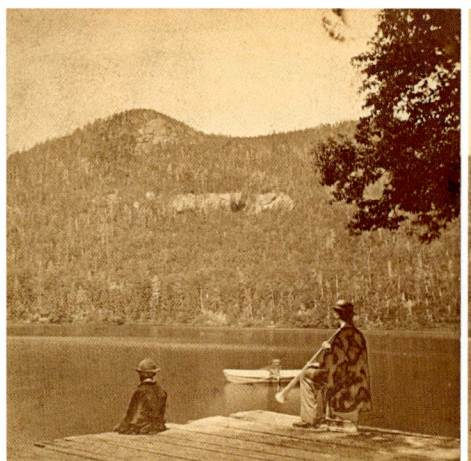

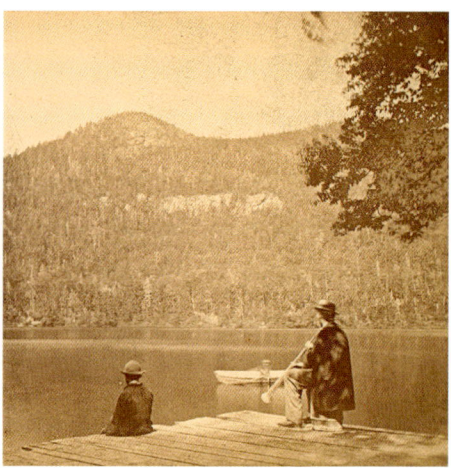

Kilburn Brothers, 'Echo Lake, Franconia Notch', n.d.

curving off in the distance. It appears settled, that is, claimed for farming, organised and self-contained. Since, overall, the rolling vistas of the New England mountain ranges are not so dramatic, the picturesque remained relatively unchallenged.

CONTEMPLATING THE PICTURESQUE

As noted earlier, interrogation of the desire to picture certain types of places (and, by implication, not others) is central to John Pfahl's *oeuvre*. From 1993–97, developing *Permutations of the Picturesque*, he visited and rephotographed at viewpoints in England and Wales, and Italy, made famous through eighteenth- and nineteenth-century sketches and watercolours (Pfahl, 1997). Pfahl was not primarily interested in the sites *per se* – although he tells us he was thrilled to visit them – but in the picturesque as an idea that fostered transcendence whereby particular places came to stand for much more than actual site. Modes of representation established a set of expectations that acted as criteria for judging the characteristics of place; indeed, whether views were noble enough to be defined as picturesque. Pfahl's photographs are scanned and digitally adjusted, with a line of pixels left in, like a watermark, but certifying *inauthenticity*. Each image is framed by a thin black line, conventionally taken as a signifier of lack of cropping, but pixelation contradicts any such authorial statement. Contours of hills and lakes may be emphasised with a fine black line that further testifies to the compositional structuring of images. At first glance, the work does not seem photographic. Gallery prints appear more like watercolours wherein the contours of the landscape observed have been sketched in, followed by development of texture and tone. The line of pixels indicates the colour palate in play, thereby referencing questions of perception, interpretation and symbolic deployment of light and shade, as well as reminding us of the constructed basis of the imagery. The views may be from Europe, but the critical intent relates to Pfahl's interest in how the American landscape has been pictured. In the series *Niagara Sublime* (1996) close-up viewpoints take us into the power of the Falls. The tactic is non-interventionist, and, as such, less successful than *Permutations of the Picturesque* in inviting the viewer to consider processes of viewing. Perhaps Niagara, as a momentous natural force whose status is enhanced through sheer numbers of pictorial reference (paintings, photographs, postcards …), imposes its own sublime regardless of means of picturing? Some titles are subtler; for instance, in 'Spectral Vapors' we perceive a full moon behind ominous dark clouds. Other titles are descriptive. For example, in 'This Roaring Surge' water cascades, a billowing vertical force of foam hitting the foaming white surf flowing amidst the rocks, causing a mist of spray; in 'Silent Thunder' the focus is on a central horizontal line, over which the water flows; 'Heaven's Fire' is split between intense amber sunset above, turbulent waters below. As a rendering of the power of Niagara the work is stunning, but unlike much of his work, there is no subversive critical tactic. It is perhaps because of this that the series has been widely shown.

Pfahl describes *Altered Landscapes* (made 1970s) as his first serious body of work, and notes the influence of the concerns of Conceptual Art. Here he intervened in the actual landscape, for instance, stringing brightly coloured ribbons through trees or laying out patterns on the ground, drawing attention to pictorial geometry, and thereby disrupting it.[13] For example, in 'Red Setters in a Red Field', Charlotte, North Carolina, April 1976, a grid of large blue squares, indicating 12 sections, draws attention to composition, including viewpoint, as two dogs are placed in the two central grid squares, one in the foreground and one in the middle distance. All the other sections lead

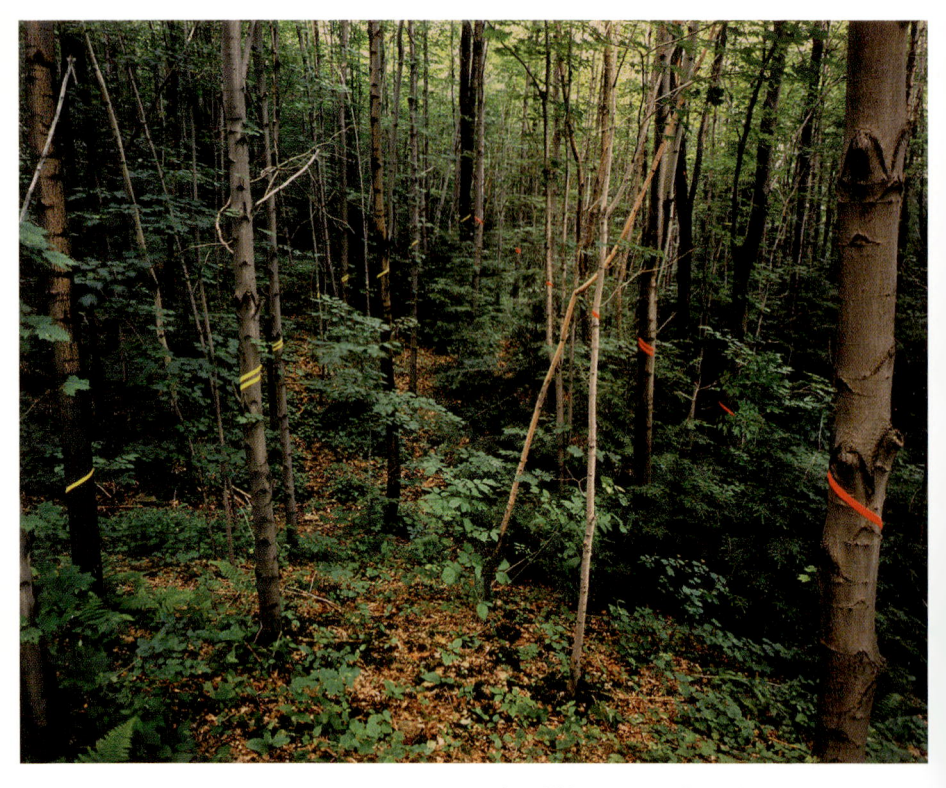

John Pfahl, 'Music 1, Elliotsville, New York', May 1974, from the series *Altered Landscapes*.

off out of the image, so frame, or edge, is also in question. Likewise, in 'Music 1', tapes tied round trunks of trees, in pairs or singly, yellow to the left of the image and red to the right, create a triangle which leads our eye towards an apex. But there is a tree trunk in the middle distance, with more trees behind, and no sky visible except slightly discerned through the foliage. Perspective leads the viewer into the woods, but the vanishing point is missing; visual resolution is disconcertingly denied. In effect we are asked to consider the picture differently, perhaps in terms of the inter-relation of trees now linked together through the tapes. Effects of the geometry of the image are centrally explored. The title reference to music reminds us of musicological concerns relating to the affects of space between notes or notes as interruption of space (silence).[14] In 'Moonrise over Pie Pon, Capitol Reef, National Park, Utah', October 1977 – the title obviously a reference to Ansel Adams – a dot, the size of the moon, with a circle around it matching the golden haze surrounding the actual moon, has been placed in the foreground, tempting us to look down rather than up at the moon in its central and dominant position. The composition is otherwise harmonious; the dot is central between darker browns of the earth in the foreground and lighted browns of rockface (the side of the hills), but by drawing attention to the harmony of composition, it upsets it. Sometimes, tricks of perspective are overt. In a later sequence, 'Wave Theory, I–V, Puno Coast, Hawaii', March 1978, we look out to sea, but vertical lines, in five-bar-gate fashion, register wave intensity through indicating levels of spray. Although the composition emphasises horizontal planes (horizon, water's edge and rocks in foreground) the vertical marks, maybe 2 inches high, encourage us to consider our position at the slippery (insecure) water's edge. Exhibition prints, mounted, are a standard 20" x 24", adding to the pictorial effect (although, they seem oddly small by today's gallery standards). In 'Tracks, Bonneville Salt Flats, Wendover, Utah', October 1977, two parallel lines give a feel of a ladder, although there are no crosspieces; the flat land seemingly acquires an incline. Here the golden (compositional) rule of thirds is disobeyed, and sky constitutes only a one-seventh horizontal strip (a rather distant goal for those seeking Jacob's Ladder). Or the intervention may be homely yet uncanny: in 'Six Oranges, Delaware Park, Buffalo, New York', October 1975, oranges recede down a pathway, tricking perspective as the fruits don't get smaller and, discomfortingly, lead us into the dark recess of the leafy path as it vanishes towards the top of the picture. Many of the pictures succeed in being simultaneously serious and playful. Pfahl comments that through this work he realised that you could show one thing (optical illusion) in dealing with another (landscape pictorial).[15]

In a similar vein, MANUAL (Ed Hill and Suzanne Bloom) takes historical notions of arcadia as one starting point for a complex and multi-layered interrogation of the ecological and the pictorial.[16] The *Arcadia Project* represents a culmination of many years of video, photography and site-specific installation exploring nature and culture, usually in a North American context, but engaged through a European Renaissance philosophical framework. *Et in Arcadia Ego* is one of relatively few examples of site-specific work commissioned overseas (Fotofeis, Scotland, 1993). It involved a series of panels placed along a path through the woods at Craig Phadrig outside Inverness. The panels were made digitally, but recount stories of a mythical sylvan community, becoming re-manifest for the twenty-first century. As artist and writer, Stephen Hobson, remarked in relation to this installation:

> MANUAL's forest 'landscapes' set out questions about the modern 'Arcady' of digital dialogues and virtual reality, but more important, they also offer versions of the artists' traditional concern with representing fate and mortality, such as the traditions of *Vanitas* paintings (emanating from the middle ages) and the less moral *momento mori* works (from Roman art to the present day).
> (Hobson, 1994: 75)

The installation that occasioned his comment took the audience on a journey following a circular pathway through woodlands. The visual pixelated stories and written panels reference legends of woodland communities, thereby animating the place as a space of intersecting stories. For instance, one wooden panel, installed along the forest trail, depicts a white chess pawn inverted and 'suspended' in front of tall tree trunks. What might we make of this? Time appears arrested, as the falling pawn is isolated in space. A text panel at another point along the track referenced an object found on the '93rd Summer Solstice of the Third Millenium' and a further text panel concerns the 'Council of Trees' wondering at new forms of life evident in the forest. Us? Our ancestors? Through devices such as storytelling or improbable imagery, 'woodland' as pastoral space subservient to human influence is brought into question. Their title references a rural scene painted in two slightly different versions ('Les Bergers d'Arcadie' and 'Et in Arcadia Ego') by Nicolas Poussin in the 1630s. The pictures depict shepherds and a shepherdess inspecting a tomb, and are commonly interpreted as meaning that death occurs even in Arcady. As with all MANUAL's work, contexts, aesthetic form, theme and medium are articulated complexly. That installations may be located in public space extends audiences. The art historical references may elude those unfamiliar with the field, but the storytelling mode is surely inclusive. To what extent preconceptions are then challenged is less easy to determine; as with public art more generally, audience response is difficult to ascertain.

In his introduction to MANUAL's more recent work, *Errant Arcadia* (2002), Edward W. Earle aptly comments that their works 'delight the eye while teasing the mind' (MANUAL, 2002: 11). The arcadia here in question is the American landscape pictorial, re-fitted as setting for alien objects or as a hyper-designed pictorial. Digitally enhanced or manipulated references to landscape as an art historical genre become a vehicle for a range of musings and meanderings on ideological themes of Romanticism, ecology, and land use which together operate to interrogate the illusory foundations of the genre. For example, 'Arcadian Landscape: the Elegiac Tradition' (1998) centres on the back of a clinically white-clad figure looking into woods, with snow in one half of the image and autumn leaves in the other. The image is framed to exclude branches and, indeed, the head of the onlooker, so we look downwards from tree trunks to the ground. Unlike Friedrich's man in the woods, small by comparison with the height of the trees, there is no romanticised sublime belittlement of humankind. Rather, modern objects and materials invade the landscape; an alien blue-grey metallic frame – perhaps of a garden shed – hovers above the snow. Settlement raises complex issues of interaction with and within our environment. How to reconcile the visual impact of technological objects and materials, cultural expectations in terms of lifestyle, and a desire for an untrammelled pastoral? References in 'Et in Arcadia Ego: Observer and Tomb' (1998) are even more elliptical. A metallic stick person, with a pole echoing the shepherd's staff in the original Poussin paintings, leans against the tomb, which in the right half of the image melds into chipboard, on which extracts from the title read 'ARCADIA GO'. Logging impacts on forests; chipboard is compressed from that which remains from sawmills rendering logs into planks. Again, tensions between settlement and cultivation, and the natural environment. The video version opens with a shot of Suzanne Bloom photographing a classically composed landscape, but there is the noise of a plane overhead, and the photo-image is then torn in half. The effect is one of simultaneous homage to land and critique of Romanticism.

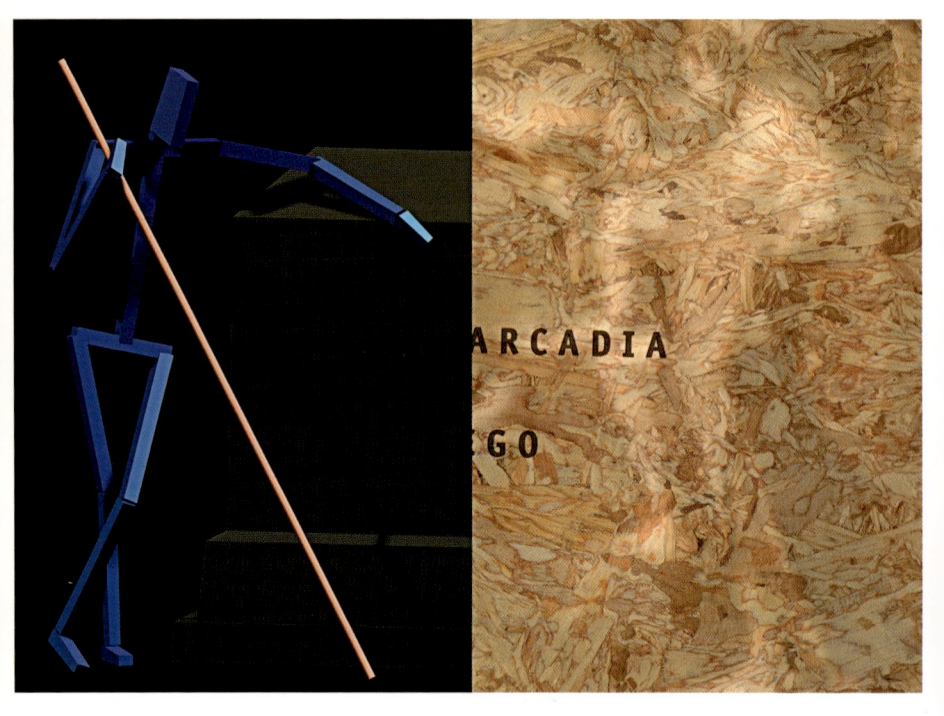

MANUAL, 'Et in Arcadia Ego: Observer and Tomb, 1998', from the series *Arcadia Project*.

SETTLEMENT NOW

A number of photographers have variously focused on the impact and import of contemporary culture for land and environment, urban and rural. For instance, Joann Brennan directly interrogates environmental issues through investigating the engagement of science and technology in the management of land now. As she remarks,

> The extent to which we manipulate nature is surprising, and like many others I am reluctant to let go of the romantic myth of nature. But I have come to understand that there is a price to pay for wildness. To guarantee wildness in our ever growing backyards we have no choice but to intervene. To become the best possible

stewards of our dwindling and battered wildness we must embrace a new definition of the work 'wild' itself. For the 'wild' to survive we must come to acknowledge its complexity, vulnerability and the difficult challenges of maintaining a future where wildness can exist.

(Brennan: 6)

The distance between Thoreau's eulogisation of nature and contemporary acknowledgement of the difficulties of the inter-relation of contemporary economic, industrial and lifestyle priorities and rural environments could not be stated more clearly.

In *Managing Eden* (ongoing) Brennan documents devices introduced into rural areas as means of investigation, control or containment of nature especially in relation to the wild animals with which we share the rural environment. For example, she shadowed 'Paul', a biologist, documenting his work to reduce the population of prairie dogs inhabiting garbage landfill sites in Colorado and eliminate those with fleas which have been known to carry the plague. In New Hampshire, she interviewed and photographed 'Karen', a hunting guide working with a bow and arrow who only kills deer for meat (not for antlers as trophies). As documentation the imagery induces questions concerning conservation and scientific experimentation in relation to moral debates about intervention and wilderness, defence of agricultural or fishing lands, and hunting and trapping as long-standing means of human survival. The imagery details equipment and methods used, for instance, to trap animals for purposes of habitat control or to ring-fence food-producing areas from predators. Portraits of people at work, staged in their rural work environments, fit within a tradition of 'naturalistic' rural documentation, with colour drawing attention to literal detail (by contrast with the sometimes more abstract effects of black and white). Taken individually a few of the portraits might seem over-pastoral but any such effect is undermined by the broader context of the series and its investigative approach. (Although some work has been shown in exhibition, the long-term objective is book publication with a view to reaching out to audiences beyond the arts institutions.)

Brennan's focus is on rural areas. By contrast, in his series *Landscapes (for Antoine)*, photographer Ron Jude, who is based in Ithaca, New York State, explores the transitional spaces of contemporary settlement, everyday liminal areas which form local landscapes in urban and sub-division areas. Antoine is Sartre's anti-hero in *Nausea* (1938).

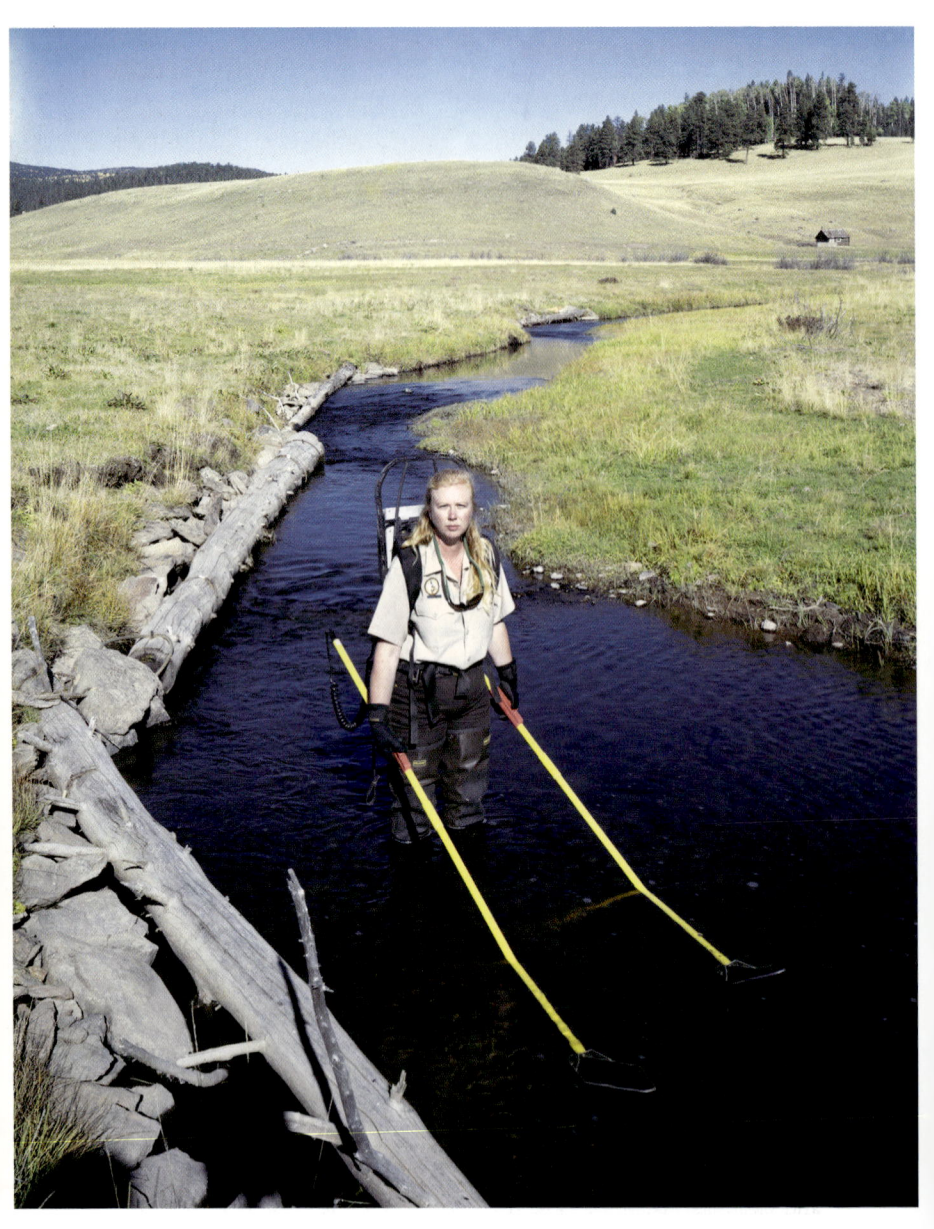

Joann Brennan, 'Electro-shocking for Apache Trout on the West Fork of the Black River, Apache Trout Project', Arizona, September 2003, from the series *Managing Eden*.

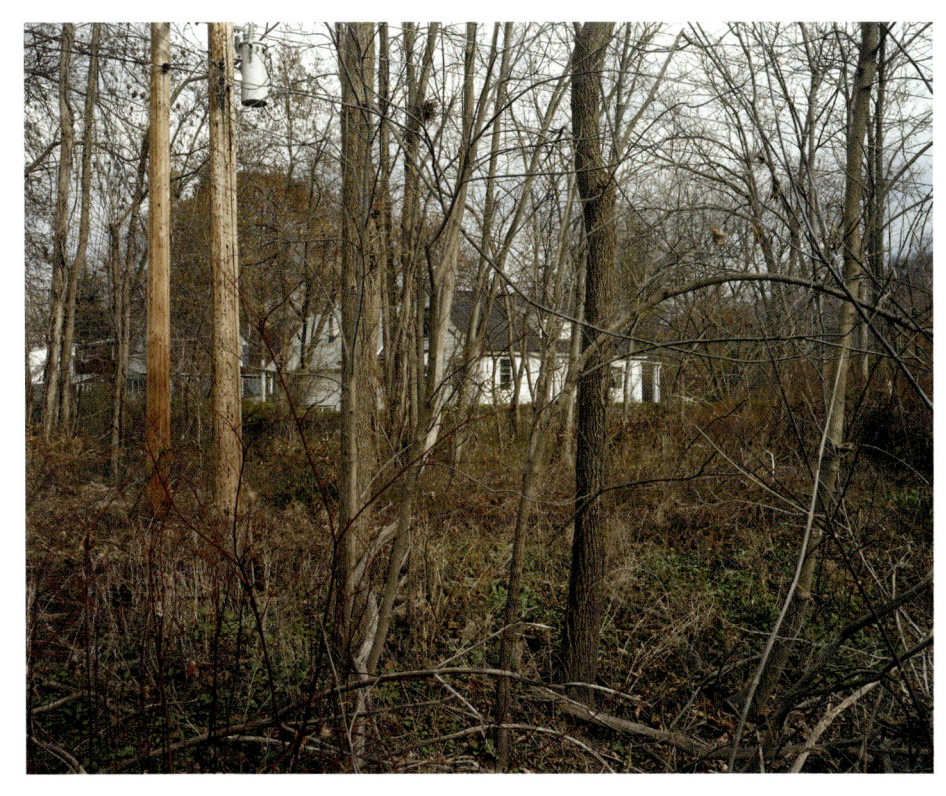

Ron Jude, 'Plain St., Ithaca, NY', from the series *Landscapes (for Antoine)*, 2000.

The novel explores storytelling modes as well as the existential issues that preoccupied Sartre as a philosopher. In Jude's work, being and nothingness are investigated through focus on the apparently inconsequential: the roots of a sturdy tree, a roadside bush, litter in the woods, a glimpse of an anonymous suburban house beyond autumnal trees whose summer foliage must offer some degree of obscurity. The greenery hints at the woodlands and clearings that must have given way to the monotony of dormitory areas. Tones are muted; nothing in the image particularly catches the eye. The exhibition catalogue essay opens by quoting a comment in *Nausea* on an ordinary, inert root: 'this root, with its colour, shape, its congealed movement was … *below* all explanation' (Jude, 2004: n.p. – my emphasis).

This idea of that 'below' explanation, too insignificant for us to bother with it, is central to Jude's work. Something exists because it exists; it is there. Jude draws attention to phenomena offering 'descriptions that pass directly into ontological sensation' (Muellner in Jude, 2004: n.p.).

His work may unsettle as the banality of the observed points to the ordinariness of the everyday. Places where we live, walk or drive are important to us, as are our life experiences and the ways in which we make sense of them. The act of depiction draws attention to complexities of detail and natural form that are marginal, easily overlooked. The act of depiction draws attention to complexities of detail and natural form. The directness of depiction resists the poetic or the transcendental. Rather, the images provoke reconsideration of the act of looking and of what so often remains unobserved. Paradoxically, photography, in drawing attention to items or events, always risks fetishising through aestheticisation. As Duchamp might have remarked, context transforms. Exhibition prints are large, which enhances the fetishistic affects of 'presence' within the reified context of the gallery. In the catalogue images are full-page and centred; there is no design device in play to intercept the emphasis on content rendered significant through the attention of the eye of the artists. Modernist questions about form and beauty arise almost inevitably, even though the photographer's philosophical preoccupations stem from elsewhere.

The art market is well established in North America, and artists inevitably have one eye to audiences and sales. Jeff Wall's work, much of which concerns landscape, offers an extreme example of photographic installation made for the gallery context.[17] Two aspects of his work are of particular relevance here. First, he investigates culture and settlement through depiction of people and places. Scenarios are often set in marginal or transitional locations on the edge of town. From a landscape perspective this phrase in itself is interesting. The town is central, and liminal settings are on its margins. This tells us something about contemporary human geography and economy. (I would like to phrase the observation in terms of 'where town interrupts country', but the phrase then sounds quaintly mediaeval.) At minimum it draws attention to the metropolitan as starting point for Wall's work. Second, and related to this, is the extent to which his work is informed by, and critically engages with, art historical tradition. The most evident example of this is his reference to early nineteenth-century woodcuts by Japanese artist Hokusai, whose series, *Hundred Views of Mount Fuji* (1835) has been extensively reproduced internationally (and who was an acknowledged influence on French Impressionism). It is the precision of the woodcut along with the emphasis on study (of the movement of light on the mountain) which Wall brings into play. In formal terms 'A Sudden Gust of Wind (After Hokusai)' (1993) echoes the flatness of a Dutch landscapes; the canal curves towards a vanishing point and a line of electricity pylons replaces the windmill which might formerly have symbolised mercantile – now industrial – power. The flight of paper is ambiguous. Paper is associated with bureaucracy, the oft-heralded 'paperless office' notwithstanding, and this wadge of paper is flying over and will litter the lands at the edge of the city in the distance that no doubt exerts public authority over its surrounding countryside. Colours are muted; in common with Ron Jude, Jeff Wall offers no easy visual anchoring point for the spectator, requiring us to scrutinise the scenario as a whole. Wall comments,

> I make landscapes, or cityscapes as the case may be, to study the process of settlement as well as to work out for myself what the kind of picture (or photograph) we call a 'landscape' is. This permits me also to recognize the other kinds of picture with which it has necessary connections, or the other genres that a landscape might conceal within itself.
>
> (Morris, 2002: 2)

His images are deliberative. Some are 'straight' landscapes. Many are staged. When Wall sees something that catches his attention, rather than photograph it then and there, he researches and re-creates scenes. His first landscape, 'Steves Farm, Steveston' (1980), was a large-scale light-box rendering of a semi-rural farm with rows of houses beyond, reminiscent in scale and stillness of a traditional realist landscape, for instance, a Courbet, in its insistence on everyday detail and on the relative banality of the scene. Wall is interested in photography as fiction, and resists any assumption that photography represents 'truth'. Everyday actuality is his starting point, and, although highly formalised, the centrality of content and the observational aesthetic extend critique of modernist preoccupations with medium in itself. Images often seem like stills extracted from some more extended sequence of events. Of course, all photographs are precisely this, but we are normally less likely to remark this as it is not usually so clearly indicated. His landscapes are not the grand lands of the West, the Rockies, or Canadian winter snowscapes. Rather, liminal spaces at the edges of cities become a focus

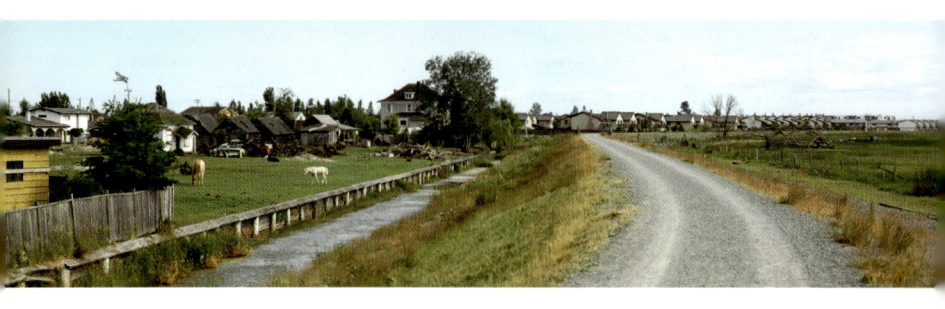

Jeff Wall, 'Steves Farm, Steveston', 1980.

of explorations not, like Jude, in terms of banality but rather in terms of a fascination with the bleakness of places and with people's behaviour. By implication, settlement comes up for interrogation, as places may seem 'unsettled'. Such perimeters throw up questions about cities and the reach of the urban as surrounding areas, once woodlands or agricultural spaces, increasingly become networks of asphalt highways, uniform suburbs, and wastelands in between.

PEOPLE AND PLACE

The photographers whose work is discussed in this chapter take history, myth and aesthetic convention as inter-related conceptual starting points, using rather different research processes and material means for realisation of projects. All of them work within the context of the gallery or art museum, and book publication. All draw attention to aspects of the history of settlement that underpins the emergence of the United States and Canada as particular and complex cultures. One of my concerns has been to indicate something of the specificities of 'Americanness' (Canada notwithstanding) as marked historically in photographic representation, taking European art as one influence, but blended with a photographic realism. A further concern has been to consider the effectiveness of the tactics variously adopted by those discussed, given the hegemony exerted by the gallery and book as particular sorts of contexts of viewing. The focus in this chapter was upon histories of settlement, Edenic notions of the rural, and, in addition, critical observations on the effects of urban sprawl. The next chapter acts as a companion to this through engaging notions of wilderness, the frontier, and contemporary explorations of attitudes to the expansive lands of the West and Midwest.

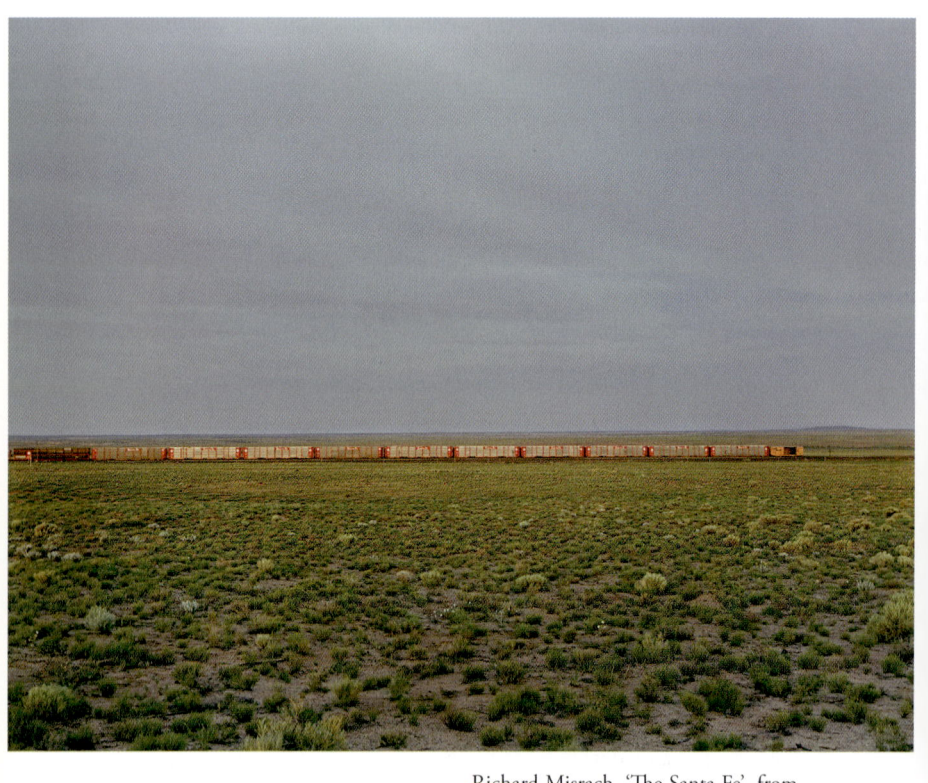

Richard Misrach, 'The Santa Fe', from the series *Desert Canto I: The Terrain*, 1982.

3

AFTER THE FRONTIER

ENVIRONMENT AND THE WEST

In the mid-nineteenth century, the wilderness of the American West was viewed as 'virgin territory', ripe for conquest and exploitation. Now, environmentalists acknowledge inter-dependence of urban and rural areas, viewing demands on natural resources made by human settlement as threatening the sustainability of wilderness regions. Attention is paid to 'wilderness management'. The latter is, strictly, a contradiction in terms, but the phrase is common within US contemporary green movements. If we take ecology to refer to inter-dependency of organisms, then ecological analysis and campaigning are concerned with integration and sustainability. This chapter is concerned with the emergence and influence of landscape imagery from the American West, and with critical appraisal of projects by contemporary American photographers as they relate to the landscape tradition, not of their making, within which they now work?

San Francisco-based photographer, Richard Misrach, is known internationally for his Nuclear Landscapes shot in the Nevada desert (Misrach, 1999). His interest in plants, water, and the night-time environment of the American West, as well as his studies of the effects of light or the movement of clouds, for instance, on the *Golden Gate*, San Francisco, is likewise widely respected (Misrach 2005). His work has been described as 'ethereal images of clouds, rock formations, and desert seas ... juxtaposed with sobering photographs of nuclear test sites, bomb craters, and desert fires'.[1] Typically his pictures are large, and slightly muted colours underline the scale and desolation of the landscape within which a presence, for instance, dead animals, or an event, such as smoke, catches attention. The impact of his work emerges from tension between, on the one hand, pictorial beauty and, on the other hand, subject matter. His 1999 retrospective exhibition and publication, *Desert Cantos, 1979–1999*, fundamentally explores human exploitation of desert areas. The work is complexly layered in terms of theme and implication. Affects are subtle. The import lies not in the single image but in the accumulation of references to nuclear test sites, animal death, emaciated vegetation and the impact of the mechanical on the natural. Misrach himself has stressed 'pure' photographic communication and his concern with form and the impact of the visual is marked.[2] The operatic title, *Desert Cantos*, further emphasises poetics. The 'Cantos' are themed, some arias seemingly acquiring biblical resonance, for instance, 'The Terrain', 'The Flood', 'The Fires', 'Heavenly Bodies'. Other section titles are more prosaic: 'The Event', 'The Inhabitants and The Visitors', 'The Salt Flats'. Classically composed landscapes are thus juxtaposed with imagery explicitly testifying to human presence – whether people watching a space launch, skeletons of farm animals, or remnants of magazines and huts indicating military camps. Occasional imagery seemingly implicates a weight of histories – for example, the train streaking across the desert in the distance reminds us of the frontier and colonisation of the West and of nineteenth-century technological achievement as distance was overcome through the development of the railroad and the steam train.

Misrach's engagement with the politics of land use, specifically military uses and the consequence of military presence in the Nevada desert, sometimes seems incidental to his priorities as an artist. One section title, 'Clouds (Non-Equivalents)' clearly references Alfred Stieglitz's expressionist explorations in his 'Equivalents' series (1920s–early 1930s) thereby reinforcing Misrach's methodological emphasis on observation rather than metaphor. His prints are medium scale, carefully considered in terms of colour balance, and expensive to purchase.[3] His work is high profile within the art market. He treads an uneasy line between, on the one hand, critique, and, on the other hand, a fatalistic sublime with gothic resonance; humankind rendered transient and powerless relative to natural forces such as, in one image, a fire snaking across the desert horizon. For this reason his work offers a good example with which to begin an examination of ways in which North American photographers have engaged with issues of land and wilderness environments.

Misrach himself does not discuss his work in overtly political terms, but concerns over US governmental attitudes to land and resources surely contribute to our response to his work. We are reminded of – to use a cliché which becomes difficult to avoid – 'the forces of nature' and the consequences of human action for the environment of which we are a part. Indeed, it was Misrach's subject matter, as much as the visual poetics, which brought this body of work to international attention, perhaps because his work in the 1990s reflected emergent concerns relating to environmental futures. He has frequently returned to areas of military activity; the explicitness of the title of a previous publication, *Bravo 20, The Bombing of the American West* (1990) in itself indicates critical stance.[4] The pictures in *Desert Cantos* likewise stem from personal fascination with desert wilderness. Introducing *Desert Cantos* (1999) Myriam Weisang Misrach contextualises the project through commenting on Misrach's wilderness camping forays, with van as darkroom, alone or accompanied by herself or by his dog. She also observes procedures within the environment, for instance, a bulldozer used to push dead animal bodies into a pit and cover them with sand, before digging a new pit for the next mass grave. Bodies are re-absorbed into the desert. Misrach's work testifies to a complexity of uses of and attitudes to vast desert spaces. Indeed, the profile of his work is indicative of a set of paradoxes often associated with critical landscape practices. The success of his work in terms of his status within art institutions perhaps testifies to more widespread fascination with wilderness and the space of the American West that can be satisfied vicariously through art. The content of the series may question attitudes to and uses of such spaces, but the beauty of the prints renders this into a contemporary sublime, allowing for existential responses that provoke little in the way of political debate. The issue is twofold: first, production values, and second, the form in which work is distributed. Ecological and political implications emerge through the imagery within groups, but they are sold and hung as single images, thereby privileging paradoxical beauty over the accumulative effects of repetition that creates a certain un-ease. It is certainly possible to imagine Misrach's work gracing the walls of the offices of those responsible for, for instance, chemical testing or the production of equipment for military purposes.

LAND, LANDSCAPE AND THE WEST

The train streaking across the desert is, of course, now a well-worn motif within the history of photography. The making of the railroad occasioned some of the earliest documentation of mountains, forests and drylands in the West. The railroad subsequently supported the tourism that would popularise post-card imagery offering a range of iconography, from the celebrated snowscapes of Banff in winter to the idealised tropical sunsets of California. This is supplemented by popular accounts of exploration within which text and pictures testify to an awesome but accessible sublime. The stories are often somewhat 'boy's own'. For instance, photographer and writer, Stephen Gorman, describes a canoe expedition:

> We were in the Boundary Waters Canoe Area Wilderness in northern Minnesota, a rugged region of forests, rivers, exposed bedrock ridges, and countless lakes … Somewhere along the southern shore, about three miles distant, the portage trail began at the bottom of a small, featureless bay. Only a foot or two wide and concealed by thick trees, the trail was as invisible as a thread laid across a living room carpet. Yet in all that vast open space, we had to find that one path.
> (Gorman, 1999: 37)

This account is typical of outdoor adventure writing wherein the story concerns a person, or group, surmounting a challenge. This account deploys two key forms of pictorial rhetoric: a sense of intimacy created through close-up shots of vegetation, and one of grandeur through, for example, photographing mountains from below. Whatever the viewpoint, there is also a 'timelessness'; there is no indication of date, or even century – except that the pictures are in colour.[5] Such accounts of exploring what is now often termed the 'great outdoors' persist. Arguably they romanticise the rural environment in ways which echo nineteenth-century notions of land as timeless, available, sublime yet tamable with persistence and endurance, and, indeed, they reaffirm North American ideals of rugged individualism historically associated with masculinity and with Republican emphasis on self-sufficiency.

'West' resonates complexly. At one level it came to represent an ideal – space with domestic, agricultural and commercial prospects. It resounds with ideas of wilderness as place of spiritual sustenance, and with stories of journeys, settlement, agricultural engagement and exploitation of natural resources such as timber or minerals. Native American histories intersect with this, as do histories of military expedition, conquest, training camps and nuclear testing stations. Many photography projects have been pursued in the vast space of the North American West or in the prairie lands of the Midwest. Notions of Manifest Destiny continue to inform attitudes to land and, indeed, contemporary debates about land, ecology and environment. Such tensions are not new; concern with environment is also evident in the establishment of national parks as protected places in the latter decades of the nineteenth century and the early decades of the twentieth. For example, Ansel Adams (1902–84) was a member of the Sierra Club, whose purpose was conservation of the Sierra mountain area. His photography was centrally motivated by investigation – and celebration – of natural phenomena.

Landscape, as a genre in photography, has been influenced extensively by North American photographers, particularly those working in the West. The long shadow cast by Ansel Adams and other early twentieth-century photographers continues to influence American landscape imagery in terms of subject matter, form and metaphor.[6] One purpose of this chapter is to note and comment upon a range of modes and contexts within which photographs made in the nineteenth century and, later, mid-twentieth century, became adopted as icons of American landscape photography. A further objective is to critically consider ways in which this legacy influences and maybe constrains more contemporary takes on landscape. Those whose work is discussed in this chapter are concerned to a greater or lesser degree with a politics of environment. Their primary focus is on land use, historically and now. As photographers they are also preoccupied with image-aesthetics, not in terms of landscape picturesque but as pictorial rhetoric. My interest is in the varying photographic methodologies that have been adopted to enhance the criticality of work? As with the previous chapter, this is not a comprehensive survey of photographers or overview of work emanating from this area. Rather, through evaluating examples of projects with critical edge, I consider themes and strategies that have preoccupied photographers whose concerns are at some level socio-political and who certainly contribute to challenging any over-simplified mythologisation of the West.

GOING WEST

'West' is simultaneously geographical and utopian. A longitudinal line bisecting the map of the United States would place what is now termed 'Midwest' in the Eastern half. Midwest is a legacy of the frontier (as new lands opened up in the 'far' west the central area slipped from being viewed as 'West', to being designated 'Midwest'). In early photography, regions such as Illinois appear as vast flatlands. Nowadays, they are extensive agri-industrial areas with cities such as Chicago, or Edmonton in Canada, that developed as key trade and industrial centres and railroad inter-changes. The map of the United States reveals that 'West' encompasses the area from the middle of the US landmass (Texas; Colorado) across to the Pacific coast, and that 'Midwest' includes states not far inland from the East coast.[7]

'West' is thus a concept, a geographical imaginary. To 'go West' was to leave newly established coastal cities and farmlands, and to risk adventure; it was visionary. 'Going West' was about mission as well as about place; the frontier was viewed by many as the border between civilisation and savagery. The injunction to go West to seek improved economic prospects was underpinned by Manifest Destiny. Single men, or groups including whole families, men and women and children, set out to found new settlements, in many instances seeking a new start after the dissent and destruction of the Civil War (1861–65). The journey, undertaken in summer, was hazardous, and preparations were arduous, as supplies for a family for six months had to be made, stored and then packed into wagons in which the families would also live. Risks of illness, injury, and (in the case of women) childbirth, whilst on the move were compounded by fear of attack by Native Americans. On arrival, men and women, families and neighbours, worked together to build homesteads, cultivate new and sometimes unforgiving pastures, and, indeed, battle with Native groups over land rights. Migrants had to come to terms with the harshness of the Western climate, and the extensiveness and diversity of the land, which includes forest, desert, arid plains, and the mountains and canyons of the Rockies. John Mack Faragher drew upon travellers' diaries and on folksongs to articulate something of the rigours and difficulties experienced by *Women and Men on the Overland Trail* (Faragher, 2001). The accounts are oral (songs) or written; there is no mention of photography apart from one letter in which the correspondent writes of getting out daguerrotypes [sic] to remind themselves of people back east (ibid.: 169). Indeed, it is impossible to imagine cameras, chemicals and darkroom tents being carried and used on such journeys, encumbered as the travellers were with food, tools, bedding, clothing and other treasured possessions.

For commercial organisations, going West involved cutting road tracks and railway lines through rugged country, establishing camps for logging and mining personnel, setting up lines of communication for the movement of people and goods. The journey offered a complex of economic potentials for commercial prospectors and for explorers, as well as for farmers and settlers. Canada and the United States each offered opportunities for photographers variously engaged in recording the progress of railroads (the Canadian Pacific Railroad was completed in 1884), documenting mineral explorations, supporting botanical and geological explorations, mountaineering and early arctic exploration. As photography became used to chart new territory, and to document people and places, many jobbing photographers moved West, eventually setting up studios in newly expanding towns and cities.[8] Aside from a few photographers later taken up by the Art Museum, such work now largely resides in local and regional history collections, used as social history documents for museum or hotel displays, or as booklets, typically subtitled 'a photographic history', available for purchase in tourism areas. That most such work is of uncertain provenance, with the photo-company or a commissioning commercial company as likely to be acknowledged as the individual jobbing photographer, reminds us of the ordinariness of photography as a nineteenth-century trade. If the visual language transcends the basic conventions of composition and detail required, thereby marking it out from the everyday vernacular, that is an intriguing bonus.

The inland South, the Midwest and, later, the West, developed as pioneer communities appropriated and parcelled out land, neighbours gathered to build cabins or homesteads, and local trading stations or townships were established.[9] If photographs from the time show dwellings that now seem makeshift, odd or distinctly eccentric, this testifies to the independent-mindedness that characterised frontier settlement. In fact, 'the frontier' was transcended relatively speedily (in a couple of generations). But the journey west also represented a move from the European-influenced mores of the East Coast to self-sufficiency and more a immediate relation with the natural environment. This involved a mystical sense of possibilities of redemption through communion with nature and, paradoxically, a simultaneous commitment to the struggle to transcend and tame land for productive use. This inter-relation of the Edenic with the injunctions of Manifest Destiny is distinctively North American. Rugged – and masculine – individualism came to characterise independence and a self-reliance that is perhaps best symbolised by the homestead (centre of a working ranch) and the collective endeavour of local communities.

Settlement of the West thus ran in tandem with industrial development and with the economic imperative to establish cross-continental communication and transport systems linking inland to coastal cities and shipping ports. In 'Of Mother Nature and Marlboro Men: An Inquiry into the Cultural Meanings of Landscape Photography' Deborah Bright notes a cluster of landscape photography publications in the mid-1980s within which ideological notions of harmony, form and beauty are regular currency (Bright, 1989). She argues that photography history and theory needs analytic models in which landscape is seen as historically constructed rather than somehow timeless and immutable. She also reminds us of patriarchal attitudes wherein nature, like the maternal, is viewed as a source of replenishment. Echoes of a nature/culture binary persist: women remain viewed as somehow closer to nature, and men are represented as rugged individualists – perhaps pausing only to light a (Marlboro) cigarette as they survey territories quelled. In addition she argues that the idealised landscape panders to small-town North American attitudes, precluding identification with rural space for a significant majority of urban and non-White inhabitants, yet contributing to perpetuating North American foundation myths that are highly selective and ideological.[10] Her comments relate to exhibitions and accompanying catalogues, both of which are necessarily selective; indeed, arguably such exhibitions tell us as much about their curators (often based in urban art museums) as they do about the interests and motives of those photographing in the complex space of the West.

Crossing the Frontier: Photographs of the Developing West, 1849 to the Present (San Francisco Museum of Modern Art, 1997) contributes to this complex agenda relating to histories of the West. Introducing the exhibition publication, Sandra S. Phillips traces the history of conquest of the West in terms of mining, the railroad, agriculture, industrial ranches, lumber camps and oilrigs, urbanisation, irrigation and tourism. She thus relates photographic representation to socio-economic context. She also observes tension between Manifest Destiny with its imperative to make productive use of land and Edenic utopias (more along the lines elaborated by Thoreau):

> The mythology of the West embodied two basic, contradictory tenets: one, that the individualist, agrarian ideal of continuous, divinely ordained progress would transform wild nature into a civilized garden; the other, that man's materialist, capitalistic development and the technology it possessed (its machines, its engineering) would be the agent that would harmoniously open the West.
>
> (Phillips, 1996: 16)

Such tensions persist, for instance, as environmentalists now battle with the giants of military and nuclear industries. Phillips also distinguishes between work such as that of Ansel Adams or Edward Weston which, as she describes it, 'looks to the land as a source of aesthetic, transcendent subject matter' (Phillips, 1996: 13) and, in a more vernacular tradition, photography documenting land use. *Crossing the Frontier* brought together work by nineteenth-century photographers, including Evelyn Cameron, Alexander Gardner, Timothy O'Sullivan, Carleton Watkins, and that of contemporary photographers based in the West such as Terry Evans, Peter Goin, Mark Klett and Richard Misrach. It encompassed nearly one hundred examples of work by named artists or photocompanies, including many examples of unattributed work, or of photodocuments made by pioneers and settlers in their locality. Through bringing together a range of themes, perspectives and aesthetic approaches, and placing the ephemeral alongside the carefully framed pictorial, the collection invites us to focus on histories and issues – rather than, for example, work by individual photographers presented as artist *oeuvre*. The emphasis in the essays as well as the selection of images is on land use historically through to the 1990s.

Evelyn Cameron was a pioneer; she is an interesting example of someone for whom photography was a serious pursuit whose work now has become of sociological value. A British immigrant, she took up photography (*c.* 1894) as a semi-commercial pastime to supplement meagre earnings from horse ranching. Martin W. Sandler comments that

> Hers was a remarkable story: of a woman carrying heavy photographic equipment enormous distances on horseback; of a woman standing at an outdoor pump washing her negatives and prints during a blizzard; of a woman continuing to carry out all the demanding chores of ranching while pursuing her photographic career.
>
> (Sandler, 2002: 7)

Her photographs included topographical landscape imagery, but also studies of men and women at work and at leisure that must have involved asking people to pause or pose for the camera. This would seem to indicate respect for her work and for photography – regardless of the gender of the photographer. She is one of several women – pioneers both as settlers and as women photographers – based in the plains or in the West at the turn of the twentieth century whose work has re-emerged for scrutiny as a result of research by feminist historians since the 1970s. (Others in the USA include Frances Benjamin Johnson, Laura Gilpin and Elizabeth Ellen Roberts.) Due to her homestead commitments, much of her imagery is concentrated within a relatively small geographic area, becoming in effect a detailed portrait of a pioneer rural community. But Sandler's comment reminds us of difficulties faced by all photographers working under primitive or makeshift conditions.

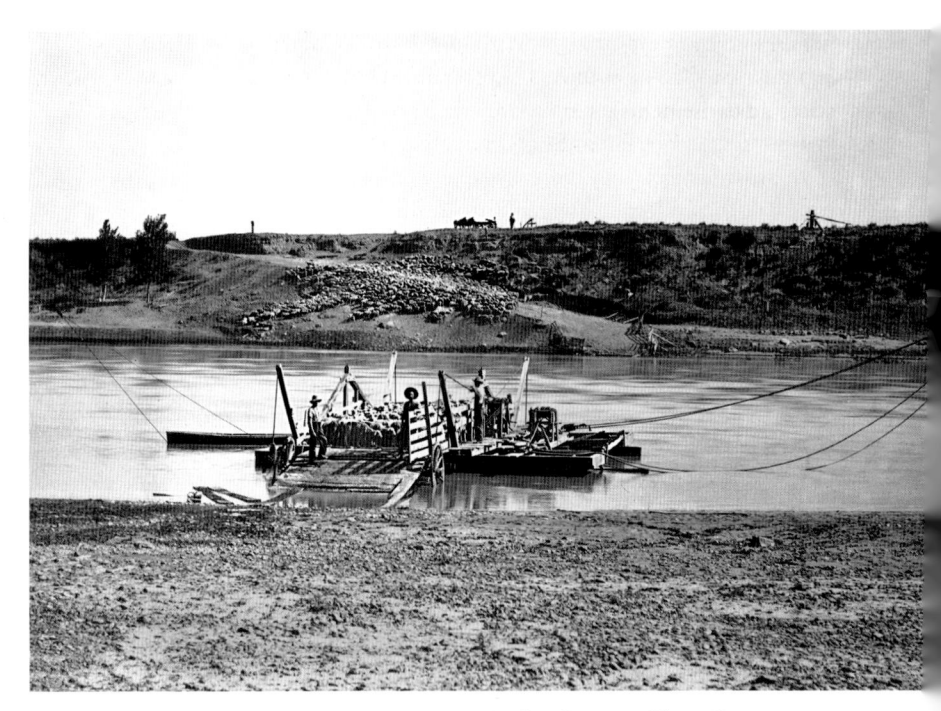

Evelyn Cameron, 'Sheep Crossing on Scott's Ferry', Yellowstone River, 1905.

We are also reminded that, by contrast with Europe or Asia, for North America – Native Americans excepted – 'history' is relatively young. Arguably, contemporary emphasis on the 'great outdoors' not only echoes the independence of spirit involved in the struggle for land and survival experienced by the early settlers but also testifies to that which became central to North American cultural identity (at any rate, outside of the major cities). Hence the stories of struggle and survival told and retold through the Western, that great Hollywood genre of historical mythologisation. Ranch hands, or 'cowboys', appear in photographs taken by Evelyn Cameron and her contemporaries. They also figure in contemporary critique.

Richard Prince is among a number of late twentieth-century North American artists interested in the mass reproducibility of images whose work is founded in photographic appropriation.[11] One of his best-known series explored the iconography of the cowboy.[12] Through relocation within the gallery attention is drawn to that which might be overlooked in more banal settings (for example, another of his series concerned street advertisements). Critic Andy Grundberg has commented that Prince's works unsettle as at first glance they appear as a direct blow-up but

> something about it – the presence of enlarged half-tone dots, the strange scale, the slightly displaced color and contrast – clues us that it is not quite what it seems to be. These shifts from the well-crafted, purportedly authentic 'originals' are relatively minuscule ... but they are enough to give the work an eerie, unlikely presence.
>
> (Grundberg, 1999: 132)

In *Untitled (cowboys)* (1980–86) we see men, each with their horse, usually alone or in small groups, portrayed in close-up or set against immense vistas that serve to emphasise the hero status of cowboys, lone rangers looking on the frontline in erstwhile frontier lands. Re-appropriation allowed Prince to crop and re-frame elements within found imagery. Whilst such fluidity is extremely common within contemporary practice, it seemed more radical then not only because of pre-dating digital production methods but more particularly because of the implied critique of American modernist emphasis on form. Through rephotography and enlargement the iconicity of 'Marlboro Man' was foregrounded. Furthermore, in choosing not to originate his own material but to re-use imagery already in circulation, Prince reminded us that such myths and stereotypes were, in effect, common knowledge that anyone could collect and reconsider. The context was prescient in terms of the broader intellectual debates of the 1970s within which questions of representation and stereotyping were raised (especially from feminist perspectives, but also in terms of ethnic and

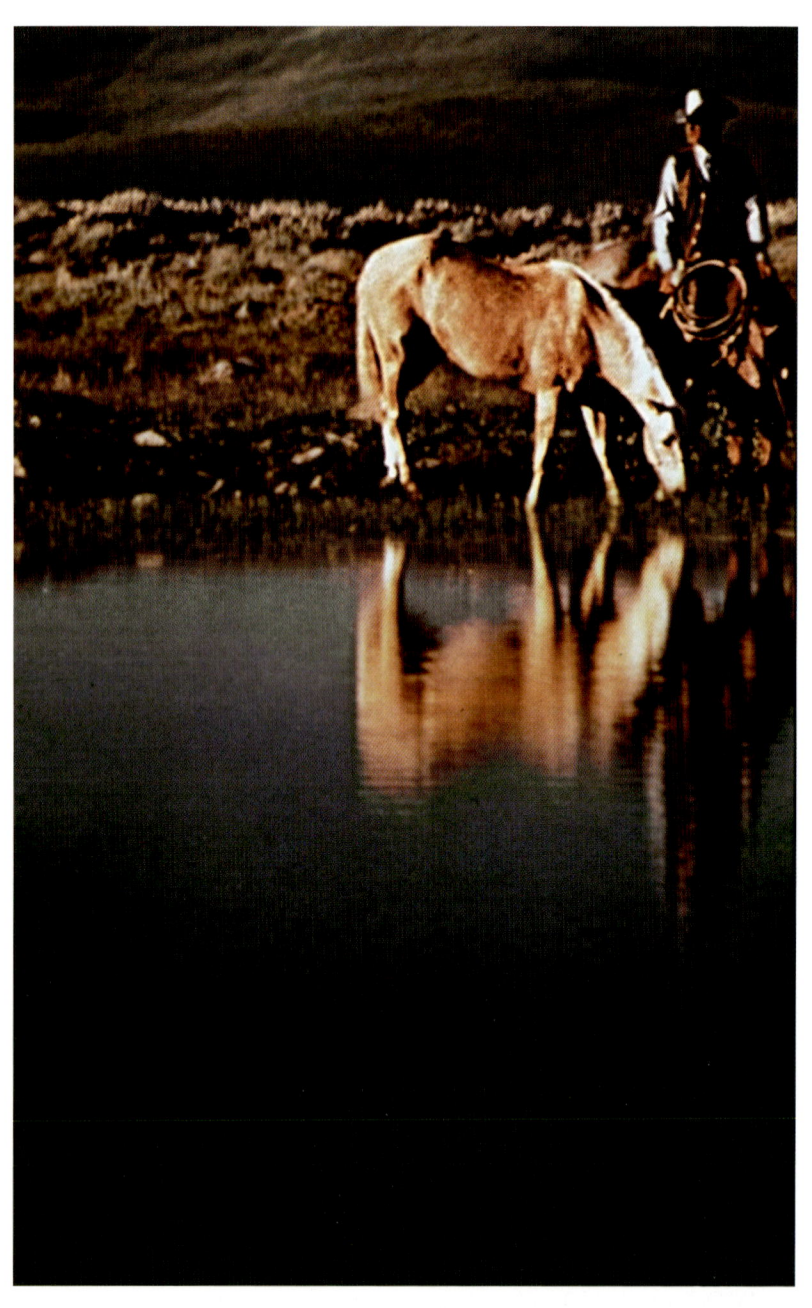

Richard Prince, from the series *Untitled (cowboys)* 1980–86.

other diversities). In drawing attention to the continuing resonance of the cowboy as icon, Prince's work pointed to the persistence of myths of self-reliance and heroism, perhaps questioning their endurance.

Phillips asserts that it is wilderness, rather than history, that is the source of identity for North America (Phillips, 1996: 15). She goes on to suggest ideological tensions inherent in the individualism that characterised the West:

> The Marlboro Man, alone in the wide open expanses, tough and self-reliant, continues to be effective in selling cigarettes around the world. In Oklahoma City, Timothy McVeigh, the resilient individual gone awry, will try to dismantle the government in an effort to bring about his own maverick version of 'law and order'. The conflict between individual ideals and corporate enterprise that shaped western history still informs our present. The added question of community needs or the general good and its relationship to western traditions of individualism and corporate industry have special relevance in the West.
>
> (Phillips, 1996: 14)

As will be seen, tensions between self-reliance, corporate concerns, land rights and common interest resonate as themes explored by a number of contemporary photographers and photography projects.

Re-appraisal of the history of clearances whereby lands previously occupied by native groups were presented as 'virgin' territory for conquest and settlement, is thematically central to the work of Native Canadian photographer, Arthur Renwick; his suite of eleven images, *Delegates: Chiefs of the Earth and Sky* (2004) draws attention to the impact of colonisation on existing inhabitants. The series pays homage to the leaders of tribes from the Plains, delegates invited to Washington in 1868 to sign a treaty conceding land to government, written in a language that they did not read or speak. Each image is a large, open vista from South Dakota, presented in 'portrait' format, a slice of the land that had traditionally been their territory. Renwick cuts punctuation symbols into the skies, quote marks (") or elision dots (…) hovering as a signal of doom as they reference the flow and pauses of the otherwise incomprehensible English of the colonisers. Each is named after one of the chiefs, for instance, 'ZIN-TAH-GAT-LAT-WAH (Spotted Tail)' or 'MO-TA-VAH-TO (Black Kettle)', many of whom were later killed in battle or by bounty hunters, or died in prison or on reservations. The

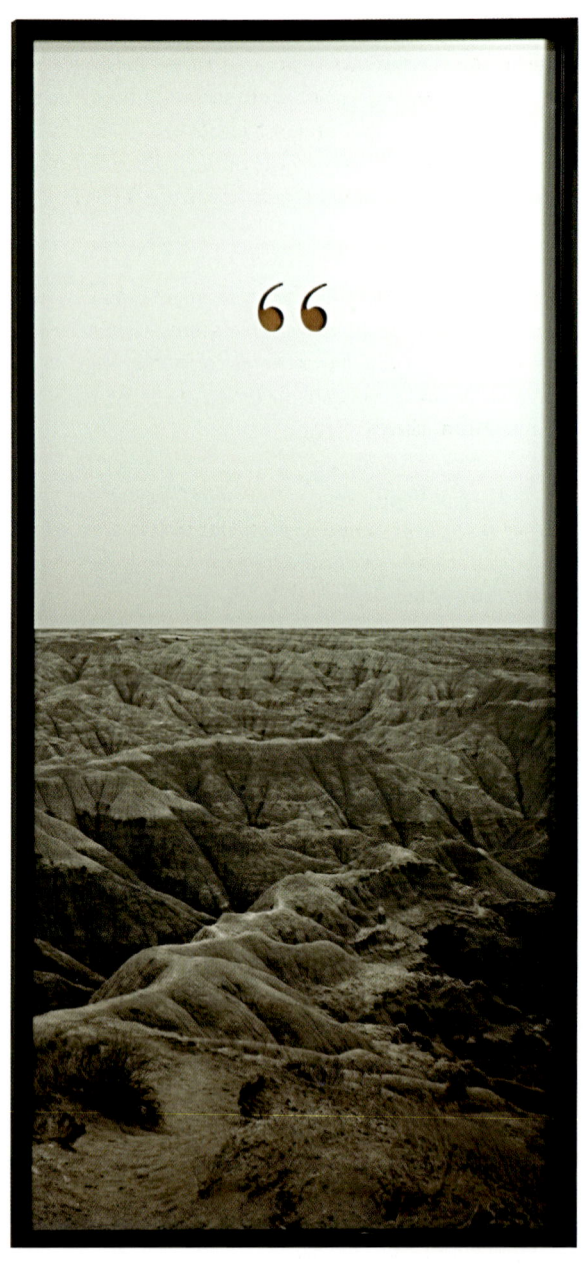

Arthur Renwick, 'MO-TA-VAH-TO (Black Kettle)', from the series *Delegates: Chiefs of the Earth and Sky*, 2004.

work is made for gallery exhibition; silver prints are mounted on anodised aluminium, with copper. Within this context, through recalling forgotten histories, they interrupt taken-for-granted associations of plains and prairies with capitalist agri-industry.[13] Martha Langford, director of *Mois de la Photo*, Montreal, 2005, which included Renwick's work, describes the cuts into the sky as 'signs of silence', commenting that

> The warmth of the copper, untouchable, yet felt, reignites the presence of the exiled leaders. A system of markers, repeated yet different for each name, instigates the telling of the leaders' lives. For the tellers, as for the listeners, life stories are acts of the imagination that emanate from silence.
>
> (Langford, 2005: 195)

Storytelling centrally relies upon audience familiarity with rituals ('Let us pray!'; 'Are you sitting comfortably? Then I'll begin …'). Renwick frequently references the shapes of totem poles, associated with Native ritual, thereby, in Brechtian terms, estranging non-Native audiences. He effectively deploys visual symbols to unsettle any easy sense of familiarity with, and response to, the pictorial. The theme for *Mois de la Photo* was *Image and Imagination*. The rhetorical play between imagination, and image-nation, couldn't be more appropriate.

Struggle over territory in South Dakota is also noted by Joel Sternfield, who remarks that in 1868 millions of acres of territory in the Black Hills were ceded by treaty to the Sioux Nation, only to be reclaimed by Congress nine years later when gold was found in the area (Sternfield, 1996: n.p.). In 1920, the Mount Rushmore monument was created there. The first picture in his book, *On this Site: Landscape in Memorium* (1996), looks from behind the three tiered lines of spotlights towards the sculpture, a dominating presence in the middle distance. He tells us that the Sioux have refused compensation. The four Presidents look out over lands for which Native American title continues to be asserted. Sternfield's project directly addresses hidden histories. *On this Site* documents urban and rural places where violence in some form has been committed. In most instances little visual hint remains; contrary to the specificity or sensationalism of photojournalism, it is the ordinariness of the site that remains which is memorable. The book is an effective form for such a project as the story or incident is summarised on the left-hand page accompanying the image on the right. In turning the pages, the images appear first, with the possibility of looking sideways (to the left page) for explanation. The point is to stake a claim for the historical significance of events. Occurrences are of rather different orders: the parking lot at Kent State University where the police shot students during anti-Vietnam war protests in 1970; a wasteland in Arizona intended for planned community development by a banker who fraudulently misused and lost life-savings deposited with the bank; the state highway where Karen Silkwood's car skidded off the road; the test site in Utah where, in 1986, managers gave the go-ahead for the launch of the Challenger rocket despite unsafe (cold) conditions, and all eight people on board were killed. The colour pictures are uniformly even in focus and depth of field, with the key element of the image (a building, a bridge) centralised. The import arises from the brief accounts of incidents combined with the ordinariness of the place, and the affect is cumulative – the overall impact of the book is unnerving as it reveals that otherwise concealed within the North American landscape.

Tensions over language and territory did not only relate to migration from the East. The gold rush of 1848 attracted immigrants from Mexico and South America and across the Pacific (from China). In states such as Arizona and California Native Americans were displaced by Hispanic and other prospectors, as lands were appropriated for boring mine shafts, establishing townships and means of transportation.[14] As settlement reached the West coast, and the frontier was declared void, a heightened tension emerged; the Manifest imperative of subduing and utilising natural resources, as already noted, Edenic views of nature, and emphasis upon individualism and survival were in complex inter-relation. Economic interests in mining, logging and agri-business do not lie easily alongside respect for natural environments and, related to this, emergent nature tourism. Relatively early on after the transcontinental railroad had been established, hoteliers started to market views of the West to entice Eastcoasters to visit as holiday destination. Photographers set up studios in tourist areas, supplying photographs for purchase and providing movie shows, shot locally for on-the-spot entertainment.[15]

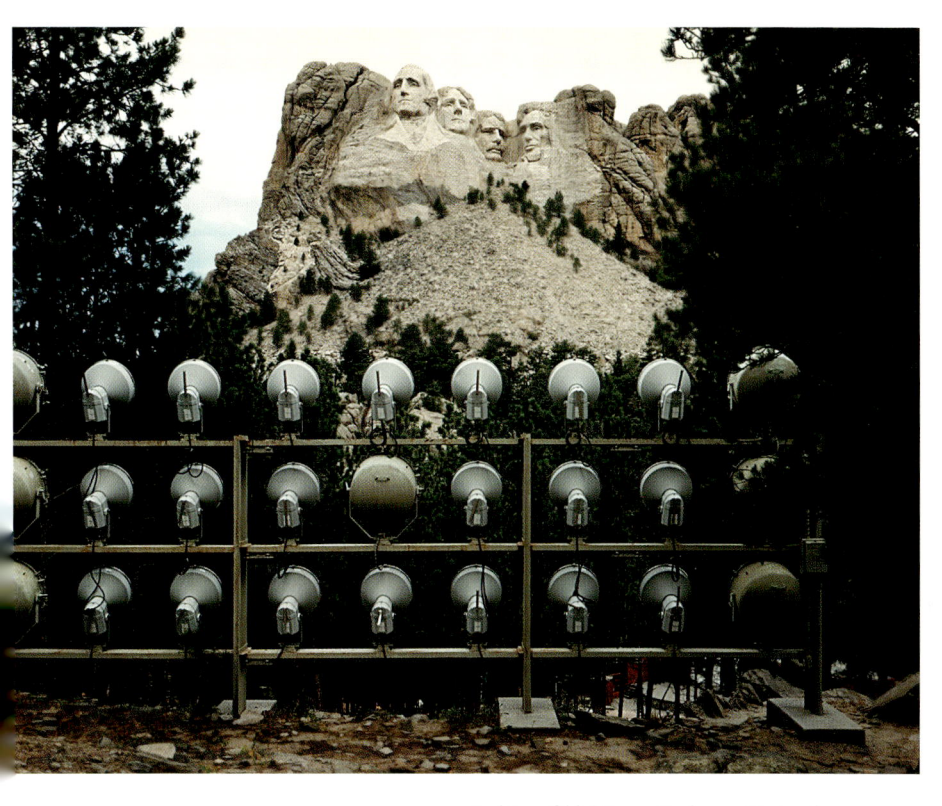

Joel Sternfeld, 'Mount Rushmore National Monument', Black Hills National Forest, South Dakota, August 1994.

In 1868 the federal government deeded millions of acres in the Black Hills of South Dakota to the Great Sioux Nation. Nine years later, when gold was discovered in the area, Congress broke the treaty and took the land back. In the 1920s the state of South Dakota, eager to attract tourists, commissioned a sculptor to carve a colossal monument into Mount Rushmore. The Sioux still considered the Black Hills their own sacred land. In 1980, the Supreme Court awarded the Sioux $17 million plus interest accrued since 1877 as compensation. The award is now valued at nearly $300 million, but the Sioux continue to refuse the money and to seek title to their land.

LANDSCAPE AND PHOTO-AESTHETICS

Photographers and painters were both employed on the early geographic surveys and sometimes worked together, for instance, Thomas Moran helped William Henry Jackson set up his 1871 photograph of Castle Geyser, Yellowstone.[16] But by the final decades of the nineteenth century, photography had largely supplanted topographic aspects of the work of painters, inheriting not only the role of representation but also sets of aesthetic conventions re-articulated to take into account specific characteristics of the photographic. How photographers pictured the West contributed centrally to the construction of knowledge about the region.

The idea of 'wilderness' had shifted within American consciousness during the second part of the nineteenth century, perhaps reflecting confidence in the imminent end of the frontier (which was superseded *c.* 1890). Kornhauser suggests that, no longer fearful, wilderness became a distinctively American sublime that symbolised future possibilities for the nation, as well as its past.

> Over the course of the nineteenth century, landscape painters in the United States investigated the transformation of the wilderness forests to cultivated fields, as European settlement took hold from the eastern to the western edges of the North American continent. In their aesthetic inquiries these artists explored the nation's geography, including its picturesque river valleys and sublime natural wonders; wilderness mountains and forests; and swamps and vast deserts. As Americans laid claim to the land, inscribing it with property lines, artists painted the newly built houses, recently settled towns, and flourishing cities.
>
> (Kornhauser and Ellis, 2003: 16)

Landscape as a genre had begun to incorporate distinctively American references not only through imaging specific iconic scenery, for instance, Niagara, but also through reference to particular histories, for example, the presence of Native Americans as inhabitants of the lands depicted. Kornhauser remarks that artists, in effect, documented the forthcoming extinction of Native Americans as they were forced to move from their lands. She adds that

> As the century progressed, landscape and landscape painting served as a vehicle for therapeutic retreat from an increasingly industrial,

urban-based society. By the end of the century, the transformation process was seemingly complete. Humanity's changed relationship to nature – from subject to master – was revealed in landscape art, and figure painting effectively replaced landscape as the leading artistic genre.

(Kornhauser, 2003: 16)

In *Perpetual Mirage, Photographic Narratives of the Desert West*, Whitney Museum (1996), section headings suggest that the exhibition curators likewise perceived changing attitudes to wilderness. The first part is titled 'Surveying an Unfamiliar Land, 1840–1880', thereby foregrounding observational characteristics of photography, whereas the next title, 'Discovering a Human Past, Inventing a Scenic West, 1880–1930', implies construction of ways of seeing (Castleberry, 1996).

Pictures do not directly replicate the physiological act of looking; whether painted or photographed they are selective, constructed images. Photography in effect constructs the image through selection; only a part of that which can be viewed panoramically is actually framed within the image, and focal devices replicate the act of concentrating on one element or section of the landscape pictured. That which is at the edge of the photograph may be potentially as interesting as that which is *fore*grounded, but the photographer directs audience attention through camera and exposure principles such as focus, framing, depth of field and tonal (or colour) contrast. One of the key distinctions between photography and painting is that the painter is not constrained by fidelity to actuality, and can invent or eliminate detail. Painters such as Moran or Bierstadt made sketches on site as preliminary studies. They later worked up a final and usually larger picture back in their studios, perhaps some months after their trip, but which time memory of detail may have faded. They certainly took advantage of license to dramatise. Photography has more limited editorial latitude, hence the verisimilitude attributed to photographs as documents. Furthermore, unlike painting, that which the photographer may not have noticed, or not actively sought, is revealed as the camera omnivorously records all within the viewfinder. This contributes to the characteristics of the camera as an exploratory tool. The work process also differs, with consequences for image content. The photographer has to seek out vantage points, preconceive image composition, then judge and await the desired angle and intensity of light before releasing the camera shutter. Picture possibilities are constrained by weather and accessibility. Photographers were encumbered by equipment, commonly travelling with a wagon as darkroom, carrying chemicals, cameras and glass plates in a range of sizes (as pictures were generally made as contact prints). They also might carry equipment necessary for 'amending' views – cutting down trees or bushes found at viewpoints.[17] Many of the photographers who moved west had covered the battlefields of the Civil War, which undoubtedly proved a useful training for working in difficult conditions.[18] Landscape photography was – and remains – something of a challenge. The sheer intensity of daylight in the West bleaches detail, whilst shifts in the height and direction of the sun impact dramatically on the contouring effects of light. In addition, movement caused by wind risks loss of sharpness in the image, and mist, rain or snow prevent photography or significantly alter the picture. Photographers may repeatedly visit a particular viewpoint carrying heavy equipment with a desired image in mind only to find adverse conditions. Also, exposure possibilities remained – and, indeed, in some respects still remain – limited. Most pictures from the post-Civil War period (1860s–80s) are characterised by solid grey sky because plates were exposed for detail on the ground rather than intensity of light above.[19]

With the end of the Civil War attention returned to the opening up of the frontier, and, as is well known, a number of the earlier American landscape photographers were employed by government or commercial companies as surveyors of lands prospected. Ellen Manchester suggests that at this time the US needed a renewed sense of national identity and that the more monumental landscapes of the West provided this (Goin and Manchester, 1992: 5). Photographs from this era became centrally implicated in imaging what was, from a migrant point of view, previously unmapped territory and contributing to new momentum in terms of the frontier and Manifest Destiny. Examples of photographs from the West included in the Kilburn Brothers collection (George Eastman House – see Chapter 2) are indicative. A few stereoscopes from California depict everyday rural scenes; for instance, a man with rolled-up trousers and stick traversing 'Merced River, Yosemite, Cal.'. Trees are reflected in the water, and the U-shape of sky, which is framed and interrupted by the trees, echoes the shape of the river as it narrows perspectivally into the distance. Content is pictorially contained, and it can be assumed that this imagery was intended for sale back East. Pictures were either made by travelling photographers from the East or commissioned from photographers already based in the West, so familiarity with terrain, and, even, personal style, were further factors influencing content and photographic coding. However, most images from the West evoke the sublime; indeed, the sheer scale of features of the region itself, with deep canyons, soaring trees and the power of waterfalls, renders the actual experience of being there somewhat awesome. This is enhanced by difficulties of access on foot, especially with camera, tripod and other equipment. Photographers were often forced to work from a distance, perhaps climbing one peak to look across a ravine to another. In images from places such as Yosemite, mountains soar upward out of pictures and canyons void the ground before the camera, reinforcing the expectation that nature will dominate and we will look up. For instance, the title 'Cloud's Rest, Yosemite, Cal.', implies a visual effect, that the rock is high and regularly enveloped by cloud. The circle in the rock is shot from slightly below so that we look upward across the boulders we shall have to climb. In principle (assuming accessibility) this image could have been shot from the other direction, looking slightly downhill; my point is that it was not. For practical, aesthetic and ideological reasons, photography in the craggy Sierra at this stage already emphasised what coffee table books might later term 'majesty of nature'.

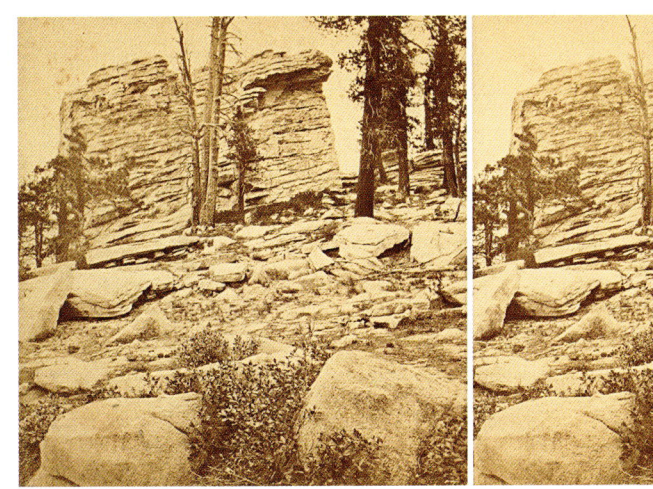

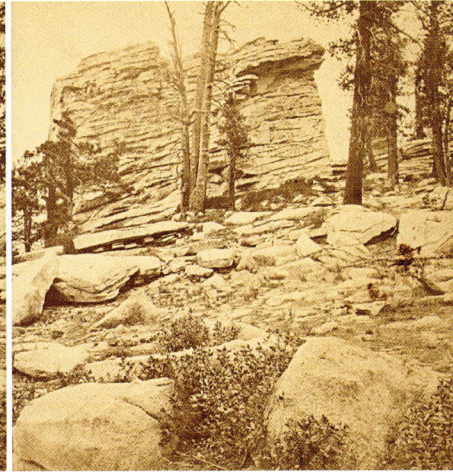

Kilburn Brothers, 'Cloud's Rest', Yosemite, Cal, n.d.

Photographer and writer Robert Adams comments that for him one of the most striking characteristics of the early photographs is an 'implication of silence' suggested metaphorically by visual stillness and the relative lack of visual clutter (Adams, 1983). He reminds us that photography was then a new way of seeing, one which involved the photographer in quietly observing objects or surroundings, waiting for the moment when the wind is still and light contours the image desired, and preparing for processing on site. In other words, this new way of seeing embodied a contemplative way of being within space. Discussing the work of nineteenth-century photographer Timothy O'Sullivan, arriving in the West after photographing the chaos and carnage of the Civil War, Adams associates his engagement with open space as a part of a struggle to find 'a proper silence'. Adams suggests that the nature of the medium itself enhanced such possibilities, commenting that:

> The chief reason the photographers did better than the painters, however, was that when the painters were confronted with space they filled it with the products of their imaginations, whereas photographers were relatively unable to do that. The limits of the machine saved them. If there was 'nothing' there, they had in some way to settle for that, and find a method to convince us to do the same.
> (Ibid.: 7)

He adds that:

> The photographer's experience was, it seems to me apparent from the pictures, finally not just of the scale but of the shape of space, and their achievement was to convey this graphically.
>
> What they found was that by adjusting with fanatical, reverential care the camera's angle of view and distance from the subject, they could compose pictures so that the apparently vacant center was revealed as part of a cohesive totality. They showed space as itself an element in an overall structure, a landscape in which everything – mud, rocks, brush, and sky – was relevant to the picture, everything part of an exactly balanced form.
> (Ibid.: 7–8)

The ensuing pictures crucially contributed to the construction of the imaginary West, to transforming the unknown into sets of images indicating a particular sort of place – whether prairie, mountain or canyon. As the most immediate form of pictorial record, such interpretations centrally contributed to mythologising the West as a place of prospects (in every sense of the word). Unlike the East, much of which had been extensively pictured by painters, at the time of the spread of photography the West was still relatively uncharted topographically. The verisimilitude of photography further supported its role in the documenting of newly emergent areas and natural phenomena.

MAN-ALTERED LANDSCAPES

Mapping land use and interrogating attitudes to environment is central to the work of a number of contemporary photographers. Explicitness of socio-political concern is relatively new, although many photographers have been associated with documentation of changing environments since the mid-twentieth century. This was particularly evident in the renowned exhibition *New Topographics: Photographs of a Man-Altered Landscape* mounted at George Eastman House, Rochester, USA, in 1975, which included work by Robert Adams, Lewis Baltz and six other American photographers plus that of Bernd and Hilla Becher from Dusseldorf. The exhibition title references nineteenth-century empirical investigation and visual mapping (particularly of the West). Through reference back to the earlier period 'new' topography also claimed the neutrality associated with photographic seeing. By contrast with the expressivity of work by those such as Edward Weston or Imogen Cunningham who had become acclaimed within the art museum, the series included in *New Topographics* was intended to be anti-metaphoric and, crucially, asserted objectivity, although of course there was emphasis on form as well as content. But, for example, Baltz stated 'I want my work to be neutral and free from aesthetic or ideological posturing' (Adams et al., 1980: 23). Yet the act of framing phenomena photographically choreographs ways of seeing, even though these are found objects, situations or scenarios. With hindsight, the new topographic interest in urban sprawl and environmental degradation, as settlement further expanded in the West, appears as social critique, but this reading emerges more from late twentieth-century re-evaluation of earlier planning priorities than from photographic intention.

At around the same time as *New Topographics*, ways in which the landscape of the West had been constructed became the focus for the major research project, *Second View* (1984).[20] In examining the photographic construction of land as landscape, Mark Klett and associates spent much of the 1970s collecting nineteenth-century photographs of the American West, noting dates, determining time of year, visiting sites, seeking the original viewpoints and rephotographing. *Third View*, completed in 2000, involved a further set of visits to more than 110 sites, using audiotapes and digital video as well as still photography. Sound and video offer a further sense of how earlier occupants may have experienced places. The overall project (still ongoing) marries interest in social change with investigation of photo-histories, particularly the technical history of photography and the integral emergence of a distinctive photographic aesthetic. The research explores issues such as accessibility, movement of light and effects of weather that influenced and limited the achievements of our predecessors; also ways in which light and shade lent drama to the original images. Technical limitations had played a part. Nineteenth-century photographers usually photographed at midday, as available light meant that length of exposure could be reduced (unlike in early morning or late evening light). This in part accounts for strong contrasts and compressed shadows in many such examples. The work involved in *Second* and *Third View* was extensive, and painstaking in terms of method; it can be a long wait until shadows replicate the 'correct' time of day! It follows from this that in introductions to publications associated with the project concern with image construction can seem to be given priority over consideration of social change (as implied in image content). This focus is perhaps inevitable as analysis of form is integral to rephotography as method, especially in this instance wherein re-appraisal of how photographers operated historically is one central objective. In effect, form is a part of the fulcrum via which the project explores aesthetic issues and photographic histories and methods alongside topographies of social, geographic and geological change.

Photographs indicate manifest changes, as well as continuities, but photography cannot *account* for social developments. Some *Second View* examples are surprising. For example, where we might have expected increased human habitation we may find the opposite. In some cases, despite repeated attempts, the research team found themselves unable to reproduce the original image due, presumably, to slow geological shifts and to climate change. William Henry Jackson's famous 1873 crucifix of snow (Mountain of the Holy Cross, Colorado) refused to reappear, despite attempts to rephotograph it on two consecutive years![21]

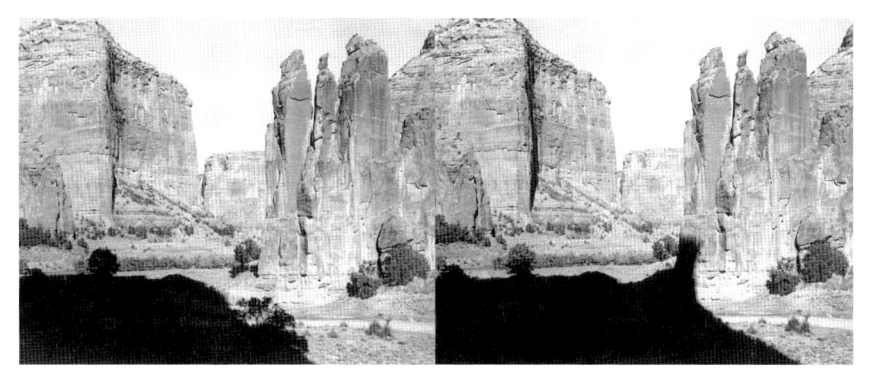

a) 9:50 am

b) 10:20 am

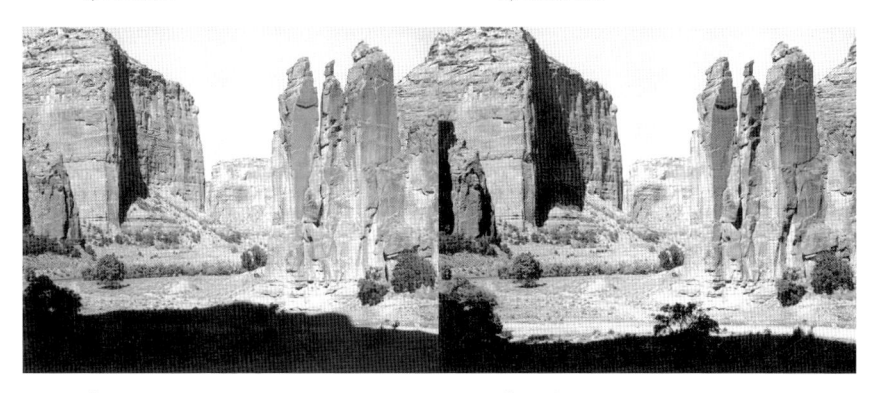

c) 11:08 am

d) 11:50 am

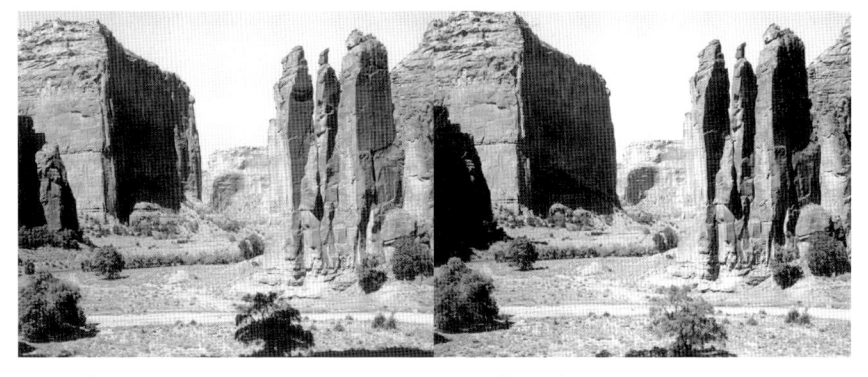

e) 12:20 pm

f) 12:54 pm

Mark Klett for the Rephotographic Survey Project, 1978. Six views of Monument Rock, Canyon de Chelly, AZ.

That the snowy crucifix cannot now be replicated implies climate or geological developments to which we should be alert. Metaphorically we might also read this in terms of a loss of the sense of the sublime and of destiny that must have so fascinated those who witnessed this phenomenon a century previously.

Rephotography also enhances understanding of pictorial priorities. For example, Rick Dingus rephotographed Timothy O'Sullivan's 'Tertiary Conglomerates, Weber Valley Utah' (*c.* 1868). In the O'Sullivan the unusual rocks appear to be sitting vertically on the summit of a hill. But when Dingus re-traced the site in 1978, it turned out that the rocks sit at a slight angle on the slope of a hill. Indeed, perhaps because of the inter-relation of the observational character of photography and the acknowledged interpretative latitude deployed by these early photographers, landscapes of the West have been highly influential within debates about aesthetics and photographic seeing. For example, John Szarkowski, curator of photography at the Museum of Modern Art (MoMA), New York (from the early 1960s to 1991), remarks that Dingus's picture, 'Witches Rocks, Weber Valley, Utah' demonstrates that O'Sullivan made the original photograph at an off horizontal angle of 9 degrees. For Szarkowski, this testifies to O'Sullivan's artistic singularity, his 'genius' of a 'purely intuitive order, operating … within the outer protective cover of a simple record maker' (Szarkowski, 1981: 9).

In the nineteenth century photography had occupied a space within the exhibition gallery as a technological development and for its visual storytelling capabilities. It was not until nearly a century later that art museum curators took up early landscape imagery. Szarkowski characterised the nineteenth-century Western landscape photographer as a heroic figure, struggling in adverse circumstances to achieve remarkable imagery. Stories abound of photographers anticipating images and heroically taking risks to achieve spectacular views – legend has it that Muybridge suspended himself by ropes from cliffs, although one might wonder how the camera was held still! Indeed, there is a whole critical discussion to be had about gender and landscape which I cannot engage here. Suffice it to note that accounts of ventures in the West tend to be overlain by gender. For example, expeditions by both Klett and Misrach, despite their very different working methods, tend to include some 'boy's own' element of driving into mountainous or desert areas, setting up camp, opening the beers, etc., alongside, of course, fascinating details of their work processes (Fox, 2001; Weisang Misrach in Misrach, 1999). Szarkowski remarks:

The photographer-as-explorer was a new kind of picture maker: part scientist, part reporter, and part artist. He was challenged by a wild and incredible landscape, inaccessible to the anthropocentric tradition of landscape painting, and by a difficult and refractory craft. He was protected from academic theories and artistic postures by his isolation, and by the difficulty of his labors. Simultaneously exploring a new subject and a new medium, he made new pictures, which were objective, non-anecdotal, and radically photographic.

This work was the beginning of a continuing, inventive, indigenous tradition, a tradition motivated by the desire to explore and understand the natural site.

(Szarkowski, 1963: 3)

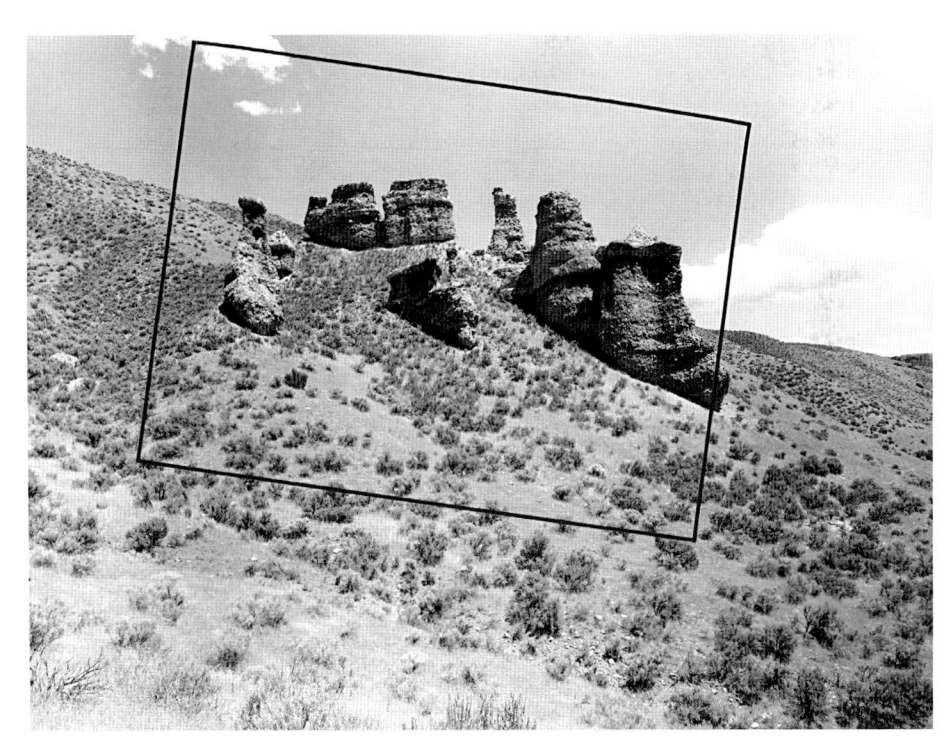

Rick Dingus, 'Tertiary Conglomerates (Witches Rocks No. 5)', 1978.

Szarkowski's statement opens his introduction to the catalogue for *The Photographer and the American Landscape* (1963), an exhibition which was one of many which he curated for MoMA. Later, in *American Landscapes* (1981) he distinguishes between the exploratory role of the survey photographers charting the frontier, and, on the other hand, the function of the photographer on the West Coast and throughout California as 'laureate' commemorating lands which had been long settled by the Spanish and by Yankees. Implicitly acknowledging ideological processes he comments that the latter 'was perhaps a little like photographing the Parthenon: certain understandings prevailed and certain expectations were satisfied' (Szarkowski, 1981: 9). In line with other photo-historians re-examining the emergence of a distinctively American landscape (see Kornhauser and Phillips above) he comments that for photographers the frontier lasted only one generation, remarking that the observational demands of frontier photography soon gave way to more poetic or eulogistic responses to nature.

Szarkowski thus described the initial project of imaging American landscape as fundamentally topographic, and also 'radically photographic'. In *The Photographer's Eye* (1966) he indicates what for him is specific to photography which, by contrast with pre-existing visual media, was founded on principles of selection and thus centrally articulates the real, detail, frame (selection), time (exposure) and vantage point. In discussing the camera image he makes a distinction between the 'factuality' of pictures, and actuality. He also argues that the photographer not only sees what is present, but also preconceives the ensuing picture. Working within the art museum this was a crucial point as emphasis on pre-envisioning contributed to elevating the status of photographers. His primary interest was in exploring photography history and identifying practitioners whose work could be argued to be of particular aesthetic import in order to claim photography as a specific art practice (and, indeed, photographers as artists). Such emphasis on preconceptualisation, along with project research, is a key element for art curators in the distinction between vernacular photography and the work of photographers as artists. Interpretation was also a key factor, involving knowing deployment of photographic coding which for Szarkowski included, in particular, the black and white framing and rendering of a world which was actually experienced in colour, using focus and depth of field for mood and emphasis.

The immediate intellectual context of such claims was, of course, American modernism with its emphasis on medium and method.

Szarkowski's primary purpose was to raise the profile of photography within the art museum; as such, focus on the medium as *modernist* was a useful tactic. Szarkowski does not specifically acknowledge the influence of European movements of the 1920s in which form and vision were emphasised. But his interest in ways in which the form of the object or view that constitutes the pro-photographic event interrelates with the formal properties of the camera image suggests similar concerns, at any rate in terms of aesthetics and perception.[22] It did indeed lead him to identify that which photography did differently from painting and other visual modes, most specifically, working with that actually present. In line with the emphasis within the art institution on individual named artists, the case was also made in terms of the contribution of specific photographers selected for poetic seeing as well as craft excellence. Interesting therefore to note that the 40 photographers selected for *American Landscapes* only included two women, Laura Gilpin and Dorothea Lange, both of whom, as Bright has commented, were dead (Bright, 1989: 131). The project of incorporating photography within the concerns of the modern art institution thus ultimately stressed formal characteristics of the image at the expense of sociohistorical context and – whether purposefully or inadvertently – promoted a male canon of landscape photographers.

The art museum's developing interest in photography as an aesthetic medium was broad, not restricted to landscape practices. But bringing landscape photography into the realm of modern art had consequences for landscape as a genre within photography. First, as noted, imagery became disassociated with precise geographical and historical context. Pictures whose more obvious home might be the regional museum became socially dislocated and eulogised for aesthetic reasons. Of course the reproducibility of the photograph allowed for imagery to sit simultaneously within local museums, and major art institutions. In his initial research for *Second View* Mark Klett approached regional and local museums and curators were apparently happy for him to remove, borrow or copy original prints. Given the current enhanced (art) market value of vintage prints such generosity would be less likely now! More to the point, perhaps, is the semiotic distinction between encountering imagery somewhere close to their origins, for instance, within the state or region pictured, and encountering imagery detached from place which can only feed into often romantic myths and discourses about wilderness spaces. Photographs viewed in urban centres, contextualised in terms of craft and aesthetics rather than history and politics, may tend to reaffirm dreams and myths rather than alert to dangers and dilemmas. Third, reification of photography in terms of poetics of seeing has had lasting influence on landscape as a genre within photography wherein some photographers as artists have taken an investigative stance but others merely seek to reflect and reproduce notions of natural beauty. This distinction can be explored through discussion of the influence of Ansel Adams within landscape photography and that of Robert Adams (no relation).

THE LONG SHADOW: ANSEL ADAMS, AND THE EXAMPLE OF YOSEMITE

The designation of national parks was a government response to continuing tension between commercial (or military concerns) on the one hand, and conservationism on the other.[23] From the point of view of photography history it is the third national park, Yosemite, which is most significant. This is not only because of the number of nineteenth-century photographers who visited the Sierra mountains, but, more particularly, because Ansel Adams, whose legacy remains highly influential within landscape photography, set up studio there.

Yosemite was declared a national park in 1890 (which more-or-less coincides with the end of the Western Frontier).[24] The designation is generally attributed to the efforts of naturalist John Muir and *Century* editor Robert Underwood Johnson; along with others in 1892 Muir formed the Sierra Club, dedicated to the conservation of the Sierra Nevada area.[25] The stated aim of the National Park was to 'conserve the scenery and the natural and historic objects and the wildlife therein, and leave them unimpaired for the enjoyment of future generations' (Yosemite National Park Guide). At this time the railroad ran into the valley, although visitors also arrived by stagecoach. Ansel Adams first visited Yosemite in 1916, and joined the Sierra Club in 1919, later becoming an active board member (Hammond, 2002; Alinder, 1996).

Yosemite is an interesting example of a national park, not only because Ansel Adams chose to live and develop his photographic practice there, but also because aspects of the history of the West remain residually evident. Mariposa, on the Western edge of Yosemite, was a gold rush (1848) settlement. The most famous hotel in Yosemite Valley, the Ahwahnee, which opened in 1927, replaced a ranch, which had been established on the ground of an Indian, Ahwahneechee village. Native American land was taken over for pioneer farming, which in turn was supplanted by tourism.[26] Whilst the hotel name acknowledges this history, it arguably also signifies triumph of dispossession. The Ahwahnee hotel did not exist when Ansel Adams first visited the valley as a teenager, but, as an accomplished musician, he later regularly went there at teatime to play the Steinway.[27]

As is well known, many nineteenth-century photographers, including Carlton Watkins (1829–1916) and Eadweard Muybridge (1830–1904), made work in Yosemite Valley. The Park area had been extensively photographed prior to the arrival of Ansel Adams.[28] Adams photographed throughout the Southwest, including the Arizona desert, the Grand Canyon, and other parts of the Sierra Nevada, but unlike the many other photographers who variously documented the region, he actually lived in Yosemite.[29] Being based in a particular place creates a different set of perceptions that contrasts with the innately voyeuristic position of visiting and viewing as outsiders. Living in woodland areas, by rivers, or close to tidal waters enhances awareness of rhythms and powers of the natural. His subsequent acclaim as a photographer is an example of the art institution adopting the work of particular individuals and thereby enhancing the influence of what is, in this context, often defined in modernist terms as their 'vision'. He was an active and committed environmentalist. Finding ways of expressing photographically something of his feelings towards his environment centrally motivated his work.[30] One of his principal legacies was his contribution to (chemical) phototechnique; his commitment to exploring process and method stemmed from desire for effective control over photography as means of expression.

Adams was co-founder of the f64 group (along with Edward Weston, Imogen Cunningham, and others, in the early 1930s). In referencing smallness of aperture and consequent length of exposure, 'f64' indicates concern with form and detail; the idea was that such attention could reveal the 'essence' of a place or object. The quality of the image thus emanated from choice of object (a tree, or canyon, or sand dunes, or vegetables), and from the technical proficiency involved in recording detail that would reveal something of the characteristics of place or object. That the work fits comfortably in relation to Edenic ideals may partly account for the high status accorded to the group historically. f64 was also a reaction against any lingering legacy of pictorialism wherein morality and myth informed scenarios depicted, often romanticised through soft focus. Adams also explicitly acknowledged the influence of the New York photographer/curator, Alfred Stieglitz, who emphasised a notion of *equivalence* in photography. For Stieglitz, the photograph offers an equivalent to the feelings and responses experienced by the photographer on seeing something of significance. In other words, the subjectivity of the photographer as artist is clearly credited. For Adams, formalism was not a matter of objectivity; rather it was a complex event or engagement within which the photographer expresses something of that which has caught attention or preoccupied. This opens possibilities for biographical or psychoanalytical re-readings of the imagery made by various f64 members. Edward Weston, in particular, has come up for discussion in terms of the sexualisation of objects photographed (McGrath, 1987). Also, within feminist photo-histories of Cunningham's 'nature' work, there has been extensive discussion that often slips into a sort of double essentialism wherein nature is characterised in an essentialist manner and woman (by extension, women photographers) viewed as essentially closer to nature.[31] Thus, formalism may have prioritised the geometry of the image and the tonal rendering of detail but the objectivity to which they subscribed had little in common with a 'new objectivity' of looking dispassionately, let alone politically.[32] Sandra S. Phillips succinctly suggests:

> Adams was a man of contradiction. He was eminently of his time, believing, on the one hand in the good and wise technological mastery of nature and the possibility – even necessity – of multitudes to enjoy it, and, on the other hand, the special spiritual benefits of its untouched state. Yet for so stalwart a believer in the spiritual necessity of wilderness, Adams was a mechanically burdened photographer with a sophisticated collection of gadgets … Adams' vision, essentially a nineteenth-century idealism, became profoundly influential as his interest shifted from making personal, expressive art to using his pictures in a more focused engagement with environmentalism, as the work of Carleton Watkins and William Henry Jackson had been used earlier in establishing parks. His wilderness vision still informs most of the photography published by the Sierra Club.
>
> (Phillips, 1996: 37)

It might be added that his vision of landscape remains influential internationally, as a starting point for students and, more generally, as

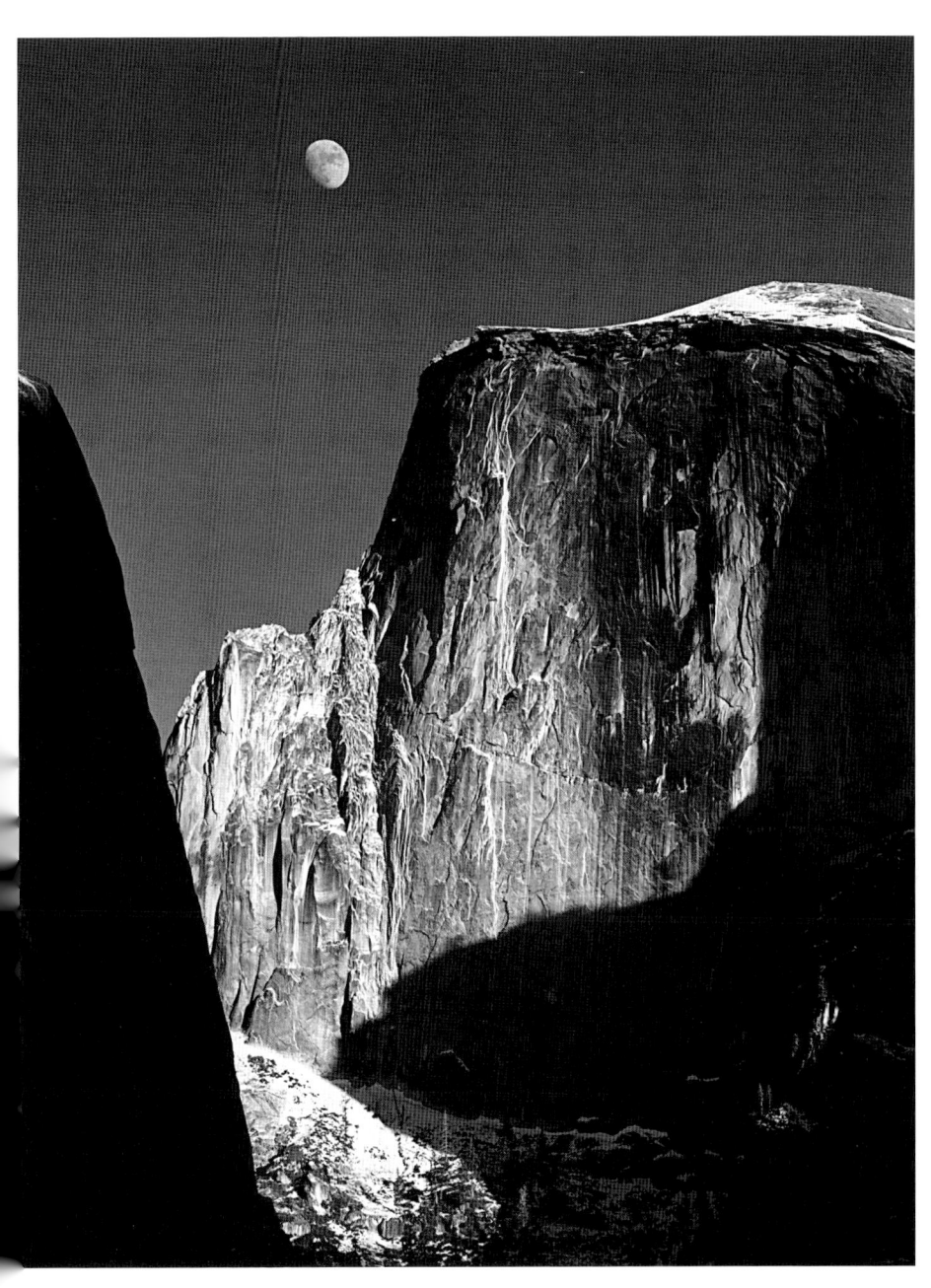

Ansel Adams, 'Half Dome and Moon', Yosemite, 1960.

a continuing eulogisation of the sublime. Although in later years Adams did experiment with colour, the work for which he is best known is monochrome, exquisitely rendered in terms of tonal contrast. It is this that was later foregrounded within art establishment acclaims for his work.

In effect, the status of Adams' work testifies first to modernist preoccupations of gallery curators in the mid-twentieth century, and second to persistence of desires for views which reaffirm the utopian centrality of wilderness within North American identity. It might also be noted that the national parks, with log cabins and carefully monitored 'wilderness' trails, pander to utopian aspects of the Edenic vision. In so doing they distract attention from how land is being used elsewhere. This is not to condemn the pleasures of the parks; rather it is to point to associated effects of political consequence.

CONSUMING THE AMERICAN ENVIRONMENT

The title of John Ganis's series, *Consuming the American Landscape* (2003) aptly points to concerns that variously preoccupy a number of contemporary photographers based or working in the West. This particular exhibition and publication draws on nineteen years of travel and photography across the USA within which the camera became a tool of discovery. The first image was serendipitous. In 1984 Ganis happened to drive past an earthmover that was creating a cloud of red soil. He apparently drove on for ten miles or so but could not get the image out of his mind, so he turned back and made the picture. This became the starting point for this expansive exploration of, what he terms, 'the beauty and complexity inherent in any situation' (ibid.: Endnote). This initial picture at first glance centres on the trees in the foreground, but the trees also act to frame the machine and the effects of the action of the machine in the middle distance. The dust serves to remind us of so-called 'dustbowl' areas and of dust-storms which were caused – or exacerbated – by logging in woodlands and the digging up of grasses in the prairies, thereby loosening the top soil and giving winds free rein. Picture composition aligns with the 'golden rule' of thirds – the sky occupies two-thirds of the image, and ground, the bottom third – thereby lending an aura of harmony that operates to contain the subject matter pictorially, and risks distracting from the thematic implications, especially as the colour tones are gentle in gradations. Here the book format is crucial, as it is the amalgam of pictures – rather than any specific single 'signature' image – which builds a repetition that indicates matters of social-political concern. But the visually harmonious construction of individual images points to tensions between aesthetic pleasures and environmental themes. Several issues arise. Foremost among these (as with examples discussed in Chapter 2) is the risk that pictorial modes reaffirm aesthetic pleasures, in effect distracting from, or over-riding, social implications of scenarios depicted. Ganis remarks on the 'ironic beauty' that he finds in many of the sites he photographs (ibid.). His strategy risks pandering to a 'dystopian sublime' within which we can only gasp at the awesomeness of an abandoned mine shaft or sigh at the geometry of roadways leading to a new housing development in a now punctuated desert.

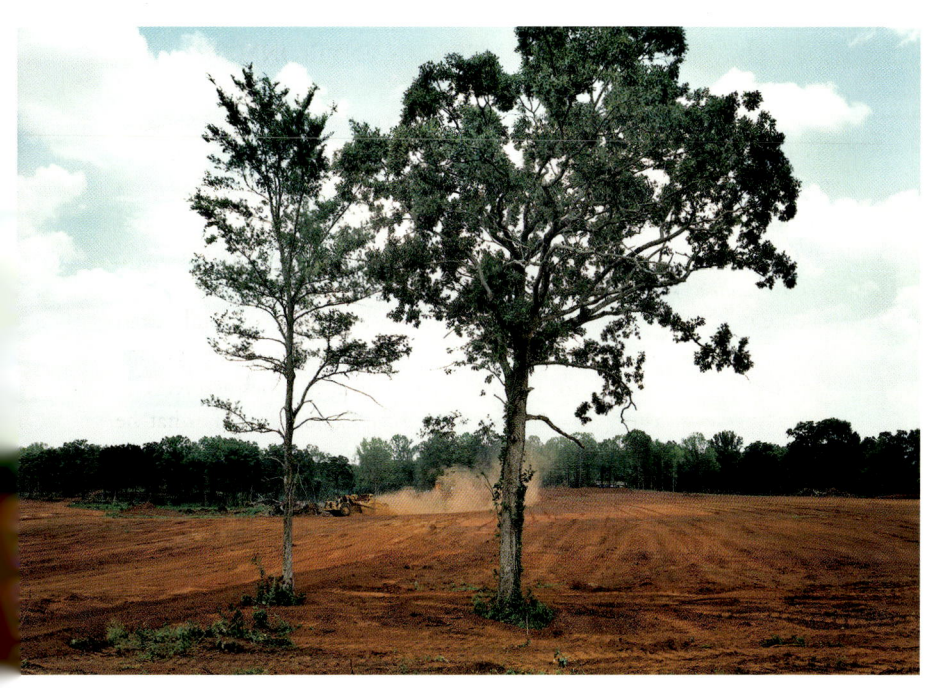

John Ganis, 'Earthmover', Texarkana, Texas, 1984, from the series *Consuming the American Landscape*.

Photography in itself cannot comment on the unseen implications of, for instance, the piping off of yet more water to support newly created domestic and leisure demands – although arguably the golf course in the desert has emerged as an icon of contemporary critical environmental photography. It follows that titles, captions and contextualising data or essays have a significant function in exhibitions or publications. If for Ansel Adams nature was somehow separate, under threat, and in need of conservation, for many contemporary practitioners land is a focus of tensions over visions of community and cultural futures. As with Misrach's work, we are forced to note the impact of human action and its legacy as marked within our environment and to consider the implications of past and present socio-economic decisions now arguably dystopian in import. Where photographers previously might have pictured the silence of the space of the West they are now more likely to document the consequences of human invasion. Ganis's imagery includes waste dumps, quarries, oil drilling equipment, dirt bike trails, highway barriers, mining and industrial sites, and whole sections on logging and on new housing estates in desert surroundings. This subject matter is not uncharacteristic; a number of photographers in the last few decades have contributed to what is now an extensive visual archive of destruction. But this risks adding up to a new post-industrial and post-idealist sublime in relation to which we feel over-awed and dis-empowered. How, then, can artists effectively contribute to asking the questions that need to be asked and find different ways of doing so in order to keep issues live?

The work of Robert Adams is of particular interest here. As a photographer he has been exploring and questioning the legacy of the impact of humankind since the late 1960s. He was included in *New Topographics*, but it is difficult to believe that he fully subscribed to the notions of neutrality and objectivity claimed at the time. He was among the first of the post-war generation to take what might be termed the 'messiness' of the environment as a starting point, documenting urban as well as rural places, particularly in Colorado. Indeed, critique is explicit in his discussion of photographing on the plateau, northwest of Denver, which became the site of the Rocky Flats Nuclear Weapons Plant, an area that he describes as 'beautiful', 'damaged' and 'discordant' (Adams, 1994: 180). In common with many photographers who question uses of land, whilst he specifically indicates legacies of human presence and intervention, people rarely appear in his images. Aesthetically his work follows in the tradition of black and white documentation, muted in terms of tonal contrast. Precision of detail renders the image compelling and the sense of a systematic approach to the documentation of environmental adjustment or decay enhances the import. A block of monochrome images from *Turning Back*, a series on the effects of logging in the forests in Oregon, held its own in *Ecotopia* (International Center of Photography, New York, 2006), alongside large-scale colour work, video and other forms of installation by a number of less long-standing artists.[33]

Series and book titles often simply dispassionately name locations, for example, *The New West, Landscape along the Colorado Front Range* (1974) or *West from The Columbia* (1995); others imply more nostalgic responses to environment, for instance, *Perfect Times, Perfect Places* (1988). But even where titles seem literal they are hardly neutral. For example, *Summer Nights* includes nightscapes shot on the eastern edge of the Rockies in Colorado, in and near Denver, where, he asserts, 'neglected peace' may be found (Adams, 1985). The square format monochrome pictures in *Summer Nights* are exquisitely carefully composed and detailed through tonal contrast, and offer a clear example of Adams' own interest in the relation of beauty to form. As a title *Summer Nights* is simultaneously literal and resonant: the phrase, 'summer nights', might also be taken to reference warmth, lazy days and short nights. The series not only concerns the region where he lives, but also reflects an aspect of photography of particular interest to him. From his writings on nineteenth-century landscape photography in the West, we know that he is interested in 'silence'. As he remarked, 'Among the most compelling truths in some of the early photographs is their implication of silence. Western space was mostly quiet, a fact suggested metaphorically by the pictures' visual stillness (a matter of both their subject and composition)' (Adams, 1983: 1–2). Adam's focus is on environmental beauty and degradation in the American West now, but in terms of photographic form his exploration implicates a much longer history of photography in the West.

The visually varied mountain ranges of the West or the deserts and oases of the Southwest contrast with the relative uniformity of the Midwest which is further emphasised through industrial-scale farming which means that fields for many miles may be planted identically. As such the region poses issues for photographers concerned with visual dynamics. Relatively few photographers have built their reputation through taking the prairies in themselves as the focus of investigation. This may be in part due to the methodological problems. To return to

Robert Adams, 'Fort Collins', Colorado, 1976, from the series *Summer Nights*.

the example of Wright Morris's journey back to his Midwest roots (Chapter 1, pp. 51–2), only the farmstead buildings, or a haystack, hold the eye of the viewer which would otherwise roam the image seeking a place to settle. For the photographer, journeying in North America must feel latitudinal. Since land colours and contours may seem unchanging for many hundreds of miles, the horizon becomes the dominant

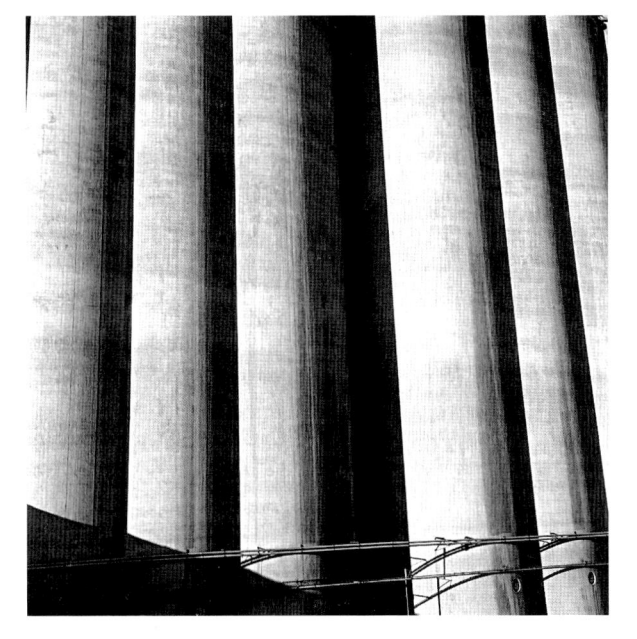

Frank Gohlke, *Grain Elevators*, Series 1, No. 26 – Minneapolis 1973.

geographic feature. Aesthetically this poses a challenge; it is necessarily a key geometric element within the image, drawing the eye into the distance, but, despite the perspectival construction of the camera lens, there is no apparent vanishing point; the plains appear endless. Without buildings or other visual interruptions, land would be emptied into a formal presence, typically expressed through monochrome tones and fluent contours rolling on into the distance with no discernible specific features, whether natural or human interventions. No doubt this is why Wright Morris, in topographic idiom, included buildings in the foreground and in the distance, ensuring that the fall of the light brought out whites in the walls in ways that would hold the attention of his viewer. Similarly, Frank Gohlke photographed grain elevators in the Midwest, echoing the Bechers' interest in industrial edifices in Europe. (Indeed, work by Gohlke was included in *New Topographics*, 1975, alongside that of the Bechers.) The man-made objects sometimes fill the frame; sometimes the flat Midwest landscape acts as backdrop.

The grain store is, of course, a symbol of extensive and productive wheat farming in prairie areas. Arguably the mid-range grey tones which typify this series express something of the relative uniformity of the environment as he perceived it (Gohlke, 1992). In keeping with the topographic idiom, the style is descriptive and ostensibly non-committal, although, given the monumental size of these edifices, photographs from ground level inevitably stress scale, and the angle of vision reminds us of modernist interests in form and the affects of photographic coding – framing, point of view, focal depth – even if that was not what concerned the photographer at the time. The example included here draws attention to the sculptural qualities of the grain elevator, which are emphasised not only through framing but also through the flat light on the metallic surface. Although the edifice fills the frame, and we see nothing of the landscape that must stretch out behind it, the shadow of the hand-rail and the intensity of the light reflected on the surface remind us of the remorselessness of the summer sun in the prairies.

Midwest photographer Terry Evans has responded to the challenge of scale through deploying contrasting and complementary aesthetic strategies. *Disarming the Prairie* (1998a) draws attention to the long-term consequences of the militarisation of landscape even where no battle has actually been fought. In this series of single images, Evans juxtaposed aerial photography, mapping the contours of the land and buildings on it, with colour pictures of sheds, walls, vegetation, woodlands and animals in documentary idiom, which include more historic elements referencing the Civil War or even a prehistoric burial mound. We are reminded that history is multi-layered; tall wild grasses and flowers were mown into farmlands in the nineteenth century by New Englanders moving West intent on taking advantage of the rich soil below; the lands were then re-appropriated a century later for military installation. The context was plans for the regeneration of the former World War Two 'Juliet Arsenal', about 40 miles southwest of Chicago, as prairie-land. This chemical works and bomb-making factory was one of a number of vast 'GOCO' – Government-Owned, Contractor-Operated – military sites which, as Tony Hiss comments in his introduction to the book, 'have their own special irony – because, though largely unmarked by destruction, they constitute a series of hugely successful places that for decades have been peacefully producing substances that can destroy other places thousands of miles beyond the GOCO horizon' (Evans, 1998a: 3).

Evans' central concern, thus, is with histories of changing land use, and with contradictions:

My aerial photographs are not about abstract visual design; they are about specific places. They show marks that contain contradictions and mysteries which raise questions about how we live on the prairie.

(Chicago Art Institute leaflet, 1998b, introducing *In Place of Prairie*)

For example she notes that the Smoky Hill Weapons Range in central Kansas, a 34,000-acre bombing target practice range, keeps two-thirds of its area as grassland for pasture and wildlife. She has also commented that

> The prairie is a subtle landscape; it demands our attention. When we look at it closely, we can see amazing details. Sounds, smell, the wind, the light changing every second – there's no way a photograph can capture that totality of experience.
>
> (Grundberg, 2001: 68)

In her contribution to the 2001 exhibition, *In Response to Place*, she likewise juxtaposed large-scale aerial overviews of tall prairie grasses from the Tallgrass Prairie preserve, Oklahoma, with ground-level documentation, in this instance, small botanical studies. The expanse of colours, contours and track markings shaping the land seems oddly out of kilter pictorially with the analytic illustrative detail of flora (reminiscent, for instance, of the work of Anna Atkins). But the one informs the other; aerial shots allow for an overview that would not be possible from ground level, thereby contextualising the detailed phenomenological interrogation, whilst the close-up shots indicate something of the constitution of what appears in the aerial overview as an intense shape and block of colour. Indeed, the aerial imagery can appear painterly! For instance, in one image, 'Gravel Pit, Kanopolis, Kansas', April 1990, the browns and greys of lands are patterned by curves of the road and by intense amber glints from the reflection of the sun; the effect is almost that of a modernist abstract exploration of colour and texture. Her work is issue-based in interrogating land use, and she has commented that her work starts from land itself and that she has become quite intuitive in her approach (Goin and Manchester, 1992: 28). She also remarks, 'I am not a lobbyist. I am an artist-photographer who is passionately committed to social and environmental issues' (ibid.: 22). She is interested in how earlier settlers examined and made sense of the land. For her *Field Museum* series (2000) she photographed sheets from herbarium museums, including dried

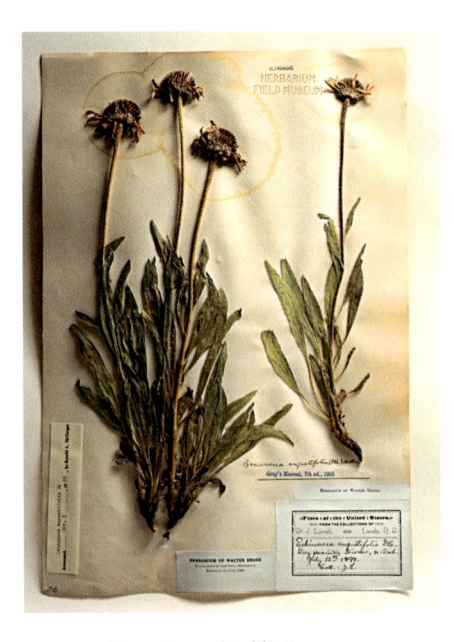

Terry Evans, 'Field Museum, Echinaccea, 1899', 2001, from the series *Prairie Specimens*.

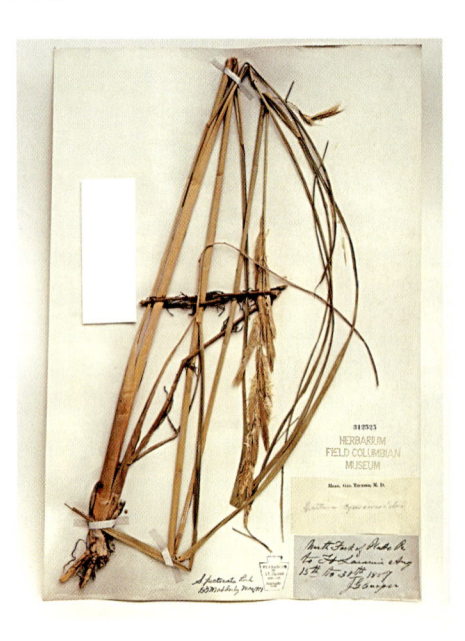

Terry Evans, 'Field Museum, Spartina, 1857', 2000, from the series *Prairie Specimens*.

flowers and the original accession or information notes. Once again she started from observed data but found a strategy whereby social context is implied through image juxtaposition or, in this instance, through montage within each piece. What is particularly striking about her work is her ability to deploy aesthetic strategies in ways that allow for political implications to be woven through with relative subtlety.

The impact of humankind on our environment has also centrally preoccupied a number of practitioners based in the Far West. For example, in *Humanature* (1996) Peter Goin, who is based in Reno, Nevada, shows workers moulding polystyrene boulders destined as sets within cages in zoos, or sprinklers maintaining the even green of a lawn in a newly built housing estate. The square format colour photographs are in direct observational mode, tightly framed; there is no escape into any romantic landscape reverie or memory. Image content and associated brief texts confront or construct inescapable questions about land use and management. Chapters encompass Trees, The Zoo, Beaches, The Mine,

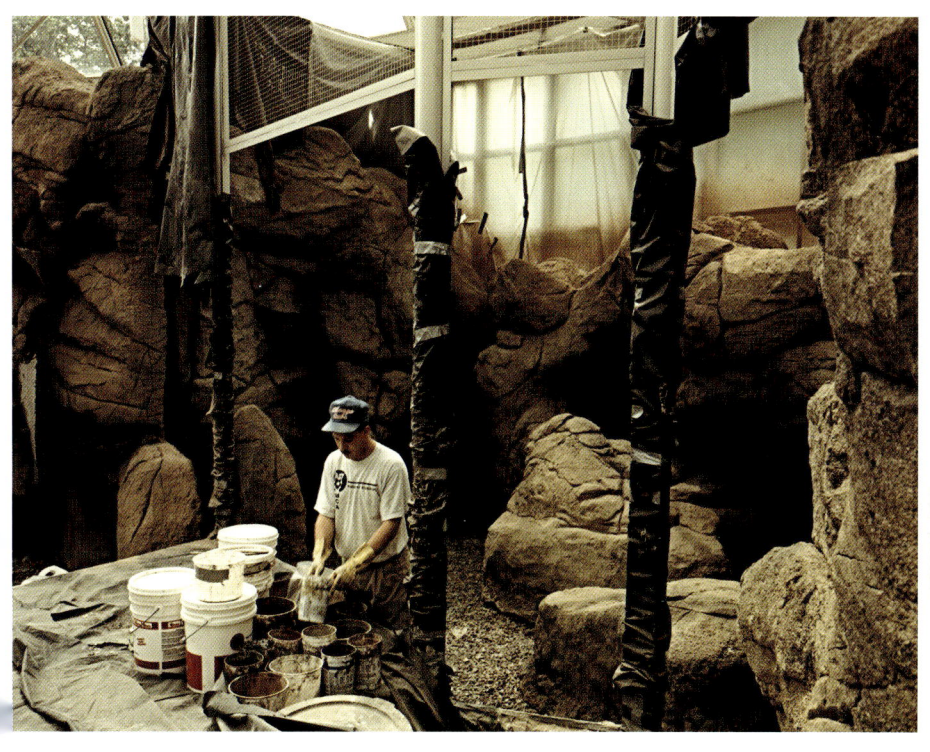

Peter Goin, 'Artificial Boulders', from the series *Humanature*, 1996.

Steve Runnfeldt, assistant design technician, mixes paint for the human-made rocks in the Sonoran Desert area. Most of the design staff at the zoo were trained as painters or sculptors at leading art schools. A few of the landscape technicians travelled to the renowned Arizona Sonoran Desert Museum near Tucson where they took photographs of rocks over a three-day period. Most of the technicians had never been west of the Mississippi. Using these photographs, these experts were able to develop a palette of colours that heighten the sense of reality in this zoological desert landscape in North Carolina.

Reclaimed Land, The River, Dams, Wildlife, as natural areas corralled and re-shaped in accordance with the demands of contemporary lifestyle and leisure expectations. We see trees marked for felling, controlled forest fires, dump trucks adding tons of sand on the beach, or flood control gauges beside rivers. Questions arise in relation to each image. Are trees being logged for timber trading, or – maybe, and – to create a space for yet another gated community? What intervention has caused river floods to become a problem – have flood plains been removed upstream, or the river been re-routed, or developments been imposed on adjacent areas further downstream? For instance, in a long statement montaged with an image of the by then almost stagnant Kissimee river in South Florida, Goin remarks that, alive with fish and birds, it used to meander for over 103 miles, linking lakes and irrigating the ecosystem for a large area. Following floods in the 1940s, and to defend post-war housing development on the flood plains, the army was brought in to re-route the river into a straight ditch. Marshland has dried up, numbers of birds and fish are significantly reduced, and the water is polluted with pesticides. The relatively mundane shot of greenery with shrubby trees in the middle distance cannot in itself tell the story. The rhetorical power lies not in the individual images but in the overall accretion of images of intervention and associated comments that together induce questions about land use. Any lingering notion that nature is somehow 'out there', outside of human influence, is refuted. Instead it is made clear that, through decisions on pesticides and crop control, land management, leisure and sport management and property development, along with failure to fully consider the implications of pollution and resource consumption, human action fundamentally impacts on our environment. This general thesis is reinforced through Goin's own essay that introduces the collection. Whilst some of this may seem obvious, in the early 1990s such issues were less central to the international agenda than they are now. Besides which, this is the West of the United States. Unlike Canada, the USA has been notably reluctant to sign up to international agreements on energy consumption and greenhouse gas emission limitation, so contribution to debates on such issues remains urgent. Goin's previous work includes *Tracing the Line* (1987), a major project tracing the barbed wire and watch points that characterise the Rio Grande, the river which marks much of the US–Mexican border; also a black and white documentary project, *Nuclear Landscapes,* that is often cited alongside the work of Misrach. As is evident from his choice of themes, Goin's work is explicit in its political position.

Water is a scarce commodity in the West. Without water, communities cannot exist. Use of water is thus highly political. A decision to dam or divert a river to create a reservoir to service a nearby city has profound implications for those who may live further downstream. In recent years tensions have run high as the interests of property developers building retirement homes as gated communities have come into conflict with the concerns over social and eco-balance of particular regions. Beautifully manicured green lawns and golf courses come at a high price. Terry Evans, Peter Goin and Mark Klett were among those involved in the 1990s' collaboration, 'Water in the West', which operated through a loose affiliation of twelve photographers, each independently pursuing a specific project. Individual subject matter and style varied; differences within the group are manifest through choice of focus, theme and aesthetic mode. For instance, Wanda Hammerbeck traced the straight

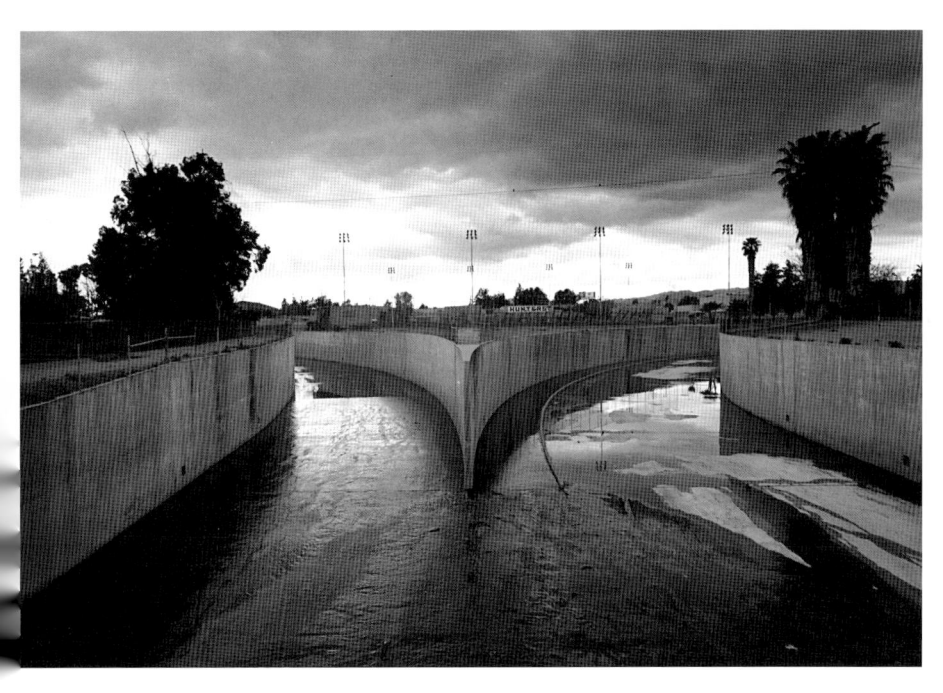

Wanda Hammerbeck, 'Confluence of Arroyo Calabasas & Bell Creek Canyon', 1991, The Headwaters of the Los Angeles River.

lines of concrete that now contain the water and mark the edges of the Los Angeles River. This runs 'from the headwaters above Sepulveda *Dam*, through the movie studios, past Forest *Lawn* Memorial Park, through the oil-pumping fields, into the *industrial* bowel of the Southland, past the Queen Mary, and finally, into the Pacific Ocean at Long Beach' (Manchester, in Goin and Manchester, 1992: 29 – my emphasis). The demand for water as a resource is manifest through this description of the river route. The detailing of the waters from source via the urban to the sea estuary again reminds us that rivers link the rural and the urban and that what occurs upstream has ramifications for developments further downstream. Hammerbeck remarks that the river is the site of human activity including teenage graffiti, riding horses or bicycles, boating or bathing, sleeping rough, murders and dumped bodies (ibid.). Goin's approach and commitment is perhaps the most explicitly political. As already indicated, he has worked extensively on the decline of the availability of water as a resource. His prologue to *Arid Waters*, the publication which accompanied a 'Water in the West' conference and exhibition (by eight of the photographers) in Reno, Nevada, 1991, expresses concern about water as a resource but also raises the question of how photographers as artists can contribute to public debate. This was, in effect, a sub-theme of the project. It is interesting, therefore, to reflect that much of the work that ended up in the publication is primarily documentary in idiom, although most of the photographers extend the idiomatic boundaries by some means. For example, Klett includes a close-up of a footprint in the sand, an index of human presence and symbol of human intervention. He also deploys the rhetoric of emphasising the frame of the image (for example, through black edges) in a manner that unsettles. Historically such framing has been variously associated with pictorialism, and with documentary authenticity. In this instance the inter-play of form and content refuses easy association with either tradition as, for instance, concrete roadways leading to an unbuilt housing estate or an arid river offer an anti-pictorial content whilst the distance from the subject is such as to defy documentary detail. Goin subverts 'straight' documentary through juxtapositions of images with differing distances and depth of field, blocking imagery together in groups that cause us to puzzle at the connections. Hammerbeck emphasises narrative continuity, which I take to reference the continuing flow of the water, through blocking six pictures each with a slightly different geometry of riverline demanding individual scrutiny. (This work was originally in colour. Reproduction in black and white for *Arid Waters* tends to stress formal qualities at the expense of local detail.)

One of the key contributions within 'Water in the West' was an extension to an already established project on the Pyramid Lake and its tributary, the Truckee River, pursued jointly by Robert Dawson and Peter Goin. The issue is that – to echo the title of their 2000 publication – the river is *A Doubtful River*. Its source in the high Sierra Nevada mountain range makes it seasonal, and reliant on snowmelt. The Pyramid Lake, where the river ends, was Paiute territory, and is now the site of a Paiute (Native) Reservation. The background is that the Truckee was dammed in 1905, the first river in the West to be diverted for human use. The original objective was agricultural irrigation to support the establishment of new farmlands in this otherwise desert region. But there have been ramifications for regional wildlife, as well as, of course, for water provision for the Reservation, as the lake level has fallen dramatically, and its sister lake, Winnemucca Lake, which relied on overspill from Pyramid Lake and supported an extensive waterfowl migratory population, is now entirely dry (Dawson et al., 2000).

Dawson and Goin note that they started the project in 1988 and spent six years exploring the river as a 'complex piece of western hydrology' (ibid.: 7) on foot, by car, and by plane, as well as researching neighbouring urban areas, agricultural ranges, regional Native cultures and the varying relationships with the river. The ensuing publication is more akin to a cultural geography text than a photobook, as it brings together old photographs, work by each of the two photographers, and that of writer, Mary Webb, who was brought in to research local histories. These are recounted factually, but also through fictionalisation in the form of composite characters expressing what were found to be common responses to the experience of this arid area. Thus the book is complexly woven, informational and rhetorical in intent. In effect the book challenges celebration of the 'new' West and, as a project, powerfully testifies both to concern over use of water as a scarce resource and to ways in which photography can draw attention to and illuminate contemporary issues. But the photographs, in documentary idiom, risk standing primarily as illustration for an argument pursued through chapters which are organised geographically in terms of the flow of the river, starting with its mountain source.

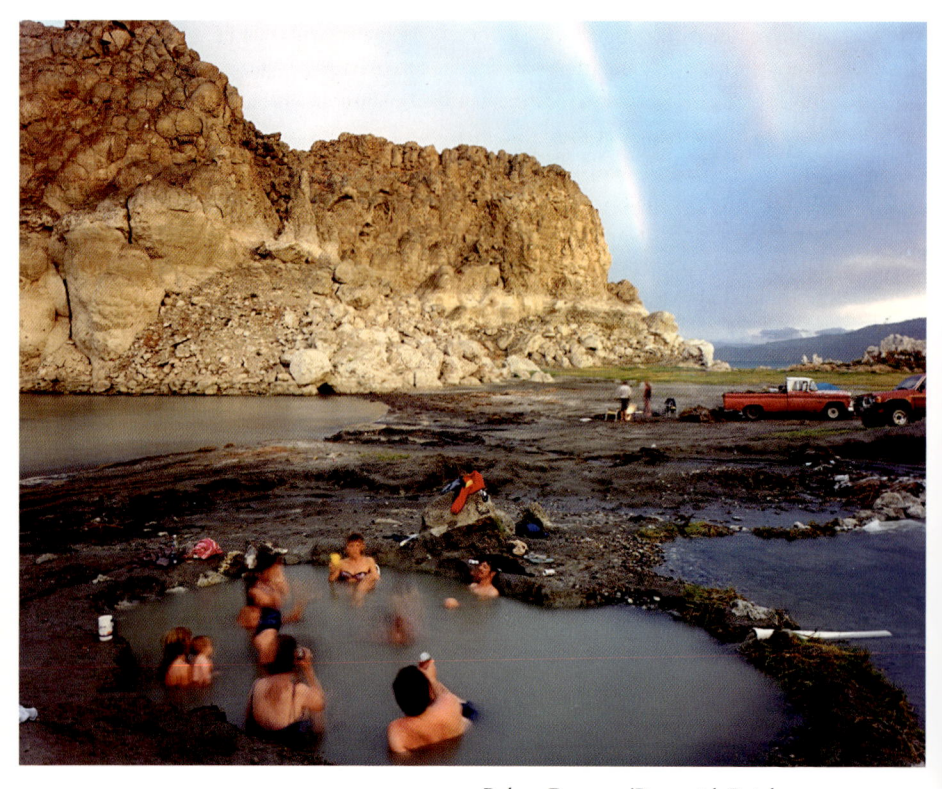

Robert Dawson, 'Party with Rainbow at Hot Springs', the Needles, Pyramid Lake, Nevada, 1989, from *A Doubtful River*.

As mentioned, Terry Evans was also one of twelve photographers, all based in the USA, included in the 2001 exhibition, *In Response to Place*.[34] They were invited to photograph in areas maintained by the Nature Conservancy and defined as 'last great places'.[35] Curator Andy Grundberg invited the photographers to respond to a 'last great place' of their choice. 'I wanted to investigate new ways of thinking about how the camera could depict our relationships to the land, to beauty, and to nature in general' (Exhibition website). He added that 'There is a cultural and historical need to find new ways to describe our place in the natural world, and this need is a matter of importance not only for photography, or for art as a whole, but also for our lives. A landscape may show us what is worth saving, but it does not always reveal what the stakes are in human terms' (ibid.). Grundberg explicitly supports an integrated model of the inter-relation of humankind and the natural world, resisting the legacy of Enlightenment notions of a nature/culture binary.

The work included in the exhibition was quite diverse in theme, method and aesthetics; indeed, the signature style of each photographer was evident. For instance, William Wegman photographed his Weimaraner dogs in Cobscook, Maine. Karen Halverson pictured oak trees in the Cosumnes River valley, California; this river is the last free-flowing river on the west slopes of the Sierra Nevada. Farming references such as a hosepipe, a house in the distance, or a cylindrical tank indicate human presence and the oaks and grasses suggest the fertility of the valley. Richard Misrach made large-scale pictures of the movement of light and shadows on the surface of Pyramid Lake in the Wetlands area, Nevada. Misrach's series includes images captioned 'Battleground Point'. He comments that the work he does often has political connotations but that in this instance he was simply intent on exploring light and water. However, given the scarcity of water as a resource in the West and the tensions and battles that have emerged, celebration of water in the desert is hardly neutral. Water plays a double role. On the one hand, political tensions become articulated around questions of access to water; on the other hand, water crucially contributes to shaping the environment, creating the visual forms that fascinate photographers. Lee Friedlander made a return visit to southern Arizona for this project. As he comments:

> I don't go looking for twisty and sprawling images, but I find them. I guess it suits my personality. When there's not much water available, plants will fight to grow, and all hell breaks loose. I like that. It is all so different from Olympia, Washington, where I come from, which is just the opposite, almost like a rain forest.
> (Friedlander in Grundberg, 2001: 90)

Grundberg asserts that the work commissioned for the exhibition represents a rupture with the more traditional approach to landscape, distinguishing between this and the work of those, such as Ansel Adams, in the Modern era, for whom the landscape was largely empty of human presence. In many respects it is closer to the origins of American landscape photography in the West wherein the point was to remark that which seemed exceptional. Grundberg rightly observes that American

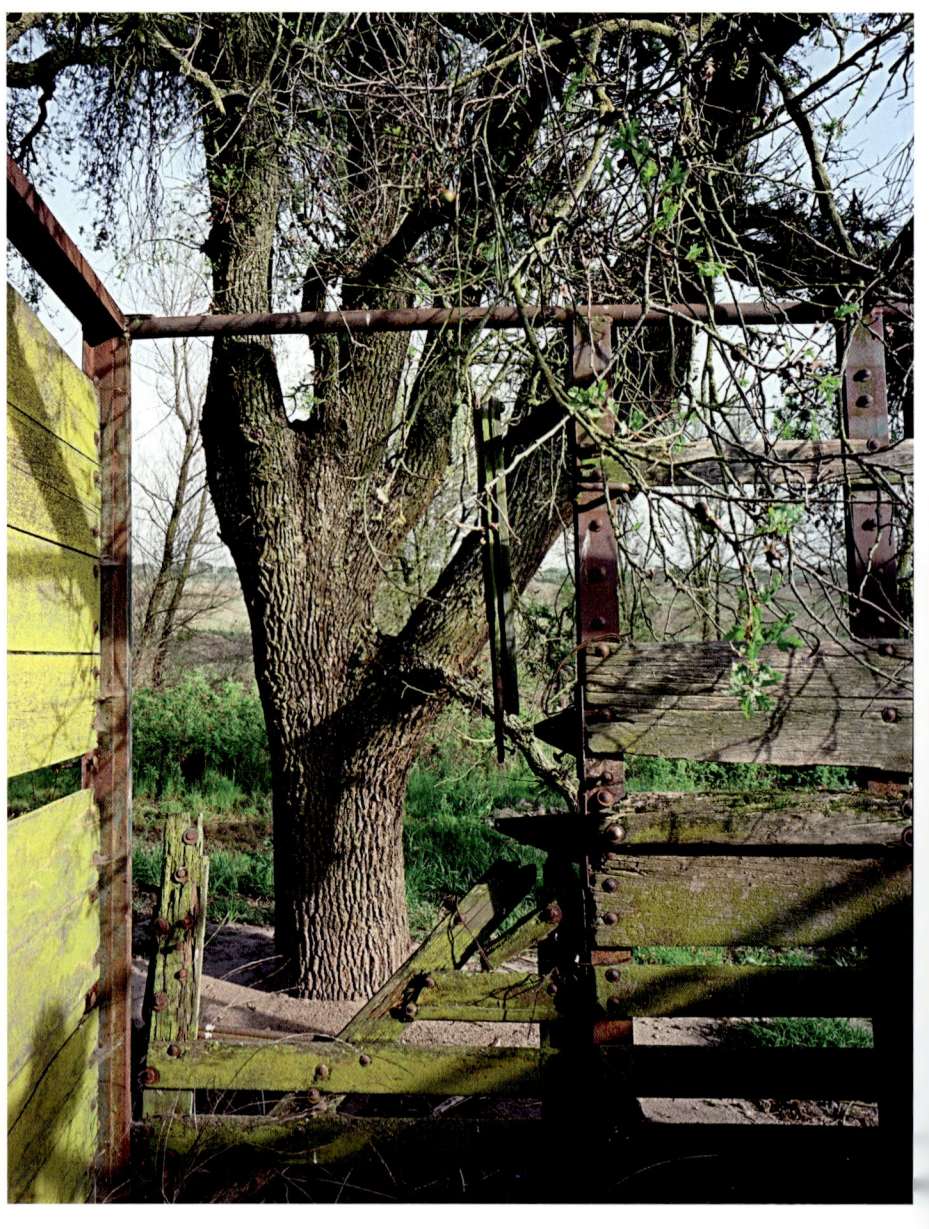

Karen Halverson, 'Valley Oak Tree, Cosumnes River Preserve', California, 2000, from the series *Trees*.

frontier photography does acknowledge human presence, for instance, through recording the railroad and early settlement. What is being challenged is not so much the observational uses of early photography as ways in which the art museum relocated work in terms of landscape as genre, romanticising wilderness as sublime. He comments:

> Feeling a part of nature makes one responsible to it, and ultimately for it. Our responsibilities are in large part a matter of who we are. For visual artists, they might involve symbolic representations of natural beauty or natural order, or working directly with natural materials. Environmentalists often talk about the ethical basis of caring for the land and water, but there is an aesthetic of well-cared-for places that artists recognize and sometimes seek to emulate. Indeed, one might argue that in our tangled relationships with nature, ethics and aesthetics are equal partners.
>
> (Grundberg, 2001: 13)

This aptly summarises some of that which is at stake for photographers and others concerned with issues of environmental management, continuity and change.

If historically ethics has been associated with religion, and 'nature' has been seen as a place of spiritual replenishment, in contemporary culture ethics pertaining to land is more associated with ecological and environmental concerns and with debates about conservation and sustainability.

In terms of theme the most obvious difference between *Water in the West*, and *In Response to Place*, is that the former in effect comments on that which has already occurred whilst the latter more pre-emptively demonstrates something of the importance of nature conservation. Research processes differed as *Water in the West* stressed collaboration and dialogue between participants and externally; the exhibition hosted in Reno in 1991 reportedly included extensive work-in-progress notes and background materials as well as new exhibition prints. This contrasts with the more conventional commissioning of individual photographers to make work for a group exhibition intended for a public museum context. The major colour publication along with the tour to high-profile city-centre institutions with developed school educational programmes means that the show will have been widely seen and utilised as a resource by educators. As a project *Water in the West* was less high profile, but the work process was more radical; those involved not only raised questions about the (mis-)use of water as a resource in the arid West but also debated ways in which such questions can most effectively be raised through photography.

IMAGE SPACE

Visual images can resound memorably. For audiences they may be retained as memory long after the precise rhetoric and statistics of political arguments have faded away. This is perhaps particularly so when the extensive and striking lands of the West form the image content, especially given the historical significance of the region in the American imaginary. Photographers whose work has been discussed in this chapter all variously deploy photographic methods and aesthetic modes not only to respond to particular places but also to engage in some respect with questions of people and place, histories and environmental futures. Perhaps because of the sheer scale of natural phenomena in the West, however critical the enquiry landscape imagery retains potential for abstraction from questions of politics of place and for eulogisation as contemporary sublime. One of my interests in researching this material was to consider the inter-relation of aesthetics and representation, and identify some of the ways whereby photographers are revisiting and re-energising enquiry; also to situate this historically and ideologically. The natural environment of the West has been extensively consumed and reformulated in response to contemporary demands which articulate corporate and consumerist priorities, and a continuing spirit of independence and self-sufficiency, along with a certain romanticised persistence of earlier Edenic ideals. Perhaps it is too late. But if not, then photographers have a significant role in exploring how to renew vision and revitalise ways of seeing in order to contribute effectively within contemporary environmental debates, whether in North America, or elsewhere.

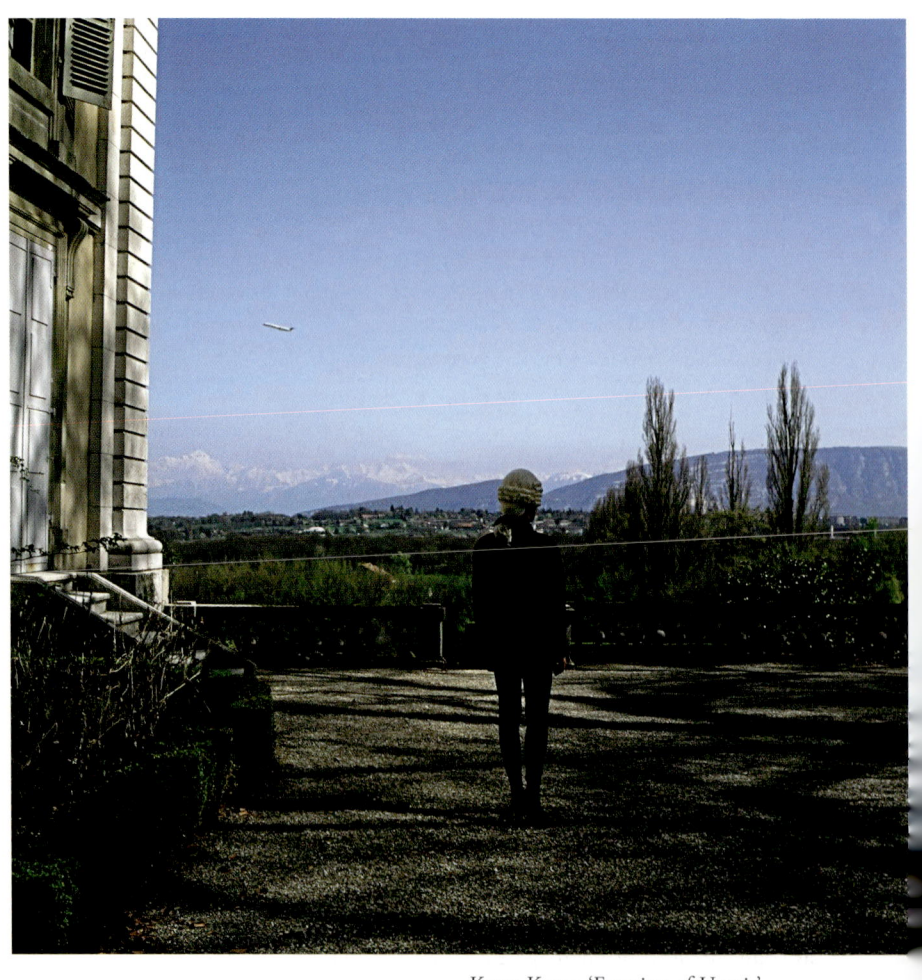

Karen Knorr, 'Frontiers of Utopia', from the series *The Virtues and the Delights*, 1992.

4

PASTORAL HERITAGE

BRITAIN VIEWED THROUGH A CRITICAL LENS

> For some minutes Alice stood without speaking, looking out in all directions over the country – and a most curious country it was. There were a number of little brooks running across from side to side, and the ground between was divided up into squares by a number of hedges that reached from brook to brook.
>
> 'I declare it's marked out just like a large chessboard!' Alice said at last. 'There ought to be some men moving about somewhere – and so there are!' she added in a tone of delight …' It's a great game of chess that's being played – all over the world.'
>
> (Lewis Carroll, *Through the Looking Glass*)

Karen Knorr's series, *Connoisseurs* (1986), on museum and gallery collections, critically reflects on history, culture and the museum as a space of display. In one picture a man in an art gallery, wearing a suit, looks at a landscape painting. He stands, stemmed glass in hand, contemplating a pastoral scene, in effect, an example of contemporary 'gentry' enjoying the pleasures of the visual. Knorr's picture reminds us of the influence of Albertian perspective within British painting and photography. Typically paintings depict land as a vista in relation to which the painter – and, by extension, the viewer – is standing centrally looking out over land which has become the object of his gaze thus, metaphorically, rendered subject to his ownership. This is male territory; landownership in Britain traditionally passed from father to son. Woman's social and economic status depended on that of her husband or sons (hence, for instance, in Jane Austen novels, the concern that a young woman should marry well). It follows that representation of land as landscape historically may be interrogated in terms of critique of the patriarchal. In the case of Britain (and many other parts of Europe) feudal histories and conventions are also in play.[1] Knorr explicitly linked history, philosophy, aesthetics, landscape and social class, and women's position. Her series *The Virtues and the Delights* (1992) is dedicated to Mary Wollstonecraft. The work consists of two triptychs with quotes and captions referencing late eighteenth-century philosophy. We see a woman, in Georgian male leisure attire including a white wig, staged on a terrace overlooking estate lands. In the first picture she regards herself in a looking glass, which must also frame a landscape behind her; in the other she looks out from the terrace of a country estate, presumably contemplating the order of things. Each central image is juxtaposed with visual emblems referencing landed estates (a brass watering can on a plinth; a Romanesque statue) or philosophers (Voltaire; Paine). The parody lies in the seeming impossibility of English history encompassing a scenario centred on a female figure. Knorr comments:

> [It] vindicates and celebrates the cultural achievements and intellectual rights of women with recourse to parody and humour. It … attempts to reinvent the past through the eyes of the present. It reinvents history, proposing an experimental form of history writing, a hybrid between the spaces of images and words: a reframing of history.
>
> (Knorr, 1994: 49)

Her evaluation usefully reminds us that radicalism in arts practice draws upon present debates and discourses, which, however critical, are nonetheless in various respects formed and informed historically. We make our own history, but not under circumstances of our own creation.

This chapter takes contemporary British photography relating to land and landscape as a case study through which to consider ways in which ideological discourses relating to class, region, gender and ethnicity may be articulated. This is a potentially extensive subject, so the discussion is necessarily selective. Specifically, questions relating to region are articulated through two examples: the north of England, and Northern Ireland. As with previous chapters, the focus is upon the politics of representation, ideological discourses, and aesthetic modes. In what ways are contemporary practitioners contributing to questioning notions of place and identity?

In principle, land is a natural phenomenon. Britain offers a particularly interesting case as all land has been mapped and subjected to human intervention, producing something akin to Alice's chessboard of cities, agricultural land, housing, woods, mountain ranges, coastal areas, and so on. 'Landscape' as a cultural construct is deeply rooted socially and historically. Legacies of the presence of the Romans two millennia ago remain marked, not only as sites of interest (Hadrian's Wall; the amphitheatre at Caerleon, Wales) but also as transit routes shaping our experience of travel as new tarmac has been laid along the lines of old Roman roads. Standing stones, often on hilltops, testify to pre-historic presence – although considerably less is known about earlier cultures, hence, *pre*-historic. There are many respects in which the ground on which we stand has been multiply trodden.

In relation to England, social historian Patrick Wright remarked on 'a country … full of precious and imperilled traces – a closely held iconography of what it is to be English – all of them appealing in one covertly projective way or another to the historical and sacrosanct identity of the nation' (Wright, 1985: 2). This might equally apply to Scotland or Wales. Raymond Williams commented that in the English language 'country' is an exceptionally powerful concept as it signifies both nationhood and land – the whole society and its rural parts (Williams, 1975). The weight of association between Britain and the rural is indicated in this double meaning and rural ancestry resonates within this. The British landscape therefore comes to stand metonymically for the nation, an island apart from the rest of Europe. 'Britishness' articulates a strong sense of heritage, multi-layered in time from the pre-historic to legacies of the industrial era (nineteenth and early twentieth centuries), all variously marked within the everyday environment. Britishness as a concept is further complicated by tensions over the positioning of the separate nations, England, Wales and Scotland, as a part of Britain, yet distinctive in themselves. Similar ambiguities relating to identity resonate for those whose ancestry is rooted in formerly colonised nations – particularly in Asia, Africa and the Caribbean.

Broadly, the notion of 'countryside' in England designates sea and coastline, moorlands and meadows, fields and farms, rivers, villages and gardens, rural buildings, canals, and so on. Property ownership is highly significant, legally and socially. It is no accident that Marx and Engels selected Britain as a focus for their analysis of class and the economic operations of Capital, and that Engels' commentary on social class and working conditions is focused on Manchester which was at the heart of industrial entrepreneurship.[2] Questions of social class and heritage are particularly marked and became even more complexly articulated as British Imperialism spread its net in the nineteenth century. The British landscape encompasses emblems of land ownership, such as hedges, fences and gates as well as dwellings of various scales (from the castle, manor house or rectory to the field worker's cottage). Harbours, mines, factories and warehouses testify to industrial histories. There are also moorlands, mountains and valleys (the latter two, especially in Scotland and Wales). Relative to some other parts of the world, little is on a grand scale. In a talk in 1877, William Morris succinctly described England:

> The land is a little land; too much shut up within the narrow seas, as it seems, to have much space for swelling into hugeness: there are no great wastes over-whelming in their dreariness, no great solitudes of forests, no terrible untrodden mountain-walls: all is measured, mingled, varied, gliding easily one thing into another: little rivers, little plains, swelling, speedily-changing uplands, all beset with handsome orderly trees; little hills, little mountains … neither prison, nor palace, but a decent home.
>
> (Morris, 1993: 245–6)

The scale may be small but rural vistas are extraordinarily varied. A traveller taking in the flatlands and panoramic horizons of north Norfolk, the red cliffs of the southwest coastal path, the cragginess of Snowdonia and the ruggedness of the Yorkshire moors would no doubt testify to this. But British land is managed – there is no wilderness; even the coastal littoral is overseen (by the Environment Agency). It follows that landscapes and vistas are human constructs, which means that aesthetic principles, as well as social mores, were and are in play within the actual shaping of land (see Chapter 1). Pictorial renderings of countryside as pastoral depict Britain as undisturbed and undisturbing, thus contributing to constructing a simplified and benign rural imaginary, to picturing countryside as *safe*. No matter that the last hundred years have witnessed harvest failures, hunger marches, war, river floods, mass incursions into green space for roads, housing and various types of industrial enterprise, not to mention more recent mass culling of animals due to disease!

Current emphasis on rural 'boutique' hotels, country cottage holidays, caravan parks and campsites, as well as the expanding network of Center Parcs, testifies to a continuation of the pastoral idyll. Indeed, in Devon, in the southwest of England, where I live, local shops sell postcards that presumably pander to tourist taste: Dartmoor has interesting stones, green craggy hillsides, streams, and blue skies with fluffy cumulus clouds

– no hint of a storm to interrupt the welcoming picturesque. One current postcard, captioned 'England', depicts a road leading past a row of half-timbered thatched cottages towards a church foregrounded against the distant horizon; the land is green, there is not a car in sight, and, although the sky is grey rather than blue, rural cliché is rehearsed once again. This is *now*, the beginning of the twenty-first century! In fact, the majority of people live in cities, towns or suburbs, and many villages encompass bungalows, small housing estates, and, sometimes, minor industrial conclaves. One wonders at the persistent resonance of such twee imagery and at its influence within the geographical imagination.

THE EMERGENCE OF BRITISH LANDSCAPE PHOTOGRAPHY

The inter-relation of painterly aesthetics and methods, and the development of early photography in Britain are too complex and extensive for discussion here.[3] But broadly there are two key lines of inheritance within landscape photography. On the one hand, there is 'straight' photography, topographical in intent, composed on the principles of Albertian perspective, with focus and depth of field as distinctively photographic elements within the overall representational method. Mid-nineteenth-century depictions of the English landscape by Roger Fenton or Francis Frith offer prime examples. On the other hand, there are pictures that are explicitly illustrative, poetic, allegorical or mythological, for instance, the work of Julia Margaret Cameron or H.P. Robinson.

Of course, any such binary over-simplifies; many photographers developed distinctive styles and became preoccupied with specific (often regional) subject matter. For example, Peter Henry Emerson is known for his lyrical renderings of life in East Anglia; his emphasis was upon what he termed 'Naturalistic Photography' (the title of his book published in 1889). He advocated realism and 'truth-to-nature' as opposed to the impressionist or the idealistic, and thus has been viewed by some critics as a forerunner of modern photography. Yet his concern with composition and differential focusing, including use of soft focus, would have allowed him a place within – more traditional – pictorialist circles had he so desired. But his depiction of rural workers actually working locates his *oeuvre* in terms of the realist; one could imagine his farm workers painted by Courbet!

Bill Brandt's depiction of the British countryside in the mid-twentieth century seems similarly ambivalent. On the one hand, he specifically indicates something of the everyday experience of his subjects; for example, his photo-story, 'Over the Sea to Skye' (1947) shows people at work indoors and outdoors in this, for him, remote island community. But his imagery transcends straight documentation, and his overall body of work testifies to surrealist and formalist influences – for instance, the whiteness of the duck on the lawn at twilight in 'Evening in Kew Gardens' (1932), which is among his better known single images. Atmospheric use of outdoor light characterises his documentation of people and places. Tom Hopkinson, former editor of *Picture Post*, comments:

> I saw many of Brandt's landscapes at this time. I did not realize that it was space which was his chief concern, but I did realize that he was producing landscapes which were not simply photographs of a place, but which summed up a whole type of country in a single picture.
>
> (Hopkinson, 1993: 99)

Hopkinson goes on to distinguish between what he terms 'postcards', or views, and, on the other hand, pictures, such as Brandt's, that crystallise the emotional dimension of our relation with land. He ascribes this to research, to finding particular viewpoints, making judgements about space and use of available light. It follows that pre-meditation and selectivity are central to the impact of landscape imagery and crucial within critical practices.

Brandt himself selected an exhibition, *The Land*, for the Victoria and Albert Museum, London, in 1975 that has become legendary. It brought together work by a number of key photographers historically, of whom the greatest single group was from the USA, from Ansel Adams, Emmet Gowin and Jerry Uelsmann to Edward Weston, most of whom had also been shown in landscape exhibitions at MoMA, New York. British photographers included Bill Brandt himself, Frederick Evans, Fay Godwin, Raymond Moore and George Rodger. All the work is monochrome and the event tells us more about modernist preoccupations with form and the geometry of the image in terms of framing, focus and tonal contrast than it does about land and environment. Themes include textures and visual contours of the land or of land-related phenomena such as tree trunks (Lartigue; Man Ray) or cliff faces (Moore; Shirakawa), furrows in fields or dunes (Midorikawa; Giacomelli; Weston), failing light (Adams; Wynn Bullock), and reflections of trees or clouds in water (Brett Weston; Siskind; Atget). Only three images explicitly reflect human intervention within the environment: a road snaking through woodlands (Caponigro), fences separating snow-covered fields (Renger-Pätzsch) and a farmhouse amidst ploughed fields (Lange); and where humans or animals appear they are contoured into the landscape. Only three of the forty-six photographers (Bourke-White; Godwin; Lange) were women. The juxtapositions of pictures on the pairs of pages in the book are organised visually, not thematically. In keeping with modernist formulations of the time, photography is treated as a universal language and images lack specific socio-historical context. As an exhibition it was also curiously detached from its contemporary context, London in the 1970s.

The 1970s witnessed seeds of change in the position of photography as an art practice in Britain. The first half of the twentieth century was characterised by experimentation in publishing, by excitement over possibilities for storytelling through pictures on the page. But the 1970s witnessed the opening of a number of independent photography organisations, thereby establishing the gallery as a potential site of critical engagement.[4] The move from the book or magazine as key means of publication towards the gallery as space of exhibition influenced shifts in photographic thinking. Gallery prints are often larger, enhancing the potential impact of the single image. Indeed, exhibition can operate as a form of theatre within which photographic installation plays with the semiotics of scale, hanging height, spacing, image–text relations, and possible trajectories of the journey from one image, or series, to the next; as I shall suggest, this contributed to opening up innovative possibilities for those exploring more radical or interventionist aesthetic strategies.

The 1970s was also the era when many now well-known British photographers, including Raymond Moore, Paul Hill and Fay Godwin, were beginning their respective catalogues of the British environment. They photographed what they saw and, although classically rigorous in formal composition, variously came to question romantic notions of landscape as harmonious and timeless. Their work can be seen as an early turning point between modernist explorations of form and phenomena, and more recent critical engagement with land seated in particular cultural histories.

CLASS AND REGION

Raymond Moore's extensive black and white documentation of countryside began a break with formalist preoccupations through including marks of domestic and industrial habitation. The effect was to refuse the rural idyll, and to draw attention to how the countryside actually appeared – a murky pastoral! Moore, who was born in Wallasey, Cheshire (1920), photographed places in Britain and Ireland from the 1950s until his death in 1987. We don't see people, but we are aware of human presence. These are not journalistic images; no specific story is being told. Captions merely record year and location. The pictorial is markedly geometric and depth of field is used to flatten or expand relations between different visual elements within the picture space. Indeed, space is one of his interests pictorially, and metaphorically; his tendency towards a uniform sky is not only anti-picturesque, it also means that little distracts from the land-level content of the image.[5] His work offers a unique documentary record of rural Britain and Ireland at that time. The prints tend to be sized *c.* 8" x 10" which was in keeping with documentary conventions (and dates from the days of contact printing when the image could only be the size of the glass plate used).[6] Through directness of engagement with what he saw and through his ability to make the banal appear extraordinary, his work avoids appearing either romantic or patronising, although the black and white idiom does risk absorption within the questionable idiom of 'timeless' imagery.

Moore was not alone in his concern to include everyday marks of human habitation within a catalogue of the British rural, thereby implicitly challenging romantic notions of the pastoral. Others, including Fay Godwin, Paul Hill, Chris Killip, Graham Smith and John Davies, likewise worked in traditional black and white in topographic mode. But content and pictorial strategies differ. Paul Hill has worked primarily in Derbyshire where he lives.[7] *White Peak Dark Peak* (1990) explores two geologically different areas of the Peak District (in the English Midlands), associated historically with farming, mining and quarrying as well as, more recently, leisure and tourism. His focus is upon everyday realities of the rural – a dead mountain hare, badger runs, pathways and cart-tracks, the water reservoir, and signs warning walkers away from fields or the Ministry of Defence firing range. The photographic idiom is monochromatic, grey-toned, no (melo)dramatic black and white highlights. The style varies from the overtly pictorial (mists in the

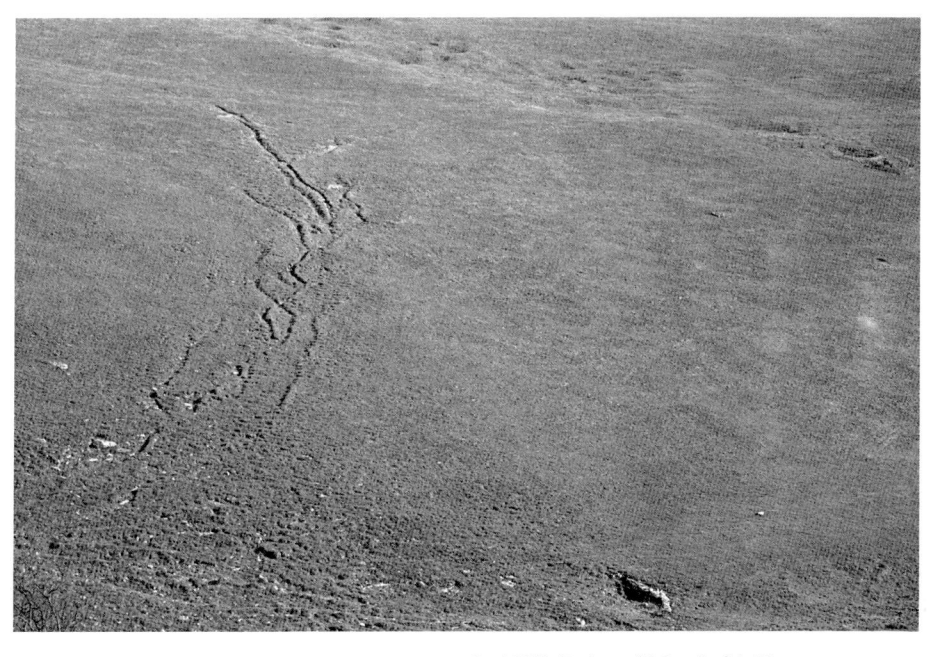

Paul Hill, 'Paths and Mineshafts', No. 1, Bradbourne, from the series *On Land*, 1979.

distance; reflections in water) to more matter-of-fact depictions of phenomena observed. On the whole we look down at the ground; the horizon rarely appears. The series indicates some legacies of human presence and implies experience of being in this particular environment, one which in his work is not romanticised. Jean-Claude Lemagny has suggested that 'Paul Hill's photographs take us through a mysterious, fascinating, but disquieting land … a land which reveals to us the marvels of Light' (Cooper and Hill, 1975: n.p.). Fascinating and disquieting, yes, but conversely it is photography (light) that reveals contours and complexities of the land, including legacies of human activity past and present.

In the preface to his poem, *Milton*, 1804–08, William Blake asked,

And was Jerusalem builded here
Among these dark Satanic Mills?
I will not cease from mental fight,
Nor shall my sword sleep in my hand,
Till we have built Jerusalem
In England's green and pleasant land.

His words were intended as a critique of the materialist consequences of the Enlightenment; paradoxically, the lines subsequently became taken up as a hymn to England. In 1987 John Davies referenced Blake in his title, *A Green and Pleasant Land*, for a series in which he challenged the rural idyll through applying picturesque modes to the industrial and post-industrial landscape. For instance, he photographed edges of cities with hills beyond, or villages nestling in valleys in former mining areas (Davies, 1987). As social historian Derrick Price has commented, by contrast with the visual pleasures of Snowdonia, the mining valleys of South Wales have long challenged those seeking a conventional pictorial (Price, 2007). Davies' interest is in an anti-pastoral pictorial; the critical vein of the work emerges from the content of the image. In effect he responded to the challenge of photographing the rural without rendering it picturesque through a strategic reversal; his imagery draws attention to the consequences, residues and margins of industrialisation and honours the ordinary through pictorial framing of subject matter previously usually excluded. His work extended from Wales to encompass the north of England including the mining regions of County Durham and industrial areas of cities such as Sheffield, Stockport, Manchester and Liverpool. Histories of labour and the artifacts of industrialisation are centrally remarked; his imagery in effect documents visual legacies of industrial modernity. Like Moore and Hill, John Davies has worked primarily in Britain (although he has also explored the post-industrial landscape elsewhere in Western Europe, applying his style to a range of rural and urban sites). In his 2006 publication *The British Landscape* – a retrospective selected from series made between 1979 and 2005 – each picture is accompanied by a brief written statement detailing the history of industrial change at that location. A particular story is noted; his work operates as a visual archive of post-industrial Britain. But his personal style is so marked that content risks becoming subservient within a generalised vision of industrial legacy in ways that work against any sense of the specificity of each site. There is a risk that political commentary is diluted rather than distilled, as the industrial becomes a strand within a new picturesque. By contrast with Moore, Davies' skies are sometimes Turneresque, thereby enhancing the drama of the pictorial, further distracting from content. His gallery prints are now larger (71 x 104 cm) than when first shown, de-emphasising documentary idiom and, more particularly, drawing attention to pictorial composition. This is not surprising as, by contrast with Moore whose work was primarily published in book or magazine formats, Davies started work in an era of expansion of photography galleries and commissions, so gallery exhibition was always a consideration.

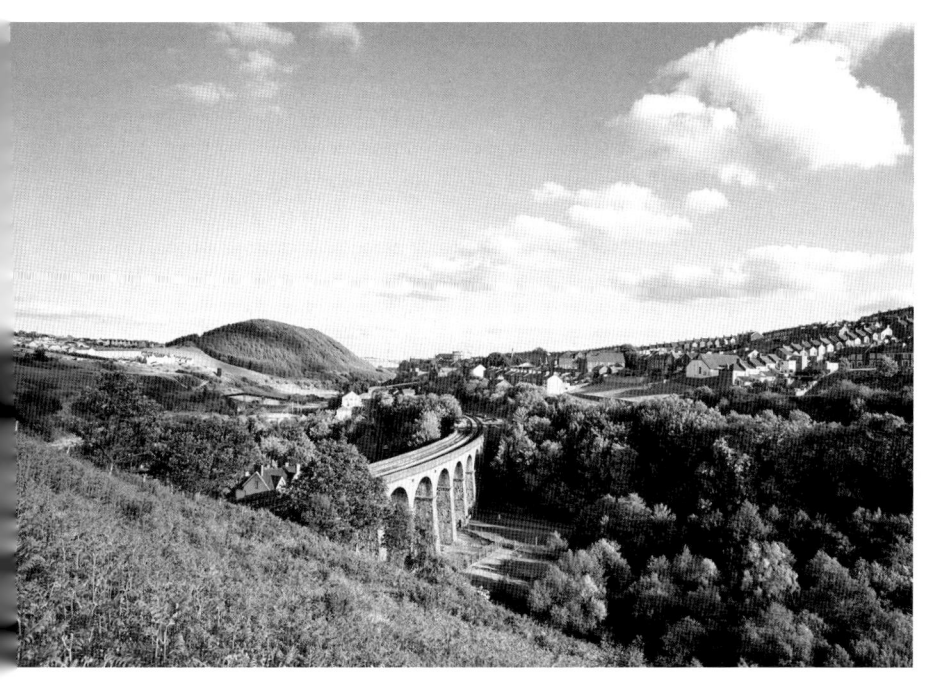

John Davies, 'Bargoed Viaduct', Rhymney Valley, Mid Glamorgan, 1984, from the series *A Green and Pleasant Land*.

Davies continues to work primarily in monochrome, but many of his contemporaries use colour. The 1980s witnessed a crucial turning point in the grammar of the photographic image as colour came to supersede monochrome as the new 'authentic' mode of documentation. This was not without controversy; black and white had become associated with 'serious' documentary and some viewed colour as trivialising. Debates raged.[8] Yet we see in colour. In this respect, black and white abstracts, rather than offering naturalistic representation. That this should have become a matter of dispute testifies to the extent to which representation is a matter of convention and, therefore, mutable. This shift was only a couple of decades ago, yet colour is now taken for granted within genres such as landscape or documentary. Indeed, the speed of idiomatic change has been remarkable. Arguably, new uses of colour, along with developments in digital imaging, contributed to shifting a semiotics of black and white from implications of authenticity towards referencing the past (nostalgia, or timelessness). Now, to work in monochrome, in standard pictorial mode, out in the landscape, is to risk producing imagery that cannot be viewed as critically engaged because it seems so anchored in history.

On the other hand, the rhetoric of black and white may come to indicate continuities, not in terms of a romantic timelessness, but indicating situations or work methods that persist. James Ravilious' extensive documentation of the agricultural landscape of North Devon offers one such example. In the early 1970s he was commissioned by the Beaford Centre in North Devon to 'show the people of North Devon to themselves'. He subsequently spent 17 years documenting places, people and rural activities in the Exmoor region, producing over 80,000 photographs as well as rephotographing about 5,000 old images for the Beaford archive.[9] This is one of the most exhaustive existing records of rural life; the criticality lies in the extent and detail of the documentation. To view a single image from this very extensive series would be to miss the point. Rather the archive acts as a social history, a visual diary of continuity and change. By contrast with Davies or with Moore, specificity of place fundamentally anchors his work, contributing to historical perception through offering a degree of insight that the more roving landscape photographer would not aspire to achieve.

Class and region are complexly inter-connected; rural land ownership, local industrial possibilities, and proximity to cities determine regional rural economies in terms of tourism, fisheries, agriculture, mining, industrial enterprise, and energy plants (nuclear or wind power), and so

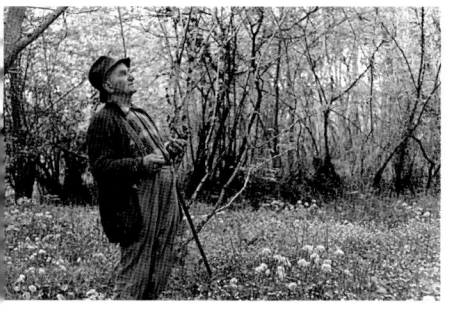

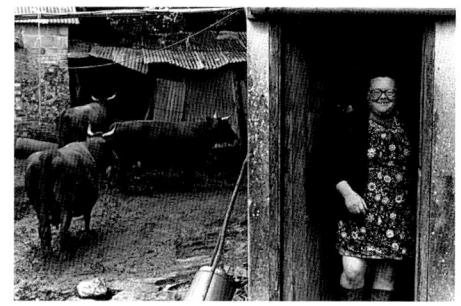

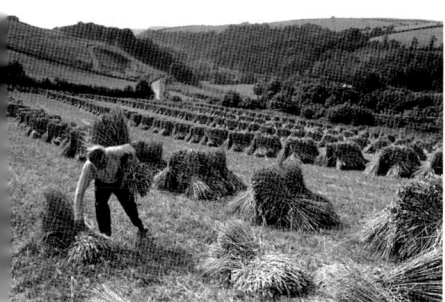

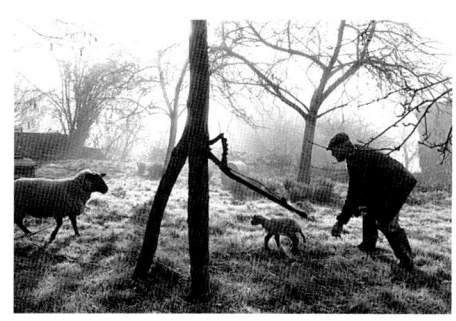

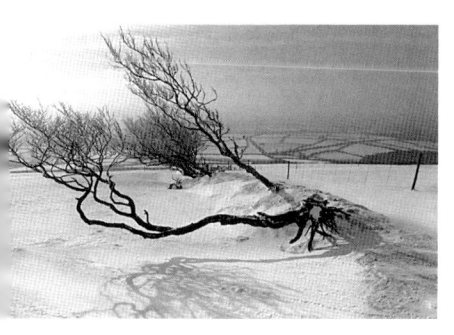

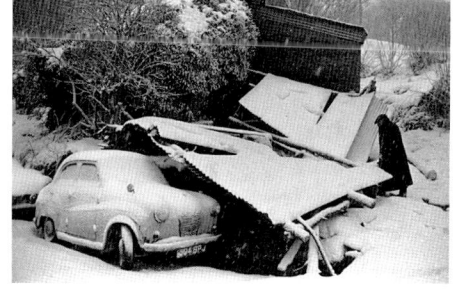

James Ravilious, From the series *An English Eye*, 1974–1986.

Top: 'Archie Parkhouse in a wood near Dolton', Devon, 1974.

Middle: 'Wilfred Pengelly setting up stooks', Woolleigh Barton, Beaford, Devon, 1974.

Bottom: 'Looking southwest from Five Barrows under snow', Exmoor, 1986.

Top: 'Olive Bennett with her Red Devon cows, Cupper's Piece', near Beaford, Devon, 1979.

Middle: 'Alf Pugsley returning a lamb to its mother', Langham, Dolton, Devon, 1982.

Bottom: 'Collapsed sheds during the Great Blizzard', Millhams, Dolton, Devon, 1978.

on. Rural towns and villages may continue to operate as regional or local centres, but may also act as dormitory satellites for city commuters. Although Britain is relatively small geographically, regional difference is significant. Class and region resound particularly complexly in the Midlands and the north of England, that is, in regions historically associated with the Industrial Revolution. For southerners, 'the North' remains a concept associated with industrial enterprise – and, later, industrial decline. In his discussion of *The Idea of North*, Peter Davidson traces notions of the north in history and myth, especially in the Northern hemisphere, including Canada and the Nordic region as well as Britain. Regarding Britain, he comments that:

> Everyone carries their own idea of north within them. To say 'we leave for the north tonight' brings immediate thoughts of a harder place, a place of dearth, uplands, adverse weather, remoteness from cities. A voluntary northward journey implies a willingness to encounter the intractable elements of climate, topography and humanity ... [south] brings associations of travelling for pleasure – leisured exiles in the world before 'the wars'.
>
> (Davidson, 2005: 9)

He adds that the idea too easily becomes gendered, with 'north' associated with the masculine by contrast with the feminine of 'south' – but he does not elaborate on this. Such gendered discourses are complex to unravel (but myths and stereotypes do indeed abound; the northward-bound explorer may be stopped in his tracks by the snow queen or the ice witch!).

Of course people travel north for many reasons including visits to friends and relatives or to holiday resorts that would not fall within the type of challenge that he suggests. But his concern is with the *idea* of north. In England, twentieth-century curiosity about 'the North' emerged in the 1930s when painters, filmmakers, photographers, sociologists and anthropologists became interested in regions which had been central to the general strike or starting points for the Hunger Marches of the early 1930s. Some came together to form the (in)famous Mass Observation project. Humphrey Spender was the principal photographer for Mass Observation. His photographs, with smoke, grime and grit, arguably set a trend towards realist imagery that contributed to a prevalent stereotype of northern-ness. Stereotypes operate through having some basis in actuality and this view of 'the North' inter-weaves topographic accuracy with caricature. Yet, stereotypes seemingly become self-perpetuating; photographers, writers and artists travelling as observers risk only noting what they expect to see. 'North' perhaps starts (or ends) at Derby, and runs up to (or down from) Hadrian's Wall. It encompasses hilly borderlands, the Lake District, the wild Yorkshire moorlands so sublimely characterised by the Brontes, as well as extensive farmlands, seaside resorts, mining towns and villages, woollen mill cities such as Bradford, pottery towns, coastal docklands east and west, and expanded industrial cities. No single characterisation is adequate.

The title of the 1985 exhibition, *Another Country*, asserted a view of the northeast of England as different from elsewhere.[10] Chris Killip and Graham Smith depicted people and places, urban and rural, in monochrome social documentary mode, telling stories about that which is otherwise often overlooked. Killip primarily chronicled people, place and community. Several series were made in rural environments – North Yorkshire; Seacoal Beach, Lynemouth, Northumberland; and most particularly, the Isle of Man, where he was born and schooled. Land figures not simply as setting but as a key determining influence on the way of life of each of these communities – whether settled agricultural labour (Isle of Man), or migrant seacoal pickers. Introducing a retrospective publication of Killip's work, photography critic Gerry Badger notes the influence of Paul Strand's documentation of South Uist in the Hebrides (1955). In a phrase redolent of 1930s stereotypes, he suggests that Killip 'follows the same strategy of linking portrait studies with views of the land, the sea, the sky – the whole ecology that shaped those grave, serious faces and their sturdy, elemental buildings' (Badger in Killip, 2001: 7). But, as Badger also notes, Killip is interested in ways in which photographic storytelling in realist vein can operate metaphorically. The sealine creeping closer to a derelict house at Cranstal, Bride, Isle of Man, might be seen as testimony to the power of nature as it reclaims the thatch and the stone. But it might equally be viewed as a critical observation of the consequences of the shifting economy of the Island, increasingly used as an offshore banking centre and tax haven whilst agrarian dwellings are left to rot. If Dutch landscape painting celebrated windmills, ships and waterways as icons of mercantile success, then photographic landscapes such as these point to the pervasive encroachment of 1970s service industry entrepreneurship in some rural areas.

Critique emanates from Killip's clear eye for the social impact of economic tension and change, and from the documentary immediacy of the photograph, in other words, from subject matter. In an era when more conceptual work was emerging, especially in London, this style was not particularly fashionable. Killip's 1988 exhibition, *In Flagrante*, which included some of the Northeast work previously seen in *Another Country*, opened at the Victoria and Albert Museum in London (then toured in Europe) (Killip, 1988). It offered a grounded view of the North of England that starkly contrasted with the post-structuralist critique that informed the work of many London-based practitioners at the time. But projects (and titles) such as *Another Country* reinforce a sense of separation between north and south.

In the late 1970s and throughout the 1980s, Newcastle had become (and remains) a major centre for cultural activity in a region historically more associated with mining, seafaring and heavy industry as well as agriculture. The timing is no accident; it precisely coincides with the ascendance of the new Right in Britain, the Thatcher decade, in which more traditional industry – and the power of the unions – was under attack, dismantled in favour of consumerism and a service industry economy. *Futureland* (1989), a joint exhibition by Chris Wainwright and John Kippin, stood in contrast with the examples discussed above. It included two separate bodies of work that challenged external perceptions of the Northeast, interrogating ways in which past, present and future are inter-woven. The challenge emanated not only from subject matter but also from the aesthetic strategies deployed by each of the photographers, both of whom work large-scale, and in colour. In *The Navigation Series*, Wainwright poses individual shipyard workers, holding tools of their trade, as red silhouettes, echoes from the past, looking out over a landscape now bereft of ships. Teesside, Sunderland, Tyne and Wear form part of a chain of former major ports on the northeast coast of England, now re-formed as industrial development zones. His work simultaneously celebrates and questions industrial edifices and legacies, implicitly interrogating political power and explicitly demonstrating something of the physical scale and impact of power, through the sheer impact of the scale of sites and artifacts pictured. The effect is underpinned by the large scale of the pictures on the wall. The figures – in one case a light aircraft – are red, burnt into history; spectres of hard-hat workers past and present haunt the sites. Red is, of course, a danger alert; in Europe it is also the colour of socialism – the red flag. Wainwright was among pioneers experimenting in digital printing, using a four-colour separation spray method that enhanced intensity of colour and shadow play. At that time digitally produced prints did not saturate paper, so there was also an interesting sense of the image as a superficial

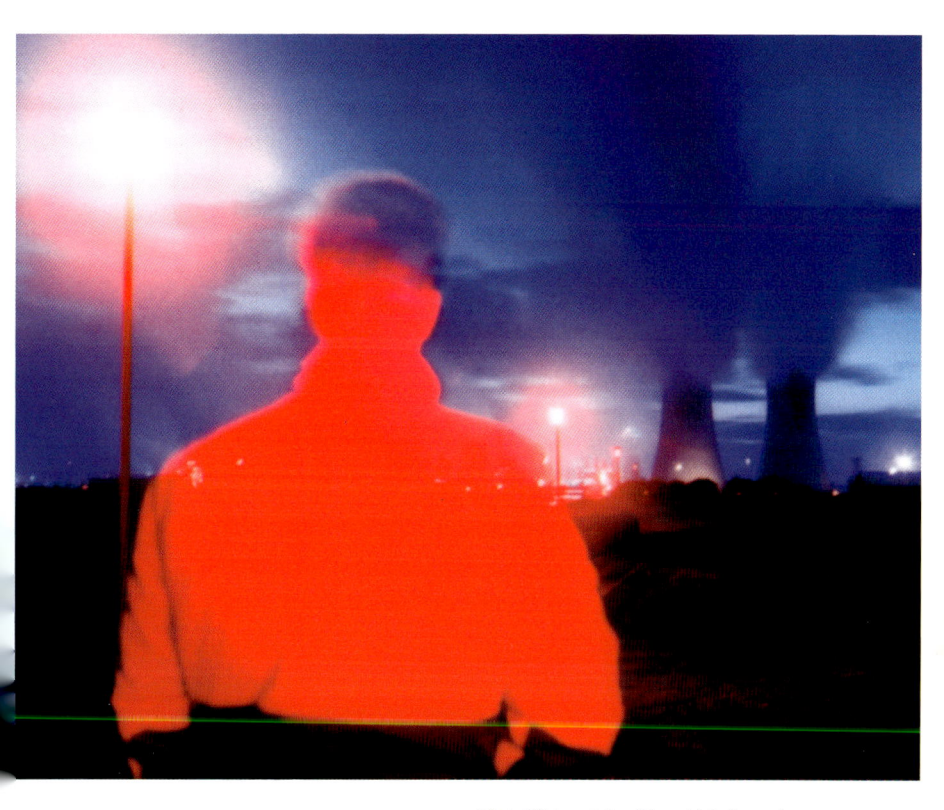

Chris Wainwright, 'Teesside', from the series *Futureland*, 1989.

layer, imposed over a landscape within which lighthouses, furnaces and other industrial elements remain silhouetted.

John Kippin's series, *Nostalgia for the Future* (included in *Futureland*, but later presented as a full-scale solo show and publication) likewise questioned stereotypes of the northeast. In keeping with a trend in the 1980s towards using written text to anchor meaning or to set up further links and resonances, titles are inscribed within the picture as a play of words. The iron bridge over the river at Sunderland, in a former dock area with skyscrapers in the distance, is captioned 'North Light' and a disused barge behind a caravan on Blyth beach with a group of people looking at it is 'Nostalgia for the Future'. 'Nature Reserve' transforms an image of cows in a bleak, fenced, muddy field foregrounded against industrial chimneys into a questioning of historical inter-relations of agrarian and industrial economies at Cowpen Marsh, Teesside. There is no mistaking the irony, or, in some examples, the political point. A gathering of people at a history reconstruction event – a joust – at Alnwick Castle, Northumberland, is captioned ENGLISHISTORY in red, white and blue so that it reads as ENGLISH (red) IS (white) TORY (blue).

Both artists repeatedly return not only to their respective themes but also to questioning the effects of aesthetic strategies. How can critical questions best be posed and when is it necessary to pose them differently? For instance, 'industrial sublime' has become a familiar feature of contemporary gallery practice; abandoned mining plants, factories or shipyards in regions wherein unemployment soared as local economies were left to decline have paradoxically acquired an awesome sublimity that, arguably, distracts from social implications. In returning to issues it is not enough to replicate aesthetic strategies previously deployed. Wainwright, now based in the Thames Estuary, continues to work with the industrial legacies of the maritime, sometimes introducing perfomative elements which heighten metaphoric impact (for example, using red flashlight to 'paint' into water). Kippin has extended his reach to look not only at histories marked in the everyday, but at more specific visual legacies; examples include the country house and estate, Compton Verney, associated with appeasement meetings pre-war, or the now empty site at Greenham Common, previously occupied by the American military. For both Kippin and Wainwright landscape is always a site of histories, with questions of aesthetics and photographic strategy as well as political and economic resonances to be explored.

Indeed, the environment is never unequivocally benign. Coastal and river areas are subject to flooding, fogs cloud the moors and mountains, and landslips eclipse pathways, all this without human intervention! Stinging nettles proliferate annually; they have medicinal and culinary uses, but the flipside is the pain they are capable of inflicting. John Darwell's work relates to contemporary northern documentary; with Kippin, he was one of a number of British photographers who initiated colour documentary. Past projects have included several exploring Cumbria and the northwest coastline (like Ravilious, or Emerson, and many others, focusing on the region where he lives, which he has come to know intimately, in part through photographic research). He has also investigated the impact of the post-industrial on employment conditions

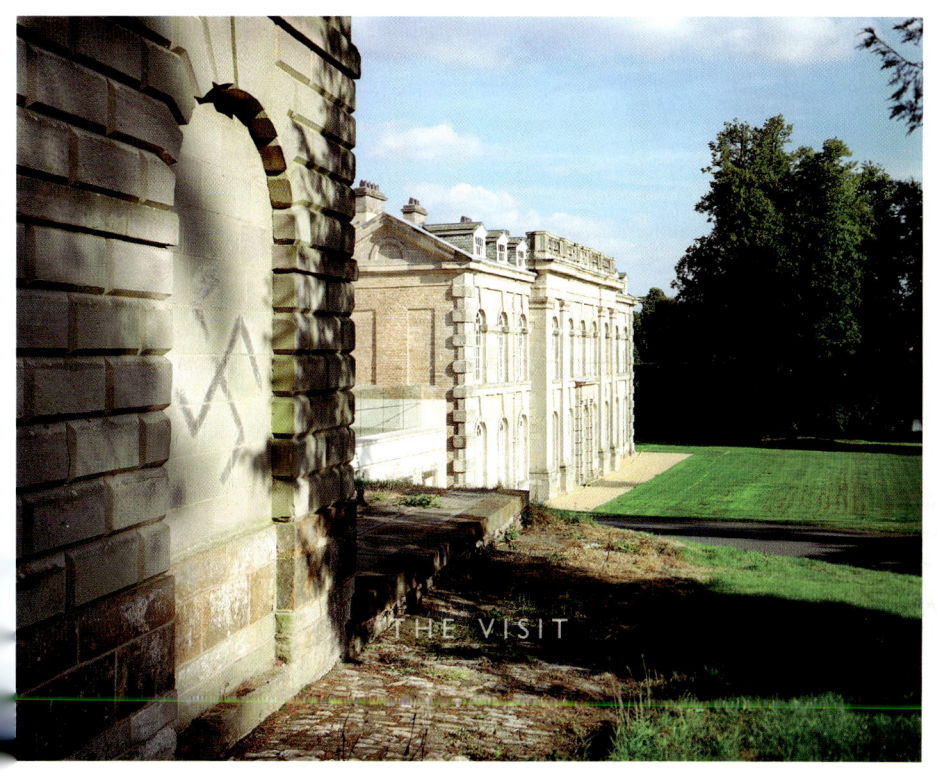

John Kippin, 'The Visit', 2000, from the series *Compton Verney*.

and practices, for instance, in Liverpool docks, and questioned nuclear power developments internationally. The nuclear power stations are carefully composed to heighten pictorial landscape settings of which they now seem to form a part. Both the architecture and their function as power production plants reinforce modernist industrial economic aspirations whilst, of course, carrying the implicit threat of seepage, explosion, terminal illness, annihilation. These are large-scale exhibition prints, theatrically installed along with other markers of debates; for instance, a souvenir mug from a visitor centre, or, in one memorable example, live cockroaches scuttling across a print laid flat in a horizontal glass case. The exhibition installation left no doubt that the picturesque composition was not intended as celebratory.

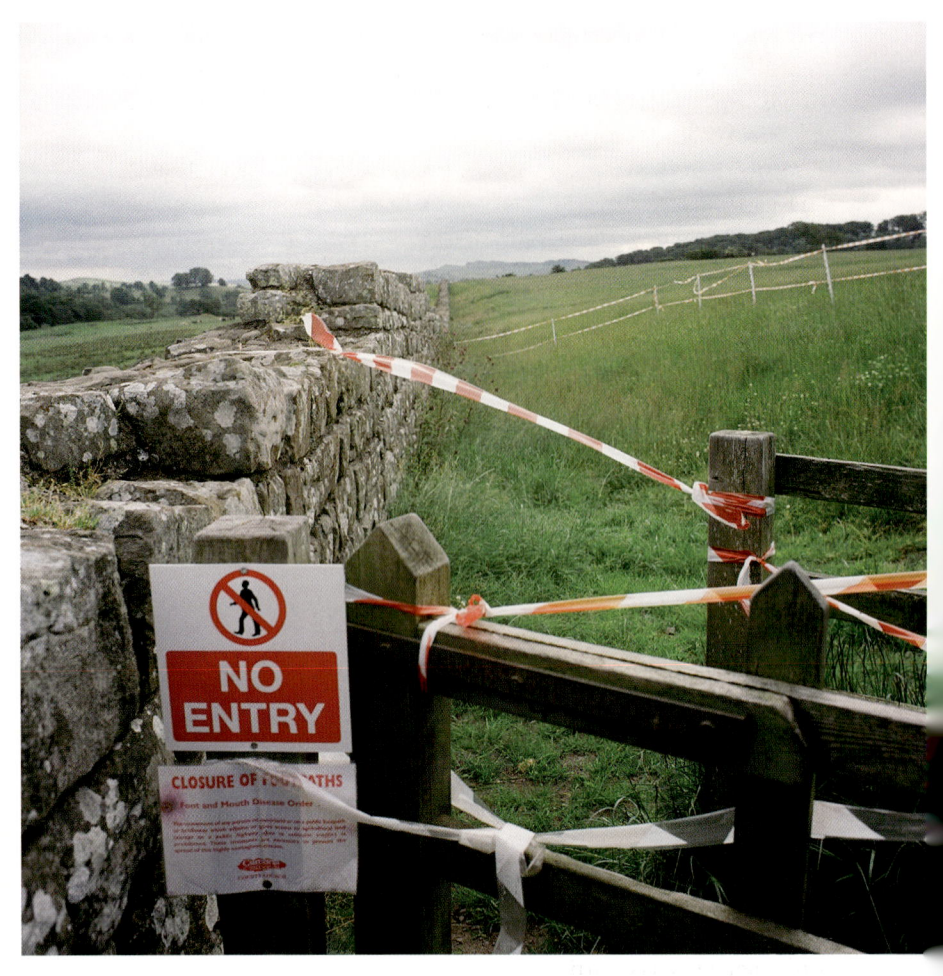

John Darwell, 'Hadrian's Wall', from the series *Dark Days*, 2001.

Darwell's documentation of the impact of the Foot and Mouth crisis in Cumbria in 2001 likewise used pictorial framing to set up tensions as he documents details of that which occurred at a moment wherein landscape came to be seen as a source of threat and dis-ease (Darwell, 2007). *Dark Days* has a three-part structure. The first part documents the blocking off of roads and footpaths – signs of enclosure and exclusion! Tensions between aesthetic harmony and discomforting content resonate; in one image smoke atmospherically mingles with clouds whilst people in white protective gear work the killing fields. The second adopts a more closely framed documentary idiom; the story of the cleansing of farmlands is told through focus on individuals and particular places. Most don't actually pose for the camera and nobody is smiling. Sheep pens and cattle sheds stand empty; food troughs have been incinerated. This is a grim reality, with immense economic and emotional impact for individuals, that the camera allows us to witness. Colour draws attention to semiotic detail – the intensity of fire, the texture of mud on boots, and colour-coded sacks and buckets to be used for disposal. In the third act the Lake District is open once again, but walkers step through disinfectant, and 'for sale' signs remind us of the personal impact of the crisis and of adverse effects on an economy heavily reliant on tourism. Gates hang wide open – there are no animals to keep contained. The Arcadian pastoral does not allow for crisis!

The above examples draw on the north of England as a region within which class difference remains marked. But several other regions – the Midlands, East Anglia, the Southwest – could equally have been noted. By contrast, the North of Ireland offers a unique and obvious instance through which to consider landscape practices and conflict as addressed in contemporary photographic practice.

LAND AND LEGACIES OF CONFLICT

Irish photographers, particularly those based in Northern Ireland, have been acutely aware of ways in which legacies of conflict are variously marked in the landscape. Daniel Shipsides' photograph of an intervention on a hillside, wherein the word 'SORRY' dominates the local landscape, reminds us that land is space within which histories are made, remembered or forgotten. Sorry about what exactly? Based in Belfast, Shipsides – who is also a rock climber – makes environmental interventions as well as documenting graffiti and other marks of conflict. The strategy is two-pronged, implicating direct action as well as documenting the acts of others.

Derry-based artist, Willie Doherty, works in video as well as still photography, using image, text and sound to express something of the

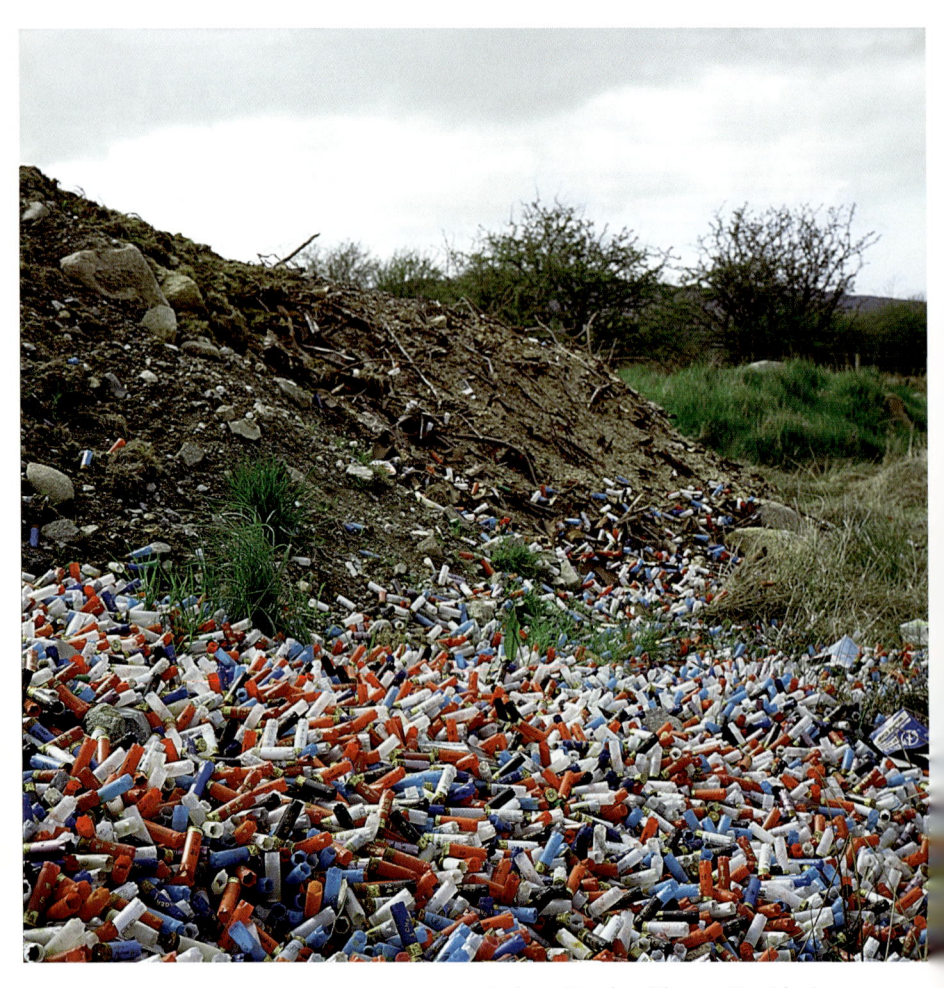

Anthony Haughey, 'Shotgun Cartridges', Armagh/Louth Border, 2006, from the series *Disputed Border*.

political complexities of the region and the impact of this on people as individuals or communities. In one installation footsteps keep on running on a bridge, never reaching the end – imagery with metaphoric overtones if one is familiar with the history of struggle in the region. *Somewhere Else* (1998) offered a retrospective in which his continuing focus on the implications of conflict for everyday experience is clearly evident. Doherty works in monochrome and in colour; he often montages pictures as diptychs or inserts text into the image, like John Kippin deploying colour associations as well as typeface to symbolic effect. For example, green is associated with the notion of Ireland as the Emerald Island and thus with Sinn Fein (a political organisation committed to the re-unification of Ireland). Upper-case lettering emphasises the militaristic connotations of phrases such as 'STIFLING SURVEILLANCE'. In one panoramic image shot across the city to the hills beyond, the central text is 'THE OTHER SIDE'; 'WEST IS SOUTH' and 'EAST IS NORTH' sit in the middle distance. (Derry is the border town, the Republic – the 'south' – does indeed lie to its west.) In the book this is set beside an image of lines of city streets, with a small open space, possibly a parkland, to the left; the caption is 'THE WALLS' and the sub-captions, in green, 'ALWAYS WITHOUT' and in blue (symbol of the British Conservative Party) 'WITHIN FOREVER'. The walls are literal – prison walls or the walls built to demarcate particular communities, Protestant or Catholic; the ideological discourses are, of course, hegemonic.

This north–south divide in Ireland reinforces the idea of north as rugged, masculine, not only in terms of conflict but also in terms of Belfast's industrial history (shipbuilding having been one of the main industries). David Farrell's *Innocent Landscapes* (2001) suggest further complexity. The series documents sites and testimonials to the disappeared, and the clues that informed the police search for locations in the Republic of Ireland where a number of Catholics from the North, executed by the IRA, were buried. Use of relatively muted colour and documentary idiom draws attention to the ordinariness of the landscapes within which, some 20–30 years after the killings, the police pursued this macabre hunt. Farrell remarks that the 'South' has often been seen as a benign pastoral and, apart from Dublin and Cork, agrarian country, by contrast with the 'troubled' North. He notes his experience of being taken to one of these places,

> We walked slowly towards 'the spot', now marked by a large stone and a crude wooden cross. The contradictory feelings of presence and loss were intense – overwhelming. We were silent for some time, before I began to make a few perfunctory photographs – my attempt to deal with the sensations and emotions I felt. But my camera was not its usual shield. Here was a paradox of beauty and savagery, tranquility and sorrow.
>
> (Farrell, 2001: n.p.)

Farrell's work thus upsets any simplistic demarcation, as we are reminded that Republicans sought to reinstate the six northern counties as part of the rest of Ireland.

Indeed, as Anthony Haughey (who himself lives near the border, and works in both the north and the south of Ireland) states clearly, the North has been *Disputed Territory* (Haughey, 2006). The book charts his work on the aftermath of conflict in three regions of Europe, of which Northern Ireland is one (along with Bosnia and Kosovo). Alien objects in open rural areas testify to surveillance, the appropriation and militarisation of space; for instance, a security camera, barbed wire, or an open landfill site almost entirely full of red, blue, white and black (but not green) spent bullet cartridges. The documentary idiom is standard, operating through a careful pictorial economy whereby key subject matter is central, and there is little extraneous information to distract from purpose. Like Farrell, Haughey registers symbols of underlying tensions. For example, a wreath, with red and blue ribbons, tied to a dead branch at the side of a field of puddles and scrubby grass, simultaneously claims the location where it hangs and, in paying tribute to one death, testifies to many. The Irish examples cited each deploy different aesthetic strategies: Doherty's utilisation of text, Shipsides' interest in direct engagement with land, Farrell's focus on contradiction between everyday landscape and hidden histories and Haughey's precisely framed markers of conflict. But each example relies on, and gains a sense of immediacy from, our knowledge that this is a site of very recent – and not yet fully resolved – struggle, with detailed stories often still remaining unnervingly concealed.[11] The instance of the North of Ireland reminds us that the power of the photograph lies partly in what the reader brings to it; also that the photographer may assume some prior knowledge on the part of the audience. This has been extensively discussed in terms of reportage, documentary and family album genres (Sontag, 1979; Evans, 1986; Barthes, 1982), but much less so in relation to landscape practices or rural social documentary. The above examples remind us that as viewers our familiarity – not to say identification – with particular regional histories contributes to informing and inflecting our response to imagery and stories told.

WOMEN, LAND AND THE GAZE

John Berger famously observed that '... *men act* and *women appear*. Men look at women. Women watch themselves being looked at. This determines not only most relations between men and women but also the relation of women to themselves' (Berger, 1972: 47). In similarly rhetorical style, American artist, Barbara Kruger, asserted in one of her renowned photomontages that 'we will not play nature to your culture'. These two comments act as useful points of departure for considering how women are positioned in relation to land and landscape.

An association of women with nature certainly figured within modernist form and themes. The naked women lying on a beach, in the woods, or on a lawn, is a familiar trope in Western Art. Bill Brandt's *Perspective of Nudes* (1961) offers a key British photographic example. His central concern was to experiment with lenses in order to explore the relation between camera mechanisms and vision. But two of the six groups within this publication place the 'nude' in the natural light of the seashore – the watery landscape which Kruger reminds us to resist. In effect the female figure becomes the object of his gaze. As Roberta McGrath has argued, even if no actual figure is present, viewpoint and framing of natural phenomena may – consciously or unconsciously – invoke female anatomical reference.[12]

Indeed, since the 1980s feminist theory has become confident in challenging patriarchal notions of woman as closer to nature within a culture/nature binary that in itself became dismantled through post-structuralist scrutiny. The debates are extensive, encompassing human geography as well as the creative arts – where they range across literature, theatre and poetry to film and fine art practices. The field is too broad to be rehearsed here. Suffice it to note that feminist art theory in Britain and elsewhere fundamentally contributed to critiques of both classical and modernist aesthetics and practices (Chadwick, 1990; Parker and Pollock, 1987). As a result, it is now generally accepted that modernism privileged vision over other, more tactile, senses; also that it perpetuated ways of seeing that privilege male authority. Women artists and art historians internationally have variously questioned the positioning of 'woman' as object, rather than agent, of 'the look', suggesting that women may have particular ways of seeing. As Luce Irigaray suggests, authors (writers or artists) draw upon their own experience, and being a woman within a patriarchal society is a crucial constitutive element within this (Irigaray, 1993). Many women artists have been primarily concerned to assert a right to a voice and to acknowledgement of themes articulating women's experience. Others have explored and experimented in the formal interstices opened through operating, as it were, in between or off to one side of patriarchal traditions.

Such critiques informed practice. Yet with hindsight it seems that relatively limited attention was paid to gender and landscape within these debates. In the UK one reason for this lay in the relative absence of British women, aside from Fay Godwin, who had become well known as landscape photographers (botanical illustration aside). A further reason was almost certainly the focus within feminism on issues in representation, ideology and stereotyping (in advertising as well as art) and also on the family album as a realm of women's creativity and a particular form of documentation within personal and social history. In terms of art practices, women's experience has clearly been formative when it comes to work on the family album, or themes such as birth and motherhood. Such influences may be less immediately evident in genres such as landscape or, indeed, documentary, although a number of editors and curators in the 1980s and 1990s (myself included) noted tendencies for women to focus on the inter-relation of people and place, rather than, for instance, on land as vista more-or-less devoid of indicators of human habitation. But this was, precisely, a *tendency*. Likewise, it was noted that when women do explore natural form, their viewing position and scale of imaging tends to be more akin to the close-up scrutiny of botanical illustration than to the grandeur of the sublime, albeit perhaps implicating the bodily and the haptic. For many artists exploring our environment involves *being within* rather than *looking at*. Nowadays this might be contextualised in terms of the ecological, but at that point, a couple of decades ago, environmental concern was not central to political debate, so did not present as a key theme for radical engagement as it does now.

But land did figure occasionally within more conceptual explorations of regimes and relations of looking. For example, in 1981–82 Jo Spence and Terry Dennett made a series of staged images under the critical title, *Re-Modelling Photo-History* (Spence, 1986: 118ff). One pair of images shows Spence, lying on her side in a field, naked, back towards the camera. Shot in black and white, the composition is classical, with hedges and trees leading the eye into the distance towards the grey sky, and branches in the top quarter of the picture, in sharp focus above the camera. The setting is idyllic, but the naked body is not that of a young slim woman; she is middle-aged, sturdy of flesh. In the twin image the same body, sectioned from shoulder to thigh, spine to arm, is foregrounded while a line of pylons holding power cables takes our eye into the distance towards the vanishing point. This is a landscape of industry and labour, not one of abstract formal synthesis. Bill Brandt would not have posed his nudes here!

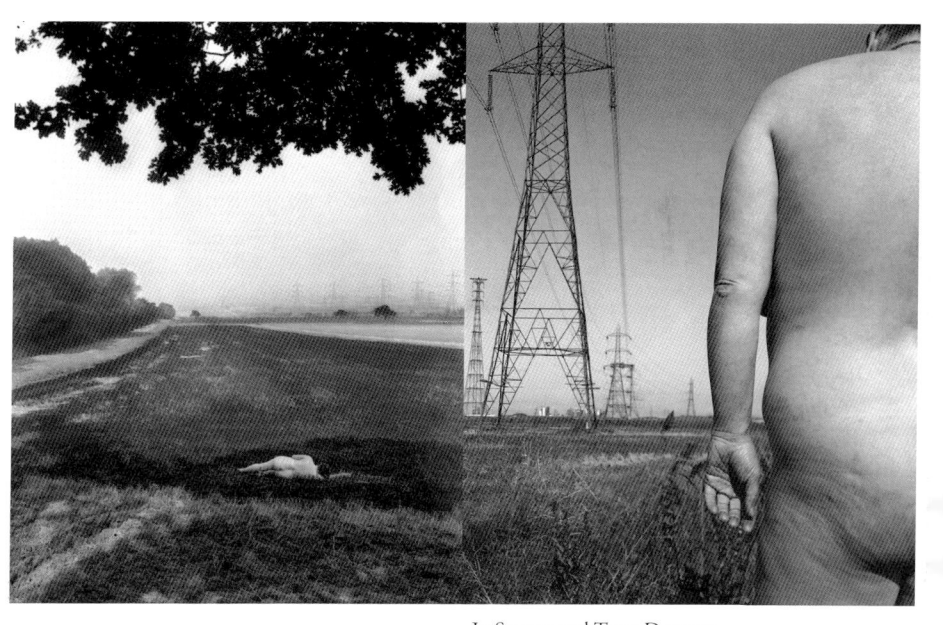

Jo Spence and Terry Dennett, 'Industrialisation', from the series *Re-Modelling Photo-History*, 1982.

In Britain historically the 'otherness' of women is complexly articulated with social class – which makes the UK an interesting case study through which to reflect upon women as landscape photographers. The first women to work with photography were largely aristocratic and upper-middle-class women (that is, women associated with the professional classes, in most cases, as wives or daughters of professional men). Since the 1970s feminist art historians have drawn attention to the work of many erstwhile overlooked women artists; in line with this, photo-historians and critics began to expose the work of women photographers previously hidden from history (Williams, 1986). But, historically, women landscape photographers have been relatively rare in Britain and there are few examples of British women making landscape work until after the First World War. As I have argued elsewhere, reasons for this included social convention: nineteenth-century middle-class propriety limited the extent to which women were free to wander unescorted beyond the gates of family houses and estates (although no doubt some did) (Wells, 1994: 43ff). Furthermore, the cumbersomeness of nineteenth-century clothing did not facilitate challenging excursions – although again, there were exceptions and some accounts of the exploits of women travellers of the time are delightful. Nonetheless, whilst nineteenth-century British photographers such as Roger Fenton and Francis Frith were out and about internationally, Anna Atkins was documenting flowers and ferns, Julia Margaret Cameron was staging mythical scenarios and Lady Hawarden was photographing her daughters.

Lady Hawarden is particularly interesting: as a member of a landowning aristocratic family she might have been expected to relate to and picture land. But in England, in that period, women were not themselves landowners. Their relation to land was mediated via a father or a husband. This may contribute to explaining a less territorial attitude to land. It is not that women were unaffected by property ownership and estate management; rather that the investment is from a satellite position. When Lady Hawarden photographed on the family estate in Ireland, the property concerned was legally her husband's. More generally, when women photographed out of doors, it was largely for the family album: leisure (picnics, walks on family estates) or travel (the royal family included several keen photographers) or visits to colonial family estates (Swingler, 2000). These were not intended as landscape pictures; rather they were a part of the domestic diary.

There were, as always, notable exceptions. For example, Englishwoman Constance Astley voyaged to New Zealand with her companion, Margaret Shaen, in 1897, and kept a travel diary which included her own watercolours and sketches as well as photographs made by Shaen. Comments in Astley's diary indicate that Shaen was a keen photographer, travelling with a big camera and a smaller one, and often stopping on their various treks into the New Zealand mountains to make 'many photos' (de Fresnes, 1997). One picture (which must have been taken by their guide) shows the two of them in full ankle-length Victorian dress with walking sticks, climbing the Tasman Glacier. Connie Astley describes trekking up beyond the glacier and looking down on it, then rejoining the others: 'I accomplished the descent in about 15 minutes, getting some fine slithers in places, & only losing both buttons from my wristbands & tearing a hole in my petticoat' (de Fresnes, 1997: 102). Sewing and mending was presumably an occupational hazard for such intrepid travellers!

There are a number of cultural reasons why it is still the case that relatively few women have become known for landscape imagery. Exploring the countryside involves long walks, lots of time, much trudging about, possibly with heavy equipment, with the attendant risks of bad weather and consequent hazards (fog, flooding …).[13] Of course this is true for all ramblers. However, photographers often work alone so there may not be help to hand to deal with accidents, adverse conditions, wild animals or, indeed, other humans; whether such threat is perceived or actual it can act as a deterrent. Fay Godwin once commented that the rural is threatening as well as beautiful and that she was 'quite often frightened out in the landscape' (*South Bank Show*, ITV, 1986). She became particularly well known for a number of reasons including, first, that she was prolific; second, that her aesthetic was classically pictorial and thus generally accessible, and third, because her work was widely circulated in book form, often including essays by well-known writers, not necessarily only those whose primary critical interest was in photography. It was the directness or the content of her images that enhanced her reputation as she increasingly allied herself with organisations such as the Ramblers Association concerned to highlight the effects of contemporary culture on rural areas and to defend common rights of access to countryside.[14] Godwin's work, detailing what she clearly saw as desecration of the rural, includes a caravan park near Salisbury Cathedral, a roadside hoarding advertising Stonehenge as a tourism destination, waterways used as waste tips, and public footpaths closed to walkers by farmers or the military. At one level, her work was conservative; it argued for a pastoral heritage that she feared was now disregarded. But she was aware that, historically, this pastoral was a selective and idealised view of the rural, certainly from the point of view of small farmers, rural workers, innkeepers and others subsisting within the limitations of the rural economy. At another level, her work asked questions about conservation, and about access, thereby challenging exclusive rights asserted by landowners. Her set of

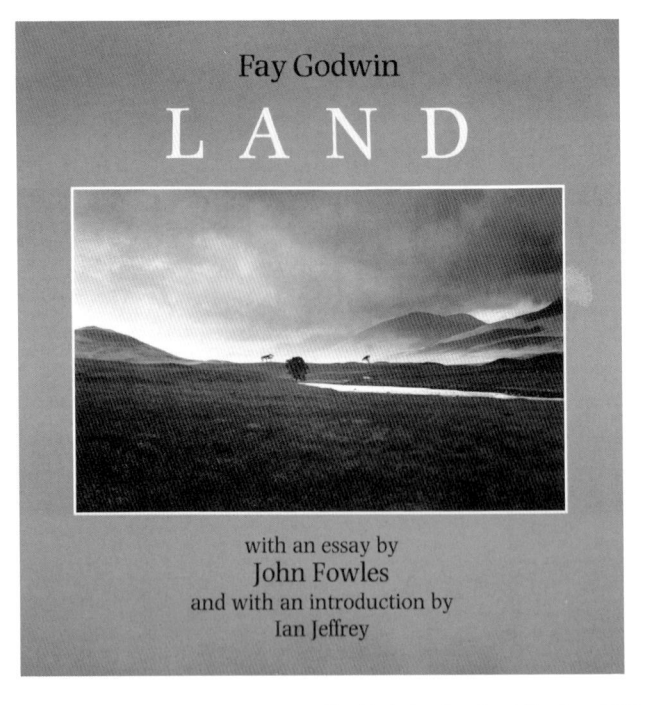

Fay Godwin, *Land*, publication, 1985.

publications, *Land*, *Forbidden Land*, and *Landmarks* together offer a complex profile of the British landscape at the end of the twentieth century. Godwin did not view herself as a 'woman photographer', rather as a photographer who happened to be a woman. She is also one of few examples of women who include territorial vistas although, as in the cover image for *Land*, often shot from a slightly low angle, enhancing a sense of being *within* the landscape (rather than looking down on it). She viewed her critique more in terms of environmentalism than gender, but she was nonetheless a pioneer within concerns with environment and ecology that now recur in women's work.

We are all influenced by Western aesthetics; notions of the pleasing picture are hegemonically sedimented. Photographers have to consciously adjust or refuse pre-existing aesthetic modes if the traditional landscape pictorial is to be critiqued. Being a woman operating within visual terms within which patriarchal attitudes have been formative renders this complex. A number of women photographers have engaged conceptually with questions of the female gaze; in effect, gender has been implicated in the interrogation of aesthetics. But all biographical experience influences our relation to and understanding of our environment. Few parts of Britain offer the sublime scale of natural phenomena that typifies landscape imagery elsewhere. However, to grow up on a farm, in a fishing village or in a mining area means that everyday knowledge, or 'common sense', takes into account facets of nature that are less immediately pertinent to the cultural circumstances of towns and cities. Hence, factors such as biography, social history and regional circumstance are as influential as gender in respect of attitudes to and ways of seeing land and environment.

In many instances, as with Fay Godwin, critique emerges from image content; classic pictorial modes are easily read and, indeed, may contribute strategically to paradoxical tensions between harmonious composition and more interrogative subject matter. For example, in

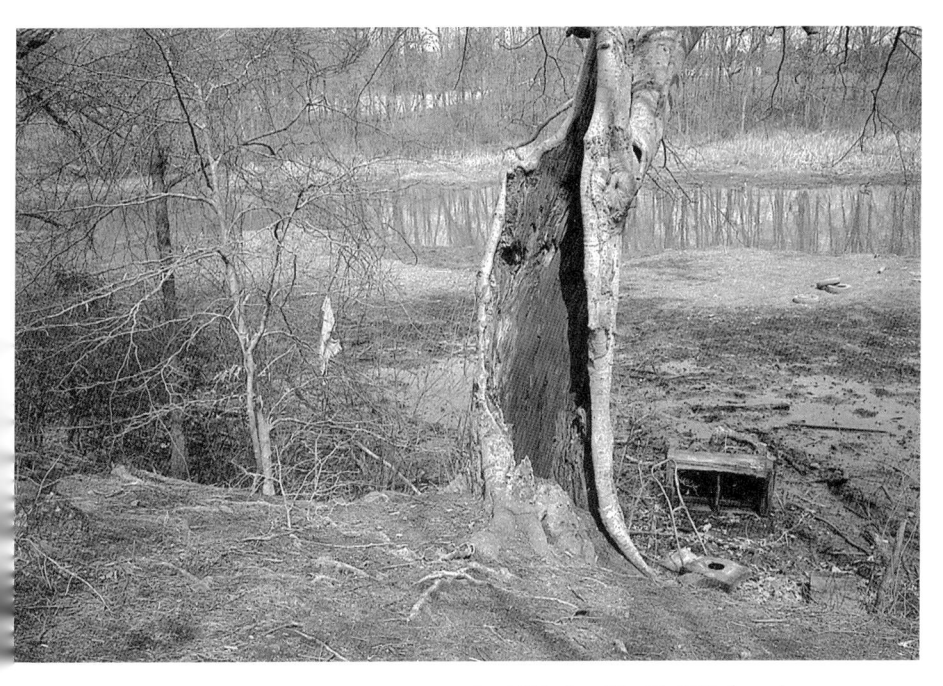

Ingrid Hesling, 'Creek', 1994, from the series *Anarchy in Arcady.*

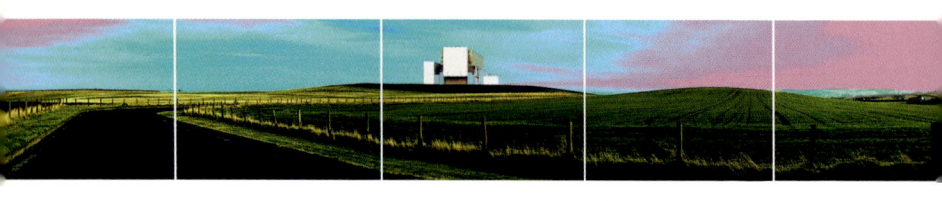

Su Grierson, 'Torness', 2001, from the exhibition, *Eyeshine*.

Anarchy in Arcady (1994) Ingrid Hesling depicted a series of disturbances in the local (Somerset) environment, which included tyres and track marks in a muddy field, building materials stacked in woodlands, and a piece of cloth caught on an aspen branch (Wells, 1994: 17–23).[15] This is a localised mucky pastoral; not the large-scale intrusions, such as mineshafts or transportation systems (canals, road, rail …), that leave a more permanent impact geologically and botanically as well as re-shaping the visible landscape. Here, what we see is transient. Use of monochrome references classic documentary, but the content of the image points towards intervention and change, however slight, as traces of human presence mark the environment, albeit temporarily. By contrast, in *Eyeshine* (2001) Scottish artist Su Grierson used video as well as still photography to document nuclear power stations, sites of dis-ease interrupting otherwise orderly countryside vistas (Grierson, 2001). The imagery is serene; the pastoral rhetoric and classical pictorial composition, but with enhanced colour saturation, lures us into visual contemplation, then snares us into acknowledging the disturbing implications of these industrial edifices, usually depicted in the middle distance, to which we may previously have turned a blind eye. The strategy is similar to that deployed by Darwell to document effects of the Foot and Mouth crisis in Cumbria, and is equally effective as, again, Arcadian ideals are brought into question, in this instance through reference to invisible threats of chemical pollution and of radiation.

The contrast between the work of Hesling and Grierson involves a range of distinctions that include colour and video versus monochrome 'straight' documentary idiom, global concerns versus local observation, artists based in two very different regions of Britain (Scottish Lowlands; the Southwest). However, the aesthetic strategy is similar: tension between what we see and the mode of vision causes pause for reflection.

Also, both artists draw attention to the environmental impact of human habitation. But, whilst it has been argued that women particularly consider the interaction of people and place, and the social implications of how particular sites or regions are developed and utilised, this concern is not exclusive to women's work (Sandweiss, 1987; Wells, 1994). Environmentalism is now central to the contemporary political agenda, nationally and internationally. Engagement with politics of the environment transcends gender. When women look, we might notice degrees of difference in theme and aesthetic strategy, but, as I have already noted, such differences are tendencies, not essential in the sense that Irigaray's work has often been taken to suggest. Gender is but one of a complexity of influences on ways of seeing.

All photographers (regardless of gender) have more limited freedom to travel extensively if constrained by childcare responsibilities; arguably this still disproportionately affects women. As a result, some have been inspired to explore and develop work reflecting on that which obtains close to home. Such environmental explorations may become variously inter-woven with other concerns, for instance, reflecting upon the family album, or questioning psychological states of being, or considering the visual and conceptual shifts effected by digital technology. Sian Bonnell is known for scatological observations and installations; Mark Haworth-Booth appropriately titles a catalogue essay on her work, 'high jinks and black jokes' (Haworth-Booth in Bonnell, 2004). She photographs domestic objects re-inserted into the landscape; for instance, *Putting Hills in Holland* (2001) is a series of close-up shots of jelly moulds in grassy fields – perhaps previously trodden by the hooves of cows (gelatine). Earlier, in *Groundings* (1997) she took domestic objects, such as a tin biscuit cutter and children's cuddly toys, back to the settings referenced; the ensuing images remind us of the extent to which the idealised pastoral penetrates the everyday. The undertones seem murky, perhaps surreal; we encourage children to eat lamb-shaped biscuits and go to bed with cuddly sheep! In *when the domestic meets the wild* (2001) garishly plastic everyday objects such as pan scourers, clothes pegs, mops and feather dusters, are relocated to exterior and sometimes extreme locations – an ironing board appears precariously isolated on the top of a cliff, pegs adorn the leaves of a tree. As Haworth-Booth comments, having no studio at home, she took her home outside. The household objects that she collects as props are cheap and ordinary, ones generally associated with the feminine in terms of domestic division of labour. Bonnell is not the only woman photographer to have remarked on ways in which family situation and care responsibilities impinge on work – particularly for a period of years when childcare responsibilities are paramount, restricting focus to more immediate environments.[16] But a madness of enforced domesticity is particularly manifest through her practice!

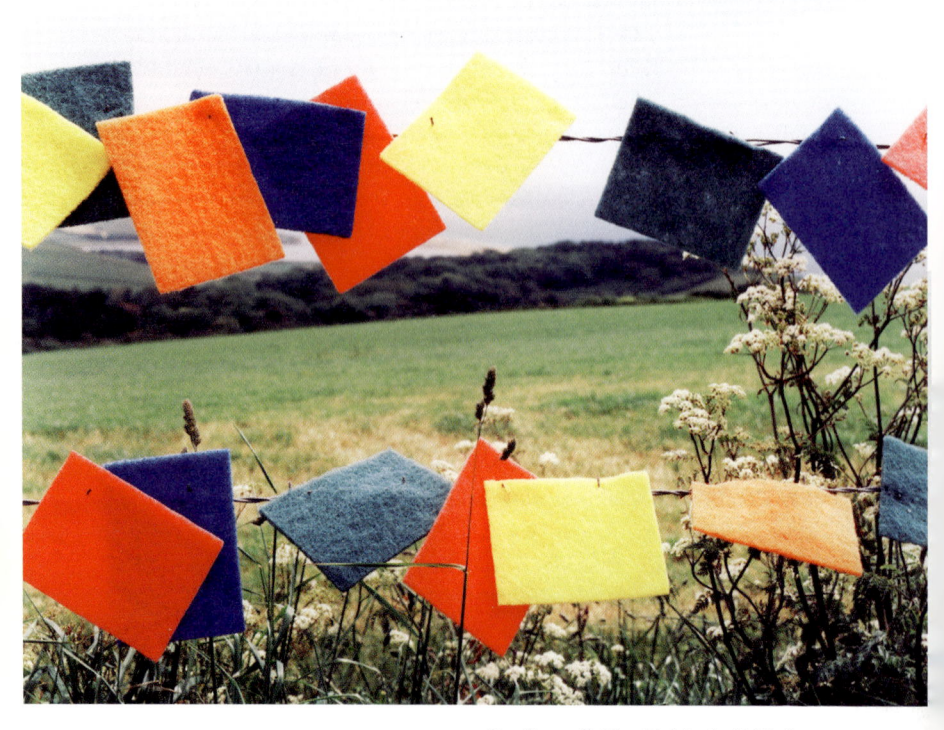

Sian Bonnell, 'Scrub', No. 1, 1999, from the series *when the domestic meets the wild*.

Gina Glover's land-based work likewise reflects upon immediate surroundings (although as someone who has worked as a photojournalist and also runs photo-workshops in mental health contexts, she is not unintrepid). Her series *Tunnels* (1998) explored the space of the greenhouse, alive with plants, so often a place of refuge and contemplation as well as, of course, nurturing plants. In this series the confined spaces depicted also stand metaphorically for states of mind. Gardens and allotments are not specifically male or female domains, but they are familiar grounds, an extension of domestic territory (and possibly of domestic dispute), often a place of retreat. They are also designed spaces, places where statements are made, consciously or unconsciously, about self, status and lifestyle. Gardens demand attention: weeds, brambles, snails and slugs lie in wait; we dispute our land rights with the first battalions of nature. In *Pathways to Memory* (1999) Glover returned to her childhood home, exploring memories through revisiting this sanctuary. We see spacious grounds, statues, walls and hedges; shadows of tall trees fall over areas where children play. More particularly, for her, we see a place that triggers

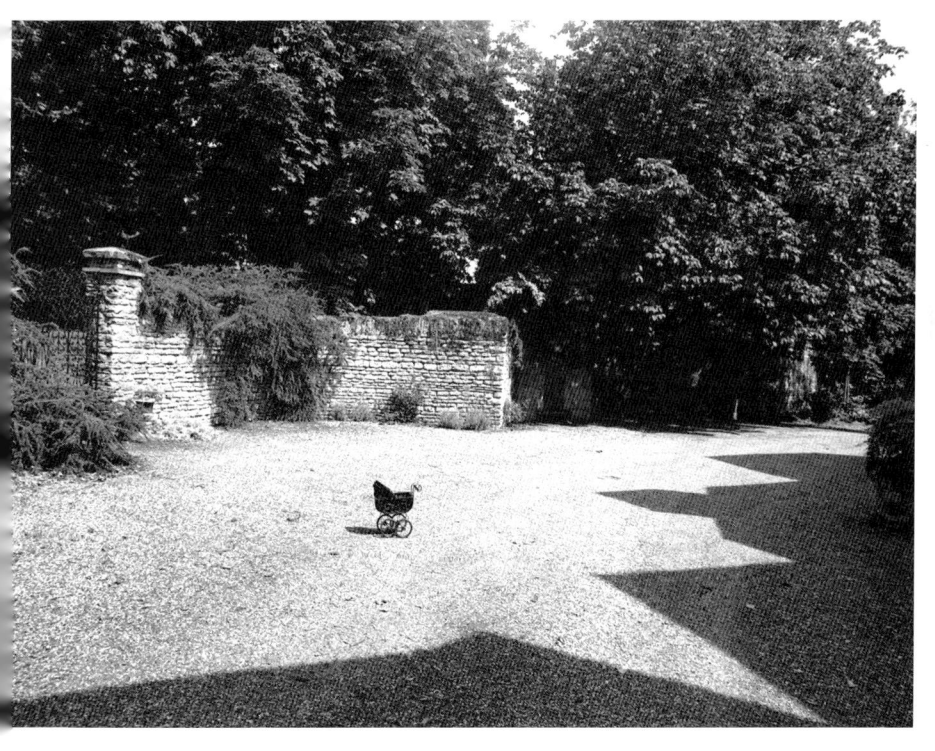

Gina Glover, 'Pram', 1998, from the series *Pathways to Memory*.

deep-seated recollections. The installation, which takes the form of a circle of images (mounted on stands), surrounds us as we look down on them. The work is literal in that it is the actual garden of her family home. But it also operates analogously. Like family history, the garden is a space of concealed layers; soil characteristics reflect local geological conditions as well as the chemical legacies of centuries of changing uses of land. Hidden more immediately below the surface are roots and bulbs that make themselves known seasonally, but not entirely predictably – flowers and harvests vary from year to year. All land in Britain is managed, but gardens represent a concentrated arena of intervention and reconstruction of space. In Glover's series the pram – isolated on the lawn between the shadows of the house, trees and a stone wall – surely stands for continuity, but whether the pram is bathed in a star of sunlight, or threatened by shadows pointing at it, is a matter of interpretation.

The works referenced above were selected because of content and theme, that is, in response to what the photographers had chosen to *look at*. It is also productive to explore ways in which women may *look differently* and consequent aesthetic affects. The idea of women appropriating the gaze, and questions of masculinity and femininity, are complexly inter-twined.[17] Julia Kristeva has argued that 'the feminine' has been repressed within modern consciousness and therefore has become problematic within the patriarchal order.[18] She asserts that the poetic (feminine) imagination stands in opposition to the logic of language suggesting that poetics (art) represents an eruption of the feminine which dis-concerts (masculine) social order. From this we can derive a set of links between the intuitive, the emotional, artistic explorations, and femininity. We can also posit the arts as in opposition to the sciences, basing this on the distinction between intuitive and rational conceptual modes. But, again, such binaries over-simplify. For instance, the geometric rationale of perspective as a system of representation clearly fits within the logical, although its application may be articulated in relation to more experimental modes of vision.[19] In similar vein, following Freud, we can posit masculinity (rationality) and femininity (intuition) not as opposites so much as a differential scale; individuals (male and female) exhibit a combination of traits culturally associated with the masculine or the feminine. Such a model is, of course, relational; values accumulated around certain characteristics are defined by contrast with those associated with other characteristics.

Kristeva also challenged the limitations of semiotics, noting the inability of linguistics as a science to take into account 'anything in language which belongs not with the social contract but with play, pleasure or desire' (Moi, 1986: 26). In effect, she suggested that language as operational process is always subject to slippages and exclusions, thereby reflecting Derrida's work on *difference* and the fluidity of meaning and Lacan's interest in the formations of subjectivity. This allows 'feminine impulse' to be considered in relation to woman as speaking subject, within this conceptualisation necessarily speaking from somewhere *unfixed*. It acknowledges poetic imagination. It refuses any politics of gender founded on a crude male/female binary. It also refuses the notion that women necessarily speak from the margins – although, sometimes 'she' might be marginalised and shouting. Rather the non-centred speaking – or viewing – subject operates in a fluid, in-between space. In principle this transcends gender as a social category, being related more to modes of artistic thinking 'outside the box'. Arguably those who have felt less centred have more invested in interrogating the dominant ideological discourses.

So what happens when women look? This question was central to *Shifting Focus*, an exhibition curated by Susan Butler in 1989.[20] Noting that traditionally women have been the object of the gaze, the viewed rather than the viewer, the represented rather than the author of representation, Butler was concerned to indicate ways in which, in exercising the right to look, women alter the terms of visual culture adjusting unequal viewing relations. A number of British women artists have taken questions of the gaze and the position of woman as viewer and as agent of representation as a starting point for considering how they might picture differently. Hence there is conceptual concern not only with the making of imagery but also with reading and interpretation on the part of audiences. Psychoanalysis proposes that images, through offering positions and points of identification, offer fantasy resolutions for subjective angst. For Lacan, identification refers to processes whereby the individual subject assimilates an aspect, property or attribute of that which is seen, and is transformed, wholly or partially, after the model the other – in this instance, the image – provides, thereby offering some form of identity re-assurance, or re-construction. If this is the case, then Albertian perspective re-assures through symbolically ordering the world in relation to the spectatorial ego, the male gaze. This returns us to questioning how women position themselves as articulate spectators within 'the male order of things' without fully adopting masculine modes – a set of issues also pressing within queer theory.

Andrea Liggins' recent work, snapshots made with mobile phones and disposable cameras, explores the construction of 'the look' of the more traditional camera and consequent ways of seeing. The affects of pictorial framing come under scrutiny as domestic digital cameras downplay the aesthetic conventions and technical sophistication of larger formats. How we look and what we see are in question as the snapshot informality, limited depth of field and consequent priority of content

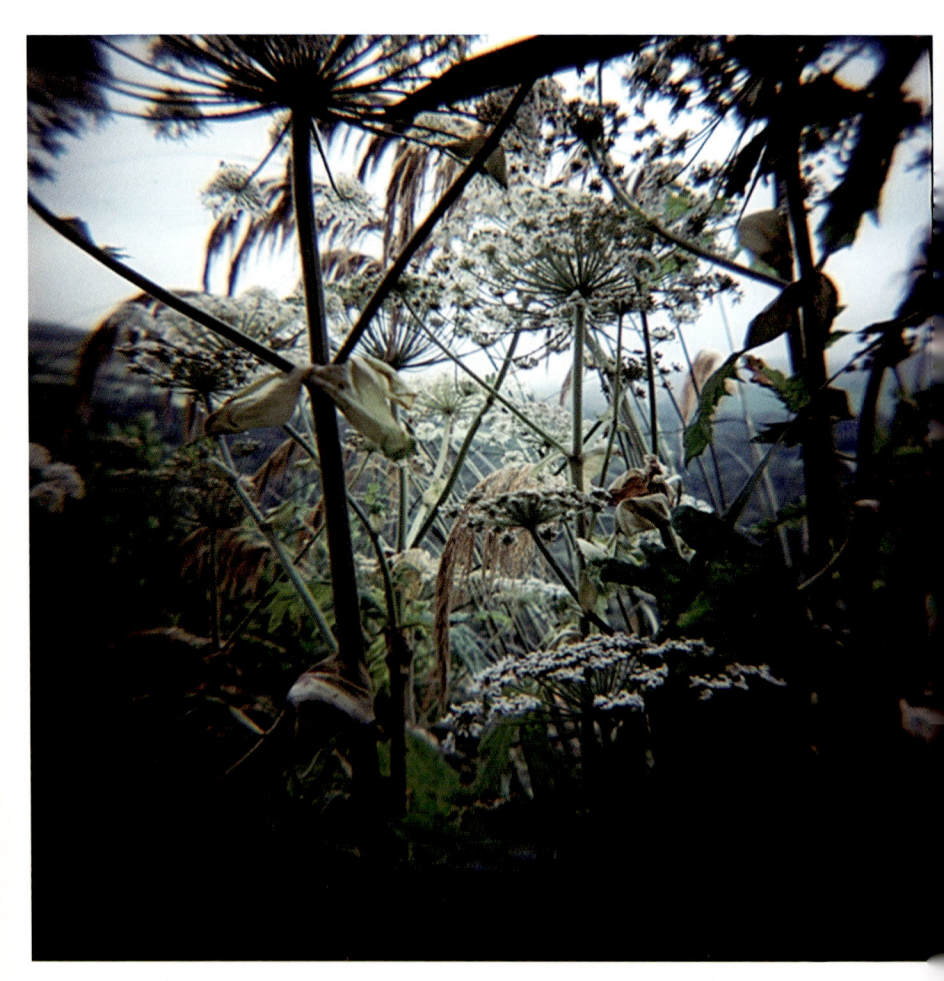

Andrea Liggins, Untitled, from the series *Uncertain Terrain*, 2003.

over form interrupt accustomed viewing experiences. For instance, in one example stalks and wild-flower heads inter-weave in the foreground – nature refusing organised geometry – while sea in the background blurs into the sky, with no detailing of contours. The technology does not allow for an imposition of organisation; it is not possible to stand further away in order to frame the flora and silhouette shapes against the movement of the sea, a clear horizon line, or to emphasise the symbolism of clouds. Liggins is interested in counteracting legacies of Romanticism, and Cartesian objectification of nature, suggesting more intimate encounters within rural and semi-rural environments, including explicitly organised spaces such as parks and gardens.

In Helen Sear's series, *Inside the View* (2005–07), Cartesian models are conceptually central. Two photographs are sandwiched together, a

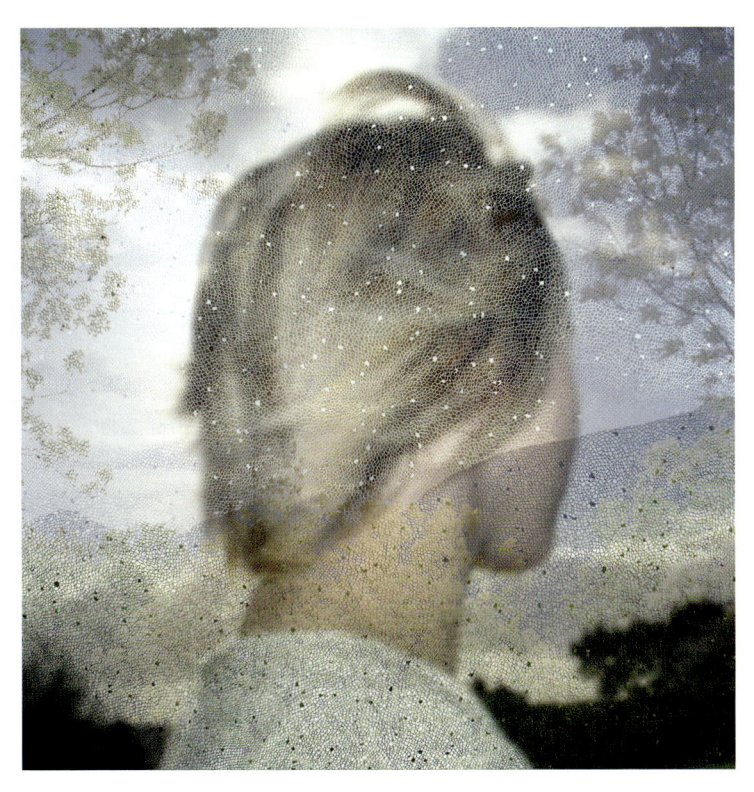

Helen Sear, 'No. 13', from the series *Inside the View*, 2005–07.

view, and the back of a woman's head, with the vista floating across the head like a net or veil on the surface of the image (the process involves hand drawing via a computer). The close-woven screen, or netting, acknowledges what she can see, but inserts distance between ourselves as spectators and the viewer framed in the image. We see some of what she sees, whilst the central part of the vista is traced but is less specific – as if it becomes more indefinite through the process of her engagement with it. There is a sense of stillness; she has paused to feel and reflect upon the phenomena. We are not offered a territorial overview, nor indeed is she, since she appears behind the mesh that both distances and encloses her. Ego-centric spectatorship is under question, as is the phallo-centricity of Cartesian models. The heads are approximately life-size; whilst distanced, we are not over-powered. That we neither look at her, nor through her eyes, effectively constructs a Brechtian alienation, causing us to question processes of looking. Sear, like Liggins, is concerned to interrogate the politics of the gaze, but the photographic methods adopted are distictly different.

In an early picture, which appeared on the front cover of the catalogue for *Shifting Focus* (Butler, 1989), Susan Trangmar confronted us with the back of a woman looking at a set of images of Elvis, poster-scale, in Western mode with gun pointed out at her/us as viewers. The series, *Untitled Landscapes* (1986), took such everyday confrontations as a starting point: we see 'her' only as a figure subject to the dominance of Elvis as material icon. Exploration of viewing modes and viewing distance, along with questioning boundaries, has characterised Trangmar's *oeuvre*. 'Amidst' (1994), a slide installation formed as a circular projection of trees, held the spectator within the darker sublime of the forest, with no obvious pathway for escape. It was interactive in that as viewers walked amidst the trees their moving shadows were cast within the imagery. It was located in the Thames estuary in the former Canary Wharf area that was redeveloped in the 1980s as apartments and office blocks. It also fundamentally questioned realities. As artist and critic John Stathatos remarked it was '… a spurious forest – a facsimile, in every sense of the word – introduced not merely in an urban context, but in an urban environment itself utterly spurious; for what else are Canary Wharf and its satellites … but a sham? …' (Stathatos, 1994). The post-modern arcades of office-based economies and the more traditional arcadia of forest were thrown into question, along with the multiple histories through which place is constituted; the installation might also have reminded us that

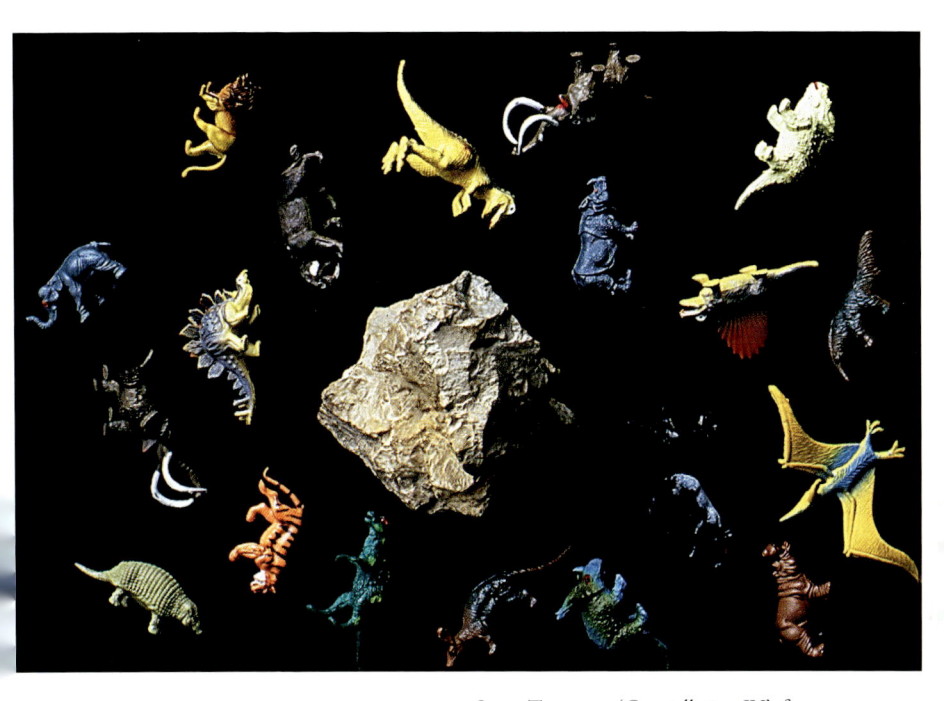

Susan Trangmar, 'Constellation IV', from the series *Suspended States*, 1992.

actual woodlands crowded these river banks many centuries ago. In *Suspended States* (1992) Trangmar explored pictorial conventions through constellations of images within which objects, colours and locations are differently arranged in relation to one another and perception is adjusted as framing, focal depth, sharp or soft focus, contribute to shifting the key element within each picture (Trangmar, 1992). The rock is a central motif; resonances derive from the primordial, the religious, the formal, and the historical. As Susan Butler remarked in the catalogue essay,

> It is not simply an object in the world, it is an object of thought, and comes into our purview as such only through those human means which we may devise to know it – means not universally available to everyone. The geologist's knowledge of the rock, for example, will differ from the architect's or the gardener's. Such specialised knowledges

have their respective histories as evolving discourses or systems of representation.

(Trangmar, 1992: n.p.)

Trangmar's purpose, then, was to explore ways in which the discourses of photography might inter-sect with discourses triggered by the concept of 'rock'. The twelve constellations of pictures each investigate the fluidities and slippages of photographic representation, attending to ways in which differing visual conventions, associated with varying contexts and audiences, contribute to constructing different points of identification. For instance, the colour yellow dominates within 'Constellation 111', a group of pictures in no particular order in which the rock is subdued by the contrasting pictorial conventions. In one it is foregrounded within a classical Edenic landscape with cattle grazing bathed in intense yellow light. In another it is barely discernible within a stylised panel in which geometry and variations of colour tone and intensity are prominent. Writing in 1992 Butler associated this with the concerns of modern art, but it also seems to echo recent stylisation in advertising. One image pastiches photojournalistic modes, or realist gangster genres; it appears blotchy, and the street in the background, blueish in tone, is barely discernible except where a hint of yellow light catches the side of the rock which here is huge enough for a man with a gun to use it as a shield. Finally, the shadow of the rock looms in the lower corner of an abstract composition of elongated figures, blurred, silhouetted against a muted yellow background. Scale and composition are central to the investigation – a hand might hold the rock or a person hide behind it. A scene constructed as a landscape in line with golden rule conventions may be juxtaposed with a close-up interrogation of form, colour and texture. As gallery viewers (or readers of the catalogue) we have to pause to consider what it is that we are looking at, and how aesthetic conventions and photographic coding contribute not only to *what* we see but also to the *ways in which* we see. We might also consider how mood inflects both making and interpretation. In undertaking a residency in Israel Trangmar remarked that she found she could not see through the eyes of others, only through her own; that indeed two people never see exactly the same thing. This led her to ask whether 'if place is a state of mind, then is it possible to be in several places at once, in several states of mind at once?' (Trangmar, 2005: 32). What would it mean to be so? Certainly we can take it that the mood of the photographer in some ways informs the mode of photographing, just as circumstances in which viewers encounter images influence interpretation and, indeed, application (the intensity with which the viewer really *looks* at the image).

Directly questioning that which is taken for granted about ways of seeing poses issues for gallery exhibition, as accustomed viewing modes are challenged. Gallery directors do not necessarily feel comfortable with the different modes of looking proposed. This, of course, is one reason why the questions are worth asking. The aim of a number of women artists, variously informed by critiques of patriarchal discourses, has been to dis-concert orthodoxy, not through simplification, or through direct accusation, but more complexly through experiments in modes of visualisation, storytelling, and explorations of alternative histories. This approach has also characterised the work of a number of artists centrally concerned with Britain, and British land and landscape, from post-colonial perspectives.

MULTICULTURAL BRITAIN

Britain was – and in many respects remains – a maritime nation; this was crucial in terms of the exercise of imperial power; the game plan was international. The 'British Empire' secured key military posts worldwide and presented itself as a benevolent protector of peoples and places. It also established and defended sources of food and industrial raw materials as well as creating an extended market for commodity distribution. British education systems – and the English language – were extended internationally (although literacy was often restricted). Regions such as India and the Caribbean became military recruiting grounds as well as reserve armies of labour for the UK (for instance, those encouraged to immigrate to the 'mother country' as health or transport workers immediately after the Second World War). As a former imperial power, as well as a member of the European Union, Britain is ethnically diverse with many citizens deriving their sense of identity as British from a complexity of geographical sources and historical lineages that lie elsewhere. Place of birth, place of birth of parents, place of habitation, sense of roots, gender, race, skin colour, class, caste, first language, level of education, employment status or occupation, domestic role, all contribute to identity formation. Each factor draws on particular clusters of ideological preconceptions forming complex and fluid tapestries of subjectivity. Many of the discourses operate in terms of binaries constructed through a sense of difference – being female is defined in part through not being male; being British is simultaneously to be not Italian or not Greek, although it might encompass the idea of being European. But the binaries are never absolutes; rather they are twin poles around which discursive notions flow. As Stuart Hall has remarked, black and white photographs are actually composed of many tones of grey (Hall, 1997b: 235).

Just as the – perhaps never visited – 'mother country' operated as a sort of fiction from the perspective of colonials (colonisers and colonised) for a couple of centuries, so 'home country' offers an alternative and perhaps similarly fictionalised imagined community. It is possible to inhabit – 'be' in – one place, yet take another as a key source of identity, thereby inducing a rupture within the notion of 'be-longing'. Given historical tensions over British citizenship, not just in legal terms, but also in terms of social status, ambiguities over cultural identity are hardly surprising; in England white 'colonials' were seen as somehow secondary (even as recently as the mid-twentieth century) and those with Asian or Afro-Caribbean appearance are still all too often viewed as 'other'. Since the May 2004 extension of the European Union to include nations from the former Eastern Bloc, tensions over Britishness and multiculturalism have been exacerbated through recurrent (journalistic) references to asylum seekers and economic migrants and as a result of impact upon local socio-economic infrastructures (jobs, housing, school provision, etc.).

Social class, rural/urban location, gender and ethnicity interact politically and psychoanalytically to inform perceptions of place. As Hall also remarks, to understand Britain in terms of its imperial history, one has to consider not only what Britain thought of the 'colonies' but also how those from India, Ireland or the Caribbean viewed Britain. Identity relations are not static, and specific biographic factors operate in and around broader cultural currencies.[21] As Bailey and Hall have remarked, 'Post structuralist thinking opposes the notion that a person is born with a fixed identity … It suggests instead that identities are floating, that meaning is not fixed and universally true at all times for all people, and that the subject is constructed through the unconscious in desire, fantasy and memory' (Bailey and Hall, 1992: 20). Furthermore, in an era of enhanced mobility nationally and internationally, and the internet as a parallel virtual 'world', perceptions of place, subjectivity and identity blend with an – illusory – sense of global reach. *Illusory* in that all information is highly mediated. The internet also further marks social and economic inequality since it privileges those in regions of the world with electricity and telephone lines, often highlighting urban/rural divides.

A number of contemporary photographers have explored questions of ethnicity and cultural identity in relation to landscape. They have been concerned with land on which one stands, literally and symbolically. Most notably, Ingrid Pollard interrogated history and identity through asking what happens when Black people occupy a space, such as the Lake District, so clearly central to an English sense of its pastoral heritage. In a postcard-style image (1993, made as a hoarding poster) we see 'Ms Pollard's party', a family of walkers, all of whom are Black, enjoying rambling, sharing a picnic, and generally appreciating 'Wordsworth's Heritage' (the postcard title). The presence of Black figures in what has become viewed as a quintessentially English landscape disrupts as it questions who shares this heritage. Likewise, in *Pastoral Interlude* (1987) Pollard drew attention to hidden hierarchies of citizenship by pointing to the singularity of the Black person in the Lake District landscape. Whilst the multiculturalism of many British cities is acknowledged and celebrated, the rural retains an association with Anglo-Celtic lineages which is simultaneously literal (the rural population is less evidently multi-ethnic), imaginary and, perhaps, desired. The rural becomes a refuge for 'little England' associations. 'Postcard England' can be seen as an attempt to hold on to something that never quite existed, that seems to represent a resistance to modernity – let alone post-modernity – and certainly does not acknowledge contemporary heterogeneity in terms of ethnicity and identity.

Pastoral Interlude was included in *D-Max*, one of the first British exhibitions to bring together work by Black British photographers (curator, Eddie Chambers, 1987). One body of work, by Dave Lewis, included a map of Africa, divided up somewhat like Alice's chessboard, as a game to be played by selected European players. The analogy is not unique; for example, Scottish artist Ron O'Donnell depicted a map of Scotland with a noose round the Highlands (*I-D Nationale*, Portfolio Gallery, Edinburgh, 1993). The point about Empire was, precisely, to play the game of chess all over the world. The psychological consequences of this in terms of subjective sense of place, identity and otherness have been particularly central to the critical engagement of a number of British Black photographers since the 1980s.[22]

Several photographers, not just Black and Asian, have interrogated the idea of the sea as boundary and what it means to be an island race. But the sea as border resonates differently for those with links beyond. Pollard, in one of the images from her series, *Seaside Stories* (1989), remarks that the name of Hastings is associated with the last successful invasion of Britain. Arguably being an 'island nation' feeds into a sense of national autonomy. It also underwrites the sea as a psychic divide from which stem desires and longings for perceived homelands that cannot be satisfied. In *Oceans Apart* (1989) Pollard (who was born in Guyana but moved to London aged four), expresses something of the longing for family left behind felt by many migrants.

The idea of crossing the Atlantic articulates a range of historical undercurrents. These include myths of exploration, the fears of those transported on slave ships, the pride of entrepreneurial colonialists sending food and raw materials to 'the mother country', the excitement of the many who emigrated to Britain post-war full of expectations of enhanced quality of life, the fears of those embarking on transatlantic flights in an era of Anglo-American alliance and terrorist threat. To cross the ocean is not a neutral act. As Paul Gilroy has noted, ships were political and economic entities (Gilroy, 1993). In his discussion of *The Black Atlantic* he defined the ocean as not only a physical divide but also a psychic one; this contributed complexly to the formation of modernity in terms not only of the economic but also of consciousness. His focus on the Atlantic as a space of transit (which is not uni-directional) feeds into more general interrogation of the economic, political and ideological foundations of modernity implicating hegemonic processes that, he argued, were inherently racialised.

Roshini Kempadoo has explored this conceptual territory through photomontage and, recently, interactive sound/video installation. Gender, ethnicity and the multiplicities of identity, articulated in terms of the subjectivity of those born British, with colonial lineage, are centrally questioned within her practice. *Sweetness and Light* (1996) most evidently echoes Paul Gilroy's comments on ways in which colonialism became integral to modernity not only economically but also in terms of cultural currencies whose import was central to the artistic and literary imagination of the era. Edward Said clearly

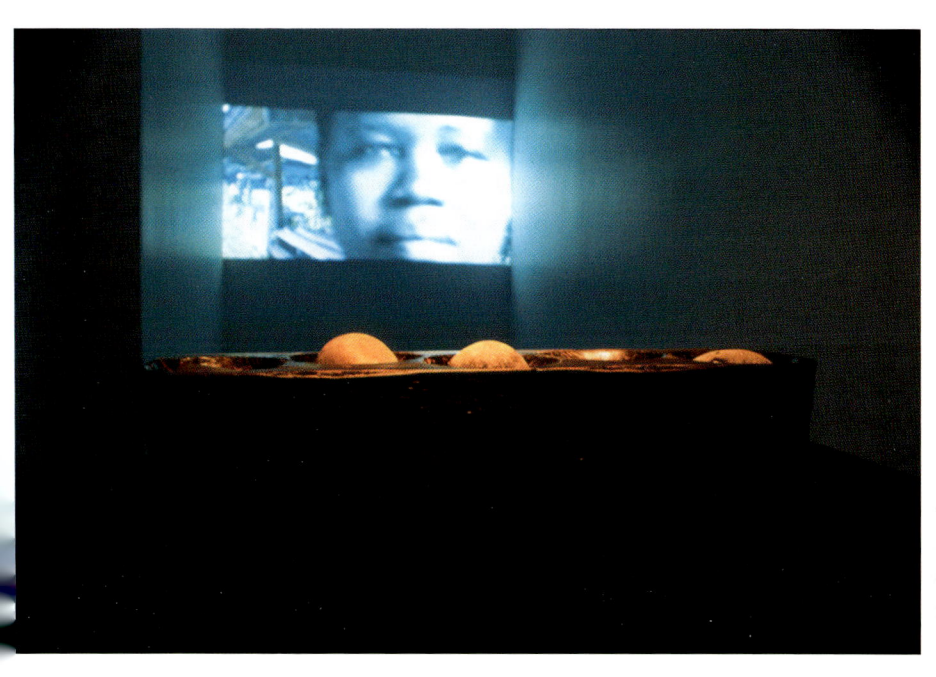

Roshini Kempadoo, video still from *Ghosting*, 2004. Installation shot, Susanne Ramsenthaler, New York, 2006.

acknowledges this in pointing to the culturally constitutive effects of orientialism (Said, 1995). Conversely, that we can talk of post-colonial literature in terms of difference of voice and point of view acknowledges the centrality of colonial perspectives within the modern. In Kempadoo's work, the continuing inequality of power relations and the operations of capital in cyberspace as well as legacies of colonial relations manifest through consumer demands for cheap imports (goods and services) are also under scrutiny. Her interactive installation, *Ghosting* (2004) offers perspectives from the viewpoint of those in Trinidad whose voices and stories were previously unheard (at any rate internationally). Sound, texture, oral history, portraiture and photo-landscapes are complexly interwoven, called up through the gallery viewer's action of moving a stone that triggers a particular set of observations and memories. Kempadoo is British-born, but clearly locates herself and her work in the context of diasporic histories and identities. This, in itself, challenges perceptions of land as landscape and authority exercised through ownership and through representation. The legacy of eighteenth-century venture capitalists, investing in Empire whilst landscaping their country estates into the English hillside, can yet still be traced.

PASTORAL HERITAGE UNDER INTERROGATION

As an island Britain's immediate territorial boundaries are clear. As a post-industrial nation, land is marked with histories of tensions over land usage, and contestation continues. As a post-imperial nation, Britain is implicated in national and international post-colonial concerns. This chapter has been concerned with Britain and the North of Ireland in terms of critical engagement with complacency over land, landscape and its representation. The purpose is to ask what happens when the dominant themes and aesthetics from a more traditional landscape are brought into question from perspectives informed by class, region, gender and ethnicity and to evaluate the aesthetic implications of various strategies deployed. Photographers' individual methods and concerns vary, but such critical perspectives clearly contributed to shifting understandings of the significance of land and the politics of representation. Of course Britain is just one example. Similar questions might be asked through investigating landscape traditions and contemporary practices elsewhere, although, as is indicated in the next chapter, the articulation of themes, aesthetic strategies and ideological currencies is always in some respects specific to socio-historical circumstances.

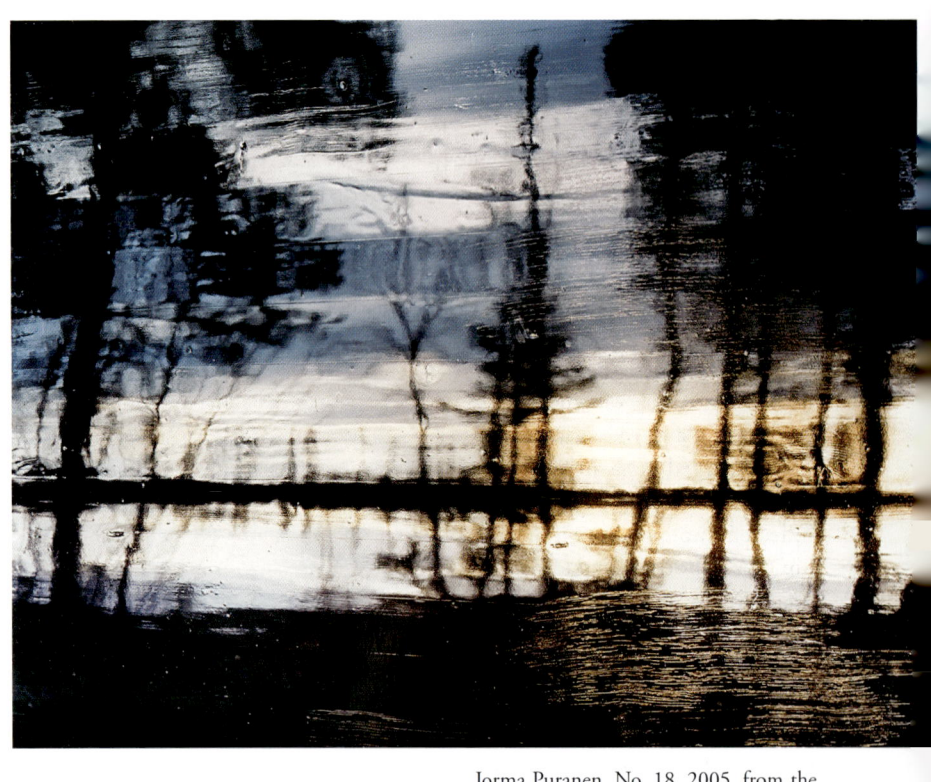

Jorma Puranen, No. 18, 2005, from the series *Icy Prospects*.

5

VIEWS FROM THE NORTH

LANDSCAPE, PHOTOGRAPHY AND NATIONAL IDENTITY

> National identities are co-ordinated, often largely defined, by 'legends and landscapes', by stories of golden ages, enduring traditions, heroic deeds and dramatic destinies located in ancient or promised home-lands with hallowed sites and scenery. The symbolic activation of time and space, often drawing on religious sentiment, gives shape to the 'imagined community' of the nation. Landscapes, whether focusing on single monuments or framing stretches of scenery, provide visible shape; they picture the nation.
>
> (Daniels, 1993: 5)

Site and space, political and spiritual identity, are complexly interwoven. If landscape is understood as cultural representation of space as place, ways in which particular lands are pictured can be conceptualised as an arena of rhetorical struggle. This often implicates tensions over national identity. The ideological discourses are complex, inflected through pictorial form as well as image content. The latter is obviously potent, as subject matter reinforces iconic nationalist imagery. For instance, the publication, *National Landscapes*, produced by the Finnish Ministry of the Environment (1993), includes photographs (and other visual materials) from 27 key locations, all of which testify variously to regional tradition and heritage. But photography may contribute to unsettling aspects of cultural identity through offering evidence which does not 'fit'. Pictures of airports, electronics factories or, indeed, industrial-scale logging would not suit the image of Finland promoted by the Environment Ministry; the national imaginary would be challenged. Ideology operates to hold together apparently contradictory discourses and knowledges, to forge a sense of nationhood out of a diversity of historical and contemporary cultural currencies.

Historical interrogation was central to the series, *Imaginary Homecomings*, by Jorma Puranen, in which he returned images of Sami people from the ethnographic archive at the Musée de l'Homme (Museum of Mankind), Paris, to their Arctic settings.[1] It was this work which brought him to international fame in the 1990s. *Imaginary Homecomings* became acclaimed for various reasons. First, his interest in Sami culture struck a post-colonial chord. Photography and anthropology were together implicated in colonial processes, and the Sami, as a nomadic group, had been the objects of nineteenth-century curiosity. Second, the performance dimension of his photo-methodology attracted attention. He rephotographed the ethnographic portraits, printed the images onto acrylic sheets and carried them to the northern slopes of Norway and Sweden, physically installing them within their 'home' environment prior to rephotographing. This series could have been made through digital amalgamation, but for Puranen the ritual of taking home the dispossessed was an essential part of the process. The British anthropologist and archivist, Elizabeth Edwards, has commented that *Imaginary Homecomings* articulates a dialogue between historical and contemporary concerns (Edwards, 1995: 317). The portraits show faces, or faces and shoulders. The composition is typical of ethnography with its requirement for systematic recording and classification of subjects as 'types'. We look at people and costumes, seeking biographical and cultural understanding, as if histories can be read from facial expression. In this series, Sami people, their bodies seemingly buried within the snow, appear 'larger than life' due to their position in the snowy hills and valleys and the photographic angle of vision. The installations become symbolic scenarios of omission, history stitched into territories otherwise marked by indicators of economic exploitation – train tracks, power lines or mine shafts. The aesthetic harmony of the images belies uncomfortable questions about dislocation, colonisation, identity, land and belonging.

This chapter critically evaluates photographic work from Nordic and Baltic areas that relates to land, landscape, environment, cultural identity and nationalist discourses. The focus is on this particular region, although, of course, the arguments about aesthetics and ideology have broader pertinence; in this respect the example stands as a case study exemplifying some of the questions that arise in considering landscape practices and nationalism. Inter-relations of aesthetic discourses and political tensions are taken into account in order to consider ways in which ideologies of nationhood are articulated and resonate through landscape imagery. Contemporary landscape practitioners variously engage with icons of identity. Such engagement is complex because, whilst particular rhetorics that have become woven within landscape practices may be critiqued, artists nonetheless in some respects identify with the region that is their homeland. Indeed, radicalism for photographers may be as much an exploration of self as of the environment. The chapter is organised into three sections, which respectively situate and evaluate contemporary practices in Scandinavia, the Baltic States, and Finland.[2] In order to contextualise critical discussion, the chapter opens with a brief socio-political history.

THE NORDIC/BALTIC REGION

The Nordic and Baltic region barely figures in mainstream histories, let alone histories of photography. This reflects a failure on the part of North American and Western European historians to look towards the margins and also to transcend language limitations.[3] Scandinavia refers to Norway, Sweden, Denmark, Iceland and three home rule territories, Greenland, Faeroes and Åland.[4] The associated notion of Nordic, or the 'Norden' region, extends to include Finland. The area encompasses Lapland, which is Sami territory, and runs across the north of Norway, Sweden, Finland and on into Russia. Baltic States include Lithuania, Latvia, Estonia, Russia, Poland and Germany. Of these, the triumvirate of Lithuania, Latvia and Estonia, smaller states not stretching south or east like Poland, Germany and Russia, are highly dependent upon relations across the Baltic Sea.

Nationalist struggles have characterised political power relations within the region for many centuries and land has figured symbolically within this. For instance, the Norwegian mountain came to stand as an icon of independence for Norwegian nationalist movements at the end of the nineteenth century. Likewise, woodlands remain significant in Swedish and Finnish consciousness and rivers/coastal regions have attracted the attention of photographers based in the smaller Baltic States, perhaps because waterways create natural boundaries whilst simultaneously offering means of travel (communications, mobility, escape …) and transportation of goods.

Nature, viewed as a source of replenishment, is particularly marked in Nordic work. Latitude is relevant: light is a key influence within northern cultures where lack of light in winter and extended days in summer centrally influence social behaviour, psyche and temperament. Indeed, light and colour are central to photography, and the extraordinary white light of the north inevitably influences Norden aesthetics. As will be seen, artists across the region are interested in specific qualities of light; there is a clarity, intensity, and cool colour spectrum (whites, greys, sharp blues) that is lacking in more temperate climates. Hence, perhaps, the photographic fascination with the effects of light and dark, snow and ice; Nordic landscape photography particularly implicates symbolic effects of light and environment. The history of photography, especially in the Nordic region, is replete with mountains and fjords (Norway), woods and lakes (Sweden), lakes and wildlife (Finland), and flat wind-swept coasts (Denmark), explored in different seasons, in varying weather conditions.

TERRITORY AND NATIONHOOD

In 1996 Estonian artist, Jaan Toomik, made a video installation, 'Dancing Home', in which, to a continuous drumbeat, he dances on the ferry deck from Helsinki to Tallinn. The installation is life-size, seemingly a ritual celebration; this 50-mile journey had become possible once again. Previously, this waterway was surveyed by the Soviet military – a carefully guarded frontier, geographic and ideological, between West and East Europe, Capitalism and Communism. During the Cold War the Baltic was silent. Now, almost 5 million people take the boats from Helsinki to Tallinn each year, statistically, almost every Finn.[5]

For over forty years in the second half of the twentieth century, the Norden region constituted a bloc of states on the ideological frontier between West and East Europe. During this time, as borderline states the Nordic countries and the smaller Baltic nations found themselves situated variously on the margins of major economic and political power blocks; indeed, Estonia, Latvia and Lithuania were annexed as part of the Soviet Union. With the break-up of the former USSR, and the easing of travel restrictions across the Baltic Sea, they now form part of the European Union, as do Finland and Scandinavia except for Norway, now the sole unaligned state in the region. The end of Russian dominance in this maritime area, along with movement towards economic union in Western Europe, combined to shift political relations and perspectives. Questions of national identity resonate through various arenas, from the socio-economic to the psychological, from the political to the pictorial, especially as the history of the region includes a number of wars of independence, and a civil war in Finland (1917–18).

Until the early nineteenth century, Sweden and Denmark operated as major imperial states. Sweden ruled Finland until 1809 and Norway until 1905. Given the long history of political mergers, takeovers and makeovers, it is hardly surprising that questions of nationhood are of import in the region. In terms of national identity, former regional powers may manifest unwarranted complacency whilst those previously subjugated may become avid nationalists. As noted, Russia has been the other significant political force in the region, impacting in particular on Finland and the Baltic States. Finland was ceded by Sweden to the Tsars, and controlled by Russia through the nineteenth century until the Soviet Revolution. In order to secure ease of access and political influence, Russians moved the capital from Turku, across the sea from Stockholm, to Helsinki, which is significantly further east, nearer to St Petersburg. At the beginning of the Second World War Finland was again invaded by Russia; Finland joined the 1941 German invasion of Russia for reasons which reflected its own history, rather than support for Nazi ideologies. Norway, which along with Denmark was occupied by Germany in the early 1940s, borders Russia in the far north. Finland shares its long eastern border with Russia. During the Soviet period post-war the smaller Baltic States, Lithuania, Latvia, and Estonia were ruled hegemonically from Moscow, in the case of Latvia, having been occupied by Soviet troops in 1940, then 'liberated' by the Germans in 1941 who remained as an occupying force until the city was once more 'liberated' by the Red Army in 1945. Latvian people, especially Jewish, were exiled, killed or put into concentration camps by both Stalin and Hitler. Since 1991 Baltic areas have regained autonomy. In common with Scandinavia and other parts of Europe, the histories of each of the Baltic States remain complexly linked with immediate neighbours. For instance, like Estonia, Lithuania is largely rural and relatively flat: a typical landscape scene would be gentle hills, blue lakes, green forests, and the whiteness of sand dunes on the Baltic coast. But its historical affiliations have been more with central Europe; indeed, the south of Lithuania, including the capital city, Vilnius, was at one point annexed by Poland (1920–39). Affiliations cut across differences. Estonia and Latvia share a Protestant heritage with Scandinavia whilst Lithuania shares a Roman Catholic heritage with Poland. All three Baltic States are ethnically diverse. Estonia, the nation directly bordering Russia, is particularly mixed, in part due to the Soviet policy of Russianisation.[6] The relationship pre-dates the Soviet era; Tallinn became a major trading centre in 1870 on the completion of a railway link to St Petersburg. There were also key links with Finland. For Estonia, current empathy with Finland is in part a response to both nations having experienced Russian domination. But there is also a language connection as Estonian and Finnish (along with Hungarian) have Finno-Ugric roots; this is distinctly different to the Indo-Germanic source of Norwegian, Swedish and Danish. Similarity of language facilitates understanding and shared structures of feeling – a further factor in Finnish–Estonian affinities. Likewise, the Scandinavian languages retain and reinforce a degree of commonality.

SCANDINAVIA

Romanticism was influential in nineteenth-century Nordic art. Analysing 'romantic nationalism' Thomas Nipperday (1983) distinguishes between 'cultural nationalism', based on the nationalising of culture and on the founding of a nation in common culture, and 'political nationalism', normally argued in terms of citizenship and shared sovereignty. Of course the two go hand in hand, but the forging of a sense of shared history and language – within which we can include visual language – operates to anchor nationalist discourses. By contrast with the universalism of the Enlightenment, romantic nationalism stresses national diversity and particularities. Romanticism centres on culture, not on the political state. But cultural discourses variously reflect and reinforce particular visions of nationhood and *Heimat* (homeland and sense of belonging); cultural emblems function within independence movements as symbols of distinctiveness and difference. Later they may come to seem kitsch, the stuff of tourist rhetoric. For instance, contemporary Norwegian landscape photography struggles against the legacy of Romanticism still rehearsed through picture postcards. Yet, cliché sometimes holds true – blue skies and bright white snow *do* render mountains picturesque, whiteouts *actually* suggest a painterly sublime. Ideological discourses selectively crystallise certain imagery, but such images can only capture popular imagination if there is some basis in reality.

Discussing forms of romantic nationalism in nineteenth-century Scandinavia, Hans Kuhn remarks that the Viking and the independent farmer offer two Nordic archetypes. He adds that these were often combined in one person since the young Viking – who might raid the Baltic, or the British Isles, or the Mediterranean in the summer – was a working farmer the rest of his life (Kuhn, 1983). Kuhn suggests that these two ideal types: 'the idealist and the realist in Schiller's terms, or romantic yearning versus classical identification with the present, or the individualist as against the socially integrated person' (Kuhn, 1983: 81), offer a useful starting point for sorting out the confusion of discourses in play historically. Myths and folklore contribute a sense of common roots, and often play a key revivalist role in independence movements. Nipperday remarks that

> Romantic nationalism begins with the discovery of the soul of the *Volk*, with the anti-rationalist accent on non-intellectual reality, with the preference for fairy tales, *Volkslied* and customs. *Volk* signifies an element of nature, signifies unconscious life.
>
> (Nipperday, 1983: 4)

Hence, for instance, the centrality of the Norwegian mountain and fjord within late nineteenth-century nationalism. In fact, artists had to go to the west coast to find such imagery; the flatter inland woodlands of the east of Norway are shared with Sweden, rendering them unsuitable as icons within Norway's nationalist struggle.

Scandinavian art has a reasonably long-standing international profile, in some respects functioning as Europe's 'other'. In Britain, Scandinavian art has been associated with the emotionally expressive and the melancholic, as well as with engagement with particular qualities of northern light. Introducing the catalogue for the 1992 exhibition, *Border Crossings,* Jane Alison and Carol Brown comment that there is a danger of stereotyping 'Nordic' art and artists, thereby obscuring variation and losing 'the sense of complexity of individual experience, not least the buoyancy, lyricism, humour, and to some degree, the rationality that runs counter to this dark night of the northern soul' (Alison and Brown, 1992: 11).

Nordic culture is rooted in relations with land. Aside from in Denmark, once away from the major cities, the population throughout the Nordic area is sparse and many live in relative isolation. Nordic sense of time and space remains rooted in the annual cycle of nature.[7] Halldór Björn Runólfsson has remarked that 'Far from being a feeling of loneliness, this solitude is rather a way of life, where nature – a silent substitute for direct social contact – plays an important role as partner, interlocutor and model of inspiration' (Runølfsson, 1992: 145). The climate is tough, and survival is challenging, especially in the far north and in rural regions. Even in urban areas the shift from snow, ice and limited daylight in winter to the long days of summer is culturally deep-seated, influencing everyday pursuits. Sea, fjords, islands, mountains, woodlands, pastures, long dark winters, and the white nights of summer, all contribute to the inflection of national cultures and concerns, and, arguably, play a key role in the construction of national psyches.

Situated on the edge of Europe, Norway has a relatively low population with a concentration of people in the south, especially around Oslo, Bergen and Stavenger. Politically democratic, it retains a sort of 'secular' monarchy. Since it is not a member of the European Union it maintains an economic and symbolic separation from the rest of Europe. That Norway has frequently been ruled from elsewhere historically is relevant to understanding Norwegian identity. As a modern nation it has only been independent for a century (interrupted by German occupation in the 1940s). For Norwegians, autonomy is important, and the monarchy symbolises national identity, hence, in London, the embassy title is 'The *Royal* Norwegian Embassy' (my emphasis).

There is a tradition of visual artists in Scandinavia travelling and studying elsewhere in Europe (Rome, Berlin, Paris). As already indicated, Scandinavians – on the periphery of Europe and echoing their Viking ancestors – expect to travel; artists are no exception to this. It follows that the Norwegian pictorial integrates a number of external influences. Johan Christian Dahl (1788–1857), who is frequently hailed as the 'father' of Norwegian landscape painting, studied in Germany, and his work is clearly influenced by European Romanticism; although he himself emphasised 'rediscovery' of the Norwegian landscape on his return.[8] Notions of beauty and of the sublime take on a particular inflection in an environment so subject to intensity of summer light, limited winter light, and the effects of reflection on ice and snow. Artists studying in Paris in the late nineteenth century encountered Realism and on their return likewise integrated this within a Norwegian pictorial. What is striking about Norwegian art history and, indeed, various websites hosting discussions of Norwegian art, is the frequent reference to the 'Norwegian romantic landscape tradition' associated with the National Romantic Movement of the second half of the nineteenth century. In the imagined community of this particular nation, *heimat* is rural.

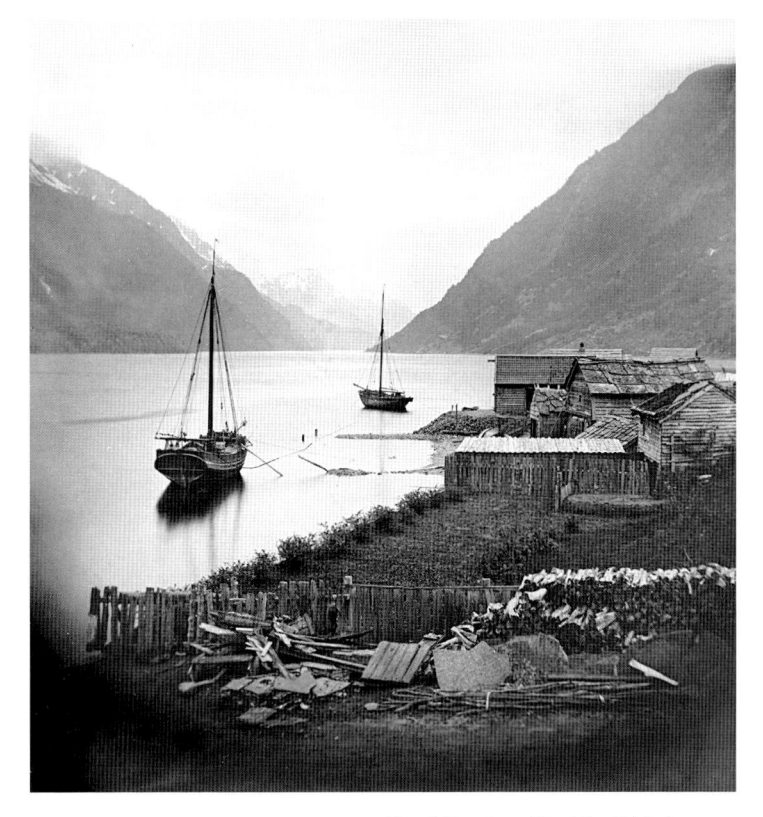

Knud Knudsen, 'Parti fra Odda I Hardanger' (An area of Odda, Hardanger), 4 June 1863.

Photography in Scandinavia developed, as elsewhere, through the involvement of artists and writers, as well as through the involvement of those with other scientific and technical interests, and through the establishment of commercial studios by those who saw potential for selling images. Foremost among the latter was the Knudsen business in Bergen. Knud Knudsen (active 1862–1900), from Hardanger, south of Bergen, was a country boy, who went to Reutlingen in Germany to study fruit farming, and there acquired a stereoscopic camera. He pre-eminently documented Bergen and his home surroundings, noting people at work, for example, fishing or farming, and roads and railways within the mountainous landscape. The studio, set up in 1864, was a general commercial enterprise; the archive is varied in terms of genre, and offers an extensive social historical record.[9] Improved roads and the beginnings of the railroads contributed to supporting a burgeoning tourist trade – Norway was particularly popular with British travellers. Knudsen journeyed north in summer to make 'views' for sale. The boat being rowed on a fjord at the foot of steep cliffs is one recurrent motif. Tourists purchased photographs (later postcards) as souvenirs. The Knudsen archive includes a number of un-peopled landscapes: photographs of ice and snow on distant mountains, or of lively waterfalls. His work became associated with the rhetorical idealisation of mountain and fjord that characterised nationalist visions of homeland. He was not alone in working on the West Coast of Norway, for instance, Axel Lindahl (1841–1906) likewise made striking views, but, as a Swede, his work was not taken up by independence movements. Overall, however, in the nineteenth century, tourism and photography articulated this particular West Coast region as space and spectacle.

Whilst Romanticism was marshalled within independence movements, Norway also produced two major Expressionist artists, Edvard Munch (1863–1944) and Gustav Vigeland (1869–1943), both of whom remained on the avant-garde fringes for many years before being internationally acknowledged, and before Expressionism became identifiable as an art movement. Gertrud Sandqvist argues that it is misleading to talk of 'Nordic Expressionism' as it easily gets confused with German Expressionism wherein, although subjectivity is central, the social and philosophical context is specific. In relation to Nordic consciousness she suggests that,

> There is no question here of allowing personality to reshape reality, but just the opposite: personality is reduced to zero; ego, hand and material are allowed to become the medium. Thus, it is not easy to speak, for instance, of the importance of the landscape or of nature, as is so frequently done. To the extent that the landscape is present it is taken up and transformed into an inner landscape; to the extent that nature is present here, it is in the desire to work like nature – and this in itself is already a dream.
>
> (Sandqvist, 1992: 15)

The definitional distinction between ego and personality is not precise, but it would seem that land is so integrated within Scandinavian consciousness that there is no clear subject–object relation. If so, this has key implications for comprehending Nordic landscape painting, photography and land art. For instance, it follows that Knud Knudsen's picture of a man standing, isolated, overlooking the valley towards mountains beyond, could be read in terms of the pleasures of space and solitude, not in the territorial vein that might influence a reading of an equivalent British image. Discussing 'Myths and Heroes in Nineteenth Century Nation-building in Norway', Sigurd Aarnes references the nineteenth-century Norwegian dramatist, Henrik Ibsen, and remarks,

> One loses a complete dimension in Ibsen's drama if one does not realize that behind his wilderness scenes there lies what is, possibly, a peculiarly Norwegian notion of the mountain as the place where a free, individual and ideal existence can be led. The mountain is seen as the place where one may freely fulfil oneself, according to one's deepest needs, without taking others into account.
>
> (Aarnes, 1983: 109)

He thus draws attention to the role of the mountain as a place of escape from the cares of the valleys, a space seen as closer to God and free of more worldly preoccupations. This is thrown into further relief when we consider the relative isolation of the valley villages through the harsh winters. For most Norwegians, the mountain remains viewed as a source of replenishment – skiing, walking, fishing are key leisure occupations.

Geologically, four-fifths of Norway is mountainous, and people live in long valleys, often along the sides of fjords which cut their way inland. The west of Norway is mountainous, the south and east are not. The mountain does not literally represent Norway in its geographic entirety, but it does point to a key geological and cultural distinction from Sweden, which is typified by central woodlands and an archipelago of islands off the southern and southeastern coasts. Rugged mountains thus came to characterise the Norwegian landscape in part *because* they contrast with the woodlands associated with Sweden, and this continues to be variously stressed. For instance, in the catalogue for *Den Glemte Tradisjonen* (celebrating the 150th anniversary of photography), Robert Meyer remarks on the iconicity of certain views; he gives the example of Knudsen's dramatic 'Skjeggedalsfossen, Hardanger' (Waterfalls, 1872) which he juxtaposes with a not quite identical scene copied from Knudsen's photograph by landscape painter, Andreas Disen (1884).

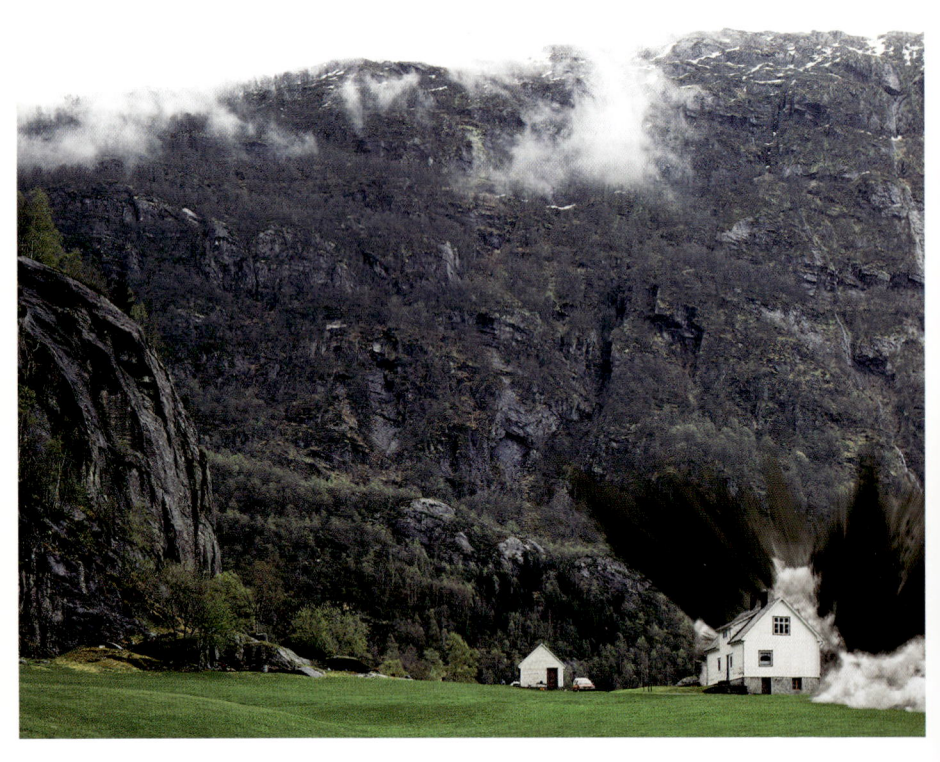

Petter Magnusson, 'Explosion', No. 1, 2002, from the series *1/3*.

It is thus no accident that Petter Magnusson, on moving from Sweden to Norway in the late 1990s, was struck by the Norwegian idyll of mountain, valley and rural solitude, which he articulates in his digital composite 'Explosion No. 1' (2002). The wooden house at the foot of the mountain by a fjord, offering solitude away from city crowds, remains part of the Norwegian dream. He explodes the rural idyll, bringing together the house, the mountain and the drama of the clouds. Scale, composition and ornate framing parody the nineteenth-century pictorial. The explosion may reference mining that, with fisheries and North Sea oil, centrally supports the Norwegian economy. But meaning is to some extent open. Magnusson remarks,

It could be a disturbance or mining in a classic romantic landscape, with a possible ecological comment, or it could be war in the peaceful north, or an absurd attempt at terrorism outside of NY; or it could be some more mystical force in action, or the dream of an explosion, or an experiment in putting sublime forces/images up against each other in an investigation into an updated romanticism, a natural disaster, or even, as someone guessed, the peasant's home brewery exploding.

(Email, 23 February 2004)

Although openness of interpretation is integral to the picture, whatever the reading the idyll of the rural retreat in the remote mountain valley is in question.

Cultural attitudes are specifically interrogated in the 1990s' work of Tobjørn Rødland whose staging of young men in the Norwegian woods and fjords became well known internationally. Rødland was the first artist to take the prevailing image of the romantic landscape as subject matter and to offer an ironic view of Norway; hence the impact of this woodlands work. Norwegian stereotypes are undercut through contemporary reference: for instance, a long-haired, blond young man, a Friedrich figure for today, carries a plastic bag, the supermarket logo clearly displayed. Contemporary consumption includes the poetic landscape! In 'Glowing Bush' (2000) what might have been a sublime view into the distance is interrupted by the elegiac bleakness of a bush, leafless, sculpturally silhouetted against a deep golden sunset. Inclusion in *The Politics of Place* (exhibition, UMEA University, Sweden, 2002) reaffirmed the contribution of his work to ironically questioning and unsettling residues of Romanticism.

Irony as a critical strategy particularly characterised Rødland's series, although he was certainly not the first to refuse the idealisation of the rural. In 1987, a group of four photographers, Per Berntsen, Jens Hange, Johan Sandberg and Siggen Stinessen, had made a two-month trip travelling extensively through Norway (in camper vans) which was brought together as the project 'Stiftelsen Norsk Landskap' (first exhibited as 'Norsk Landskap 87' at Henie Onstad Art Centre outside Oslo). The work focused on everyday phenomena in a non-romanticised manner. Pictures of mountains or seascapes, where included, are anti-sensationalist, in that aesthetic rhetoric and drama are downplayed through the topographic idiom.

In his series, *Prospects* (2002), Per Olav Torgnesskar likewise references vernacular imagery. He used 'straight' documentary idiom and postcard format to make images of ordinary places, in effect reminding us that rural and small town scenes may be dull and journeys remarkably banal, not at all the scenarios commonly celebrated in picture postcards. Like Rødland, the work critiques sublime romanticism, but in this instance the reference is more elliptical, as the re-deployment of the postcard format reminds us precisely that these are not standard postcard views. A companion video, *Norwegian Scenarios* (2000), constructed from television news footage, again testifies to the ordinariness of the everyday. These photographers variously challenge the dominant iconography of the Norwegian landscape as snowy, mountainous sublime, but their aesthetic strategies are markedly different.

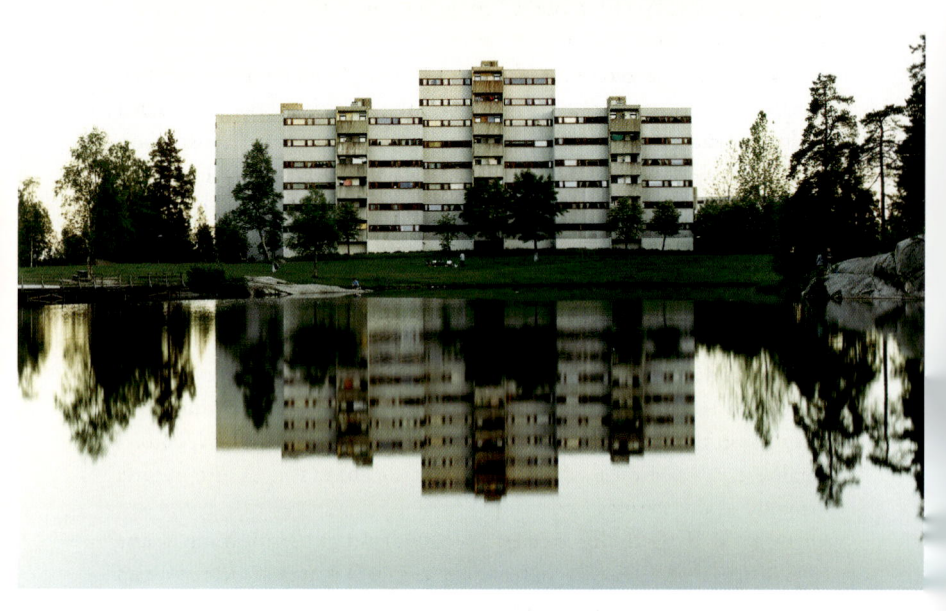

Ane Hjort Guttu, 'Untitled' (Romsas, Oslo), from the series *Modernistic Journey*, 2002.

Ane Hjort Guttu (like Torgnesskar, based in Oslo) explores interrelations of natural phenomena and new urban building. In *Modernistic Journey* (2002) she captures the effects of the movement of light on both the natural environment (the mountains, or the shore) and modern architecture. In one image the light falls on an apartment block from exactly the same direction as it falls on a mountain in a separate image. Both appear equally monumental. A further picture captures the reflection of a white block of flats in the lake landscaped into the foreground. The photographer as observer is not modernist in the sense of extolling modernity, so much as post-modern in observing ways in which nature incorporates culture – or vice versa. We may read the effects of light metaphorically, whilst noting and taking pleasure in the pictorial affect. We are also reminded that landscape pictures, however abstract and symbolic, tell us something about cultural attitudes. Likewise Oslo-based, and questioning romantic modes of viewing, Mikkel McAlinden's large landscapes, which appear almost painterly, on close inspection turn out to be digitally stitched images which refuse Albertian perspective. The shift in geometry dis-concerts; the pictures refuse any central viewing position. The scale (usually *c.* 150 cm x up to 400cm) makes this a bodily encounter, and the sheer physicality enhances the unsettling affect.

These works are pictorially dramatic. Other photographers, across all of Scandinavia, continue to work in more dispassionate observational style. In her series, *Common Green* (1999) Norwegian photographer, Marthe Ass, depicts everyday scenery and scenarios, for example, children playing in the snow. The documentary idiom throws emphasis on content, and the images work rhetorically through building a series of observations on space and human behaviour in external environments close to home. Likewise, contemporary Swedish photography features a strand of colour documentary examining contemporary lifestyles. For instance, in *Commonplace Intervention* (2000–01) Maria Lantz pictured streets of identical houses or garages which we presume are suburban as they sit on the edge of maintained common lands, some with football goalposts; the clinical observational mode draws attention to the banality of the settings.

In some respects this echoes a longer-standing Swedish landscape tradition. As elsewhere, landscape painting in Sweden towards the end of the nineteenth century reflected National Romanticism. Discussing Swedish Art of the 1990s, art historian Michelle Facos suggests that National Romanticism in Sweden was progressive in encompassing

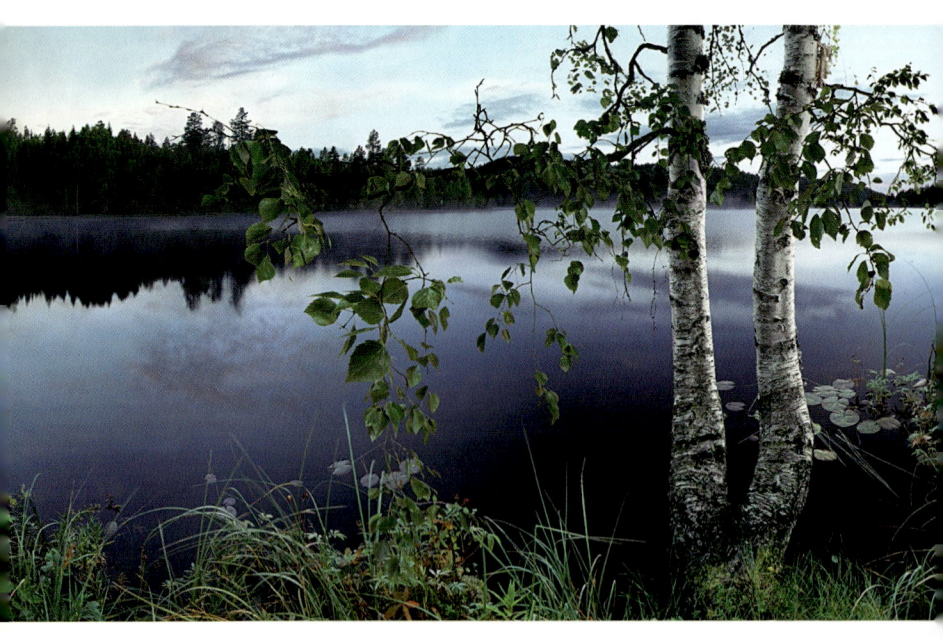

Mikkel McAlinden, 'The Evil Cottage', 2000.

change, rather than harking back to a traditional pastoralism (as, for example, in Germany or Norway). Sweden was not industrialised, but was, she argues, characterised by a social utopianism within which values such as 'simplicity, cleanliness, and social equality' were stressed (Facos, 1998: 3). She adds that for Sweden, anxious to distinguish itself from immediate neighbours such as Norway (which was seeking independence) or Finland (then ruled from Russia), regional specificity was significant within any sense of homeland; also that the social democratic ethos transcended class difference. Nonetheless, she notes the hegemonic role played by professionals in promoting a shared sense of responsibility for – as she phrases it – 'cultivating the edenic garden in which they and future generations would thrive' (ibid.). Swedes were encouraged to take responsibility for their own back yard.

Like Maria Lantz, in his humorous colour observations of the Swedish middle classes at work, at home and at leisure, Lars Tunbjörk emphasises the banality of the suburbs that now characterise Swedish towns. The series suggests a standardisation of living environments while also indicating ways in which each household has personalised use of otherwise uniform space (children's toys, sun-loungers, barbecues …) and pointing to the peculiarities of how people spend their time off. In one image someone dressed as Father Christmas looks on, presumably in summer as two children are wearing shorts, and a bare-chested man sits in a toy car on the driveway beyond which shrubland and tall trees are silhouetted against a bright blue sky. Domestic bliss? The style is ironic yet warm, but the sheer extent of his work enhances the sense of the bizarreness of the everyday. Annika von Hausswolff's work raises even more uneasy questions about the Swedish Edenic. She depicts bodies in the landscape, apparently dead, possibly murdered. In one example, from *Back to Nature* (1993), a woman lies naked, face down in a lake, surrounded by reeds, but we view this relatively close-up, looking from her feet towards her thighs, bottom and back. We cannot see her face. At one level, since these are female bodies (or, sometimes, couples) the notion that woman is closer to nature is reinforced, but this is only in order to undermine it, since physical violence towards women is also under scrutiny. The large scale of the tableaux adds a sense of immediacy that further enhances dis-ease. This happens, and can happen anywhere! That the photographer is a woman exploring patriarchal attitudes enhances critical edge – indeed, it is difficult to imagine a male photographer engaging this subject matter in such a way. As Swedish curator-critic Jan-Erik Lundström, remarks 'The images in *Back to Nature* are landscape images. They perform a waist lock upon an entire genre and without hesitating settle accounts with the tradition of nature painting in Scandinavia, which often has placed the landscape in an ideal space beyond culture and beyond ideologies' (Kouhia and Lundström, 1998: n.p.). Meanwhile, rural activities, such as berry-picking, formerly associated with family days out or community harvesting, have become organised commercially. As Swedish artist Margareta Klingberg notes, this offers seasonal employment for 'new Swedes' (from Eastern Asia and elsewhere) and for migrant workers from former Soviet areas (see Lundström, 2002). Woodlands and closeness to nature may remain a part of Swedish consciousness, but the realities of industry, city culture, and suburban lifestyles have led to a disjunction between the traditional imaginary and actual behaviour. The mode is documentary, but the work disturbs as it points to a significant social change – the depiction of berry-picking as something done by those who are nationally or ethnically other centrally challenges a taken-for-granted association of rural pursuits with Swedishness.

LAND MATTERS

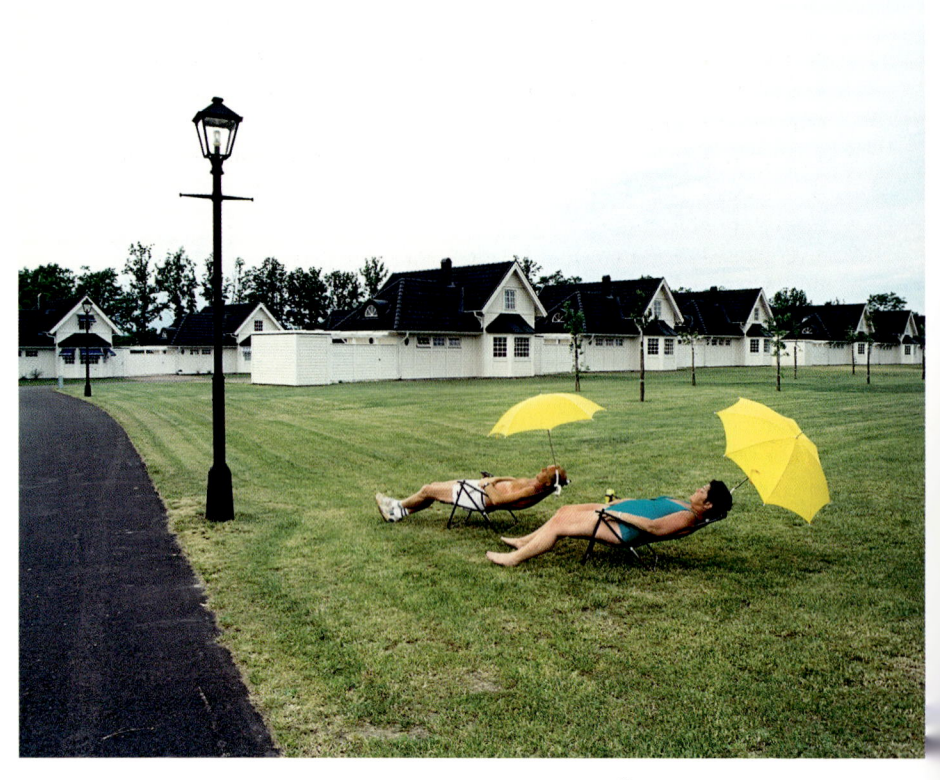

Lars Tunbjörk, 'Öland', 1991, from the series *Landet utom sig* (Country Beside Itself).

Gothenburg lies across the water from the north of Denmark, and south Sweden is closer to Copenhagen than Stockholm, not only geographically but also historically and culturally. The Øredok Sound both separates the east of Denmark from southwest Sweden and conjoins the two in shared shipping routes, vegetation, economic links, not to mention historical antagonism (possibly partly caused by so little water separating the two mercantile empires). Agriculture is now industrialised, but traditionally Denmark and south Sweden were family farming areas, rural communities, facing each other across the water. Joakim Eskildsen's series, *Requiem* (2000), pays tribute to his grandmother. It is based on a not uncommon early twentieth-century story of sisters sent from the relatively poor south of Sweden to live and work on a farm in more affluent Denmark. The full installation includes a pinhole landscape depicting a rural road through farmlands in northern Denmark, images of his grandmother as a young woman, a portrait of her soon before she died, and a study of the skin of her hand, on which years of manual labour are etched. The black and white pinhole photo-aesthetic lends a sense of historical distance and timelessness to the rural landscape; indeed, this was only three generations ago. We are reminded of the extent of the shift from local farming communities to industrial-scale farming. In *Øredok* (1998) John S. Webb documents further changes as this coastal area in southwest Sweden, previously something of a nature reserve, has now been eroded by roads and industrial plants congregated around the motorway bridge which, since 2000, has linked Sweden with Denmark (finally terminating the relative isolation of the north from the rest of Western Europe). The work is in the form of a series of 360-degree panoramas, digitally stitched, and thus disorienting for those with intimate knowledge of the local landscape. Again, the strategy is one of unsettling the viewer, asking those who know the area to consider the implications of new developments.

Denmark is relatively intensively populated, with extensive tracts of countryside now transformed into agri-industry. The era of small-scale farming referenced in Eskildsen's homage to his grandmother has given way to intensive production geared to the demands of the international supermarket. Kirsten Klein lives on Mors Island (Jutland) and much of her work is from that region, forming an extensive documentation of a more traditional rural. She is particularly preoccupied with elemental effects, with movement and change, with picturing transient moments. For example, a classically framed picture of a windswept line of trees, captures something of the character of Denmark, a country where climate is constant but weather is highly variable and winds howl across the flatlands between the North Sea and the Baltic. Recent work belies formalist and pictorialist influences: for instance, *Water* (2002) focuses on sea, waves, clouds, snow and ice, but soft focus and sepia-effect distance subject matter. Images of waves breaking after a storm or a shell sanded smooth by seawater resonate like scenes from old movies, taking us into the realms of memory rather than into a more immediate recollection of the cold and damp of wind and storms. Traditional image modes and themes together hark back to a Denmark of coast and

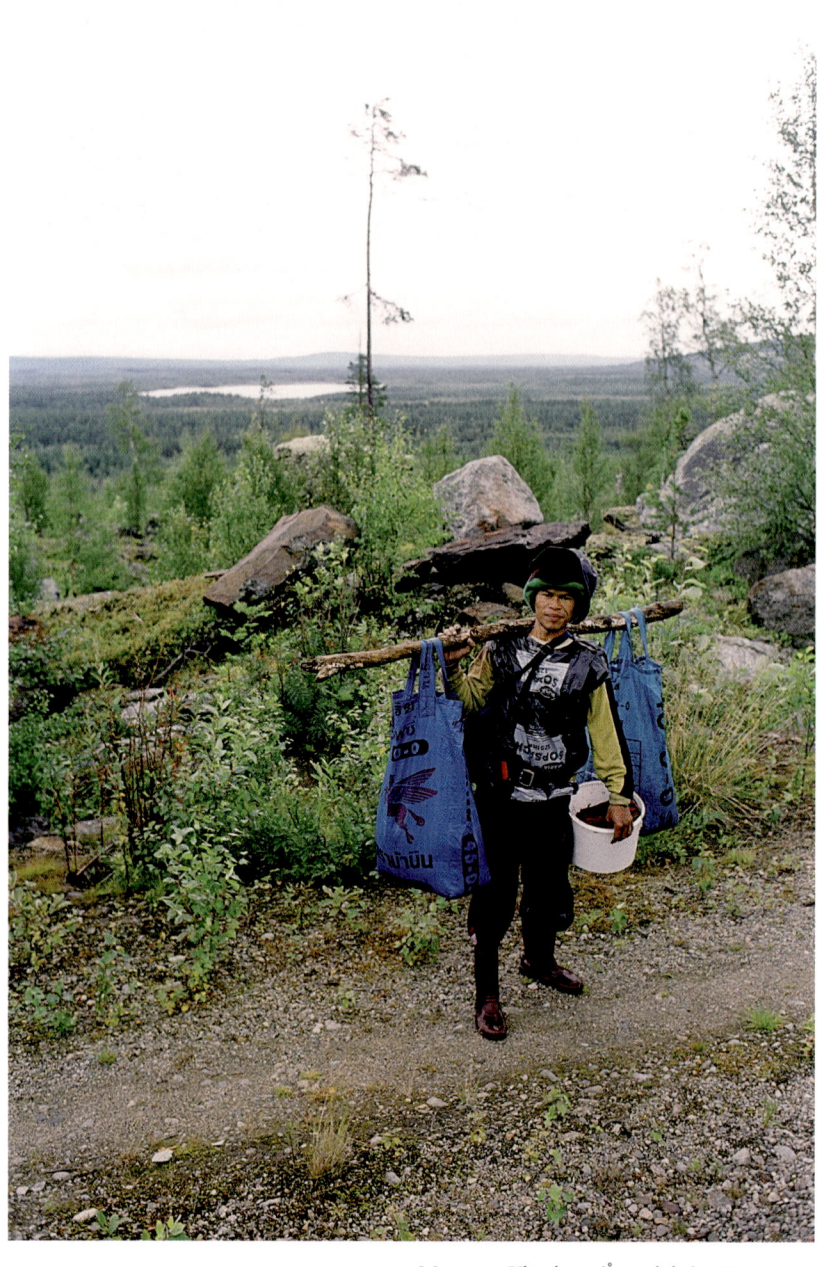

Margareta Klingberg, 'Åtjärnlider', 2001, from the series *On the Move*.

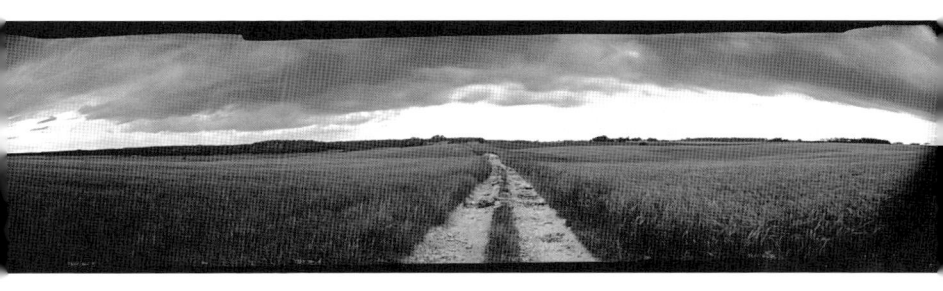

Joakim Eskildsen, 'The Road', 2001, from the series *Requiem*.

farmlands that figured in nineteenth-century Danish landscape painting but has become residual. Klein's pictures are not in themselves intended as critique, but many aspects of rural change are detailed.

The Golden Age of Danish painting, early to mid-nineteenth century, was characterised by a new precise and direct mode of depiction and a focus on everyday subject matter, which, with hindsight, seems proto-photographic. The Counter-Enlightenment had emerged across Europe in the period immediately following the Napoleonic Wars (1800–15). The classicism, universalism and mythological themes of post-Renaissance culture began to give way to a concern to explore immediate phenomena and circumstances; the seeds of National Romanticism were sown, as were the roots of Realism in painting and an enhanced desire to be able to fix the photographic images in order to enjoy its (perceived) accuracy. Denmark had been in economic decline since the mid-eighteenth century, culminating in Copenhagen becoming a battleground in the Napoleonic Wars (1801 and 1807), and in the secession of Norway to Sweden (1814). Arguably the new era in painting emerged from and contributed to a search for a new sense of self. There were two key features that might be seen as forerunners of landscape photography. First, a descriptive idiom emerged featuring direct depiction of countryside and coast. Suggesting that the Golden Age subverted the grand themes and ideologies of European academic art, Philip Conisbee remarks a concentration on 'present virtues: the pleasures of a well-ordered daily life; the quiet beauty of their country, with its islands and cliffs, woods and dunes, meadows and beaches; and the silent ships, moored in the harbors or plying the coasts' that indicate that 'in spite of the reduced circumstances of their country, the Danes were nurturing a positive sense that they had much

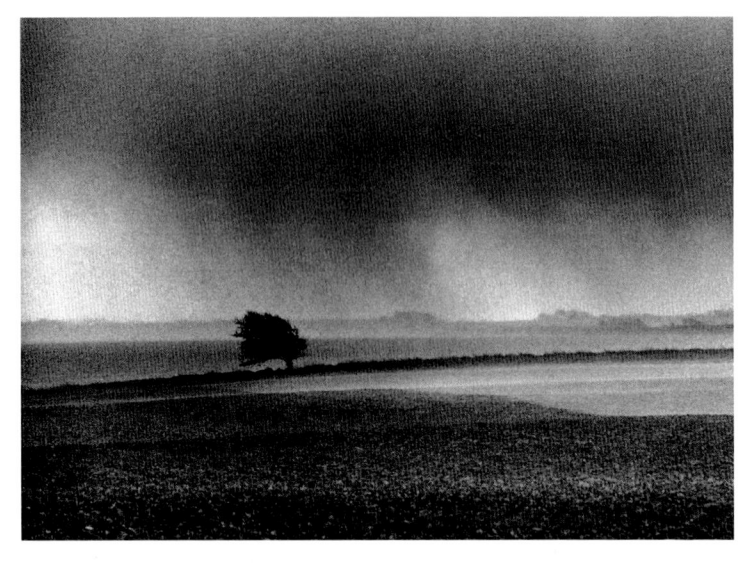

Kirsten Klein, 'Raincloud above Draaby Dove', Winter, 1994.

for which to be grateful, both in their heroic past, mythic or historic, and in the continuity provided by their native landscape' (Conisbee, 1995: 45). Nature and small-scale farming could be seen as a source of replenishment of national pride. It also chimed with the Protestant (Lutheran) work ethic. Second, in the mid-nineteenth century, a group – known as the Skagen painters after the coastal town on the northerly tip of Jutland – became preoccupied with the effects of the elements, especially the movement of light, in effect foreshadowing concerns that would become typical of landscape photography.

In his introduction to *The Danish Landscape* (Photography Centre, Copenhagen, 1996) curator Lars Schwander comments that although the genre figured prominently in the nineteenth century and 'nature' was implicated in National Romanticism at the beginning of the twentieth century, contemporary photographers generally ignore the Danish landscape. The photographs of Sigvart Werner, who made a series of books (1927–40) exploring different regions and towns, is one example of photography exploring that which is typically Danish. For example, in *Copenhagen* Werner particularly emphasised monuments and state buildings. Schwander also remarks that in recent work 'no matter how much idealisation goes into the portrayal, innocence is still missing. There is no immediate sublimity, no religious mediation, it is rather (once again) a question of concretisation, like a *momenti mori*; marked by death and therefore mortal. Nature no longer appears to be the wild expanse of freedom …' (Schwander, 1996: 7). This comment seems to indicate a juncture or turning point in landscape in Denmark; it acknowledges the vulnerability of environment which increasingly preoccupies artists, yet it views landscape in Burkian terms, emphasising religious dimensions of traditional landscape. Tom Christoffersen, one of the artists included in the exhibition, depicts individuals in everyday urban streets, each person holding a framed landscape painting within which benevolent sunlight and traditional Danish emblems figure: the cottage, the windmill, cumulus clouds, and hedges lining country lanes. The work is open to interpretation, but my first reaction was to take this as acknowledgement that such pastoral idylls, insofar as they ever existed, are now a matter of the past.

Per Bak Jensen's pictures do not fit within a specific genre, rather his work ranges between landscape, city documentary and the architectural, encompassing more formalist explorations of colour, texture, light and shade. The style is direct, observational; what we see appears unmediated – although the striking geometry of his imagery points to a concern with composition and the organisation of space within the frame. People sometimes figure, usually incidentally, but his concern is with overlooked spaces or moments, for instance, the distant reaches of Greenland (which remains a Danish protectorate). Introducing his work, critic Michael Bogh notes that Jensen's interest in photography as a mode of observation dates from childhood when he started photographing unnoticed places (Bogh, 2006). He has continued to observe the banal, and talks of photography as encounters which in some way change the photographer. His approach seemingly links Walter Benjamin's proposition that photographs allow for the optical unconscious with Lee Friedlander's interest in photographing to see what something looks like photographed. His pictures 'hold' an image in order to be able to examine phenomena; these are ostensibly external to the photographer as artist but of course speak about the artist himself. Bogh notes some echoes of the subject matter of the Golden Age landscape painters, not when engaged with the pastoral, but when exploring outlying areas of cities. Jensen's interest in light, for example, the intensity of blues of sky and sea, offers a further echo – he makes work out of season, at dawn and twilight, when available light is at its most subtle. As Bogh remarks,

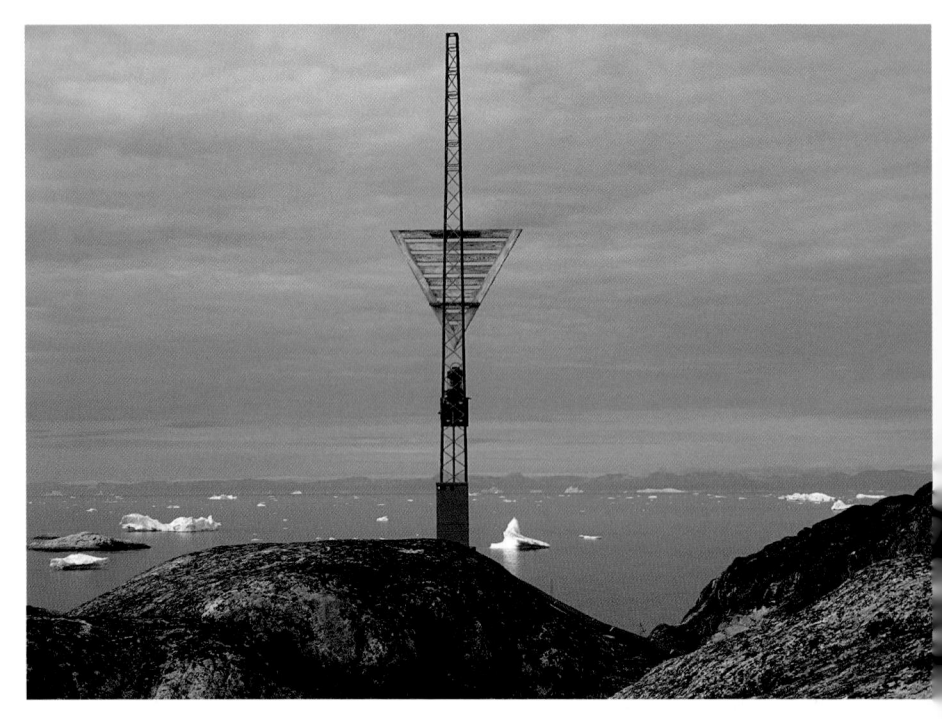

Per Bak Jensen, 'Seamark', 2006, from the series *Greenland*.

Jensen's pictures do not try to summarise or visually crystallise stories. This is partly because he pays attention to overlooked sites, and partly because the images are so open that they do not reference any single or simple idea. In this respect his work cannot really be viewed as contributing to the construction of histories of place. Nor is it deliberately enigmatic; rather, it invites reflection in terms of the spiritual.

A number of Danish artists using photography, and interested in environment, are now based elsewhere, for instance, Mads Gamdrup is based in Dusseldorf, and Olafur Eliasson (see Chapter 6) in Berlin. Gamdrup (who was taught by Jenson at the Royal Danish Academy of Fine Arts) notes an interest in *time*, in Denmark, which he contrasts with Finnish photography of 'situation'.[10] For him a photograph may indicate that something has occurred; the event may not necessarily be shown in the image, but it has changed the relation of the photographer to the place or space pictured. Travel is central to his work as an artist, as he sets up personal encounters with natural phenomena – for instance, going to Zimbabwe in 2001 to experience and photograph a total solar eclipse or in '21.06.1999' travelling to the northernmost point in Norway to experience the midsummer light. Discussing this project Anna Krogh relates his explorations to Kierkegaard's distinction between the temporal (fleeting or passing) and the eternal. Gamdrup's approach is akin to conceptual art. For example, his series, *Renunciation* (1998–2002), offers an extensive exploration of horizons, desert landscapes, textures and colour, in which it is not precise place so much as change over time and expressive affect that is at issue. He rarely makes work in Denmark, preferring the visual intensity of desert or arctic spaces. Indeed, although a number of Danish photographers are engaged with themes concerning land and environment, aside from Per Bak Jensen, many seem either to relate to traditional Danish scenarios, or to work elsewhere (albeit including Greenland or Iceland with which Denmark has historic links). Why this should be the case is not immediately clear except, perhaps, because maritime nations foster travellers. In addition, as has been remarked, the former rural landscape of Denmark has been extensively transformed through the industrialisation of agriculture. The land perhaps holds less interest now than it might once have done for photographers intent on exploring home environments.

BALTIC STATES

The geographical centre of Europe, as defined by the French National Geographic Institute in 1989, is in Lithuania, about 25 kilometres north of Vilnius, itself a mediaeval city acclaimed as a key European heritage site.[11] The journey from the city to this nondescript site was the subject of a film, *Europe 54° 54' – 25° 19'* (1997) by Deimantas Narkevicius. The journey takes us into the rural. The hand-held camera idiom suggests that this is a personal journey; but we are also reminded that principles of geographic measurement differ from those of the cultural. Berlin, London, Madrid, even Paris or Rome, would no doubt all claim cultural centrality.

If history resonates in landscape imagery, recognition of sites and familiarity with local histories become prerequisites for understanding extra layers of significance. For instance, under Nazi occupation, the majority of Vilnius' large Jewish population were killed, many in the Paneriai Forest on the outskirts of the city. A picture of a forest clearing in itself recounts little of such events; although no doubt blood could be traced in the soil. Many photographers in the 1990s documented disused Soviet military bases, enjoying the symbolism as nature reclaimed abandoned observation bunkers, perhaps with residues such as pictures on walls amidst the peeling paint, weeds and moss. Other Soviet legacies, including high-rise concrete suburban housing estates, continue to mark the landscape across the three Baltic States, as do small bleak towns once taken over for the families of Soviet troops. Among the best-known examples of post-Soviet work is that of Vilnius-based photographer, Vytautas Balcytis, who pursued an extensive documentation of rural areas and small towns in Lithuania, going against the grain by *keeping in* signs of former Soviet presence.

The three smaller Baltic States are more-or-less excluded from international photo-histories; an oversight exacerbated by similar exclusion from accounts of Soviet photography wherein – as in the arts more generally – the mainstream focus was in Moscow and Leningrad. For instance, the American publication *Photo Manifesto: Contemporary Photography in the USSR*, makes no specific mention of photographers, organisations or collections from the smaller Baltic States (Walker et al., 1991). Socialist Realism prevailed from the early 1930s onwards, and photography, in the decades from Stalin to Gorbachev, primarily served state bureaucracy. In intending closure of interpretation, Soviet Realism presumed a 'transparency' of the photographic medium; photographs served as apparently unmediated windows on a world. It was only after Henri Cartier-Bresson's work first became known in the Soviet bloc in the 1960s (the Khrushchev era), and influenced a new photojournalism which incorporated the idea of 'decisive moment', that staged Socialist Realist pictures were eschewed for a more informal street photo-reportage.

For Estonia, Latvia and Lithuania there was a dual constraint of Soviet conformity and Russian domination, with its hegemonic 'russianisation' programme.[12] Paradoxically, one legacy of socialist realism was an undermining of philosophical association of photography with 'truth'. Photographers based in former Soviet areas have long-standing scepticism relating to the ontology of the photograph and questions of authenticity. In consequence, as was remarked in *Photo Manifesto*:

Many photographers hand-color, collage, superimpose, and otherwise manipulate photographic images in many different ways. But their reasons for manipulating photographs are different from those used by the Soviet government in the past. Contemporary photographers' manipulation has more to do with freedom of expression and the re-exploration of old techniques than with the idealisation of reality in a state-approved form.

The new photographers manipulate photography not to censor but to explore the truth. Instead of creating a make-believe reality for the news, they explore their own inner reality and reaffirm their significance as individuals within the state. Their photographic series often capture present society and are a vivid reminder of the independence of spirit that has remained despite the efforts to extinguish it …

(Walker et al., 1991: 32)

Photo Manifesto focused on work from Moscow, Leningrad and Minsk, but offered little biographical or ethnic information about the photographers included. Possibly some of the photographers have origins in the Baltic States, but it is also possible that the cultural myopia of curators who search for work only around cultural centres (such as Moscow or Leningrad) led to those on the margins remaining marginalised. But margins can offer spaces for experimentation. Art historian Valery Stigneev comments that,

The new young artists developed their own creative styles … In Latvia photographers emphasized the use of symbolic images. In Lithuania 'direct photography' was explored, but with an increasingly expressive visual style, and by the end of the 1960s, first in the Baltics and then elsewhere, photographic schools had been founded as an outgrowth of the more informal photographic clubs.

(Stigneev in Walker et al., 1991: 58)

Stigneev thus presented this region as an early source of photo-innovation, although it was not until after 1985 that the prevailing distinction between official culture, and unofficial or underground culture, begins to be eroded.

In fact, as it was seen as neutral, landscape offered a relatively unconstrained genre of practice in the Soviet era, aside from restrictions on photographing in certain (military) areas. Soviet ideologists might have requested the inclusion of signifiers of industrial or agrarian achievement – electric poles, industrial tubes, herds of cows, factory sites – but it was easy to leave such marks out of the frame, claiming to document just what was observed in response to the environment in itself.[13] Photographs could stand as a form of passive dissent; photographers observe, and tell things as they appear. For example, Latvian photographer, Mara Brasmane, worked in street documentary from the 1960s on; but she also explored the changing Daugava estuary (from Riga to the Baltic coast), observing shapes made by plants within the flow of water or held within the illusory solidity of ice. Graphic surface, timelessness, repetition, and cyclical renewal speak through this extensive series of work; light is part of the 'moment' of the image, and nature seems transcendent. This appears traditional, and indeed, in terms of photography's long-standing preoccupation with recording nature, it is. But the work refused socialist realist imperatives, in effect offering a mini-challenge within the particular historical context. (This work was not much exhibited in the Soviet era.) Choice of subject and the way it is framed may imply alternative ways of seeing, but it was difficult for the authorities to condemn someone just for documenting something.

Formalist concerns with photographic seeing, with the psychological impact of imagery, and with the layering of photographic meaning, acquire critical resonance if taken in part as resistance to dominant modes. Walker (1991) notes an 'aesthetics of defect' wherein marked or scratched negatives or an amateur idiom both acknowledge the mediating presence of the photographer and simultaneously refuse the dictates of photo-realism. The tactics are Brechtian in that alienation or 'making strange' is intended to provoke critical reflection. For example, pictures by Lithuanian, Remigijus Treigys, depict rural or coastal scenes from the Baltic coast region where he lives. His *Distressed Landscapes* (1999–2003) are dark, mysterious: shadows predominate and detail is obscure. One essay on his work is titled 'The Invisible Side of the Void', suggesting search for the unknowable.[14] Surface intrigues; he not only retains 'blemishes' but also touches the paper enhancing marks of making; each image is thus unique. This emphasis on the pictorial in effect eschews influences or legacies of socialist realism, although this is not necessarily immediately evident. Taken away from the Soviet context, the work resonates through complex layering of observation, association, perceptions of time and space, nostalgia, tone and mood, and the geometry of the image. Indeed, neither Brasmane nor Treigys intended direct resistance; their concerns are more existential.

Remigijus Treigys, 'Signs 2', 2001.

Use of colour is relatively recent in all three Baltic States; equipment is limited and materials are expensive. Until the mid-1990s, 'serious' photography was monochrome. There has been a direct leap from the authoritative rhetoric of black and white to the fluidity of the digital. This is not uncontroversial. Andrejs Grants has been influential since the 1980s for naturalistic documentary. He became well known for depicting everyday life in Latvia in the late Soviet era, for instance, behind the scenes at the opera, on the edges of cities, or in the back streets of suburban industrial estates. He resists colour, which he sees as undermining 'authority of record'.[15] His comments on colour and documentary did seem to echo debates in Britain in the 1980s. But nothing directly replicates. Grants told me that he values 'mystery' in the picture; different layers, something spiritual: 'Photography is this marvelous opportunity, this paradox that can be captured and played on – the eternity of the moment. You picture a moment, and if it's the right moment, then it'll be a reflection of eternity as well' (Grants, 2002: back cover). In a post-Soviet context emphasis on the existential also implies anti-materialism (in the Marxist sense), again, perhaps, passive resistance. But Grants' analytic concerns are also formal: comparing photography to other visual arts he comments, 'In photography, however, it's the moment that is the basis, and there has to be some sort of incompleteness of form that relates to the image itself. That's why a picture that is worked to perfection can start to balance on the border of unwanted banality. You have to leave something that seems like chance, carelessness, imperfection. But only seemingly' (ibid.). In other words, he is suggesting that the illusion of spontaneity, of capturing an instant, is crucial as this is specific to the photographic. In this respect his philosophical position, and the manner of his work, perhaps acknowledge the high regard in which Cartier-Bresson became held once his work became known in this region. But Gatis Rozenfelds, who was taught by Grants, takes a different line on the advent of colour and the digital: he wants to challenge what he terms 'beauty landscape', to find something 'more truthful'.[16] His series, *Weekends*, 2002, concerns the shaping of new suburban landscapes, but also explores colour as a means of speaking about land. This was innovatory; colour equipment and materials had been prohibitively expensive before the advent of the digital so colour was idiomatically relatively unfamiliar even at the turn of the twenty-first century. The images note everyday scenes and, to those familiar with colour documentary, may appear relatively ordinary photographically. In the Baltic region his work was greeted as very original and included in the third Baltic triennial.[17]

Landscape imagery, however abstract and symbolic, is always at one level about place and human intervention. Layers of historical development are marked in Herkki-Erich Merila's wry series, *Lunaatika*, 1999 (connoting moonlight and, of course, lunacy). Estonian rural scenes are viewed by night; the presence of roads and factories is marked. Fields have been harvested but the hay now sits in the shadow of agri-industry. Car headlights (the ultimate symbol of everyday modernity) rather than moonlight, illuminate the harvest stacks and distant industrial plant. This is, of course, *somewhere*, but it also stands for *everywhere*. Each image articulates tensions – nature/culture, tradition/modernity. For a newly re-emergent nation this perhaps symbolises struggle over identity. What sort of future will be sought for woodland and agricultural areas, and how will notions of the rural resonate in terms of nationhood?

This is a fast-changing region, within which photo-practices reflect new-found freedoms of movement and the possibilities presented by the digital, not only for making images but also for (cheap) distribution via the web. Whilst landscape once offered an arena of escape from Soviet dictates or figured as a space of (passive) resistance, the contemporary

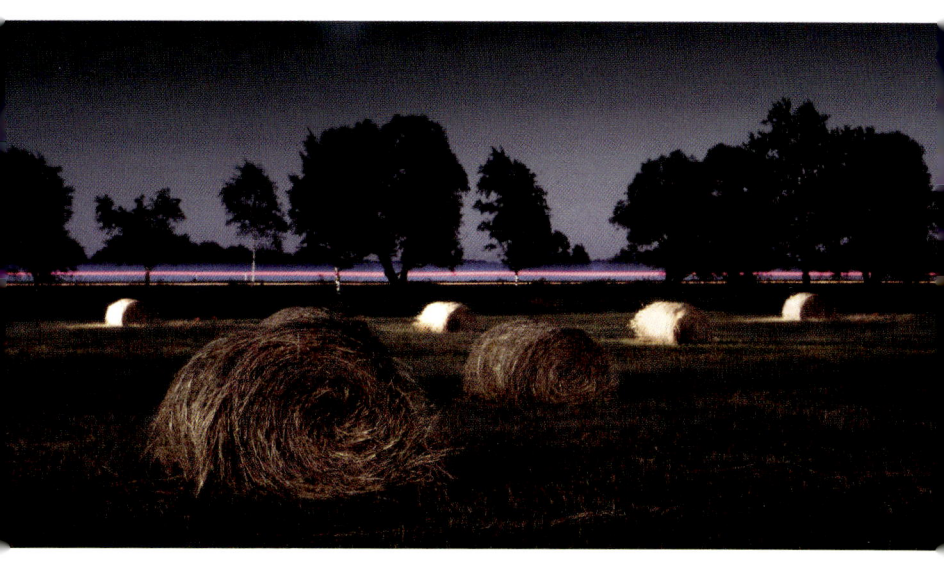

Herkki-Erich Merila, 'Lunaatika II', 2000, from the series *Lunaatika*.

focus seems to be more on the urban, the immediacy of the moment (especially in youth culture) and on new-found commercial possibilities. There is less stress than might have been anticipated on exploring land as territory and heritage. Perhaps in this transitional period the excitement for photographers lies elsewhere.

LANDSCAPE, PHOTOGRAPHY, IDENTITY: FINLAND

By contrast, imagery relating to land and environment is central to Finnish contemporary practice. Finland is also fast changing, both in its confidence as a nation with electronic industries at its contemporary economic core and as an active player within Europe (and a member of the Eurozone). But industrial development in Finland only dates from the second half of the twentieth century, and the great majority of economic activity is concentrated in the triangle between Helsinki, Turku and Tampere (including the Lakes area, i.e., Jyvaskyla). The rest of Finland, especially the extensive north, is poor and lacks investment.

Woodlands remain significant in Finnish consciousness. Woodland covers about 75 per cent of Finland and just under 10 per cent of the country is under water, mainly lakes.[18] It is the most heavily forested nation in Europe. Finland also encompasses Europe's largest archipelago, including the Åland islands off the southwest coast. Two-thirds of the population live in cities, but city dwellers retain strong links with countryside. Many have second homes where their family lived historically and where they may still have relatives. This is not a matter of social class, in the way that it might be, for instance, in England or France; most Finns retain a marked sense of region and rural roots and the seasonal gathering of berries and mushrooms remains an everyday pastime. Unlike in the UK, Finns have a right of common access which dates from dependence on slash and burn land clearance for agriculture, hunting and fishing. A sense of the spiritual significance of land resonates in the *Kalevala*, and was central to nineteenth-century nationalist movements; it remains marked in legend and myth.[19] Nature thus remains central to the Finnish 'soul'; spending summer at the lakes is still common. The sauna offers an elemental spiritual experience (transcending simple associations with cleansing and health), and 'at oneness' with the rural remains marked in the work of many contemporary artists. Jan Keila's well-known portrayal of an old man, photographed repeatedly (1985–2000), naked in a garden, sometimes reading, at one with his environment, typifies Finnish attitudes to nature.[20] Concerns about changes in rural areas and lifestyles feature prominently in contemporary Finnish practices. Forests, water, and also the Arctic region in the north, have been central to the explorations of many contemporary photographers.

Finland is proud of seascapes, woodlands and lakes, but inland is boggy and rugged; ice, snow and limited daylight in winter make eking out existence exceptionally difficult. The problem has been one of conquering land, bringing it under control and rendering it productive. Taneli Eskola has photographed extensively in Aulanko Park, a tourist centre in the south (about 100 km from Helsinki), whose origins lie in a mediaeval hill fort by a forest lake. The park represents a conquering of wilderness. But this was a barren wilderness manicured into a sublime, as a steep-sided rocky valley known for snake nests was transformed into a woodland park, with lakeside areas, viewpoints and paths through the trees, managed as a leisure facility and nature reserve. Eskola notes that, although the idea of a landscape park comes from England, the sources of inspiration were international. The park includes a castle 'ruin' constructed in the 1880s, referencing legends of Teutonic chivalry, plants imported from Russia and Japan, and a terraced area with potted trees and palms based on the French Riviera. Imported animals were used to stock Finland's first zoo (Eskola, 1997a: 13). Aulanko clearly replicated interest in landscape architecture and gardening characteristic of other parts of Western Europe in the late seventeenth and eighteenth centuries, but, this being Finland, it was envisaged as a public – not private – space. In effect, Aulanko represents a constructed 'natural' that is now 'naturalised'. That Eskola's photography is black and white adds to a sense of timelessness of landscaping and also idiomatically references an era pre-dating widespread colour photography or, indeed, the digital (the 1950s was the peak period of Aulanko's popularity). The park now facilitates outdoor leisure activities at all times of year, from sunbathing by the lake to cross-country skiing (without enduring the actual rigours of wilderness, especially as manifest in Lapland or on the northeastern forest borders with Russia). His photographic investigation is enhanced through a companion study in which he analyses photographs of Aulanko historically.[21] Art historians have often interrogated how painters and photographers have represented landscape; by contrast, Eskola started by asking how photography has *constructed* the landscape (Eskola, 1997b). He pursues this through demonstrating changing subject matter and emphasis within pictures of Aulanko over time that reflect broader social developments but also contributed to influencing shifts in perceptions of landscape as a space of pleasure. The study thus situates photography within a complexity of ideological discourses. The idea of communal access to land, and of the natural as a source of replenishment, is central to this.

Wildlife photography is a remarkably popular genre in Finland. We are reminded that the rural can be an uneasy space. Wild animals, and hunting, carry significance based on a hunter-gatherer mode of existence. The popularity of wildlife photography, involving treks to forest hides, echoes this – the photograph acting as substitute 'trophy'! Juha Suonpää's humorous, anti-pastoral *Wilderness* pictures, mostly made in the eastern border forests, interrogates this masculine pastime.[22] At one level, the work is humorous: a bear, eating convenience food, stands still to be photographed, and a photographer disguises himself behind a tree, wearing antlers, to fool passing wildlife.[23] But a number of more symbolic points are encoded: the blues of the sky and of the water in which a cow has drowned match that of the Finnish flag, and a distant line where managed forestry gives way to wilderness marks the Russian border. From a Finnish perspective the implications of this are multi-layered; Russia once ruled Finland, so comments on the unruliness of the landscape on the Russian side of the border reflect previous antagonism. Yet, many Finns support wildness and regret the erosion of Finnish wilderness as it has given way to commercially managed woodlands, and, increasingly, tourism.

Forestry is now big business; birch trees, which once grew randomly amongst the lakes, now stand regimented through organised planting. Commercial logging has cleared acres of woodland. In an extensive project on change in northern forest areas, Ritva Kovalainen and Sanni Seppo comment on the implications of this, focusing on the loss of what for many is a primary space of contemplation, a spiritual home.

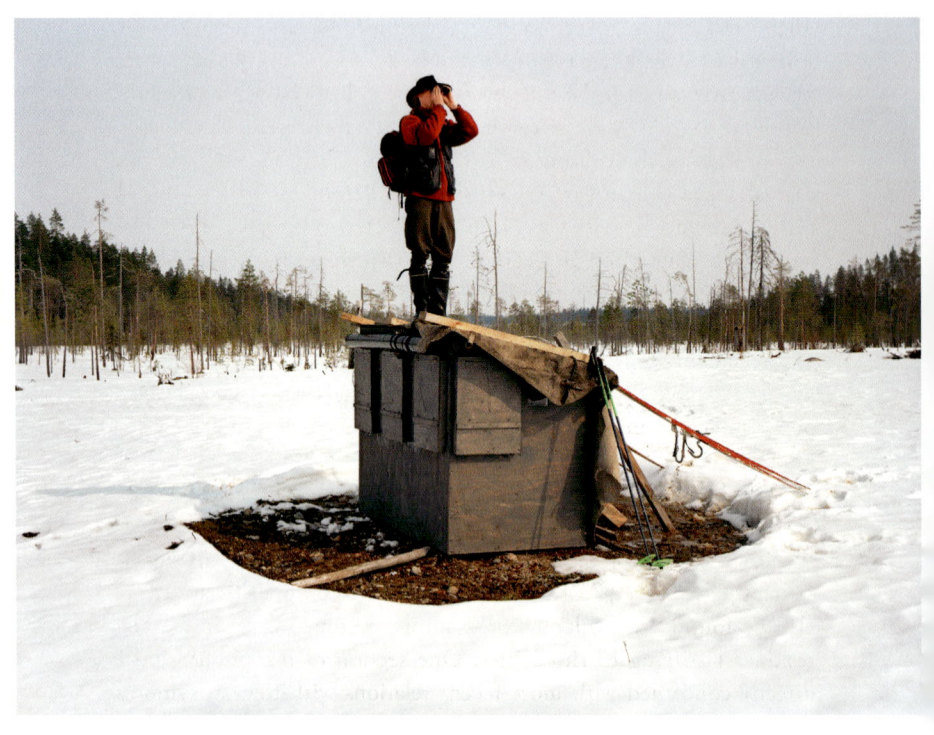

Juha Suonpää, 'The photographer standing on the hut', Kuhmo Finland, 1994, from the series *The Beastly Image of the Beast*.

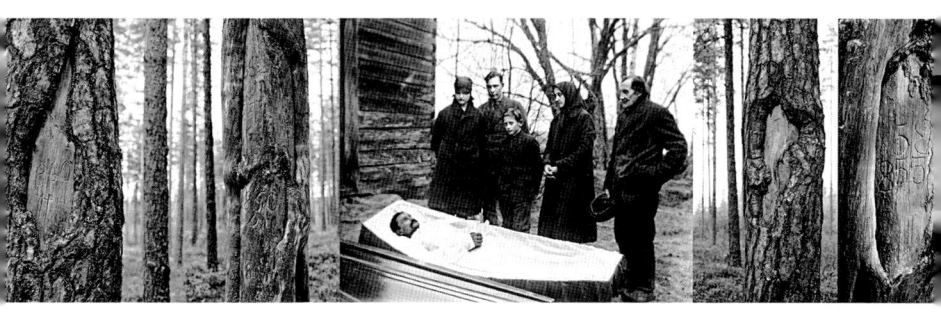

Ritva Kovalainen and Sanni Seppo, 'Memorial trees in Pyhakangas', 1997, from the series *Tree People*.

Their starting point for *Tree People* (2006) was an interest in the spiritual and the shamanistic. The initial English translation of the project title was *The End of the Rainbow*, which has more mystical connotations. As their research developed, their approach became increasingly analytical and political.[24] Most Finns view forest as a crucial space of spiritual replenishment. Before the mid-twentieth century there was relatively little commercial impact on woodland wilderness. But after 50 years of intensive logging, nearly all the natural forests have disappeared. Kovalainen and Seppo are concerned about the implications of the disappearance of forest and change in the woodland landscape for Finnish identity. The project is ongoing, and has involved extensive research into legend and myth as well as oral history and photo archives in forest regions of Estonia as well as Finland.

Sacred groves of trees apparently existed prior to the import of Christianity when they were cut down and replaced by landmarks such as a church or a cross, but their existence remains marked in ancient place names. As Kovalainen and Seppo comment, markers can also be found on the land, for example, a stone circle or charcoal residues testifying to ritual fires. One section of the publication is directly concerned with more recent relations with trees as symbols, as carriers of family history. There are a number of examples of trees planted when land was first cleared or farmed. Such trees have grown, outliving the initial settlers, carrying on through the generations. These yard-trees are seen as spiritual protectors and spaces of contemplation. The several accounts of family relations with their sacrificial tree include the remark that after a baby had been born in the sauna it would be taken to be blessed by the tree before being brought into the family home. Second, trees are described as anticipating or responding to human events – for instance, the belief that when an old farmer dies a branch will fall off the tree. In one account the good-luck tree, which had previously flourished, fell down shortly before the death of the last member of a family. Such accounts are interesting not because of whether or not they are accurate in any causal or inter-related sense but because of what they reveal about attitudes to land. They are also interesting because of their persistence despite Christian campaigns against holy trees – the authors remark that the axe was an important tool for priests (Kovalainen and Seppo, 2006: 134). Trees also act as memorial markers, with commemorative inscriptions carved into the bark, or photographs hung on the tree trunk, often found on the route between the family home and the local cemetery, presumably representing some sort of compromise of Christian and pagan beliefs. Many of these trees have been logged, erasing personal histories as well as changing local landscapes and impacting on traditional affinities.

The overall project consists of exhibition photography, the book, a poetry anthology, an education pack, with a film also in production. Thus various aesthetic strategies are involved. One section of the book comprises a series of long panoramas (up to two metres wide when shown in galleries) portraying rural spaces where woods have been cut down, with individuals isolated within what must previously have been personal Arcadian spaces. As a pictorial form the panorama emphasises the extent of change across the horizon. There are also more tightly framed images of tree houses, and of people sitting amongst the branches, places obviously special to them. The book makes extensive use of quotes from interviews with residents, as well as archive materials, which in exhibitions are replayed via headsets as viewers consider the panoramas of destruction. Overall the project is informative and reflective, inviting us as audience to consider the loss of historical links and lineage. In picturing what remains of forest retreats, along with the desecration effected by logging, the artists in effect both reassert the significance of long-standing environments within Finnish consciousness whilst simultaneously challenging complacency about woodland, nature and the Finnish imaginary through showing evidence which does not 'fit'.

Several other photographers have questioned the national imaginary through projects investigating contemporary change. For example, using a classical black and white idiom, Kapa is one of many photographers who observe legacies of human presence. His depiction of ski-slopes out of season draws attention to marks on the landscape consequent upon leisure entrepreneurship and the black and white idiom refers us backwards in time. The imagery straddles a slightly uneasy space between critique, and romanticisation, especially as the image surface sometimes carries marks of processing and the framing is pictorial. But countryside is changing, as is photography – and technological change itself can come under scrutiny. Ilkha Halso used to enclose aspects of the rural, for example, trees, then photograph the construction. Now his images are re-made in 'digital laboratories'; the woodlands appear as a stage within which landscape emblems are eerily lit. These examples, and many others, indicate that landscape photography is caught up in a complex nexus of discourses and debates. Furthermore, although photographers may critique particular ideas that have become associated with land and landscape, their work nonetheless reflects their own feelings of identification with the region that is their homeland. Projects may, in effect, be an exploration of themselves as much as of the circumstances pictured.

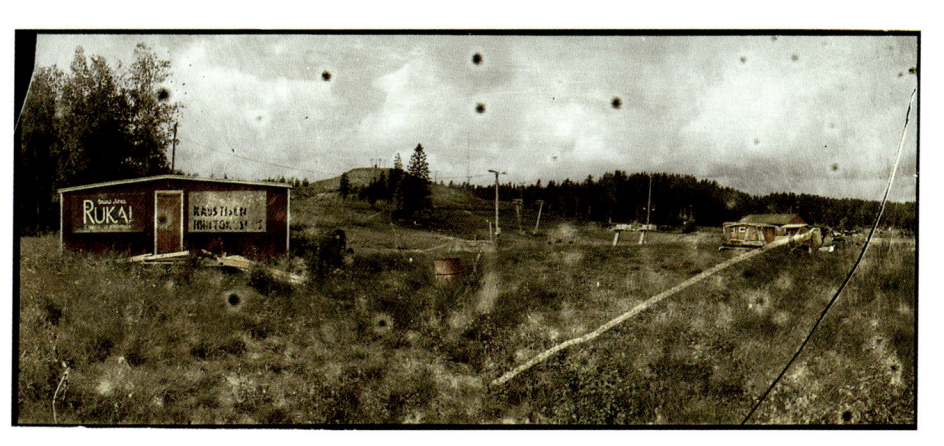

(Martti) Kapa (Kapanen), 'Kaustinen', from the series *After Ski*, 1998–2002.

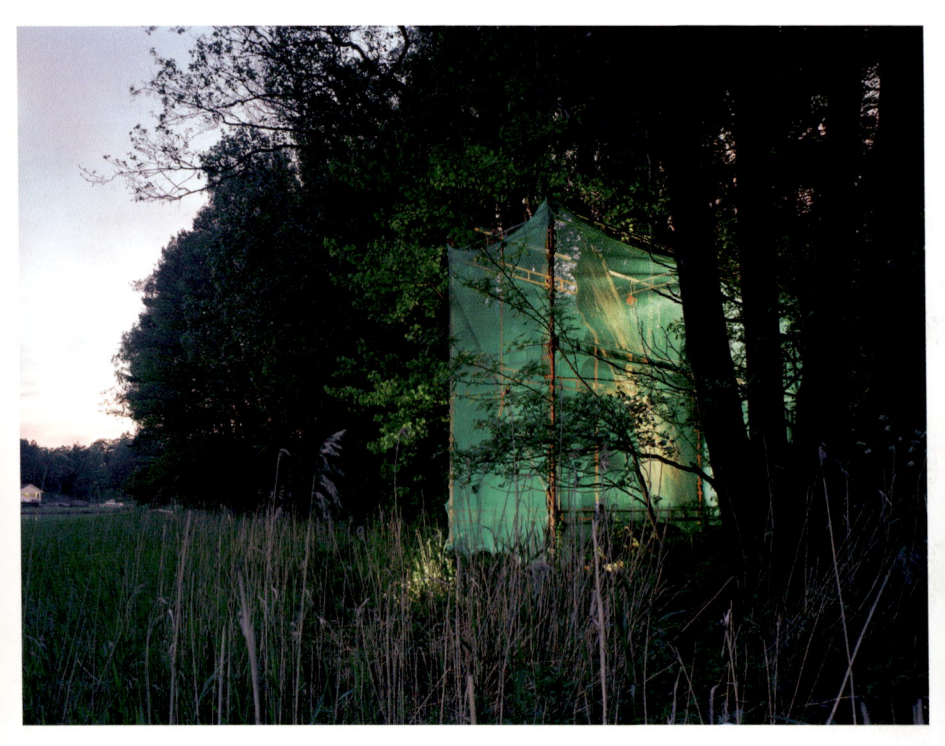

Ilkha Halso, 'Untitled 6', from the series *Restoration*, 2001.

Interior/Exterior, by Marja Pirelä, symbolises the extent to which 'the natural' is incorporated into everyday consciousness. This series uses long exposure and the camera obscura effect of reflected external scenery into internal space; the projection becomes superimposed on the domestic. Her method was to cover the window with black plastic and cut a hole in it into which she fitted a lens. The everyday room is transformed, as was Plato's cave. She then photographed the inhabitant of the room in this intermingled space wherein the reflected exterior transformed the everyday interior (Pirelä, 2002: n.p.). The effect is surreal in that the final picture could not be pre-determined, and the imagery testifies to the unexpected or unconscious amalgams. As the artist remarks: 'The photographs began to take form not only as the charting of the living environment of a human being, but also of the landscapes of the mind:

reflections of thoughts, dreams, fears and reveries' (Pirelä, 2002: n.p.). Just *being* is important. In a separate series, *Like a Breath in Light,* Pirelä's breathing is transcribed into a series of images, made at different times of year, as she sits, pinhole camera on her knee, facing north across the lake, open to the effects of elemental colours of light. Each print is based on long exposure, softened by slight movement as she breathes. The process is contemplative, and the images respond with an intensity of colour (which is unlikely to be achieved through more conventional photographic means). Each is dated, and the series is installed as a vertical block of images, seemingly ethereal as they are behind glass but unframed, supported by (almost invisible) fishing wire (taut from floor

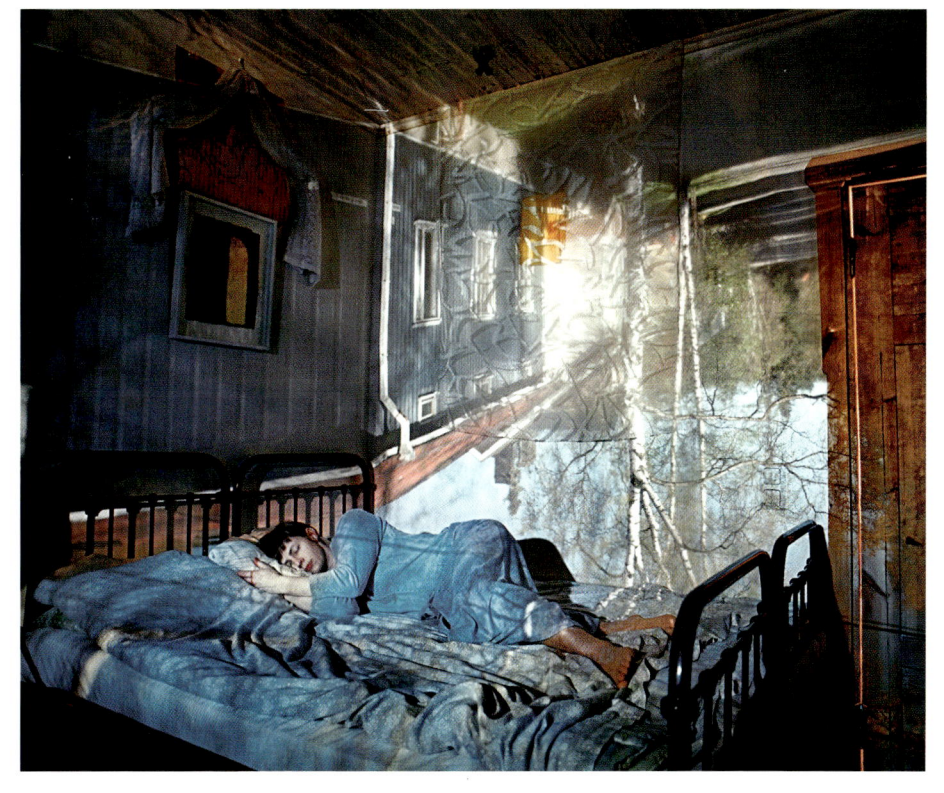

Marja Pirelä, 'Sarianna', Tampere, 1996, from the series *Interior/Exterior*.

to ceiling). We view a group of floating impressions of light and colour, shifting in intensity in response to movement of natural light within a gallery; the effect is sculptural. Symbolic interpretation is very open. One response is to consider our own space and how we occupy, impinge upon, or pass through environments.

This resonates within *Summertime*, by Martti Jämsä, in which he photographs his family at their summer home by a lake, which, he tells us, is little changed since his own childhood (although a sheet iron roof has replaced a shingle one, and electricity has supplanted oil lamps) (Jämsä, 2003: epilogue). In Finland summertime is as much a state of mind as a season; monochrome emphasises timelessness and continuity. As with Pirelä's work, process is inscribed as an evident part of the aesthetic. He uses daylight, polaroid, or a tripod and bellows camera (4" x 5") in portrait format; the latter set-up requires staged poses on the part of the boys pictured – which adds a sense of formality. Scratches and marks indicate direct handling of the exposures by the photographer and his family. They also reflect the chemistry of the particular environment as films are washed in water from the lake and dried in the sauna. Scale further points to the everydayness of being in summertime space; exhibition prints are small, retaining allusion to the family album.[25]

The north is not simply a place for summer. Esko Männikkö, who lives near Oulu (in the northwest, not far south of the Arctic), is known in particular for his 1980s series in which he portrayed rural workers in their everyday environment. The mode is straight documentary, but when the work was first exhibited he used ornate frames, made from reclaimed wood, in order to stress that his subjects, ordinary men from the north, were as deserving of a place in art history as anyone else. His more recent series, *Organized Freedom, final version* focuses on the inter-relation of people and place as abandoned items such as cars gradually rust and rot and the remains of sheds or everyday rubbish gradually become reclaimed within the environment. The images pay forensic attention to detail, but the style is that of the still life tableaux, inviting us to question where occupants went and to speculate why they left. The impact and originality of his mode of working was evident in his installation, *Cocktails 1990–2007*, which amalgamated images from various previous series as an intense block of impressions, pictures abutting one another, each uniquely framed, with no apparent order or uniformity.[26]

Lapland, in the far north of Europe, is home to the Sami people. Historically it has been – and continues to be – a space of investigation

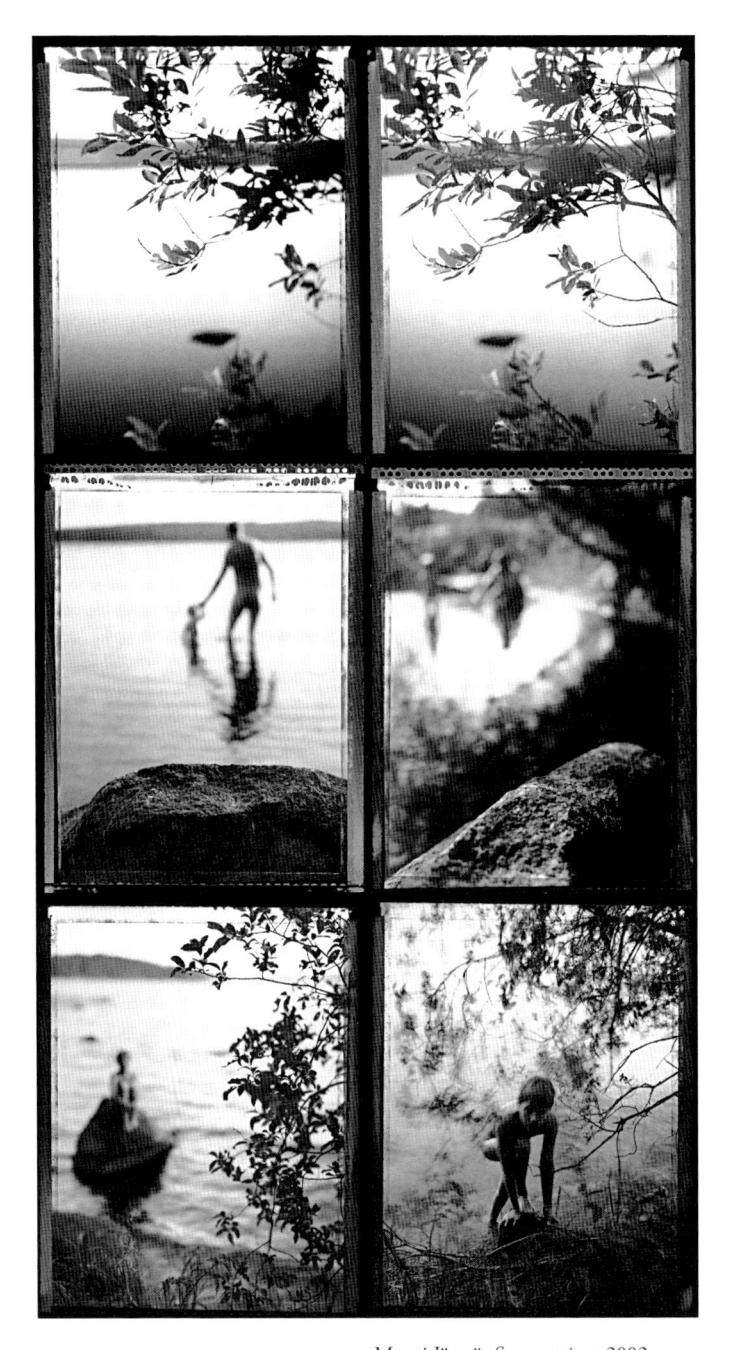

Martti Jämsä, *Summertime*, 2002.

for explorers, ethnographers, geologists. Many Nordic people view Lapland as a marginal space. Marginal to whom? Certainly not to the Sami, the only indigenous people in Western Europe; traditionally nomadic, they travel widely within the area, regardless of national boundaries. People from 'the north' are stereotyped as unsophisticated, perhaps because lifestyle there continues to be based on natural resources. Mining, logging, shipping, fishing and reindeer herding anchor the local economy. This is an area where the sun barely rises in winter, and never sets for about six weeks in June–July. Light reflects brightly on snow and ice, and the horizon seems broad. During the white nights of summer it becomes a tourist destination; camper vans congregate along the coast, especially at the North Cape (in Norway). At other times of year it remains an icy wilderness.

For Jorma Puranen the icy north is a cultural space begging interrogation. In one image 'Travels and Translations' (1998), an Arctic map, centred on the North Pole, is laid over an ice-float, like lace over a dense piece of cloth. From a European or North American point of view the geographical perspective is striking – Greenland appears near the north of Norway; Iceland and Lapland fall at approximately the same latitude. Here the world is imagined not in terms of centres of population, but in terms of geographic relations and geological formations.[27] The map delineates the territory of Puranen's work as an artist. He is one of Finland's best-known contemporary artist-photographers, and is certainly among the most critically incisive.

At one level, Puranen's imagery interrogates ways in which art, including photography, has been involved in the construction of history. His fundamental interest is in imperialism and appropriation, language and ideology, and photography as a tool within the construction of social histories. In exploring colonial attitudes, Puranen is concerned with both visual and spoken languages. This was particularly evident in *Language is a Foreign Country* (1998–2001) in which Sami and Greenlandic words are flown on flags staked in icy landscapes, and in *Curiosus Naturae Spectator* (1995–98). This series integrates Latin phrases and mediaeval script, printed onto white sheets, within Nordic landscapes. Latin references the Renaissance, an era of philosophic debate encompassing astronomy and cartography. The natural world was idealised, but also interrogated. Latin became the language of logic and classification, of poetry and of rationalism. Phrases are taken from maps: for instance, 'Speculum

Orbus Terrae' reflects the desire to view and investigate the whole of the earth. In this image, white lettering on a black sheet is set on white snow, with grey melted snow-water in the middle distance and ominous clouds. In 'Systema Naturae' from the same series, a man-made dam dominates the centre of the picture, enticing the eye towards the vanishing point. What we see is not nature, but human marshalling of natural resources. The visual organisation of the picture is in accordance with the rules of perspective, again a Renaissance ploy, and the clouds have been manipulated to connote a romantic sublime. Indeed, in Puranen's work, austere pictorial rendering of the cold blue-tinged environment often emphasises sublime strangeness. Ice, snow, sky, clouds merge, their shapes reflecting upon one another, uncanny effects of light and movement. Stark silhouettes (maybe a person, pylon or tree) and details of cracks and fissures within icy landscapes command attention as we respond to the chillingly unknowable. But wilderness, as a construct of the geographic imaginary, cannot remain untouched once we have got there. A further title, 'Terra Incognito', provokes us to question what is unknown. Unknown to whom?

In effect, Puranen's subject is European attitudes. His visual language is post-Renaissance (not the shamanistic storytelling and myth of the north). He researches social anthropology, art history, and the historical depiction of Lapland within European visual culture. The above series centrally explore the ideological operations of language (verbal and visual). More generally his work interrogates ways in which art practices, historically, have been implicated rhetorically in the exercise of power. Puranan is primarily interested in stories relating the 'otherness' of the Arctic. His work points to the limited perspectives which, historically, masqueraded as ethnographic 'knowledge' whilst also operating to legitimise the authority of the colonialist through the distancing effect of categorising peoples as ethnically 'other'. He also reminds us that the sublime points to human fears. Explorers may be under-prepared for the rigours of the environment within which they find themselves. The northern sublime is not only awesome in a classic Burkian sense, but also extraordinarily alien for those unaccustomed to such survival challenges. In *Icy Prospects* (2006) images are made by painting wood with black gloss paint, reflecting the landscape on the wood, and photographing the reflection. The method is akin to the use of the Claude mirror (see Chapter 1) so we are reminded to think again about the construction of the landscape pictorial. In *Travels within Canvas* (2002–03) he directly scrutinises the historical role of art in the representation of difference. He photographs details from eighteenth- and nineteenth-century paintings of northern landscapes by foreign travellers. Textures (derived originally from the surface of oil paint) emphasise the strangeness of the settings. Paintings showed explorers, perhaps striding out across the snow, their possessions on sledges behind them, or gathered around the fire in the middle of a tent; local people, wildlife and vegetation are relegated outside. These are the travel stories of explorers, intruders, yet painted as central. Indigenous people are included merely as iconic references, along with reindeer, huskies, and birch trees. The emphasis on otherness reinforces cultural difference, isolating the Sami region from any more collective sense of Nordic identity.

The critical foundation of Puranen's work offers an influential example of the social and philosophic edge that we can expect from contemporary Finnish landscape photography. TaiK, the University for Art and Design, Helsinki, where Puranen taught for many years (and remains an emeritus professor) has become central to the so-called 'Helsinki School' with which most contemporary Finnish photographers are or have been in some way associated.[28] Puranen suggests that the Helsinki School can be characterised as 'an arena for an exchange of ideas' about photography and, more specifically, the identity of Finnish photography which he describes as performative, meditative, as 'trying to trace poetic possibilities found in *silence*' (Persons, 2007: 223). He qualifies this through reference to the inter-play of locality and internationalism in art dialogues, but does acknowledge a quality of reflection and stillness in Finnish work. Arguably this reflects an existential desire for space that at one level is manifest in ideological tensions relating to land.

Elina Brotherus, who is among Finland's best-known younger artist-photographers, studied at TaiK.[29] As elsewhere in Europe and North America, feminist perspectives in the 1980s in Finland induced a focus on the personal and on sexual politics, often expressed through incorporation of domestic craft or aesthetics. (For example, in the 1980s Ulla Jokisalo amalgamated photography and needlework.) Brotherus's early work took her own experience as starting point, as she staged herself and friends – usually naked – within the image. Her video installation, *Baigneurs* (2003), concerns the patterns made by swimmers on the surface of a lake, and includes herself as a lone swimmer, forging a trail into the middle distance. Recent work is more academic; for instance, in 'Sarjasta The New Painting (2000–): Der Wanderer' (2003) she positions herself as viewer looking out over lands which become configured as landscape precisely through the act of framing and looking (see the front cover of this book). We look at her back and at the view beyond. There is clear reference to Casper David Friedrich's 'Wanderer above the Sea of Fog' (1818, oil on canvas). In this famous painting a solitary man on a mountain-peak commands the view and we look with him and respond to the sublimity of the mountain range. The painting is relatively small (94 x 74.8 cm) so this is not a direct bodily experience. In Brotherus's new series the figure is female, and the scale is very slightly larger (80 x 100 cm), with the figure closer, so it seems nearer to actual body-size. More particularly, the context is the Finnish environment which, as I have suggested, for Finns is a space of solace. In what respects, then, might Brotherus's new work provoke reflection on more traditional constructions of landscape through the central positioning of a female figure? The (male) gaze is, by implication, unseated. But, on the other hand, this is Finnish work and, as has been argued, Finnish culture retains a particular sense of oneness with nature. Another image in the same series, 'Sarjasta The New Painting (2000–): Nu Endormi' (2003), depicts a naked woman asleep, one hand behind her head and the other covering her crotch; she is alone and relaxed, not posing as in, for instance, Manet's 'Olympus' or 'Déjeuner sur l'Herbe'. Furthermore, she apparently does not feel threatened within the environment – the discourses attendant on her nakedness are very different from those articulated, for example, in Annika von Hausswolf's half-clothed figures awkwardly positioned on the ground (p. 227). Brotherus's new body of work simultaneously embodies a critique that reflects international feminist debates of the past three decades and reinflects this in terms that are culturally specific. Of course, to comment that the landscape pictorial articulates international and local perspectives is not critically innovative; this has characterised emergence of landscape as a genre historically. Rather I am concerned to reinforce the point that land figures particularly intimately within Finnishness.

But Finland is definitely not isolated internationally. In *My Weather Diary* (ongoing series), Jari Silomäki, also associated with the Helsinki School, points to inter-relations between the global and the local, as place, personal experience, and the distant backdrop of world events con-fuse. He makes a photograph every day, wherever he is, adding some

LAND MATTERS

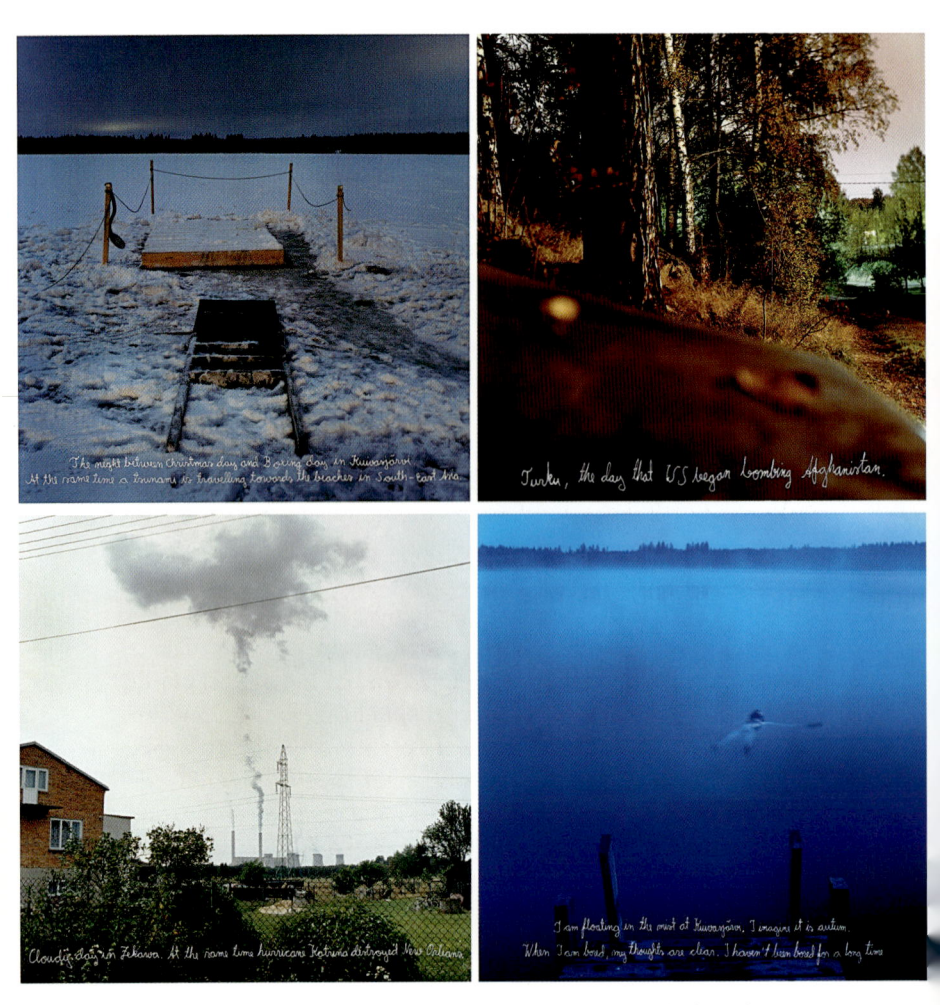

Jari Silomäki, 'Untitled', from the series *My Weather Diary*, 2001–07.

comment on it which relates to that day's experience. The comment may reference the news, or world events, or his own immediate personal situation and experience. Use of his own handwriting emphasises that this is clustered in relation to the personal. That the imagery is to be understood as of global pertinence is reflected in his use of English, rather than Finnish. (This has also allowed this series to be shown internationally – a factor that the artist no doubt took into account.) Depth of colour reflects light intensity and exposure times, sometimes linked to the day's event; for instance, for 'Turku, the day US bombed Afghanistan', he was expecting the news and had his camera set up on a tripod, ready for exposure for the length of the news item. Hence, the purple intensity of the sky. Several are shot in northern Nordic nightlight, reminding us of extraordinary qualities of the landscape during the white nights. From a non-Nordic perspective these are disconcerting as night-time (social) activities take place in sunlight. We are reminded that latitude and climate influence culture.

Likewise, Riitta Päiväläinen's evocative photographs of clothing, standing upright, frozen in the icy landscape, would have been unlikely to have been conceptualised were it not for specific conditions of climate and culture. The clothes are second-hand, bought in markets and junk shops; for the artist it is important that the clothes have a history. For this series she wet the garments, and left them to freeze, before installing the icy figures.[30] The caricatures, eerily devoid of the people who might have once worn the garments, imply human transience and vulnerability. Given current awareness of the dangers of global warming we might also remark the vulnerability of Nordic lands. The imagery – clothing, frozen, or animated in the wind – not only implies human fragility relative to the elements but also evokes the idea that human activity leaves an environmental imprint even though particular people and cultures may themselves have moved on. The implications are serious, although the body language implied in the frozen garments is sometimes wonderfully humorous!

Contemporary Finnish landscape photography reminds us that any binary between city and country is simply outside of Finnish consciousness. Finnish people (regardless of social class and status) retain regional links and the rural remains at the (symbolic) heart of Finnishness. The examples discussed above all variously ask questions about contemporary Finland; a nation that in many respects continues to stress its traditional rural roots yet is also home to the global telecommunications company, Nokia. This is of course not quite as paradoxical as it might at first seem. As Jari Silomäki reminds us in his *Weather Diary*, we are all now somehow simultaneously global and local.

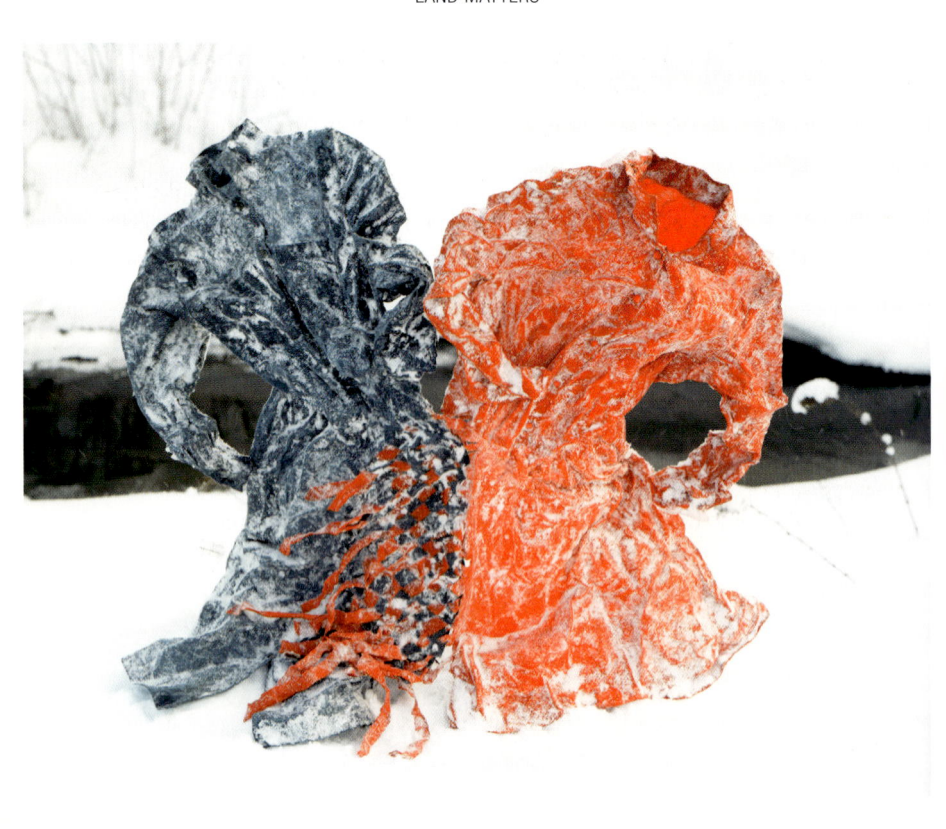

Riitta Päiväläinen, 'Relation', from the series *Vestige – Ice*, 2001.

THEMES, AESTHETIC STRATEGIES, AND NATIONAL IDENTITY

Contemporary Scandinavian work might be expected to rework or challenge the twin legacy of Romanticism and of Nordic Expressionism. Throwing off the yoke of Soviet social realism is a crucial motivation within contemporary work from the Baltic States. Some Norwegian work adopts a deliberately anti-expressionist aesthetic; it is, as it were, 'dead pan' in its approach. By contrast, in Baltic work, an 'aesthetics of defect' has been used to counter the strictures of Soviet socialist realism. This comparison serves to remind us that there is no necessary relation between aesthetic form and radicalism. As Brecht famously remarked, as reality changes, modes of representation must also change.

Struggles over personal and national identity resonate complexly, influenced by representations of place and space within which landscape imagery plays a key part. If creative and critical engagement is central to the role of the artist then, given recent political and cultural shifts, it is hardly surprising to find a number of photographers in Norden and Baltic areas exploring and questioning location and identity. Artistic expression draws upon an archipelago of personal perceptions, philosophic interrogations, and aesthetic conventions. Light is central to the construction of photographs. Dramatic shifts in illumination, from the white nights of summer to stormy winters, lend intense tones, often sharp, sometimes melancholic, as contemporary landscape photography at once both shapes, and questions, perceptions of place and national identity.

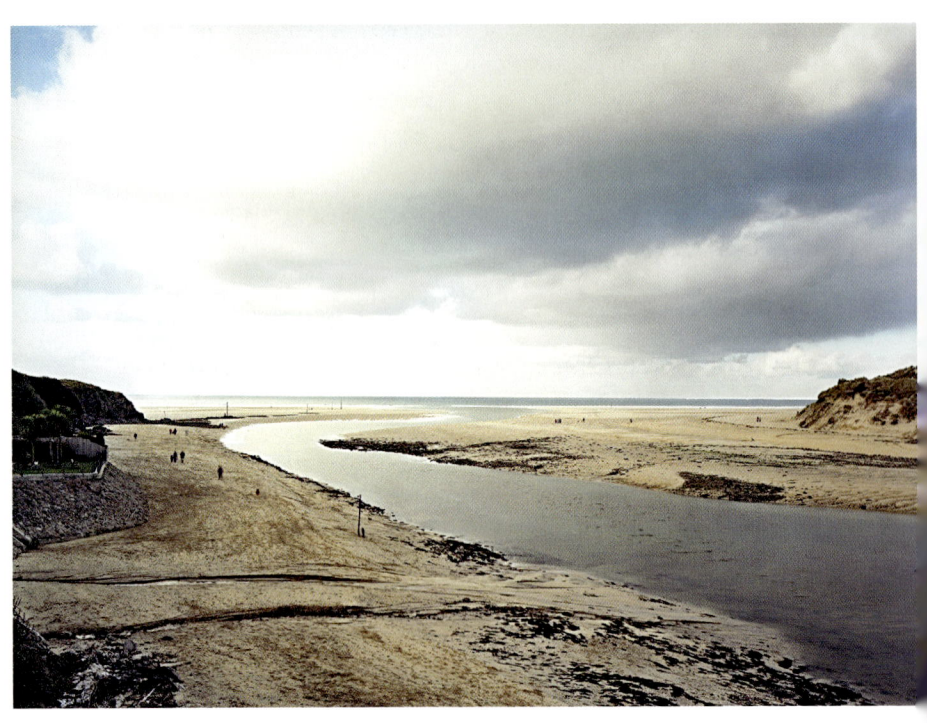

Jem Southam, 'River Hayle January 2000', from the series *Rockfalls, Rivermouths and Ponds*.

6

SENSE OF LOCATION

TOPOGRAPHY, JOURNEY, MEMORY

> Photographs are about memory – or perhaps about the absence of memory, providing pictures to fill voids, illustrating and sometimes falsifying our collective memory.
>
> (Lippard, 1998: 60)

Jem Southam's picture describes a rivermouth at the point where the estuary reaches out towards the sea. It indicates shape and height of the cliffs. Because it is a photograph the image is still, but the slight white foam implies movement of water. We can deduce heights of previous tides from seaweed deposited at the foot of the cliff in the bottom left of the image. The perches on the beach serve no current function, but at high tide will act to indicate the main channel for boats to follow. The cliff to the left has been shored up, which suggests that this is the area which the tides erode, and concrete steps suggest a local access point. Unlike in navigation charts, that which cannot be seen in photographs cannot be summarised; rather they operate allusively. Here, tidal deposits indicate that the water has shifted height, but we do not know the tidal range, currents or depth of water. The stones supporting the cliffs are, of course, natural objects but rearranged functionally and aesthetically – the new cliff-base was surely intended to look close to 'natural'. The channel markers have no obvious function, but we read them semiotically as implying a boating route. In other words, however naturalised, this is a landscape that has been subject to extensive human intervention – the markers are there for our information, whether we are physically present, or viewers of photographs which operate in observational idiom. This picture is, in fact, one of a series which records the same place in 1996 before work was done to support the cliffs, and 2000. The rephotography details changes – the stonewalling replaced an eroding wooden breakwater. People are present, distant figures on the beach. We wonder whether the photographer consciously reflected on their clothing or body language in composing the image, or, indeed, on the patterning and textures of the seaweed.

Photography documents environment and, since its inception, has been used to chart sites and note changes consequent upon human access and habitation. Photography thus has a role within cultural geography, one that is founded in realist principles, in the credibility of the photographic. Photographs tell stories, contributing to the construction of histories related to particular sites. Part of the pleasure of viewing images is the noting of rhetorical devices and strategies deployed by photographers as visual narrators. But our relation to land and the way it is recounted photographically transcends the topographic. Photographs also contribute to perpetuating myths and memories associated with place. Landscape photography complexly articulates 'objectivity' with personal vision. The latter maybe responds to more spiritual dimensions of the experience of environment, in the sense defined by Lippard as 'living the ordinary while sensing the extraordinary' (Lippard, 1998: 61). For example, bluebells in the woods in the spring sunshine, or the regular pulse of the waves against the side of a boat, are mood-enhancing; our sense of being a part of something beyond human culture is brought into play. Photographs can express something of this through form, aesthetics and photographic coding, although in terms of affects, photography cannot replicate actual experiences. But, as I shall suggest, photographs can reference, or substitute, through invoking equivalent memories.

In his well-known, extensive volume on *Landscape and Memory* Simon Schama discusses the significance of particular landscapes through forging links between his biographic experience and broader cultural developments (Schama, 1995). Underpinning this approach is the assumption – one that I share – that landscapes, real and imagined, contribute to the formation of our sense of identity, subjectively and collectively. But there are questions as to whether this can be considered universal in terms of fundamental human emotions, and, if so, how these inter-relate with or become reinflected through specific cultural formations. It does not follow from the fact that we all respond to natural phenomena that, for instance, the movement of tides, or the longevity of trees, has a universally shared symbolic meaning. What may be more general is a sense of continuity derived from patterns, for example, of seasonal change, that characterise nature. Schama reminds us that Jung viewed the universality of myths relating to nature as serving to deal with fears and desires, that is, as directly related to 'human nature'. Schama himself resists such generalisations; indeed, the ensuing thesis of his book points to particularities of cultural histories. But he does concede that 'it is clear that inherited landscape myths and memories share two common characteristics: their surprising endurance through the centuries and their power to shape institutions that we still live with' (Schama, 1995: 15). In what ways, then, are contemporary practitioners engaging such questions, implicitly or explicitly, and how might existential issues be reinflected in consequence?

Photography is often discussed in terms of time, most particularly through the notion that photographs 'freeze' a moment in time, referencing something past. Indeed, photographs indicate how particular places or phenomena appeared at specific moments. In his essay 'Fire and Ice' Peter Wollen contrasted photographs and films ('movies') suggesting that, however much they reference particular 'instants', photographs have a complex relation to time: 'is the signified of a photographic image to be seen as a state, a process or an event?' (Wollen, 1989: n.p.). He suggests that notions of time inevitably relate to narrative – or, we might deduce, history – and that photographs, although still, correspond to and operate as narrative elements. Photographs endure; in principle the image is static (print degradation notwithstanding). But time moves on. Things change. We change. Our response to that which is referenced is fluid, mediated by shifting perceptions and circumstances. If photographs provoke narrative constructions, the narratives that might be constructed may shift and change. Applied to our experience of land and environment, we might ask whether a picture of a specific seascape, or expanse of land, or canyon, provokes us to recall how it appeared when we last visited and experienced the place, or whether it over-rides recollection. To what extent, and in what respects, does the literal descriptiveness of the image which we are contemplating overlay personal memory. For example, how do images of, say, dust storms or 'twisters' in the North American prairies inter-relate with personal experiences of such places? How is our interpretation mediated via degrees of familiarity – there is a distinction between visiting the Midwest, perhaps in calm times, and living in the region through variations in weather, or indeed, struggling to make a living agriculturally from land crops disrupted by storms. Such questions provoke reflection on processes of meaning-production and interpretation.

This chapter is concerned with the complex inter-relation of image and memory. It draws together and reflects upon bodies of work that take very different approaches both in relation to land and in modes of picturing. There is a sort of fluid seesaw with topographic (or observational) photography at one end and composited imagery that explicitly draws on personal experience at the other. The seesaw simile is intended to remind us that imagery that purports to be grounded in direct observation nonetheless reflects the interests and curiosities of the photographer, whose feet are, as it were, slightly off the ground. Conversely, montages relating directly to individual memory nevertheless retain some reference to external scenes or objects. The chapter thus encompasses site and space, the topographic, journeys, history and memory. Questions already touched upon are variously expanded. First, contemporary topographic practices are investigated, as previously, through selected examples. It is suggested that the credibility of photography persists and that, despite the possibilities of digital manipulation, topographic vision retains authority and critical edge. It is argued that credibility rests not on photo-technologies (chemical or digital), nor on the expressive abilities of photographers as artists, but on the integrity of photographers as artist-researchers. As viewers we are reassured by systematic approaches to image making.

Discussion of method and the authority of the topographic is followed by consideration of more haptic engagements with the environment. Here I focus in particular upon the work of British artists, Hamish Fulton and Richard Long. I want to suggest a distinction between their work and that of those working in a documentary idiom whose journeys take an ostensibly more detached view of environment. Finally, the chapter considers image and memory, with a twin focus, on the one hand, on processes of looking and interpretation and, on the other hand, on ways in which artists actively utilise their understanding of spectator identification in the construction of imagery. Thus, the chapter moves from critical evaluation of practices whose touchstone is environmental observation through to more overtly personal responses to land and the comprehension of ways in which aesthetic conventions can be used in the articulation of such responses. If the topographic is about directness of vision, about what is seen, and the sense that can be made of phenomena, then this compass runs from more literal modes of visual storytelling to more explicitly personal envisioning.

LANDSCAPE AND TOPOGRAPHIES

The term 'landscape' is widely used. In some fields – cultural geography, for instance – it has been suggested that it has become too imprecise to be of value (Cresswell, 2003). There *are* variations in its use in the visual arts, but we cannot ignore the influence of landscape painting as a genre, which means that we cannot avoid the term. Topography might be viewed as a sub-set within landscape practices (that pre-dates photography). The *Oxford English Dictionary* defines topography as 'detailed description, delineation, or representation on a map of the features of a place' or 'the surface features of a place or region collectively'.[1] Thus the mapping of land use, including buildings, boundaries and other social phenomena, is the primary purpose of topography. The emphasis on 'surface features … *collectively*' is significant as it implies an overview. Photography is particularly suited to detailing that which can be observed. The camera is indiscriminate; although, of course, the photographer selects what is to be within the frame. But, as Walter Benjamin remarked, the camera acts as an 'optical unconscious' recording that which the photographer may not have consciously noted (Benjamin, 1931).

As is well known, in the nineteenth century photography was greeted as the visual medium most able to re-present phenomena in accurate detail. That governments, the military and commercial organisations commissioned photographers to chart the land testifies to belief in the fidelity of the photograph. Photographers, through accepting such commissions, implicitly concurred with and therefore reinforced ontological notions of the accuracy of the image. Photography was a product of modern scientific and technological development, and became a tool in the service of modern aspirations; it played an extensive role within the sciences and social sciences, particularly anthropology, sociology and geography. These fields all have histories founded in the empirical – exploration, fieldwork, case studies – and are concerned with description and analysis. As Denis Cosgrove has commented,

> If geography is a discipline that examines relations between modes of human occupance and the natural and constructed spaces that humans appropriate and construct, then landscape serves to focus attention on the visual and visible aspects of those relations.
>
> (Cosgrove, 2003: 249)

Photography fitted itself as an instrument of topographic documentation, contributing to travelogues, visual ethnography and geographic surveys. For instance, photographers, such as Carleton Watkins, Eadweard Muybridge and Timothy O'Sullivan were commissioned to chart the American West and to document socio-geographic change wrought by railroads, mining stations, and other nineteenth-century entrepreneurial developments. As already noted, their work was later singled out by the art museum (see Chapters 1 and 3). But it was originally made in a commercial context which included making stereos or postcards for sale by (family) firms involved in the production and marketing of 'views' as well as work for government surveys or private companies such as the railroads. As noted (Chapter 3) historical work is now conserved and exhibited both in the art museum and in national or regional collections. In the former it is framed in terms of the perceptions of the photographer as artist, in the latter more in terms of social history within which old photographs become called upon as illustration or evidence, all too often without interrogation of the images themselves as selective constructs.

It was assumed that photographic seeing was unmediated, that photographers responded directly to what was observed with limited latitude for interpretation. In an era of mechanisation technical excellence was welcomed as central to the *craft* of photography. But as a technological craft photography implicated aesthetic sensibilities; hence the continuing influence of notions of composition and beauty previously associated with and explored through landscape painting. It also implicates the ability to pre-visualise imagery, to be able to anticipate the pictorial *affects* of the effects both of photographic coding (focus, depth of field, tonal contrast) and of the movement of light at particular times of day or year. *Pre-visualisation* perhaps alerts us to subjective elements. However much photographers – along with their audience – saw themselves as setting out to record that which was found, selection implicates subjective interests and aesthetic pre-dispositions. Despite this, a notion of unmediated representation became a part of the ideological currency of the image, underpinning its documentary authority.

Two developments in topographic photography in the second half of the twentieth century are particularly well known and exert a continuing influence on contemporary practice. The *New Topographics* exhibition at George Eastman House, Rochester (USA) in 1975 brought work by German photographers Bernd and Hilla Becher together with a group of then-youngish American photographers including Lewis Baltz, Robert

Adams and Steven Shore.[2] The 1975 exhibition was significant for re-emphasising observational characteristics of photography at a time when formalism and abstract expressionism had impacted on the agenda in North America and elsewhere. These photographers adopted an observational mode that, as a legacy, forms a detailed record of environmental development and change in the USA post-Second World War. Steven Shore's work is in colour, forming something of a precursor of more contemporary modes, although the prints are small in keeping with photographic conventions of the era; the other series are all monochrome in line with the rhetoric of documentary authenticity of the time. In his introductory essay for the original catalogue, William Jenkins commented that the work is all about that which is portrayed, foregrounding the descriptive properties of photography. He commented that 'rather than the picture having been created by the frame, there is a sense of the frame having been laid on an existing scene without interpreting it very much' (Jenkins in Adams et al., 1975: 5). The style appears detached and objective, although the formalist characteristics of black and white renderings of environmental scenes nonetheless can seem mannerist given the extent to which we have now been exposed to equivalent work in colour.

Introducing work by Adams, Baltz and Joe Deal for a later exhibition, likewise titled *New Topographics* (Arnolfini, Bristol, UK, 1981), Paul Highnam was in a position to reference critical response to the 1975 show, which had apparently attracted 'allegations of *coolness, distance, banality* and even *anti-photography*' (Adams et al., 1981: 3). He remarked that a new sensibility was perceived both in the apparent lack of emotional engagement with land and environment – by contrast with predecessors such as Ansel Adams or Edward Weston – and also in the pictures encompassing human construction within the traditional landscape. He suggested that the new style and new subject matter made it difficult for audiences at the time to locate the work in relation to traditional landscape themes and aesthetics.[3] The work stood outside of – and implicitly challenged – both the focus on beauty in nature typical of more traditional landscape work and the concern with people in relation to work and living conditions associated with social documentary.

Jenkins also referenced a suggestion by Lewis Baltz that photographic veracity rests in imagery persuading us of its documentary authenticity, this despite (necessarily) selective representation of their subject. Baltz repeatedly focused on city margins, domestic or industrial suburbs (sub-divisions) that encroach upon the rural. For *Park City* (1980) he photographed interiors under construction, sometimes with glimpses of open land beyond; other series, such as *The New Industrial Parks Near Irvine, California* (1975) record the exterior walls and spaces of work sites; these images are usually people-less, although we know there must be employees inside. Of the photographers included in the exhibition Baltz in particular might be associated with dispassionate observation; yet he did not deny the agency of the photographer and reaffirmed the rhetorical nature of photographs as documents (Adams et al., 1975: 6). The new topographic photographers demonstrated something about the contemporary environment; verisimilitude, photographic coding and aesthetics were important because this facilitated such description. For Baltz, therefore, however dispassionate the mode of picturing, imagery does more than simply show the world through photographs; courtesy of selections made by the photographer, they also suggest something about it, albeit not judgmentally. This led Jenkins, in the George Eastman House catalogue, to ponder matters of style; this, for him, is the 'problem' central to the exhibition. The photographers whom he interviewed for his essay variously asserted the importance to them of repetition, both of subject matter and of photographic idiom, thereby denying notions of uniqueness of phenomena or, indeed, of imagery. As Robert Adams remarked, 'What I hope to document, though not at the expense of surface detail, is the Form that underlies this apparent chaos' (of the world of phenomena) (Adams et al., 1981: 7). For Jenkins there is a key distinction between anthropological interest and analysis, and judgement or opinion which, he asserts, the new topographic photographers avoid. This is, of course, a fine line; Adam's emphasis on beauty in the everyday might well be characterised as 'opinion'.

The work of the Bechers who had returned to European pre-war aesthetics and principles of 'new objectivity' influenced the Rochester exhibition. Still lives and banal objects had been central to *Neue Sachlichkeit*, or new objectivity, wherein composition, tonal contrast and angle of vision cast the everyday in new perspective. Working together from 1959 onwards, the Bechers became known for typologies, which they described as 'families' of objects or motifs.[4] Much of their work concerns industrial edifices whose function is to extract from the ground. In her extensive discussion of their work, Susanne Lange comments that criteria for their interest in phenomena included functional aspects of the object and architectural shape, but that they were also interested in the photograph in itself (Lange, 2007). The

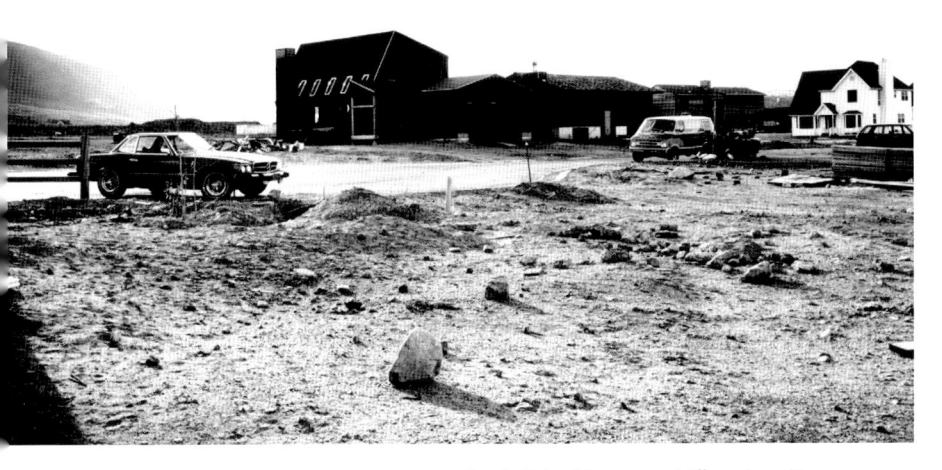

Lewis Baltz, 'Prospector Village, Lot 65, Looking Northwest', Salt Lake City, 1978–79.

composition of the typological groups takes aesthetics into account. Each image is conceptually similar: there is a uniformity of distance, framing and depth of field, shadows are minimised, and little attention is drawn to environment. The way images were grouped simultaneously facilitated comparison *between* objects of similar type and identification of *typical* characteristics, for example, of water towers, or of half-timbered houses. The Bechers in effect classified and transformed mechanical edifices and buildings into architectural curiosities.

Systems and schemes of work, along with formal precision and concern to link one image or object to the next taxonomically, are perhaps their main legacy. The apparent coherence of their work, along with the ability of the imagery to arrest attention, emerges from this inter-relation of topographic observation and photographic coding. The style foregrounds literal detail, rather than comment or critique. Noting

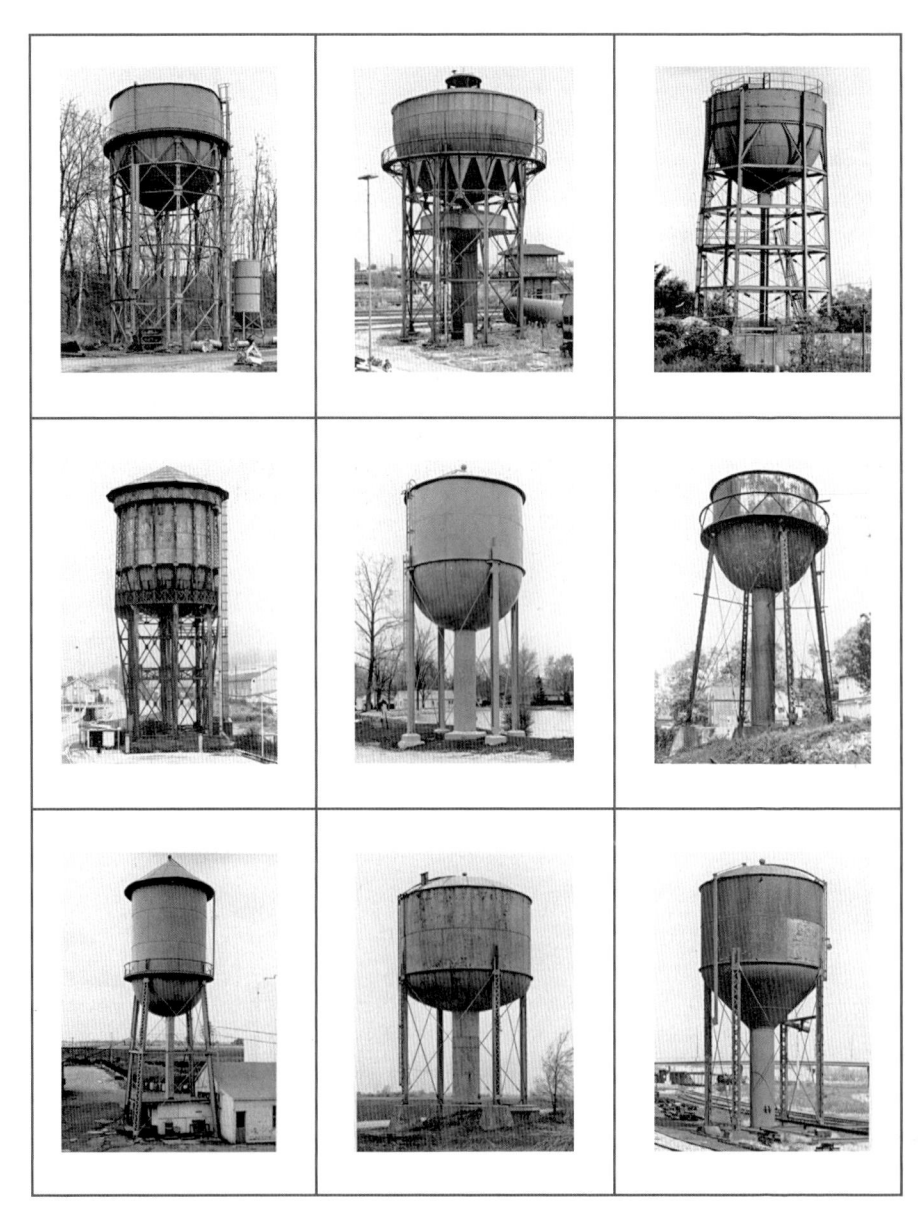

Hilla and Bernd Becher, 'Water Towers', 1980.

its basis in reportage, in the 1930s Walter Benjamin had argued that, by contrast with photomontage, new objectivity was ineffective as a mode of political intervention since, he asserted, photographic aesthetics and technique transfigured objects and scenarios, however ugly or sordid, making what he termed, 'human misery' beautiful (Benjamin, 1977: 95). Arguably, in the work of the Bechers, style transforms subject matter, rendering industrial and other edifices in terms of geometry rather than function and social implications. The work of the Bechers, and of the American new topographers, would certainly fall foul of Bertholt Brecht's stricture, cited by Walter Benjamin, that a photograph of the outside of a factory tells nothing of the socio-political relations that obtain within it (Benjamin, 1931). This does not undermine the reportage authority of the 'straight' photograph; rather it points to the critical limitations of the image in itself. Lange notes that exhibition and publication planning was concurrent with the compilation of their typologies or 'work groups', which first came to international attention through exhibition at the *Documenta* festival, Kassel, in 1972. Initially they presented their observations in blocks mounted together on boards, with individual images up to about 60 x 50 cm (24" x 20") and some images printed larger and hung singly, in effect becoming establishing shots. Later, images were individually framed, then assembled as groups.[5] Authority emanates from precision of content, systematic work method, and from the direct comparisons set up within each grouping.

TOPOGRAPHIC MODES NOW

Questions of method and context can be explored through evaluation of the approaches to work adopted by contemporary practitioners. For instance, two English photographers made work using maps as the basis for selecting observation points.[6] In *Island* (1997) Kate Mellor used Ordnance Survey Landranger maps to plan a trip round Britain exploring the coast as a boundary and an area of human activity.[7] Photographs looking out from shore were made every 50 kilometres, using a Widelux panoramic camera originally designed for survey work. Gazing out to sea is a perennial theme for artists, and writers' accounts of coastal travels are legion. Mellor's approach is distinctive for at least three reasons. First, the book includes the map, showing the grid used

TQ300041 — Brighton

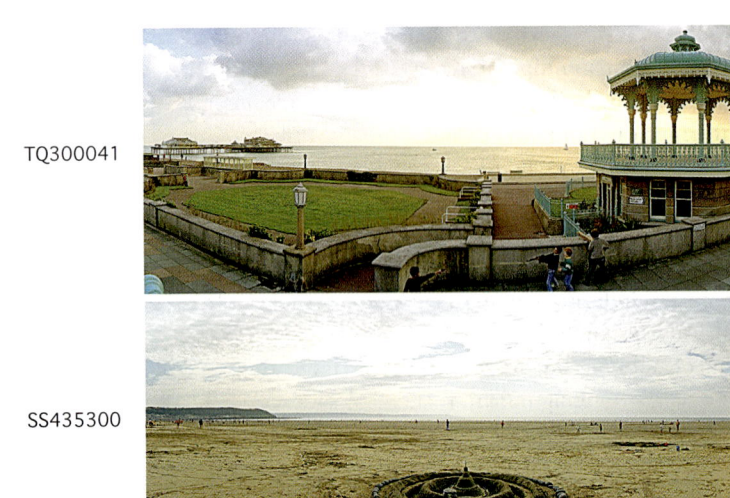

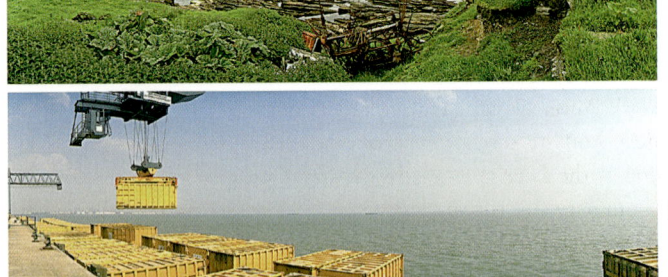

SS435300 — Westward Ho!

ND300748 — Mey

TQ698803 — Mucking Flats

Kate Mellor, from the series *Island: Sea Front*, 1989–94.

by her; the scheme is made evident. It is, of course, a ruse; there is no conceptual reason for photographing every 50 kilometres. Besides, cartography is not neutral; it involves the power to define, interpret and encode information (and, as a discipline, implicates issues of territoriality).[8] But the adoption of such a scheme provided a working method and was intended to parallel and thereby metaphorically challenge the authority of land charting systems, ownership and control. Second, the time involved in this project, which took three and a half years to complete, indicates commitment and persistence. Third, her photographs always include the shoreline, thereby avoiding the romanticism of 'looking out to sea' as well as indicating aspects of cultural activity, and offering botanical and geological detail. Much of the interest lies in human response to the maritime and ways in which different regional histories are inscribed at the water's edge. This was not the starting point for the project so much as something that emerged through the process of making. The publication proceeds clockwise round the map, not from where she lives (Yorkshire) but from south of London, that is, from a point near to the English capital, in effect acknowledging its cultural and economic centrality. We are taken on a journey through which regional differences in the lie of the land and our use of it are revealed. Aesthetic and technical considerations, as well as image content, must have influenced the precise viewing position from which each image was made. The authority of the series emanates in part from the crisp documentary idiom, but more particularly from evidence of system.

Mark Power likewise employs documentary rhetoric and systematic models. For the series, *A System of Edges* (2005), he took the 2003 edition of the *London A–Z* street map as a framework for exploring the city boundary and the space beyond. He went to the outer edge of each of the 56 pages and photographed a place just beyond the edge, paying some attention to photographic content and composition. The photographs show buses at the end of the line, new housing estates, and industrial legacies. He looks outwards, his back towards the urban centre. Often there is little sense that this location is peripheral, which leads us to wonder why this was determined as boundary. (The *A–Z* has been revised regularly since the first edition in 1936. Places once beyond the boundary are now incorporated.) As with Mellor's work, in the first exhibition the scheme was made evident through including a map, with photo-locations (although as the project was further refined the map was omitted). The photographs were in geographic order; the viewer

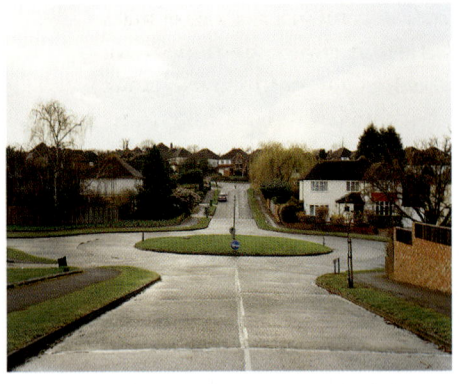

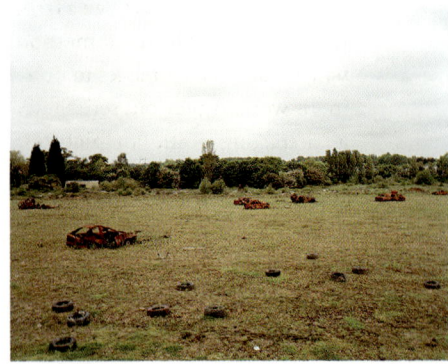

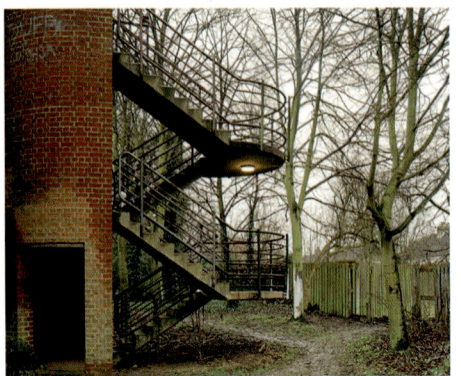

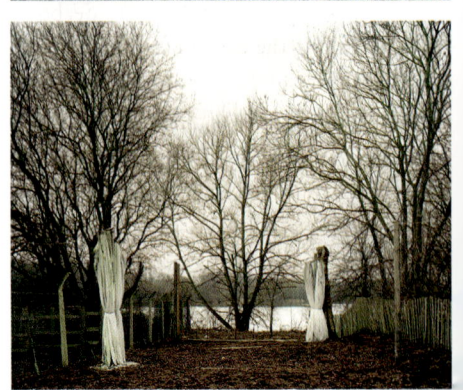

Mark Power, four pictures from *26 Different Endings*, 2003–05.

A: 148 South.

N: 40 West.

K: 13 North.

Z: 22 West.

experienced a (virtual) orbital journey. Relatively flat print tones enhance a feeling of banality. The subsequent publication was edited down and re-titled as *26 Different Endings* (referencing the 26 letters of the alphabet) (Power, 2007). The 'endings' are, of course, edges as defined from a metropolitan perspective. Power remarked that, although he had a structure, it was only once photography was completed that he realised that the project was about social identity, about inclusion/exclusion and the significance of being in – or beyond – London.[9] He added that he remembers as a child regretting not being able to claim to have been born in London; he is from Harpenden, Hertfordshire, a couple of miles too far north! However methodical, there is always some respect in which our research relates to ourselves. Indeed, the margins often feature in his work. A previous series took his fascination with shipping forecasts as a starting point for pictures made at coastal points from which regional weather forecasts take their names. Captions reinforce this, simply noting location and time of year.

Rephotography is likewise systematic, in this case, drawing on previous (often historical) photographs. A site is revisited after a period of time, in effect, recording cultural and geographic change. There are many examples of research using rephotographic methodologies. For example, in 1997 Mike Seaborne led a project documenting change along the edge of the Thames, based on a panorama made for the Port of London authority in 1937.[10] In 2001, Jem Southam rephotographed the Bristol Docks duplicating his own photographs from the late 1970s and early 1980s. Southam revisits sites regularly over a period of time up to five years, documenting the same place at different times of day and year (Southam, 2005). Through revisiting he develops an intimate familiarity with the characteristics of particular locations and with seasonal alterations. Care, detail and repetition lend authority to the work. A series of detailed observations of change as the cliffs crumble at Sidmouth on the southeast Devon coast involved regular visits over a period of 18 months (December 1995–May 1997). He comes to know a location very well, respects it and responds to it. Working is for him a way of being simultaneously an observer and a part of our environment; it also offers contemplative space. This particular sequence was first shown in *Speed*, a large group show at the Whitechapel Art Gallery, London in 1998. By contrast with much of the work included in that exhibition, it reminded us that speed is not necessarily fast. Of course, this is a matter of cultural perception. Human sense of time and geological time are somewhat different; in terms of geological time the rate at which the rockface is disintegrating, being absorbed by the sea, is probably quite alarming! The scale to which his pictures are printed contributes to our response – for instance, expansive views at rivermouths out towards the sea contrast with the smaller-scale that lends a sense of intimacy to, for example, pictures of a pond in the woods. Botanical and geological detail is revealed, as are effects of season, light and weather. He is not interested in the sharp light of summer nor in the poetics of shadow play; although what is pictured may itself seem dramatic, his landscape stories are not dramatised. Rather, the grouping of images invites us to examine minute environmental detail. Picture titles usually simply log location and date, sometimes with a brief reference to the geological. If places are sites of multiple and diverse histories then Southam, as storyteller, offers perspectives on change in particular locations.

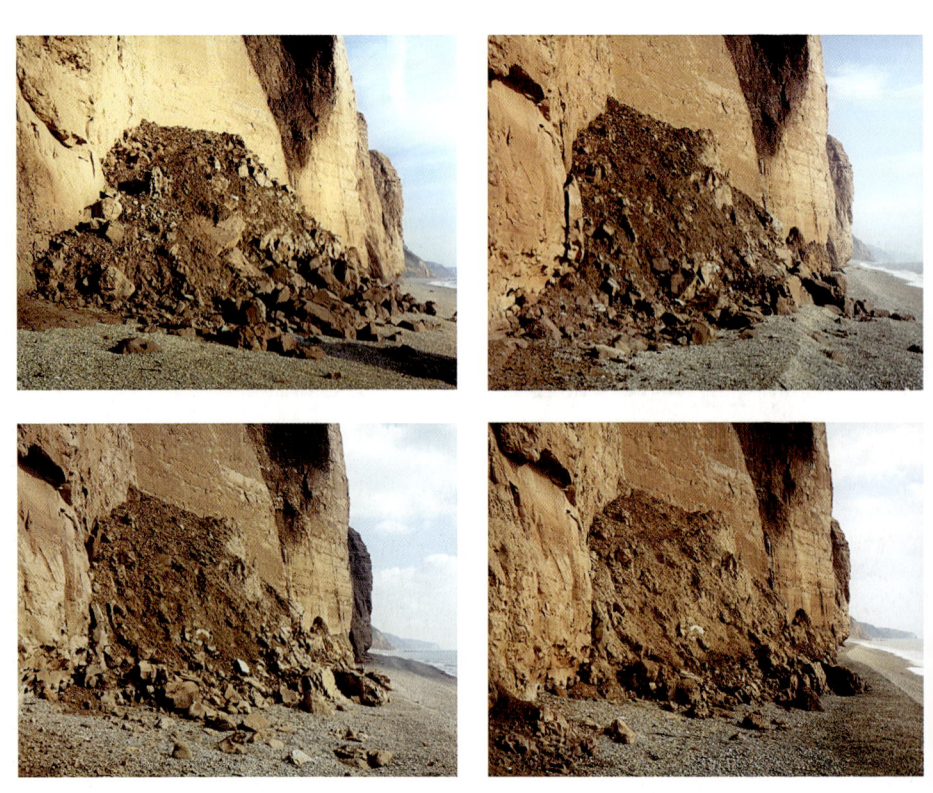

Jem Southam, 'Red Mudstone, Sidmouth', 1995–97, from the series *Rockfalls, Rivermouths and Ponds*.

Ingrid Pollard similarly makes repeated visits to particular regions and sites; her fieldwork includes interviewing people and shadowing them at work, as well as researching social history, botanics and geologies. Her methodical approach to research is typical of topographic modes, but the form of installation offers interpretative latitude. For instance, in 1994 she was resident artist at Lee Valley Park, which is a public space extending 23 miles from Bow, in urban East London, northwards to Hertfordshire. Soil samples were mounted within the frames alongside photographic panoramas; also portraits of park rangers, their sites of work and the tools they used. The exhibition, *Hidden Histories, Heritage Stories*, additionally included found objects in display cases, and a fictional account of an eighteenth-century Black worker based at the mill that was actually in the park, and later became a gin distillery. The juxtaposition of black and white photographs with

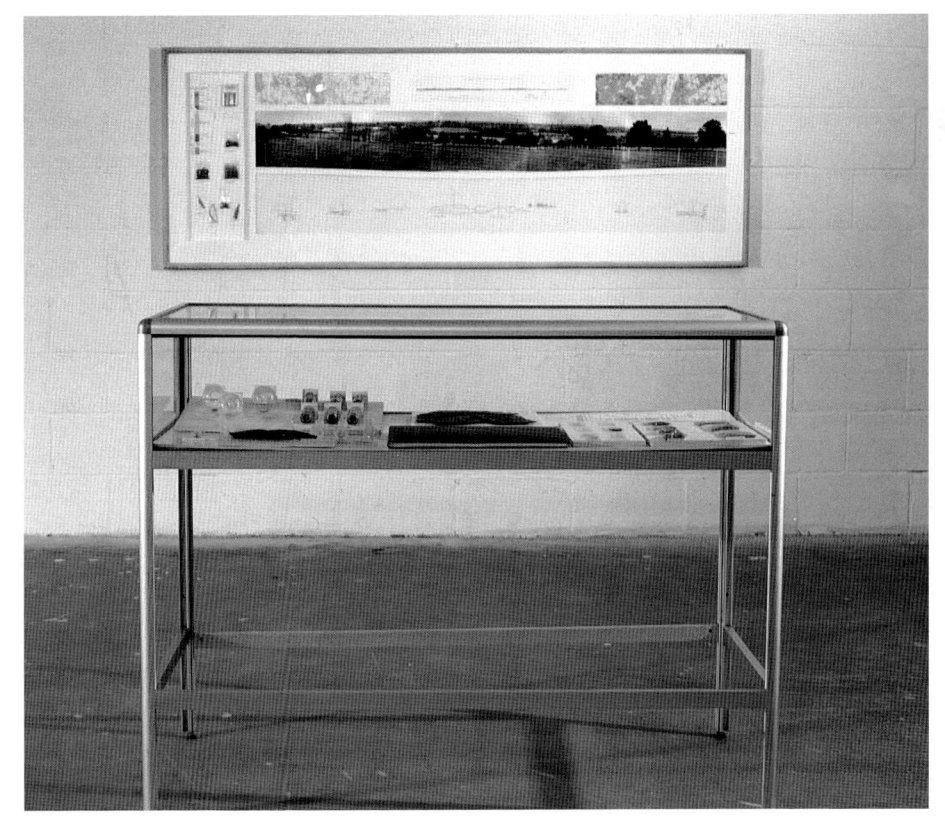

Ingrid Pollard, from *Hidden Histories, Heritage Stories*, 1994.

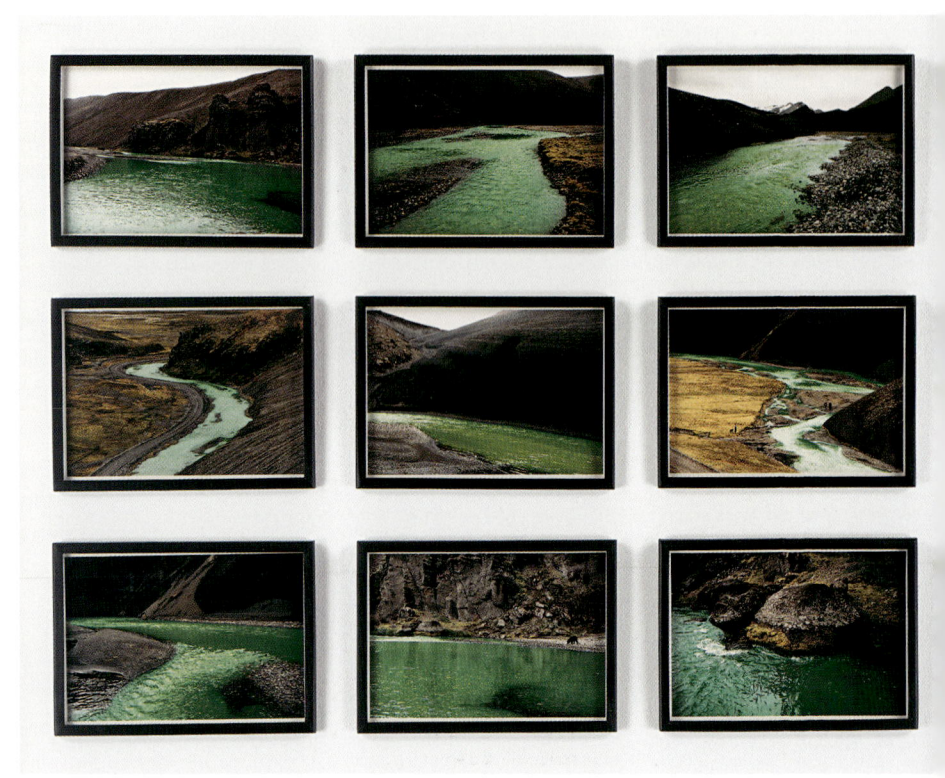

samples and stories indicates the diversity of sources and findings; it also reflects her view of place as site of competing stories, experiences and perspectives. The exhibition was in the foyer of the park visitor centre, that is, in the context referenced, rather than in a gallery detached from the site explored. This was intended to encourage local audiences to reflect upon their environment.[11] During a residency on the Farne Islands, off the coast of Northumberland. she used a similar approach: interviews, visual observation, geological and botanical exploration, the latter including visual notation of the (chemical) effects of soil that she investigated by burying film, in effect exposing it below the surface. Again, results were first shown locally (Pollard, 2005). Whilst her approach as a researcher is methodical, her findings are not presented as conventional 'straight' photographs. Variation of photo-method invites the viewer to think differently about sites pictured, and there is always something tactile about the work, whether rocks and stones displayed or abstract imagery derived from cameraless (contact) methods of film exposure. As a photo-researcher, a combination of system, fieldwork and intuition underpins her approach.

Danish artist Olafur Eliasson is known for kinetic light sculptures and ambitious light installations (including *The Weather Project* – the 'sun' – at Tate Modern, 2004).[12] He also makes photographic series, like Southam, and, indeed, the Bechers, using repetition to detail change or difference. Gallery installation blocks together separately framed images. One series shows fronts of buildings in Reykjavik (Iceland); imagery shifts from landscape format on the left of a block of pictures to portrait format on the right. Our attention is drawn not only to individual facades depicted, but also to geometric difference as the picture frame echoes the shape of each edifice. A

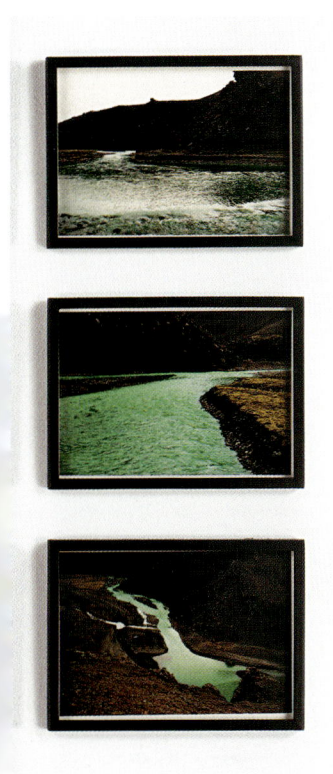

Olafur Eliasson, *The Green River Series*, 1998. 12 C-prints, each 21 x 30.5 cm; series: 84 x 146 cm.

set of horizon panoramas, also from Iceland, is unusual in integrating black and white and muted colour images; the subtlety of change means minor differences come to seem highly significant. Likewise, intensity of colour becomes a key element in the vocabulary of his series on the green river. The groups have clearly been meticulously researched and planned, not only in terms of sites, season and source materials, but also in terms of the grammar of gallery presentation.

ON THE AUTHORITY OF THE TOPOGRAPHIC

In reconsidering the authority of topographic photography it is useful to revisit notions of authorship. As is well known, Roland Barthes argued for 'The Death of the Author'.[13] He was not suggesting that writers and artists don't exist. The phrase is rhetorical; he wanted to point to the place of writers (or photographers) within systems of discourse, and to disavow modernist notions of originality premised on linking genesis and genius. In resonant tones, he stated:

> We know now that a text is not a line of words releasing a single 'theological' meaning (the 'message' of the Author-God) but a multi-dimensional space in which a variety of writings, none of them original, blend and clash. The text is a tissue of quotations drawn from the innumerable centres of culture.
>
> (Barthes, 1977: 146)

The notion of text as a 'tissue of quotations' is useful as it reminds us to consider the fluidity of cultural legacies and remnants as they become incorporated and reinflected in particular conjunctions and contexts. He adds that it follows that everything needs to be *disentangled*, rather than *deciphered* and, in a rousing final flourish, declares that 'the birth of the reader must be at the cost of the death of the Author' (ibid.: 148). But Barthes does not propose alternative ways of taking into account the fact that someone writes the words and frames the image, weaving a particular tissue. So where does that leave us when considering the photographer as producer?

French philosopher Michel Foucault is more useful. He asks 'What is an Author?' and suggests that what he terms the *author-function* has a role within discursive systems which is not merely one of cultural cipher, but transcends this since thematic and stylistic characteristics unify a body of artistic work. Focus on authorial function allows for creative perception and consistency, but, in situating the producer within systems of production, refuses modernist understandings of art and artists (1992 [1969]). If we follow Foucault's formulation, authority stems in part from consistency of ways of looking and seeing. Photographers consider subject matter, form and style, method and metaphoric implications. Projects are researched, objectives clarified, photo-methodologies tested, and images pre-meditated. Photographers also take into account constraints of production, and ways in which particular contexts of dissemination may reinflect meaning, interpretation and significance. Such systematic consideration lends authority to the photographer as investigator and storyteller.

The integrity of the topographic stems from system, consistency and commitment. This is a legacy of the Bechers and continues to be associated with what has become known as the 'Düsseldorf School'. Bernd Becher taught at Dusseldorf Academy from 1976–2000. Ex-students include Thomas Ruff, Thomas Struth, Andreas Gursky and Candida Höfer, who all also deploy an aesthetic of detached and detailed observation and let meaning accumulate through groups or series. Thematically, unlike the Bechers, they are variously concerned with social scenarios and interior environments. But the difference in scale and context of their work indicates a number of significant shifts: first, photo-technologies now facilitate large-scale reproduction. Previously, for instance, in 'photo-realist' painting, artists wanting to work large-scale used paint to simulate the photographic.[14] Second, the concern with the German post-war environment has been superseded. Third, photography has become an accepted medium and set of practices within the (fine) art institution to the extent that photographers may prioritise the art institution (and the art market) rather than book publication as the context for dissemination of work. Struth's tableaux of visitors viewing paintings in museums and churches reflect on the arts institution as a culturally authoritative space of contemplation. Contemporary photographers, including those making work relating to land and environment, can now aspire to exhibition in major museums and galleries, as well as in specialist photography venues. The pictures in this series are nearly two metres high and wide ('National Gallery, London, 1989' is 1805 x 1965 mm, unframed). Struth turned from painting to photography, but seemingly retained a painterly sense of scale. Pictures of such dimensions are designed for public spaces such as galleries, or commercial premises – certainly not for domestic interiors or smaller community museums – and the sheer size enhances authority as the image as object imposes itself on spectators. The primary fascination of this series is the body language of the viewers pictured, each appearing intent and sometimes awkward, as if the stillness involved in detailed contemplation of paintings exhausts body poise. As we consider viewers looking at pictures we become aware that behind our backs we might be the object of someone else's gaze. Although there are no examples focused on classic landscape paintings, we are reminded of landscape's trajectory from setting to subject matter as examples include more traditional academic painting (at the Louvre) as well as the early modern example of Seurat's 'La Grande Jatte' (Art Institute at Chicago). But Struth's concern is not with particular genres; rather, the series offers a commentary on the space of the contemporary art museum and on the activity of spectatorship. When shown as a group, similarity of body language of visitors in different institutions – the National Gallery, the Art Institute, Chicago, Galleria dell'Academia, Venice – brings into question the status of the gallery as international destination, perhaps akin to religious sites visited by pilgrims of the past. Struth's work, meticulous in photographic control, retains detail in book reproduction. But it becomes less imperative as the figures are no longer human scale; they no longer replicate us. Unlike the Bechers, whose work, although exhibited in museums, lent itself to book reproduction, the younger Dusseldorf generation operate primarily within the terms of the art market – picture scale is indicative. Their work testifies to this shift that occurred in the final decades of the twentieth century whereby photography not only became accepted within the art museum as a practice in its own right but also expanded to an evocative scale traditionally associated with painting.

However, a number of contemporary German photographers persist in more documentary modes, with book publication as primary means of dissemination. For reasons perhaps relating to the twentieth-century history of Germany, its particular role within the re-unification of Europe, and its central location, borders and sites of transition are a common current theme. For example, Doris Frohnapfel travelled Europe photographing border posts, both those that have fallen into disuse since the expansion of the European Union, and those that now edge the European bloc. Some crossing points between nations no longer carry the authority previously exercised, especially as the ideological tensions of the Cold War period have receded into history. Others have acquired

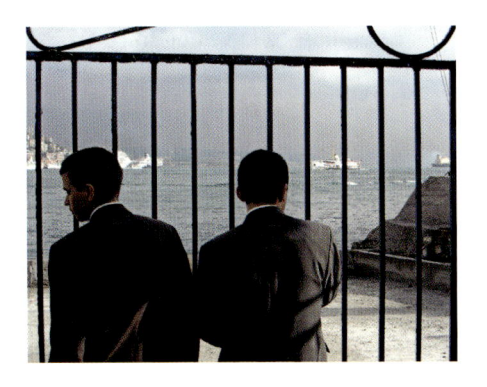

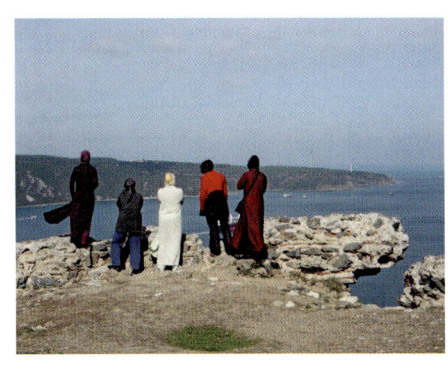

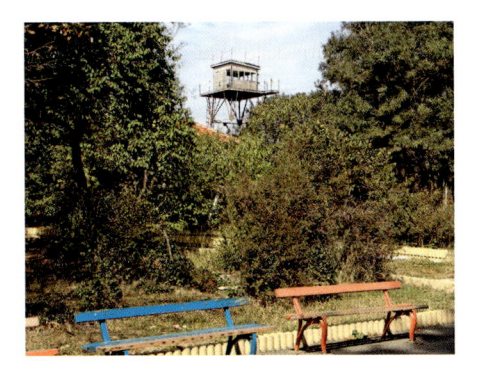

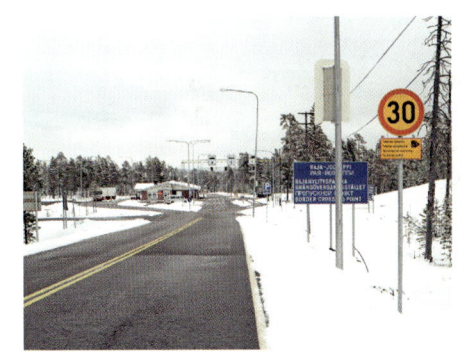

Doris Frohnapfel, *Border Horizons – Photographs from Europe.*

'Two young men waiting at Sirkeci Iskelesi', Istanbul (TR), 18.10.2003.

'Benches in a park in front of an old watchtower at the Black Sea', Tsarevo (BG), 8.10.2004.

'Looking over to the European bank of the Bosporus and the Black Sea' (TR), 19.10.2003.

'Finnish–Russian border checkpiont Raja Jooseppi' (FIN), 29.4.2003.

enhanced significance as key new frontiers (with Asia, Russia, or Africa across the sea) become the frontline against political and economic migration, as well as contributing to the import/export regulation of the circulation of goods and services. Her work offers a good example of the coming together of typification, topographic method, and the concerns of cultural geography. Her extensive series of colour photographs, muted in tone, are captioned simply as location and date. They testify to the banality of places that have been highly symbolic in terms of national and cultural identity, as well as within various group and personal biographies as points of immigration or emigration. Again, method was a primary consideration: the photographer stands back, the foreground is generally empty, the focus is on edifices and events in the middle distance whilst the horizon stands for that which is beyond the transitional space.

So, in considering the authorial function it is clear that the authority of topographic photography is primarily founded in methodology, in evidence of a systematic approach to research and of the integrity of the artist-photographer as researcher, and in stylistic consistency. The photographer's ability to deploy photographic codes, aesthetic conventions, and the semiotics of scale and titling within the context of gallery installation and book or website publication, enhances our sense of careful consideration thereby lending further authority to stories told. Earlier twentieth-century work was similarly methodical, but limited attention was paid to this; perhaps the documentary directness then associated with chemical photography seemed sufficient guarantee. If authority emerges from the research underpinning representation, then the medium – chemical or digital – makes little difference to credibility. What has changed is credulity. Awareness of virtual possibilities has induced a more critical audience. The scepticism with which we now view evidential photography is welcome as it encourages us to further examine the ontological basis of landscape practices.

JOURNEY

One attribute of landscape photography is that the photographer thought it worth travelling to a particular place in order to make a photograph. Landmarks, natural or constructed, historical or recent, signify places of specific interest, often only accessible on foot. But the second half of the twentieth century was characterised by the extension of car ownership, the expansion of cheap air travel and the speeding up of the railways. Travel has increasingly come to be associated with ease and speed of access to destinations, rather than being about the pleasures of journeys.

Walking is different. The pace is slower, and the experience of environment is more immediate. Nineteenth-century topographic photographers travelled by horse and cart, but walked or climbed to particular places in order to make images. Likewise, twentieth-century photographers may drive to a particular area, but then they get out to look and explore. Walkers pause; the experience is reflective. Birdsong, wind, sun, rain, and maybe the grind of machinery, hint at seasonal change, habitat and local land use. Impossible not to be aware of climate and weather, of soil and vegetation, of greens and browns, of sky and light, of the textures of the earth underfoot. Walks engage time and space. Walking is corporeal; the process integrates the sensual and the cerebral.

Walking is also sequential. The walker settles into a rhythm and pace determined by terrain, climate and weather that allows other concerns to fall away. Feelings may shift, from day to day, hour to hour, minute to minute, as a walk evolves through encountering new sites and sights, and a tapestry of reflections accumulates along the way. Such retrospective responses form the core of work by two British artists, Hamish Fulton and Richard Long, both of whom first made work in the context of conceptual art in the 1970s. Both artists walk, keeping notes of feelings and observations, and making pictures. Walking becomes an art act or process – not merely a means of reaching an end. Fulton defines himself as an artist who makes walks, not a walker who makes art. He usually photographs in quite traditional landscape idiom, looking out towards distant horizons, with rivers or paths enticing us towards vanishing points. Very occasionally the pictures include companions, or people encountered along the route. For him the images refer to past experience, to the journey that he undertook; for us, as audience they are fascinating fictions. His work is founded on a principle of minimal intervention within the natural environment. Observations are literal and succinct. For example, one early piece titled 'Camp Fire', reads 'A 12 day wilderness walk 100 miles between two roads Alberta Canada October 1974'. Occasionally captions indicate an incident or excitement, for instance, 'Bitten by a Dog … Nepal 1983'. His early work often took the form of photographs with words inscribed. More recent gallery installations (and book works) use the photographic as only one element. We rarely see a 'straight' photograph. Rather pictures may be transformed into silhouettes or photo-text montages, and, increasingly, he installs text-poems as images within which typography and colour are strikingly deployed. It is the action of making a walk that is the central project; exhibitions are not the event, they are the after-event. As he comments epithetically, 'A WALK HAS A LIFE OF ITS OWN AND DOES NOT NEED TO BE MATERIALISED INTO AN

ARTWORK' (www.hamish-fulton.com). The retrospective of his work held at Tate Britain in 2002 traced the trajectory of his work, from earlier photographs to later text installations, many of which took the form of large-scale lettering on the gallery wall. In this respect, his work transcends the photographic, although the imagery conjured up recalls direct experience of land through journey. Reasserting the integrity of the walk in itself, he also comments that 'AN ARTWORK MAY BE PURCHASED BUT A WALK CANNOT BE SOLD' (ibid.). This perhaps causes us to reflect that, even when sharing the experience of a walk with a companion or a group, the experience is essentially individual. Photographic interpretations of journeys are enticing perhaps because they are inter-subjective; the photographer and the viewer each enjoys imaginative latitude as senses and memories of experiences of walking are conjured up through photographic allusion. Even when Fulton is at his most objective, merely detailing destination and distance travelled, we can relate to the physicality of the experience as we know how we would feel having walked an equivalent number of miles over similar terrain.

Richard Long also walks. His sculptures, shown within the gallery context, are made from found materials and echo natural contours (for example, 'Ring of White Marble', 1993). Like Fulton, in walking he records distances and hours. In his work, for example, his exhibition, *The Time of Space* (Haunch of Venison, London, 2006), pictures of places are over-written with literal descriptions of time taken, place and date. Often there is no photograph; the alignment or flow of the visual image is made up of phrases transcribing experience and evoking mood. The texts operate evocatively through summary phrases and the poetry of the graphic shaping. For instance, the text 'All Ireland Walk' from Baltimore Beacon to the Giants Causeway, 382 miles in 12 days, is laid out with central justification; words and phrases expand in and out from a central vertical core. Single words such as 'drizzle' or 'rainbow', alone on a line, starkly reference general experience – of damp, of wondering at the effects of light – while other lines, such as 'a coffee in a flooded bar in the slieve bloom' indicate the more specific. Long also intervenes, making and documenting land sculptures which will later decompose. These are not major interventions – no spiral jetties or other monumentalist earthworks. Rather, he lays trails, or constructs patterns, sometimes contouring the land with stones, small and transient by contrast with the stone circles of Celtic and megalithic ancestry. Analysing Long's work, Ben Tufnell has remarked that the apparent

THE GIANT'S CAUSEWAY

MINCE BEEF AND ONION PIES

RATHER YOU THAN ME

DRIZZLE

FIRST BIRD OF PREY

FAST CLOUDS

LAMBS

WASHING BAY

A WRONG FORK

POTATOES BLUES FOR SALE

SHARING A POT OF TEA AT A GARAGE

A REST IN A STRAW BARN

A WRONG FORK

IT'S A BEAUTIFUL MILD MORNING

DRIZZLE

B. D. FLOUD LTD OLDCASTLE

SUPPER IN A KITCHEN BEING DECORATED

POTATOES PINKS FOR SALE

MAHON'S COSY SNUG

THE ROAD FLOODED

A COFFEE IN A FLOODED BAR IN THE SLIEVE BLOOM

THE ROAD FLOODED

OPEN TRENCHES AHEAD

WAITING WITH LOCALS FOR A MIDDAY OPENING

IT'S GOING TO BE BAD ALL DAY AND TOMORROW

WELCOME TO TIPPERARY TOWN

THE BALLYHOURA WAY

IT'S FROSTY THIS MORNING

POTHOLED ROAD

WRINGING OUT SOCKS IN A CHURCH

LONG'S BAR AND LOUNGE MALLOW

A CAMP IN THE BOGGERAGH MOUNTAINS

RAINBOW

THE ROAD FLOODED

FRIDAY MOUNTAIN BOG MEN

THE ROAD FLOODED

FOLLOWED BY A DOG FOR FIVE MILES

THE AHACRINDUFF RIVER IN SPATE

PLEASE LOOK FOR A LOOSE HORSE

A WRONG TURN

BALTIMORE BEACON

ALL IRELAND WALK

A WALK OF 382 MILES IN 12 DAYS FROM THE SOUTH COAST TO THE NORTH COAST OF IRELAND

WINTER 1995

Richard Long, 'All Ireland Walk', 1995.

simplicity of material used 'belies the conceptual and imaginative richness ... which explores complex ideas about time, space and experience', adding that the work is often witty and playful (Tufnell, 2006: 20). That Long's interventions make temporary adjustments, rather than permanent impact, perhaps reflects the transience of human presence. Projects culminate in his return, maybe some years later, to disperse his temporary traces or residues. All that then remains are the photographs or texts referencing the performative events.

For the walker, photographs and diaries act as memory aides, helping to conserve the precision of particular moments of observation for later contemplation. They record something of that which was experienced. The walk is a fact; a plan realised through time from starting point to outcome. For the audience this is a story recounted, in word and image, maybe also sound; an account that testifies to the experience of the walker but cannot replicate it. As audience we relate to it by identifying with experiences pictured and, if we too are walkers, relating imagery to our own memory of similar occasions, places and sensual responses. By contrast with the topographic, such imagery is not about *place* in itself so much as about the *experience* of place.

IMAGE, TIME, MEMORY

Discussion of landscape and memory inevitably implicates an inter-relation of space and time as memory deals both in place and in histories. There has been a tendency to separate spatiality and temporality one from the other.[15] As a consequence of modernity and industrialisation, with emphasis on productivity and making 'good' use of our time, arguably we live in an era that privileges time over space, with *speed* of action ... achievement ... communications ... travel all seemingly axiomatic within contemporary culture. Time, as we experience it through artificial divisions into hours, minutes, seconds and nano-seconds, tells us more about cultural developments than planetary cycles. International time-zones date from the needs of passenger shipping and schedules. (Greenwich Mean Time was only established in 1884.) Schedules based on time come into their own for public transport, shift-working in factory and service industries and, indeed, school or college *time*tables. For agrarian societies (including agrarian regions now) space nonetheless remains pre-eminent, and time probably has more to do with seasonal change (and weather) than with the clock. But time and region are interactive: international telephonic systems – let alone internet communications – cut across regional time differences allowing for speed and simultaneity of communication. Furthermore, perceptual experience of time may bear limited relation to the regular march of the clock. Time may 'fly' or 'stand still'. Likewise our sense of space is relative – not only literally but also conceptually in terms of psychological space, for example, 'space' to think. Arguing that 'space cannot be annihilated by time' Doreen Massey remarks that it does not follow that time assimilates space; on the contrary, what is happening is a complex simultaneity whereby two or more people participate in an action or event although geographically separated (Massey, 2005). Therefore not only moment (time) but also multiplicity (place/location) is fundamental. She comments 'space is more than distance. It is the sphere of open-ended configurations within multiplicities', so the question becomes not *whether* time will encompass space, but *what* new types of multiplicities and relations are generated through new kinds of spatial parallels and crossings (Massey, 2005: 91).

Such multiplicities also operate through amalgams of past and present. A distant sound may evoke memories and a voice on the other end of the phone may evoke an image of someone as s/he appeared when previously encountered in person rather than as s/he has become now. Jean-Paul Sartre commented on photo-portraits in relation to place and time-lapse, reflecting on why an image of his friend 'Peter', taken in Paris two years previously, should conjure up thoughts of Peter whom he knows to be now living in Berlin (Sartre, 1972 [1940]). He asks both how the image conjures up the person he knows, and whether what is remembered is Peter now or Peter then. He concludes that photographs reference that which is no longer present thereby, paradoxically, emphasising the *unreality* of that which, through depiction, seems to be made present. Images operate through association to conjure up a broad spectrum of references and memories reaching beyond the moment or event pictured.

Images do not have memory! Memory is a human faculty; it is one of the facilities we bring to the disentangling of images, when we draw both upon our individual experience and upon wider cultural discourses. Photographs appear as images removed from the flow of time. But the affects of photographs, how they work on us as we respond to them, is less clear. A number of thinkers have set about theorising photography and memory. However, there is something of a lacuna in relation to land

and landscape. Most theorists of photography have tackled questions of photography and memory either in terms of social history or in terms of the personal (for instance, Sartre's musings on his friend 'Peter'); there tends to be a focus on people, portraits or the family album. The best known example is Roland Barthes' reflection on a photograph of his mother as a young girl, on which he based the second part of *Camera Lucida*. He asserted that the image referenced her identity, but not what he terms 'her truth' (Barthes, 1982) and concluded that (family) photographs are *analogous*.

Barthes also proposed that we find some images more engaging than others due to the operations of the punctum, that is, an element that particularly pricks our attention as viewers, perhaps operating to animate memory in some more extended affective and/or narrative form (feelings, moments or stories remembered). If we take it that environmental photography operates similarly, then we need to interrogate interpretative processes. From the point of view of the photographer, photographs do more than simply provoke memories and associations; given the optical unconscious, they may *enhance* memory and perception. They also act as *aide-mémoires*; photographs remind us of moments, experiences or details that might otherwise fade. It is often stated that photographs achieve this through freezing moments in time, thereby allowing for extended contemplation of that which is depicted both for those who were present as participants or for those for whom an image indicates something of a scene that might otherwise be differently imagined. But the cryogenic model over-simplifies the fluidity of the inter-relation of imagery, personal recollection and collective history. Indeed, imagery may *reconfigure* memory. In extracting from a narrative, perhaps a place visited and a journey experienced, photographs prioritise particular moments, foregrounding them rhetorically to the extent that other parts of the experience may fall away.[16] Photographs thus may substitute for memory. For viewers, photographs of places – which may or may not have been actually visited – operate evocatively through drawing on memories of the sites depicted or of similar sights, as well as more generalised knowledge about places. As with the example of Fulton's summary statements or image-text pieces, and with Long's poetic abstractions, a sensual imaginary founded in past experience is drawn into play. If the optical unconscious sometimes takes photographers by surprise as they notice and respond to *un*-observed elements registered within the image, then as viewers perhaps there is a haptic unconscious in play whereby the image generates responses in terms of senses other than sight. For example, in looking at a photograph of an estuary such as that pictured at the beginning of this chapter, we may 'hear' the wind and the birds, 'smell' the seaweed, 'feel' the texture of the sand beneath our feet and 'taste' the salt in the air.

Proust's extensive novel, *Remembrance of Things Past*, which conjures up a private world of family and friends, includes many references to photography. Within the story, which might be likened to an extensive family album, Proust references a number of uses of photographs, including: repositories of detailed information, tokens exchanged between friends, symbols of past events and relationships, images invoking recollection. For Proust, photographs are not merely sources of information, reminders of details, later so scrupulously woven within his novels. He (in the guise of his character, Marcel) comments on the power of the photograph to transcend the experience of actual encounters, to open space for fantasy:

> Pleasures are like photographs: those taken in the beloved's presence no more than negatives, to be developed later, once you are at home, having regained the use of that interior darkroom, access to which is 'condemned' as long as you are seeing other people.
> (Proust in Brassai, 2001: Frontispiece)

Photographs for Proust, are simultaneously literal, emblematic in that they may represent a particular relationship, evocative, and erotic. For Proust they provoke reverie through the invocation of a particular (personal) scenario, and, also, fantasy as the invocation allows the viewer to enjoy imagining not only what had occurred but that which might have transpired. He did not discuss photography specifically in relation to rural landscape and memory – although there are several passages that evoke seasonal atmosphere through description of smells. But he usefully points to ways in which photographs, albeit observational, transcend simple documents or *aide-mémoires*. They reconfigure particular memories, or substitute for them, or even, as triggers, evoke images of specific places experienced in different circumstances than that depicted, or, rather like fairytales, provoke associative memories, fantasies, reveries, desires. Photographs act as a mini-haunting.

It is not difficult to understand why photographers enjoy the experience of researching and making landscape images; they construct for themselves images that trigger memories of their explorations. But why do we want to view them? Here, the ability of particular images to relate in some way to subjective experience or trigger particular feelings and associations is central. For example, Jem Southam's pictures recall my immediate environment, as I also live in southeast Devon. Besides which, these images evoke very long histories of geological and oceanic transformations. The philosophically provocative title for an initial solo exhibition of his rockface and rivermouth work was *The Shape of Time*.[17] Not only am I viewing a familiar environment, but also I am invited to consider it in terms of time, space and primordial history. By contrast, for example, for me Mark Klett's or Richard Misrach's explorations of the US West (see Chapter 3) are strictly speaking not familiar. I have never lived there. For those of us not from the United States, with the West as an idealised symbol of space and prospects, the imagery does not feed any sense of destiny or (national) identity. On the other hand, having travelled in the West I have some memory of the scale and vistas. Besides this, even without direct experience, there are cultural mediations – Hollywood Westerns, Marlboro Man – which may also be in play. There is a feeling of recognition and association, even though, as Susan Sontag remarked, this may have been falsely earned in that it is based on photographic constructions, not on personal experience (Sontag, 1979). As she implies, photographs offer only limited perceptions and perspectives.

But arguably some more elemental and more universal process is in play. Ritva Kovalainen and Sanni Seppo's investigation into *Tree People* (Chapter 5) includes accounts of a number of legends that reflect feelings of being integral to – not separate from – our environment. For instance, the idea that a person's soul remains at the site of death, becoming a part of the 'spirit' of that place. Thomas Joshua Cooper's work offers a further example of photography that operates through evoking the elemental. His work never obviously remarks human presence. He has described himself as a picture-maker and a storyteller who is concerned to 'find beauty'. His hallmark is close and detailed observation of natural phenomena, apparently untrammelled by human presence. His work certainly invites a contemplative response; whether we experience 'beauty', or something more sublime, is both a matter of definition of terms, and of subjective experience. As Susan Daniel-McElroy remarked in her essay on a series of works commissioned by the Tate, St Ives, and shot off the West Coast of Cornwall, his approach is nowadays rare and unfashionable. The influence of Stieglitz or Weston is evident in the formal expressionist qualities of the work (he was born

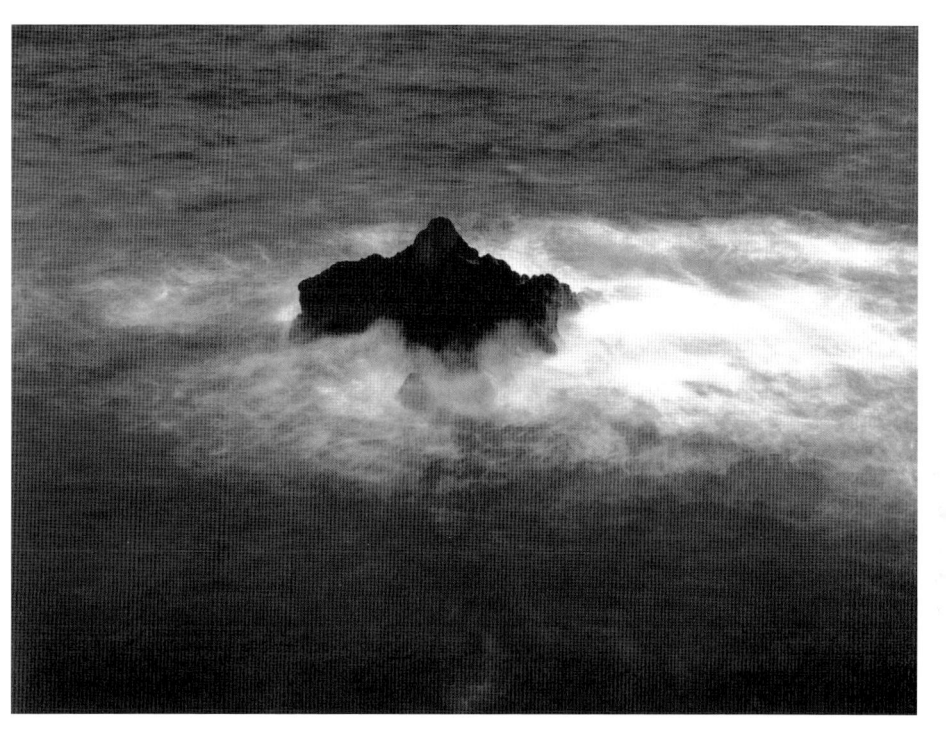

Thomas Joshua Cooper, 'Unexpected Nightfall, The Mid North Atlantic Ocean', Porto Moniz, The Isle of Madeira (near the north-most point of the Island), Portugal, 2002.

and grew up in San Francisco, although he has lived and worked in the UK for many years now). The Cornwall pictures form part of a much more extensive project looking west across the Atlantic that has taken him from Scotland to Portugal. He explores the transformative power of light in relation to water and earth; the formalist aesthetic lends emphasis and the rhetorical authority of the photographic enhances credulity – if these pictures were painted we would assume that artistic license had been liberal. Daniel-McElroy comments that in one image the surface of the sea starts to look like fire ranging across the surface of the earth. The experience of contemplating his pictures is always slightly unsettling; we never know what lies beyond the depths pictured.

Photo-historian Ian Jeffrey suggests that this uneasiness in Cooper's work is symptomatic of a longing for an unrecoverable past in which we think we had a more integrated inter-relation with the natural (Jeffrey in Cooper, 1995). This is, of course, a matter not only of history but also of desire and (in)securities. Cooper's personal engagement with the elemental perhaps reflects his Cherokee ancestry; legends and myths relating to natural environments continue to resonate in Native American cultures. Indeed, for me the work suggests a continuing spiritual oneness with natural phenomena that persists despite more populist aspects of contemporary culture. A shared awe of natural forces might contribute to accounting for the subliminal lure of his imagery. His picture titles name locations, but the affects transcend specificity of place.

Susan Derges likewise engages directly with the elements – fire, water, earth and air – and with their inter-relation, often using cameraless processes. Science, psychology, metaphor and archetypes are among her starting points. In *Natural Magic* (2001) she pictured the alchemical effects of moments of transformation, for example, water within a glass jar heated so as to turn to steam or bubbles of air rising through water. She looks for contexts in which she can explore her general interest in thinking about being, and seeing where we belong. Seeing, in the twin sense of observation, and knowledge ('I see'), is crucial. In *The Observer and Observed* (1991) her own eyes repeatedly figure as if behind a surface of water, sometimes garlanded with reflective droplets of water like glass beads.[18] The observer is simultaneously a part of the subject of her image and agent of its making. At one level the effect is narcissistic, as she must have been preoccupied with the reflection of her own face when creating the imagery. But her face and eyes swim out of definition when the image is looked at from different angles, so her situation within the picture comes to seem very fluid. In common with Thomas Cooper she relates directly to natural forces, and likewise explores form and aesthetics. But her methods, concerns and influences are radically different: the legacy of several trips to Japan is evident in the accuracy, minimalism and economy of form. She frequently makes photograms, often cyanotypes, in effect offering homage to Anna Atkins.[19] But Derges' concerns transcend scientific illustration; physical effects of light are a part of the object of exploration, not simply the means of image-making. She is open to the elements, not distanced as on-looker behind the eye of a camera. This is hands-on work; every picture is an experiment wherein results can never be precisely anticipated. Each image is unique.

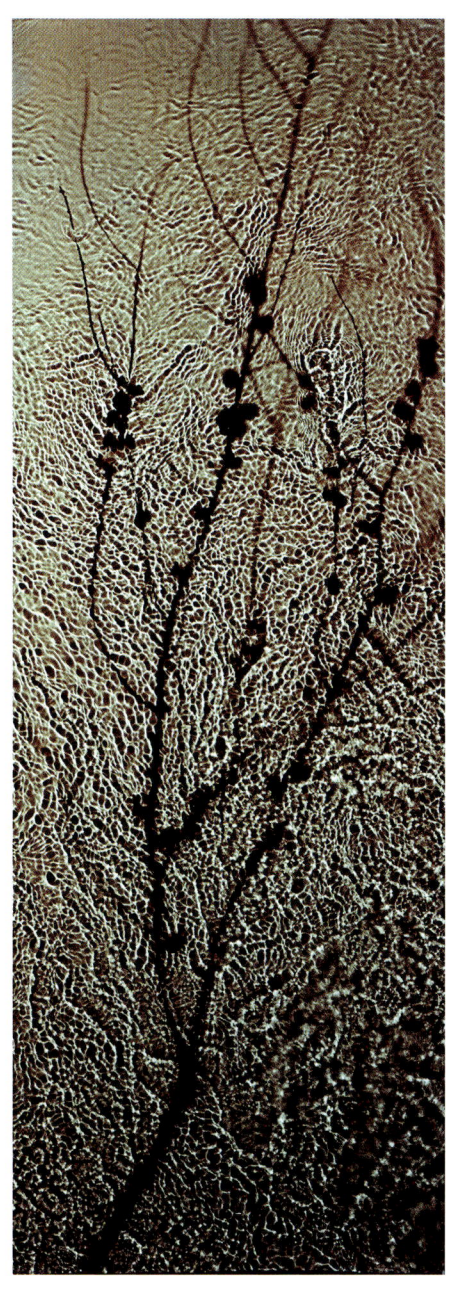

Susan Derges, 'Larch', from the series
The Streens, 2003.

Shoreline (1997–99) explores the movement of water on the coast (at Dawlish Warren, South Devon) noting the movement of the seventh wave, using moonlight (but not full moon which would be too bright), ambient light from nearby towns and villages, and flashlights.[20] The ensuing image accumulates traces of the movement of sand and pebbles during the ebb and flow of the tide. At first sight abstract, the horizontal strips stretch across the gallery wall (up to 2.5 metres wide). The pleasures are aesthetic, with patterning reflecting movement of matter in the water, and colours, sometimes intensely blue or green, evoking mood and inviting metaphoric interpretation. Perhaps an illusory cloudscape is conjured up, perhaps fungus, or cascades of human hair. Processes of making the imagery are not immediately evident. But if we pause to reflect on this, we may also be assailed by tactile memories of wet sand between the toes, and of the movement and sounds of sand and pebbles, sucked in by the receding water and thrown back out into the disarray of the water's edge. Other work is less abstract. For example, *The Streens* (2002) depicts shadows of branches, leaves and stars on the surfaces of this section of the River Findhorn, Scotland, in an open moorland area with no light pollution making the sky seem close. Derges details the process:

> Working with water again, in the darkroom of the night time landscape, was a familiar but also very new experience here; it was impossible to focus merely on the 'below', the 'above' was somehow fused with it and part of the landscape in a very real but also metaphorical sense. Moonlight was flooding the photographic paper during its brief exposure to the elements while it was immersed in the streams, colouring the prints with different casts of blue. The fine details of water and trees were exposed by a microsecond of flash but the colour variations and sense of sky were formed by the much slower exposure to this ambient changing light of the lunar cycle and stars.
>
> (Derges, 2002)

Whilst each image reflects the effects of light, water movement and reflection at specific sites, for the artist this is clearly only one moment within an overall process of familiarisation with the local environment:

> The pattern of making work became a kind of journey which began with the very fertile and murky water of ponds filled with spawn close

to the river in the bottom of the valley. The various species of trees that grew beside the streams and cascades on the sides of the valley changed from the soft flexible forms of Birch and Alder to the hardier Larches, Fir and Scots Pine higher up. High in the hills there were no trees and a sense of complete oneness with the sky that made the idea of the microcosm mirroring the macrocosm feel completely real.

(Ibid.)

Her method in this respect is performative, echoing that of Fulton or Long; process and existential experience are as important as geographic destination. She tells us where imagery has been made, but in her work the specification of place is not intended to anchor the images so much as to emphasise the authenticity of the artist's experience. Her approach is reflective; minimalist precision and intensity of colour provoke a meditative response of universal resonance. Whilst not directly invoking Christian symbolism, repeated return to explorations of the movement and mutability of water evokes myths of cleansing and re-birth. That images are made by night associates her work with the moon, symbol of the feminine, controller of the tides, and, archetypally, harbinger of various 'darker sides'. We can enjoy the formal geometry of the image, but we can also let her imagery trigger more philosophic meditation. In his extended foreword to *Liquid Form* (1999) Martin Kemp considers that her work invokes fascination with the inherent orderliness of nature and acknowledgement of deeper patterns of organic phenomena. She draws us into exploration of surface manifestations of a holistic system that is beyond rational comprehension. He suggests that 'The orders of nature respond, as it were, to our articulate scrutiny, while the mental processes of perception and deduction seem to reconfigure themselves continuously to resonate with external systems' (Derges, 1999: 9). Such processes draw upon deeply embedded myths relating to natural phenomena or events. He adds that 'we may suppose that the "aesthetic impulse" is an integral part of the feed-back system in perception and cognition that rewards and reinforces those mental procedures that allow us to make selective sense of the myriad of impressions that cascade on our senses' (ibid.). Derges' work enthralls us, focusing contemplation.

Derges is one of a number of artists whose work explores the elemental, evoking myth and symbolism. Other artists make more determined, strategic, use of nature as metaphor. For instance, Ori Gersht's exhibition, *The Clearing* (UK tour, 2006–07), included a video,

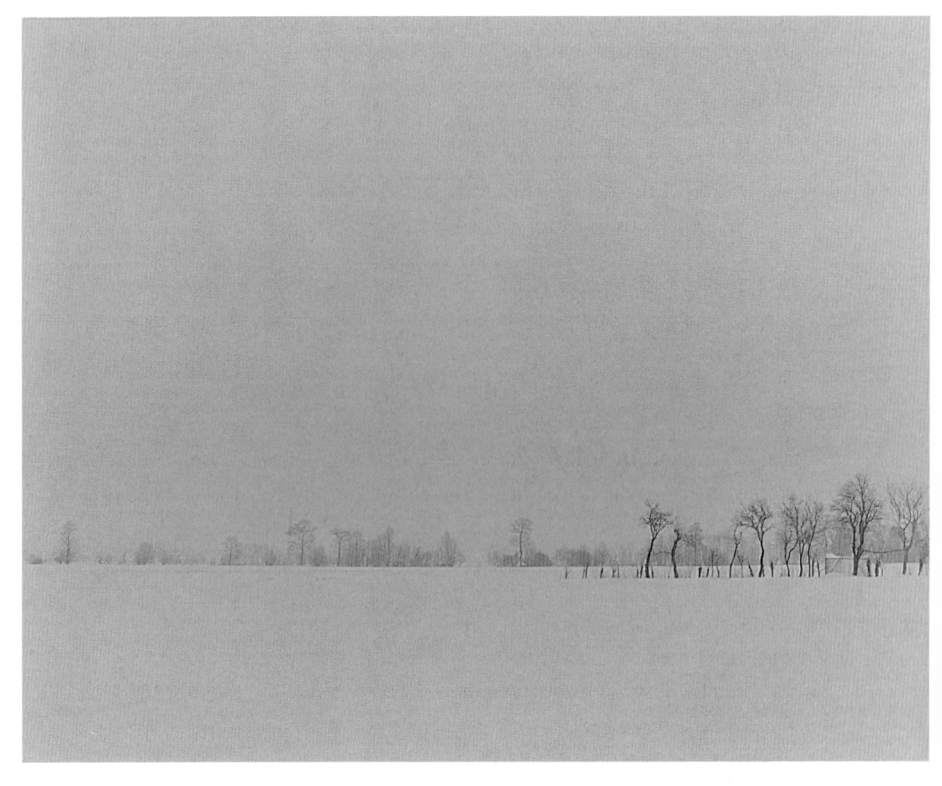

Ori Gersht, 'In Line', from the series *Liquidation*, 2005.

The Forest, and *Liquidation*, a series of still pictures made at European holocaust sites. The history is no longer clearly marked visually. Visiting and documenting sites of past events is a common theme or quest – indeed, it was central to Simon Schama's landmark *oeuvre*. But the mode of Gersht's work is complex. He is interested in romanticism, in the Romantic's fascination with the fragility of humans in relation to the sheer scale and history of nature. But he also notes the paradox of the relationship between German Romanticism and nationalism, blood and soil. The style is lyrical. The single pictures work through a form of *trompe l'oeil* – our response to the hallucinatory beauty of the image is undercut by historical information. What we see refuses to fit with what we know. In the film trees fall slowly, one by one, with an audible thump as each one hits the ground. Gersht remarks:

> Our sense of time as human beings is limited to 70 or 80 years but all these landscapes spread over a cosmic or geological perception of time. Some of the trees are hundreds and hundreds of years old; they bear with them the memory of all previous events and at the same time keep a certain silence and are impenetrable. The work is trying to make the landscape unravel, not in a dramatic way, but to somehow tell its secrets. And I think that in the film it was very important to create this tension between a sense of a disaster and the idyllic and pastoral beauty of the place. When we worked on it we were interested in the tension between the monumental crash of the tree falling and then how quickly this moment is forgotten as the camera drifts away and the harmonic sound of birds takes over again.
>
> (Gersht, 2005)

Places in themselves may reveal very little of their past especially as vegetation comes to mask historical traces. But the suggestion that nature literally absorbs history through the soil connects with the idea of a collective unconscious. Gersht deploys pictorial tradition and archetypal responses rhetorically in order to support a claim that these sites remain of particular significance as they represent the horror of not too distant histories.

Artist, Ann Chwatsky made a series of photographs titled 'WHEN I WAS A GIRL' (1999–2001). Each one montages a particular landscape with a statement about childhood experience, for example, 'WHEN I WAS A GIRL the women always waited' shows two small female oriental figurines, women in floor-length robes, their hands concealed in long sleeves are set against a barely discernable backdrop of hills and cloudy sky, with one rectangular section, scaled like a doorway, offering more clearly defined images of the hillside and clouds reflected in a lake below. The women stand this side, in the less discernable area. The landscape stands as a metaphor for the feelings and cultural circumstances implied in the individual picture titles which, we understand, simultaneously reference the photographer's own memories, the gendered nature of childhood, and loss of childhood. The landscapes are digitally manipulated. The series is not about actual places; rather, like Cooper, she deploys archetypal imagery rhetorically – 'WHEN I WAS A GIRL I worried about being buried' amalgamates burial mounds from Korea and China with funeral urns on a raised wall from Italy, reminding us of the universality of death and commemoration. In 'Mexico', she took the trees from one place and the arch from another. She describes the process:

> The Mexican one is called, WHEN I WAS A GIRL, I Kept Separate. The story is that I use images that suggest the title to me, and I was in San Miguel, Mexico, going to the outskirts and saw the bales of hay – I think that is what they are – and felt I had to photograph them. Then I realized afterwards, looking at contact sheets, that they had called to me because of their separateness. The trees were actually from Hawaii, and are manipulated to play up the separateness of the feeling. The arch is also from Mexico, from Pozos, a deserted mining town that I fell in love with visually.[21]

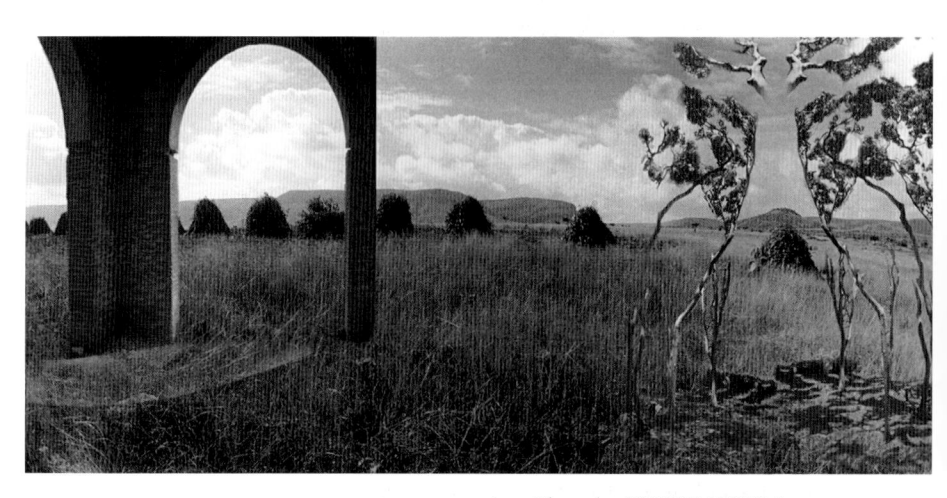

Ann Chwatsky, 'WHEN I WAS A GIRL, I Kept Separate', 2006, from the series *WHEN I WAS A GIRL*.

What she is constructing is scenarios against which her statements of memories of feelings from girlhood resonate. She defines the images in terms of 'interior landscapes' but uses what she terms 'iconic scenes' to make the particular more universal, thereby, in effect, constructing points of entry for her audience. She has visited China and Korea, as well as Mexico, and draws upon settings that – from her point of view as a New York-based artist – appear exotic, to evoke more dreamlike spaces. Some of the iconic references, for instance, Buddhist statuary, border on stereotyping 'asianess', but in so doing also draw into play a plethora of references to a long history of travel photography (Beato, Thompson, Bourne). She states that 'to bring together traditional landscapes with psychological and personal issues was my challenge'.[22] 'WHEN I WAS A GIRL I Thought I'd Watch Westerns with My Father Forever' layers the frontier landscape of histories as mediated through Hollywood with the intimacy of shared television viewing. Gender became a theme. For example, 'WHEN I WAS A GIRL My Brother Drowned My Voice' captions a photograph of a running river. The elemental association of water with the feminine is a part of the strategy deployed in this reference to her feelings about her brother – albeit perhaps ambiguously, since in this instance although 'she' was disempowered the water keeps on flowing. The montages address us very directly via the reference to childhood memory conjoined with landscapes which reference stereotypes (for instance, from movies) yet articulate elemental associations of land and water with silencing, death, burial.

IMAGE, LAND, MEMORY

This chapter has twin purposes. First, it explores two rather different modes of landscape practice, on the one hand, those that are ostensibly observational, objective, and, on the other hand, responses to phenomena that are explicitly subjective. Second, it reflects on ways in which memory is drawn into and reinflected through photography concerned with site and place. The discussion reminds us of the complexity of references implicated in making and responding to representations of environment. This involves a multi-layering of histories told and experienced in relation to particular places as well as more general ideological discourses reinflecting our understanding of our situation within our environment and how we relate to it conceptually. None of this is fixed; imagery plays rhetorically within a complexity of discourses through which we endeavour to make some sense of location.

Land matters. It matters across a range of interests and concerns, from the political and socio-economic through the ecological to subjective associations and collective identity. Through representing land as a particular sort of landscape or environment, photography contributes to reaffirming or challenging perceptions of space and place. Hence the desirability of critical evaluation of the themes, contexts, epistemologies, critical methods and aesthetic affects that variously inform and characterise contemporary practices.

NOTES

INTRODUCTION

1 The obvious example is from Christian culture wherein it is believed that Christ spent a period of time in the desert (wilderness) in order to gather strength to take on the mission with which he had been charged.
2 This incisive quote from Edward Weston (1932), *Nature, the Great Stimulus* is included in *Aperture* 98 (Spring 1985) on *Western Spaces* as a keynote statement within a small portfolio section of work by Art Sinsabaugh, and William Clift, thereby testifying to Weston's status within Modern photography.
3 The most obvious example of this would be struggles over naming of spaces or places as a symbolic refusal of territorial claims, or marks of changing power relations – *la Manche* is the English Channel; St Petersburg became Leningrad, then became St Petersburg again; 'Derry' or 'Londonderry'?
4 The chapter title references *The American Space*, an exhibition and publication that focused on the contribution of nineteenth-century landscape photography to perceptions of 'America', particularly the North American West (Wolf, 1983).
5 Oddly the division more-or-less echoes US voting patterns and allegiances prior to the Obama election. Republican individualism remains rooted in the South and the West; Democratic values are more characteristic of the coastal and urban areas. This rough division does not apply to Canada since tensions between Francophone and Anglophone regions, not to mention sensitivity to First Nation Canadians, add specific political complexities.

CHAPTER 1

1 Robert Adams, discussing form and meaning in photography as a prelude to considering the limits of the still image in 'Photographing Evil', included in his collection *Beauty in Photography* (Adams, 1996: 68).
2 Victor Masayesva, Hopi poet, photographer, filmmaker, teacher, 'Sovereign Images' – Contemporary Native American Photography & Video, symposium organised by the University of Houston Department of Art & Museum of Fine Arts, Houston, 9 March 2002.
3 Kennard was one of many photography workers engaged in a range of political activities in a decade in Britain characterised by Thatcherism, the miners' strike, an established feminist movement, and new sets of questions about post-colonialism, identity and Britishness.
4 I am indebted to Raymond Williams's discussion in *The Country and the City*, St Alban's: Paladin, 1975. His case study of changing attitudes to countryside and landscape in Britain is particularly pertinent.
5 Levi-Strauss (1969), *Conversations with Charles Charbonnier*, London: Jonathan Cape, p. 133. This comment, from the section on 'The Future of Painting', came to my attention as John Berger quotes it in *Ways of Seeing* (1972). The interview is notable for Levi-Strauss's anthropological relating of pictorial art to research, exploration and forms of knowledge.
6 Venetian Marco Polo sailed East in the late thirteenth century; Portuguese navigator Vasco de Gama sailed to India via the Cape of Good Hope in the late fifteenth century, at the same time as Christopher Columbus was traversing the Atlantic to Central and South America; Francis Drake, English sailor, crossed both the Atlantic and the Pacific in the mid-sixteenth century.

LAND MATTERS

7 For a fictional and lyrical – but nonetheless indicative – account see Tracy Chevalier (1999), *Girl with a Pearl Earring*, in which she imagines the economic context within which Dutch artists – in this instance, Vermeer – worked.
8 Arcadia, the idealised community of 900 BC – which may or may not have existed in the form in which we imagine it, but which has been transmuted into a powerful myth – has been drawn upon at many different points in history as a utopian ideal informing landscaping and agrarian husbandry.
9 For instance, Chiswick House in West London, designed in Palladian style about 1725; or Stourhead in Wiltshire, where the gardens were developed *c*. 1741.
10 Thomas Paine's *Rights of Man*, later taken up as a key egalitarian text in North America, had been written in 1791–92 in response to Edmund Burke's attack on the democratic ideals central to the French Revolution; *The Communist Manifesto* was published in 1848.
11 Vienna Camera Club, formed 1891; The Linked Ring, London, 1892; Photo-Club de Paris, 1894; and, later, Photo-Secession, New York, 1902.
12 Clarence King (1878), *Systematic Geology*, Vol. 1 of *Professional Papers of the Engineer Department U.S. Army*, Washington DC: Government Printing Office.
13 A stereoscope is a binocular gadget that makes two identical images placed side by side appear as one 3D picture.
14 Giuseppe Canella, Verona 1788–Florence 1847; Pietro Ronzoni, Sedrina (BG) 1781–Borgama 1862.
15 See, for example, Wollen (1989), 'Fire and Ice' in which he likens the flicker of film to fire and the stillness of photography to ice.
16 For detailed discussion of the late nineteenth–early twentieth-century photo-secession see, for example, Margaret Harker (1979), *The Linked Ring: The Secession Movement in Photography in Britain 1892–1910*, London: Heinemann; or Naomi Rosenblum (1997), *A World History of Photography*, London, New York and Paris: Abbeville Press, Chapter 7.
17 Arcadia has been transmuted into powerful pastoral myth of (rural) community within which nature and culture are organically integrated, functioning as a harmonious whole. Hence, in landscape gardening, 'arcades' came to define secluded spots offering peace, shade and sanctuary.
18 The American 1964 Wilderness Act concerns management of wilderness areas, inherently a paradoxical notion!
19 The association of the awesome with natural phenomena is not new – it has a particular position within Christian myth. Moses and his followers spent 40 years in the wilderness, Christ fought off temptation in the desert and Noah transcended the flood to replenish the world.
20 See Liz Wells (ed.) (2004), *Photography: A Critical Introduction*, London: Routledge, 3rd edn, pp. 13–20.
21 The *double entendre* in English (and, indeed, other languages including French), whereby to see references both viewing and comprehension, is particularly useful applied to the visual arts.

CHAPTER 2

1 Interview with the artist, 25 April 2005, Rochester, New York State.
2 Landscape painters who worked in oil made notes and sketches on site, then returned to their studios to make paintings, often waiting for specific commissions before working on final pictures.
3 In British history this is always referenced as a 'War of Independence' as opposed to 'revolution' – yet another example of language naming and claiming, in this case, a perspective on the past.
4 Eric Hobsbawn remarks that in 1860 only 16 per cent of Americans lived in cities of over 8,000 inhabitants. Hobsbawn (1975), *The Age of Capital*, London: Weidenfeld & Nicolson.
5 Abstract for his talk, 'Sacred Ground' in conference catalogue for *Fact or Fiction: Photography and Mediated Experience*, SPE, 2002: 17.
6 The mobile darkroom is 'a Suburban, not quite a van, not quite a pick-up'. Email from photographer, 4 February 2008.

NOTES

7 Pritchard explains the process: 'Beginning with a 4" x 5" Polaroid negative incorrectly processed to yield chemical stains, I then scan the image, add color from old tintypes, and make a digital print on rag paper.' Exhibition statement (Chicago, 2006).
8 See Robert W. Bermudes Jr, 'Guide to the Collection of Samuel A. Bemis's New Hampshire Daguerreotypes at the International Museum of Photography at George Eastman House', February 2005, unpublished.
9 Sweetser notes nine first-class hotels in the region plus many second-class ones, and boarding houses. Also see the New Hampshire Historical Society, www.nhhistory.org/popresorts.html (10.12.07) and www.whitemountainart.com (10.12.07) for an account of artists visiting the region in the nineteenth century.
10 See, for example, Thomas Cole's picture of 'Lake Winnipesaukee' (1827 or '28), Albert Bierstadt, 'Lake at Franconia Notch, White Mountains' (n.d.). See Chapter 1 for discussion of the American sublime including some reference to the nineteenth-century Hudson River Group of artists.
11 All the examples cited here are from the collection at George Eastman House.
12 Kilburn images include a set of ice formations related to extracts from a particular poems, and, most kitsch, a picture of a stag cornered at the edge of a river by eight dogs, title 'The Stag at Bay', reminding us of Celtic legacies of the imagination. The copyright on 'The Stag at Bay' is noted on the back as 'M. Knoedler & Co., Publishers, 170 Fifth Avenue, N.Y. and copied with their permission by Kilburn Bros., Littleton, N.H.' It is also noted that it is available as a photogravure from Knoedler, which suggests that they were selling it as an upmarket image, whilst Kilburn Bros made it more widely available (George Eastman House Collection, viewed April 2005).
13 In pre-digital days such interventions had to be pro-photographic, but conceptually one can see the foundations of his later use of digital manipulation.
14 American composer, John Cage, famously argued that silence was integral to music. Cf. John Cage, *Silence*, 1961.
15 Interview with the artist, Rochester, NY, April 2005.
16 They are based in Houston, Texas, but use the Vermont landscape in summer as their 'studio'.
17 Wall is based in Vancouver. His concern with contemporary mores and with (non-)places peripheral to the sub-urban means that his work often explores the edges between urban settlement and the immediate (semi-)rural, thereby raising questions about the impact of contemporary settlement patterns.

CHAPTER 3

1 Museum of Contemporary Art, Chicago, http://www.mcachicago.org/.
2 In 1979 he published *A Photographic Book*, in which the only words are captions stating place and date. In effect, a priority of visual semiotics and affects is asserted.
3 I am grateful to Fraenkel Gallery, San Francisco, for the opportunity to view prints (and use their library), April 2002.
4 The book is proactive in proposing turning the area into a national park commemorating the Navy's 15-year use of this land, due to expire 6 November 2001, and which was 'unlawfully confiscated'. It is – perhaps sardonically – proposed that 64 square miles of bombing range could be turned into an environmental memorial, Bravo 20 National Park. In the 1940s, Nevada, one of the least populated states in the Union, with desert, snow-capped mountains and generally clear visibility, seemed ideal to the War Department as a training area for bomber pilots; the nuclear test site was established in the 1950s, about 60 miles northwest of Vegas. By 1963, when testing moved underground, more than 235 nuclear weapons had been atmospherically tested. Now 77 square miles of desert is contaminated with radioactive substances, and the leukaemia rate is exceptionally high locally (Weisang Misrach in Misrach, 1990).
5 One of many examples is Stephen Gorman (1999), *The American Wilderness; Journeys into Distant and Historic Landscapes*, NY: Universe Publishing.

6 Until very recently students of photography still learned the zone system; they continue to work in the field with medium and large format cameras – albeit, now sometimes with digital backs.
7 The USA is often divided into Northeast, South Atlantic, The South, Midwest, Southwest, Northwest and, what is sometimes still (sardonically) described as, the 'Republic' of Texas. The first two regions were settled by the first European incomers; Hispanic influences, mediated via Mexico and South America, characterise the southern parts of the West, especially Arizona (which became the 48th State only in 1912) and California (ceded by Mexico in 1847). The West Coast also increasingly manifests Asian cultural influences.
8 For instance, as a gold rush city San Francisco expanded from 1845 onwards; Carlton Watkins moved there in 1851, become apprenticed within a daguerreotype studio, and set up his own studio in 1857.
9 The agrarian ideal of a network of small, self-sufficient, farmers was central to the federal Homestead Act, 1862, which allocated a 160-acre plot to those who would cultivate it productively for at least five years.
10 Her inclusion of a photograph of Ronald Reagan, chopping wood at the 'Rancho del Cielo' in California, 1976, reminds us that it is no coincidence that a film star, associated with Westerns, should have been voted President (as, indeed, President George Bush Jr, with his roots in Texan oil and agri-business wealth).
11 In terms of art movements Richard Prince is a contemporary of Sherrie Levine, Cindy Sherman and others who, particularly in the late 1970s/early 1980s, became known for appropriation as a method of exploration and critical reflection.
12 The series was included in the main pavilion at Giardino, Venice Biennale, 2003, which offered an opportunity to reflect upon it after a period of twenty or so years.
13 Renwick's work has been shown widely in Canada, including in *Mois de la Photo*, Montreal, 2005.
14 Such histories have become subject to active re-interrogation, with many museums and education centres dedicated to research and exhibition of native cultures.
15 Outline histories of many examples exist, typically sold (along with other tourist paraphernalia) in the various national parks.
16 Source: exhibition on the work of Thomas Moran, Bolton Museum, Art Gallery and Aquarium, Lancs, UK, June 2007.
17 Edward W. Earle notes advice from James Mullen, published in *Anthony's Photographic Bulletin* of January 1874, that landscape photographers should carry an axe and a spade (MANUAL, 2002: 10).
18 See, for instance, Stuart Alexander's brief comments on 'the American West' (Frizot, 1998: 167) or, for an earlier discussion of the work of Brady, Gardner, O'Sullivan and others in the Civil War, see Newhall (1982), pp. 89–103. Timothy O'Sullivan, along with Carleton Watkins, is perhaps the best known of those who worked with the Government Surveys of the 1860s and 1870s. Photographers did not come along and note what had happened after the event, rather they were part of it.
19 It only became possible to expose simultaneously for land and sky towards the turn of the century. By this time the replacement of wet/dry plates by film meant that it was no longer necessary to transport such heavy equipment or to process on site, although carrying large format cameras and tripods remained – and still generally remains – necessary.
20 Mark Klett and Ellen Manchester (1984). *Second View: The Rephotographic Survey Project*, Albuquerque: University of New Mexico Press. Mark Klett et al. (2004), *Third Views, Second Sights*, Santa Fe: Museum of New Mexico Press. http://thirdview.org.
21 This scene, now something of an American icon, was also painted by Thomas Moran in 1875. We have a sense of both the painter's and the photographer's interest in something greater: the sublime of the mountain combined with the symbolism of the crucifix is powerful!
22 New Objectivity particularly stressed the form and function of objects, often mass-produced, so that by extension the movement celebrated the machine age, of which, of course, photography was a part. In New Vision the emphasis was more on looking differently, on the possibilities offered by the mechanics of newer cameras for new ways of seeing. Both

NOTES

movements, which were not unrelated, developed in Europe – including Russia – in the context of the turmoil and sense of change that characterised inter-war Europe.

23 Yellowstone, in Montana and northwest Wyoming, was declared a national park in 1872. It was the first such government-protected area.

24 Initially Yosemite park consisted of 1,512 square miles of land around, but not including, Yosemite Valley or the Mariposa Grove of giant sequoias (which are up to 2,700 years old). In 1906 California ceded responsibility for the valley and the grove to federal government, thereby establishing the foundations for the park as it would be encountered by Ansel Adams when he first visited in 1916.

25 Apparently John Muir first walked (from Oakland) to Yosemite in 1868, aged 30, having already trekked widely in the West (Alinder, 1996: 26) The Sierra Club still exists.

26 Information from guided tour of the Ahwahnee hotel, March 2002, its 75th anniversary year.

27 The hotel then decided to serve tea daily, so that if ever people came to the lounge to hear Adams play, but he was not there that day, there was something provided for them (tour information). The teas continue.

28 The story is well known: as a teenager he visited Yosemite on holiday from San Francisco, and proceeded to return regularly; Yosemite is where he met Virginia, later his (second) wife. She was the daughter of the couple who ran the photographic tent (later studio) in Yosemite, and the liaison cemented Adams' involvement with the Yosemite.

29 The Ansel Adams Gallery in Yosemite Village, one of a handful of shops and services based there, testifies to the centrality of association of his photography with the area.

30 It simultaneously satisfied commercial imperatives, as visitors purchased pictures, and as Kodak took advantage of his technical expertise to commission him to test and experiment with new film stock.

31 This discussion falls into at least two modes: the patriarchal and patronising. Within this it is assumed that women would not normally make particularly good photographers but, of course, being close to nature, can express something of its 'wonders'.

32 I use the phrase deliberately to invoke the social concerns of photographers working in Europe between the wars.

33 Viewed in New York, September 2006. Adams' work was hung as a block of images, right near the entrance to the exhibition, near two installation pieces. It clearly contributed to setting the exhibition agenda, as it was both the first piece encountered on entering the show, and the last as one returned to exit.

34 The photographers were William Christenberry, Lynn Davis, Terry Evans, Lee Friedlander, Karen Halverson, Annie Leibovitz, Sally Mann, Mary Ellen Mark, Richard Misrach, Hope Sandrow, Fazal Sheikh and William Wegman. Places visited range in character from the red rock plateaus of Utah to a tidal cove in eastern Maine, and in geographic region from New York to California, as well as Mexico, Brazil and Indonesia.

35 *In Response to Place* was commissioned to mark the fiftieth anniversary of the Nature Conservancy, an international organisation committed to conservation and sustainability. Curated by Andy Grundberg, the exhibition opened in Washington in autumn 2001, and toured to seven further US venues, 2002–04 including science centres such as the Field Museum, Chicago, and Houston Museum of Natural Science as well as art institutions such as the Corcoran Gallery of Art, Washington, or the Ansel Adams Center for Photography, San Francisco.

CHAPTER 4

1 This is not simply a matter of history – organisations such as the Duchy of Cornwall remain powerful, and in some regions, for instance, East Anglia, whole villages continue to be owned and run from the manor.

2 Friedrich Engels worked in Manchester 1842–44 and subsequently wrote *The Condition of the Working Class in England* (1844–45).

3 See, for example, Peter Galassi (1981), *Before Photography,* New York: MoMA; Aaron Scharf (1974), *Art and Photography,* Harmondsworth: Pelican, rev. edn; David Hockney (2001), *Secret*

Knowledge: Rediscovering the Lost Techniques of the Old Masters, London: Thames and Hudson.

4   The Photographers Gallery, London, opened in 1971; Impressions Gallery, York, 1972; Side Gallery, Newcastle, 1977; Stills Gallery, Edinburgh, 1977; Fotogallery, Cardiff, 1978.
5   I find his style reminiscent of American photographer, Wright Morris's Midwest documentation, although Moore's USA links seemed primarily with the East Coast group associated with the Rhode Island School of Design – Minor White, Aaron Siskind, Harry Callaghan.
6   Moore's work constitutes an important visual record and social archive. In his lifetime there were only three slim publications, plus a portfolio in *Creative Camera*.
7   The Paul Hill collection – his own work, and an extensive holding of exhibition invitations and catalogues – is held in the Birmingham City Library photography archive.
8   Martin Parr and Paul Graham were among those who were particularly influential in the development of colour vision. This was not uncontroversial. Colour had been associated primarily with advertising, and new colour documentary was seen by some not only as lacking the authenticity of black and white imagery, but also as trivialising subject matter (Paul Graham's colour documentation of *The Troubled Land* of Northern Ireland particularly attracted adverse criticism.)
9   See www.jamesravilious.com.
10 The exhibition opened at the Serpentine Gallery, London, then toured in the UK, but (regrettably) there was no exhibition publication so there is no long-term record of what was a significant intervention at the time, coinciding as it did with the 1984–85 miners' strike.
11 In May 2006 I was in County Antrim at the time of the 25th anniversary of the Hunger Strikes. Anniversary banners in some villages contrasted starkly with the red, white and blue markings on the pavements in others. (Reconciliation projects are ongoing across the region.)
12 See, for example, Roberta McGrath's argument interrogating Edward Weston's writings and visual vocabulary (McGrath, 1987).
13 Large format cameras, commonly used for landscape or survey work, and associated gear (lenses, tripods …) are heavy to carry over distances; producing detailed panoramic vistas in remote places poses physical and logistical challenges (which persist despite new technologies since such cameras are still bulky, even with digital backs).
14 Fay Godwin (1931–2005) was elected President of the Ramblers Association in 1987.
15 Several of the artists discussed in this section were included in two exhibitions on women and landscape photography with which I was involved as curator/editor: *Viewfindings* (1994–95), commissioned by Newlyn Art Gallery, Cornwall, and *Shifting Horizons* (2000–01), commissioned by the Iris Women's Photography Project at Staffordshire University, co-curated with Kate Newton and Catherine Fehily. Both projects offered opportunities to promote work by women and, more particularly, to reflect upon thematic concerns and aesthetic modes articulated via work by British-based photographers concerned with land and environment. In viewing work submitted for both exhibitions, I noted a tendency for women to be interested in relations between people and place, with rather more limited interest in land as (unpeopled) landscape vista, or as geological space.
16 This is, of course, also true of male photographers with young children if they are primary or co-carers.
17 Here it is useful to distinguish between biological sex (physical) and gender (cultural). Gender is formed culturally, reflecting specific cultural histories and circumstances. As social anthropologists have demonstrated, behaviour that is deemed appropriately masculine, or feminine, varies from one cultural group or region to another. Put very broadly, Western society 'femininity' has been associated with the maternal, the emotional, the domestic, while 'masculinity' and the patriarchal order reflect regulation, the intellectual, the economic, the public sphere.
18 In her conceptualisation, the symbolic order is closely inter-related with the economic. Unlike more traditional Marxist theorists, she does not posit the economic as underlying social determinant; rather she sees the spheres of the economic and the ideological as inter-discursive. Since within this model language is inextricably founded in the material, the 'logic' of language – the intra-relational system of codes and conventions through which ideas are formed and expressed – encompasses the logic of social order, in this instance, patriarchy.

NOTES

19. For instance, the radical impact of Impressionist painting wherein the endeavour to replicate movement of light and water might be associated with the intuitive, but the organisation of the canvas was often absolutely conventional in terms of the rules of perspective.
20. Co-hosted by Arnolfini, Bristol and Serpentine Gallery, London, the exhibition also toured to Cambridge Darkroom, City Museum and Art Gallery, Stoke-on-Trent, Newport Museum and Art Gallery, S. Wales, Harris Museum and Art Gallery, Preston (1989–90).
21. To take myself as an example – I would describe myself as a Londoner born and bred, with Scottish and Canadian ancestry, who has lived in the Southwest for about 25 years. Living in the Southwest does not make me *from* the region, or even *of* it. But on the other hand, living on an estuary in a village (with a church, a chapel, pubs, a rail station, post office and shop, three small farms, and also a council estate) informs my political and social perceptions of contemporary Britain.
22. Curator Sunil Gupta has noted that the history of Black photography in Britain is brief. As a movement, he ascribes its early development to funding initiatives taken by Labour-controlled local city councils in the early 1980s-context of Thatcherism, and of inner-city racial tension (Gupta, 1990). Key exhibitions and initiatives included *Reflections of the Black Experience* (curator, Monika Baker, Brixton Art Gallery, 1986), which, as a primarily documentary show, offered evidence not only of the diversity of Black experience in Britain but also of the presence of good Black photographers. The Association of Black Photographers, later Autograph, was formed soon after this to promote the work of Black photographers across a range of fields.

CHAPTER 5

1. The originals are by a French photographer who travelled north with Prince Roland Bonaparte in 1884.
2. Several of the photographers whose work is discussed in this chapter were included in the exhibition, *Facing East; Contemporary Landscape Photography from Baltic Areas*, curated by Liz Wells, which opened at the Arts Institute at Bournemouth, April 2004, and subsequently toured to a further six UK venues (to 2007). I am grateful to the Arts and Humanities Research Council, UK, for funding to support curatorial research trips, and to the Arts Institute for commissioning and managing the exhibition.
3. Scandinavian languages, let alone Finnish or Baltic languages, are not commonly read outside of the region. (In addition it is a consequence of the limited access to information and archives in Estonia, Lithuania, Latvia, and indeed, Poland and East Germany, that obtained through much of the second half of the twentieth century, a period within which critical studies within photography developed apace.)
4. Scandinavia refers to Norway, Sweden, Denmark and Iceland as it references a linking geological formation. (Inclusion of Finland in travel publications titled 'Scandinavia' is technically inaccurate.)
5. Statistic attributed to the harbour authority reported in Liutauras Psibilshis (1997), 'Nationality Matters', *Siksi* 12:1 (Spring), p. 54. Although these expeditions are principally for shopping and leisure, this nonetheless implies cultural affinities and inter-change.
6. Tallinn, the capital city of Estonia, is 50 per cent Estonian and 40 per cent Russian; Russians form 26 per cent of the total national population. Source: *Tallinn in your Pocket*, Aug./Sept. 2003, p. 9. This statistic disguises further variation, as other Russian-speaking Slavic groups such as Ukrainians and Belarusians are included. Further non-Estonian ethnic groups date back to Danish occupation of the northern regions in the thirteenth century.
7. This is captured in a number of films and novels; the films of Ingmar Bergman, or the description of the opening up of a village, and its people, as spring arrives in Cora Sandel's novel *Alberta and Jacob* are among very many examples.
8. 'Romanticism', dating from the late eighteenth century, commonly references the lyricism of Caspar David Friedrich or the more dramatic poetics of Turner and stood in opposition to the geometric discipline of classical art.
9. The archive is now based at the University of Bergen, and includes Knudsen's own storage cabinets as well as glass plates, notes and prints, so is also a key study resource for historians of nineteenth-century studio photography systems.

10 Interview with artist, Copenhagen, August 2003.
11 'Lithuania' is first mentioned in writing as 'Litua' in 1009 (Lithuanian National Museum). The University in Vilnius dates from 1579. Lithuania shares an agricultural economy with Poland (both are known for amber mining). From 1795 most of Lithuania was incorporated into the Czarist (Russian) Empire, and remained so until, in 1920, the Soviets ceded Vilnius and the south to Poland, and Kaunas, the second largest city, became the Lithuanian capital. The Soviets only returned Vilnius to Lithuania in 1939 when Germany and the Soviet Union split Poland; subsequently the Nazis occupied Lithuania, and the majority of Vilnius' extensive Jewish population was killed.
12 The imperialist method was overtly hegemonic. When I first visited Riga (Winter 1983) street signs had been changed to Russian, with Latvian as a smaller 'translation'.
13 I'm grateful to Stanislovas Zvirgzdas, director of the Lithuanian Photoartists' Union, for his observations; interview, April 2003.
14 Agu Naru (2004), 'The Invisible Side of the Void', translation supplied by the artist.
15 Andrejs Grants, discussion with author, Riga, August 2003.
16 Gatis Rozenfelds, discussion with author, Riga, August 2003.
17 *What is Important?*, 3rd Ars Baltica Triennial of Photographic Art, opened Kiel, April 2003, toured Baltic region to 2005.
18 Aame Reunala, 'National Identity in the Forests', Finnish Forest Research Institute, Helsinki, n.d. (current 2006).
19 *The Kalevala*, based upon oral poetry, was assembled and published in 1849.
20 Exhibited widely, including in *Wasteland; Landscape From Now On*, Rotterdam photography biennale, 1992 (Gierstberg and Vroege, 1992).
21 This study was generated as a practice-based PhD at the University of Art and Design, Helsinki (TaiK/ UIAH), which is the most prominent centre for masters and doctoral-level photographic studies in Finland, and, indeed, the Nordic region.
22 Juha Suonpää's study likewise was developed as a doctorate based at UIAH (completed 2001).
23 This image was one of the two pictures favoured by the various galleries for private view invitations and more general PR for my exhibition *Facing East*. Indeed, the (badly) disguised photographer features on the front cover of the Arts Institute booklet accompanying the exhibition. It is a striking image but so are many of the others in the show; I presume it is thought that humour and paradox seduce contemporary audiences! The other image that was often used for publicity was Petter Magnusson's 'Explosion No. 1'. Again, the humour is striking.
24 Ritva Kovalainen and Sanni Seppo (1997), *Puiden Kansa*. Helsinki: Pohjoinen Gallery. Republished in English as *Tree People*, 2006. Also see http://www.puidenkansa.net/_english/TREE_PEOPLE_PROJECT/TREE_PEOPLE_PROJECT.html.
25 Viewed on exhibition in the foyer area at the Museum of Photography, Helsinki, September 2003.
26 *Cocktails 1990–2007* was first shown at Millesgarden, Stockholm, then at the Photographers Gallery, London, in 2008, when it won the annual Deutsche Borse award.
27 The map delineates the literal territory of Puranen's work: he makes photographs in Greenland and in Lappish areas of Norway, Finland, and, very occasionally, Russia. He rarely makes work in Sweden, which seems surprising given its location between Finland and Norway. (He once told me that he does not find the Swedish landscape interesting, as it is too organised – which may belie Finnish attitudes to Sweden as a former colonial power.)
28 In 2009 the University of Art and Design, Helsinki, was merged with two other specialist universities to form the Alvar Aalto University – named after the Finnish modernist architect and designer (1898–1976).
29 She now lives between Helsinki and Paris, and was short-listed for Ars Fennica, 2007 (a Finnish equivalent to the Turner prize).
30 Subsequently, during a residency in Ireland, she made a sequence within which the clothing, attached to poles or trees, was animated by the wind. See Pavalainen, 2003.

NOTES

CHAPTER 6

1. See *The New Shorter Oxford English Dictionary*, 1993.
2. Others included were Joe Deal, Frank Gohlke, Nicholas Nixon, John Schott, Henry Wessel, Jr.
3. For example, although I can no longer find a date for the event, I clearly remember tensions and lively discussion when Lewis Baltz spoke at Watershed, Bristol, UK sometime in the late 1980s, his work having been shown at the Arnolfini (also in Bristol) a few years earlier in *New Topographics* (1981).
4. www.tate.org.uk/research/tateresearch/tatepapers/04spring/stimson_paper.htm.
5. Their first key publication, in 1970, was *Anonyme Skulpturen: Eine Typologie technischer Bauten*, Dusseldorf: Art Press Verlag. This led to a series of monographs, each on one work group, for example, Mineheads or Water Towers.
6. These examples rest on the accuracy of cartography, necessarily taking maps at face value. But this is not a methodological issue as questions investigated relate to human activity and social values, and do not rest on micro geographic precision.
7. *Island* was based on the Ordnance Survey Landranger series of maps, which she borrowed from public libraries; she generally used one map per location, about 50 of them used in total (source: emails from artist, January 2006/July 2009). Originally *Island: The Sea Front* was designed as a gallery installation; the formulaic way of working was intended to reference the authority of systems which defined land and territory and governed land control, and to challenge the supposed objectivity of such systems. This emphasis is perhaps less marked in the publication. See www.katemellor.com.
8. For a critical discussion of cartography see Jeremy Black (1997), *Maps and Politics*, London: Reaktion Books.
9. Mark Power, *Peripheral Visions*, conference, University of Brighton, 29 October 2005.
10. Charles Craig, Graham Diprose and Mike Seaborne (1997–99), *London's Riverscape Lost and Found*. Exhibited variously, including at the Arts Institute at Bournemouth, 2004. Mike Seaborne is curator of photographs at the Museum of London.
11. Ingrid Pollard (1994), *Hidden Histories, Heritage Stories*, London: Lee Valley Park, Exhibition brochure.
12. www.olafureliasson.net.
13. Roland Barthes (1977), 'The Death of the Author' in *Image, Music, Text*, London: Fontana. Trans. by Stephen Heath. First published in 1968 as 'La mort de l'auteur', in *Manteia V*.
14. See, for instance, *The Painting of Modern Life*, London: Hayward Gallery, 2007.
15. For instance, in analysing cinema Gilles Deleuze distinguished between *The Time-Image* (1985) and *The Movement-Image* (1983).
16. I used to have a snapshot of myself boarding a canal boat in Amsterdam aged about three. That is my only memory of that event. I don't know if I ever remembered the event itself, but if I once did recollect the actual experience, this has been overlaid by the photographic image of the little girl climbing onto a gangplank. Of course I could not have actually seen this scene, as I was in the centre of a picture that must have been taken by my father. But if I once remembered the sounds and textures of the trip, now I can only see the little girl with short blonde hair climbing onto the boat.
17. Towner Gallery, Eastbourne, UK, 31 March–4 June 2000. *The Shape of Time* was also the subtitle for the accompanying publication *Rockfalls, Rivermouths, Ponds*, 2000.
18. This effect is achieved through use of strobe light whereby water is transformed into droplets (due to sound vibrations) and these drops act as tiny lenses. The same jet of water appears as a flow when exposed under constant light. General light emphasises movement; strobe light shimmers crystals across the picture. Hence the title of her book, *Liquid Form* (1999).
19. The 2002 calendar of the National Museum of Photography, Film and Television places 'Vessel No. 3', 1995, by Derges, alongside a leaf cyanotype by Anna Atkins, 1853, thus clearly indicating her place within a long tradition of contact image-making.
20. Pre-coated paper, placed on aluminium sheets, is exposed below water, responding to ambient light and to the effects of a bank of flash lights that she has positioned above. The sensitised paper records swirls of water, foam, sand and pebbles, all of which have to be thoroughly hosed

off in the darkroom before the exposure can be sent for processing. On stormy nights too much sand is brought in, obliterating detail; very strong waves generate too much foam, creating black blocks; strong clouds render ambient light flat and dull. Such effects are integral to the process.

21 Email correspondence with artist, Spring 2006.
22 Artist's statement. Also see www.annchwatskyphoto.com.

BIBLIOGRAPHY

Aarnes, Sigurd Aa (1983). 'Myths and Heroes in Nineteenth Century Nation-building in Norway' in J.C. Eade, ed., *Romantic Nationalism in Europe*. Monograph No. 2, Humanities Research Centre. Canberra: Australian National University.
Adams, Robert (1983). 'Introduction' in Daniel Wolf, ed., *The American Space: Meaning in Nineteenth-century Landscape Photography*. Middletown, CT: Wesleyan University Press.
——— (1985). *Summer Nights*. New York: Aperture.
——— (1994). 'Two Landscapes' in *Why People Photograph*. New York: Aperture.
——— (1996). *Beauty in Photography*. New York: Aperture.
Adams, Robert et al. (1975). *New Photographics: Photographs of a Man-altered Landscape*. Rochester, NY: International Museum of Photography.
——— (1980). *Landscape Theory*. New York: Lustrum Press.
——— (1981). *New Topographics*. Bristol: Arnolfini.
Alinder, Mary Street (1996). *Ansel Adams*. New York: Henry Holt.
Alison, Jane and Carol Brown (1989). *The Search for the Picturesque*. London: Scholar Press.
Alison, Jane and Carol Brown, eds, (1992). *Border Crossings*. London: Barbican.
Aperture (1985). *Western Spaces*. Aperture No. 98, Spring.
Arter, David (1999). *Scandinavian Politics Today*. Manchester: Manchester University Press.
Bachelard, Gaston (1994). *The Poetics of Space*. Boston, MA: Beacon Press. Original French publication, 1958, Presses Universitaires de France.
Bailey, David A. and Stuart Hall (1992). 'The Vertigo of Displacement: Shifts within Black Documentary Practices' in D.A. Bailey and S. Hall, eds (1992). *Critical Decade*. Ten/8 2:3. Birmingham: Ten.8 Ltd.
Barthes, Roland (1977). 'The Death of the Author' in *Image, Music, Text*. London: Fontana. Trans. Stephen Heath. First published in 1968 as 'La mort de l'auteur', in *Manteia V*.
——— (1982). *Camera Lucida*. London: Jonathan Cape. First published in French, 1980, as *La Chambre Claire*, Editions du Seuil.
Baudelaire, Charles (1972). 'The Salon of 1859: II, the Modern Public and Photography' in *Baudelaire: Selected Writings on Art and Artists*. Trans. P.E. Charvet. Harmondsworth: Penguin. Originally published in French, 1859.
Becher, Bernd and Hilla (1970). *Anonyme Skulpturen: Eine Typologie technischer Bauten*. Dusseldorf: Art Press Verlag.
——— (2005). *Basic Forms of Industrial Buildings*. London: Thames and Hudson.
Belting, Hans (1998). *Thomas Struth Museum Photographs*. Munich: Schirmer/Mosel.
Benjamin, Walter (1931). 'A Short History of Photography' in *One Way Street*. London: New Left Books (1979).
——— (1936). 'The Work of Art in an Age of Mechanical Reproduction' in Hannah Arendt, ed., *Illuminations*. London: Fontana. Rev. edn, 1992.
——— (1977). 'The Author as Producer' in *Understanding Brecht*. Trans. Anna Bosock. London: New Left Books. First published in 1966 from an unpublished manuscript.
Berger, John (1972). *Ways of Seeing*. London: BBC/Penguin Books.
Berman, Marshall (1982). *All That is Solid Melts into Air: The Experience of Modernity*. London: Verso.
Bermudes, Robert W., Jr (2005). 'Guide to the Collection of Samuel A. Bemis's New Hampshire Daguerreotypes at the International Museum of Photography at George Eastman House' (Feb. 2005), unpublished.

Black, Jeremy (1997). *Maps and Politics*. London: Reaktion Books.
Bogh, Michael (2006). *Per Bak Jensen: The Unseen Image*. Klanpenborg, Denmark: Bjerggaard Publishers.
Bonnell, Sian (2001). *when the domestic meets the wild*. Weymouth: Trace.
——— (2004). *from an elsewhere unknown*. Cardiff: Ffotogallery Nad London: Hirschl Contemporary Art.
Brandt, Bill (1947). 'Over the Sea to Skye'. *Lilliput* 21:5, Nov. 1947, pp. 389–96. London: Hulton Press.
——— (1961). *Perspectives of Nudes*. London: The Bodley Head.
——— (1975). *The Land: Twentieth Century Landscape Photographs*. London: Gordon Fraser.
Brassaï (2001). *Proust in the Power of Photography*. Trans. Richard Howard. Chicago and London: University of Chicago Press. Original publication, 1997, Paris: Editions Gallimard.
Braun, Stefanie (2008). *Deutsche Börse Photography Prize 2008*. London: The Photographers' Gallery.
Brennan, Joann (n.d.). *Managing Eden* (unpublished).
Brewer, John (1997). 'Culture, Nature and Nation', in *The Pleasures of the Imagination: English Culture in the Eighteenth Century*. London: HarperCollins.
Bright, Deborah (1989). 'Of Mother Nature and Marlboro Men: An Inquiry into the Cultural Meanings of Landscape Photography' in Richard Bolton, ed., *The Contest of Meaning*. Cambridge, MA: MIT; originally published in *Exposure* 23:3, Fall 1985.
——— (2001). *Manifest*. Artist's exhibition statement.
——— (2003). *Glacial Erratic*. Artist's exhibition statement.
Bunce, Michael (1994). *The Countryside Ideal: Anglo-American Images of Landscape*. London: Routledge.
Burgin, Victor, ed. (1982). *Thinking Photography*. London: Macmillan.
Burke, Edmund (1757). *Philosophical Inquiry into the Origin of Our Ideas of the Sublime and the Beautiful*. Oxford: Basil Blackwell (1987).
Butler, Susan (1989). *Shifting Focus*. Bristol: Arnolfini and London: Serpentine Gallery. Exhibition catalogue.
Castleberry, May, ed. (1996). *Perpetual Mirage: Photographic Narratives of the American West*. New York: Whitney Museum of American Art.
Chadwick, Whitney (1990). *Women, Art, and Society*. London: Thames and Hudson.
Clark, Kenneth (1976). *Landscape into Art*. London: John Murray. Originally published in 1949.
Conisbee, Philip (1995). 'Ordinariness and Light: Danish Painting of the Golden Age' in Kasper Monrad, ed., *The Golden Age of Danish Painting*. New York: Hudson Hills Press and LA County Museum of Art.
Cooper, Thomas Joshua (1995). *Simply Counting Waves*. Lisbon: Calouste Gulbenkian.
Cooper, Thomas Joshua and Paul Hill (1975). *Remnants and Prenotations, The Photographs of Thomas Joshua Cooper and Paul Hill*. Bristol: Arnolfini Gallery.
Corner, John and Sylvia Harvey (1990). 'Heritage in Britain', *Ten/8* No. 36), Spring.
Cornforth, John (1998). *The Country Houses of England 1948–1998*. London: Constable.
Cosgrove, Denis (1984). *Social Formation and Symbolic Landscape*. London and Sydney: Croom Helm.
——— (2003). 'Landscape and the European Sense of Sight – Eyeing Nature' in Kay Anderson et al., *Handbook of Cultural Geography*. London: Sage.
Crary, Jonathan (1990). *Techniques of the Observer*. Cambridge, MA: MIT Press.
Creates, Marlene (1990). *The Distance Between Two Points is Measured in Memories, Labrador 1988*. North Vancouver, BC: Presentation House Gallery.
——— (1993a). *Language and Land Use, Alberta 1993*. Lethbridge, AB: Southern Alberta Art Gallery.
——— (1993b). *Marlene Creates: Landworks 1979–1991*. St John's, NF: Art Gallery, Memorial University of Newfoundland.
——— (1994). *Language and Land Use, Newfoundland 1994*. Halifax, NS: Mount Saint Vincent University Art Gallery.
——— (1997). *Places of Presence: Newfoundland Kin and Ancestral Land, Newfoundland 1989–1991*. St John's, NF: Killick Press.

BIBLIOGRAPHY

Cresswell, Tim (2003). 'Landscape and the Obliteration of Practice' in Kay Anderson et al., *Handbook of Cultural Geography*. London: Sage.
Daniel-McElroy, Susan (2001). *Thomas Joshua Cooper, At the Very Edges of the World*. St Ives: Tate Publications.
Daniels, Stephen (1990). 'Goodly Prospects: English Estate Portraiture, 1670–1730' in Nicholas Alfrey and Stephen Daniels, eds, *Mapping the Landscape*. Nottingham, UK: Castle Museum.
——— (1993). *Fields of Vision: Landscape Imagery and National Identity in England and the United States*. Princeton, NJ: Princeton University Press.
Darrah, William C. (1977). *The World of Stereographs*. Gettysburg, PA: Times and News Publishing Co.
Darwell, John (2007). *Dark Days*. Stockport: Dewi Lewis Publishing.
Davidson, Peter (2005). *The Idea of North*. London: Reaktion Books.
Davies, John (1987). *A Green and Pleasant Land*. Manchester: Cornerhouse Publications.
——— (2006). *The British Landscape*. London: Chris Boot.
Dawson, Robert et al. (2000). *A Doubtful River*. Reno, NV: University of Nevada Press.
de Fresnes, Jill, ed. (1997). *Constance Astley's Trip to New Zealand 1897–1898*. Wellington: Victoria University Press.
de Tocqueville, Alexis (1946 [1835]). *Democracy in America*. London: Oxford University Press. Trans. Henry Reeve; edited and introduced by Henry Steele Commager. Original publication: Part One, 1835, Part Two, 1840.
Derges, Susan. (1999). *Liquid Form*. London: Michael Hue-Williams Fine Art.
——— (2002). *The Streens*. Weymouth: Trace Gallery. Artist's statement.
——— (2006). *Susan Derges*. London: Purdy Hicks.
Derrida, Jacques (1978). *Writing and Difference*. Chicago: University of Chicago Press. Originally published in French, 1967.
——— (1987). *The Truth in Painting*. Chicago: University of Chicago Press. Originally published in French, 1978.
Digranes, Åsne, Solveig Greve and Oddlaug Reiakvam (1988). *Det Norske Bildet, Knud Knudsens fotografier 1864–1900*. Bergen: Universitetsbiblioteket and Grøndahl and søn Forlag A.
Doherty, Willie (1998). *Somewhere Else*. Liverpool: Tate Gallery and F.A.C.T.
Dorrian, Mark and Gillian Rose, eds (2003). *Landscapes and Politics*. London and NY: Black Dog Publishing.
Eade, J.C., ed. (1983). *Romantic Nationalism in Europe*. Monograph No. 2, Humanities Research Centre. Canberra: Australian National University.
Eastlake, Lady Elizabeth (1857). 'Photography', *Quarterly Review*, April. Reprinted in Beaumont Newhall, ed. (1980), *Photography: Essays and Images*. London: Secker and Warburg.
Edwards, Elizabeth (1995). 'Jorma Puranen: Imaginary Homecoming'. *Social Identities*. 1:2. Oxford: Journals Oxford Ltd, pp. 317–21.
Emerson, Peter Henry (1889). *Naturalistic Photography for Students of the Art*. London: Sampson Low & Co.
Eskola, Taneli (1997a). *Water Lilies and Wings of Steel: Interpreting Change in the Photographic Imagery of Aulanko Park*. Helsinki: University of Art and Design Helsinki UIAH.
——— (1997b). *Aulanko Revisited*. Helsinki: Musta Taide.
Evans, Harold (1986). *Pictures on a Page*. London: Heinemann.
Evans, Terry (1998a). *Disarming the Prairie*. Baltimore, MD: Johns Hopkins University Press.
——— (1998b). *In Place of Prairie*. Chicago: Chicago Art Institute. Exhibition Leaflet.
——— (2001). 'Tallgrass Prairie Preserve, Oklahoma'. Artist's statement in Andy Grundberg, ed., *In Response to Place*. Boston, MA: Bulfinch Press.
Facos, Michelle (1998). *Nationalism and the Nordic Imagination: Swedish Art of the 1890s*. London and Berkeley, LA: University of California Press.
Faragher, John Mack (2001). *Women and Men on the Overland Trail*. New Haven: Yale University Press. 2nd edn.
Farrell, David (2001). *Innocent Landscapes*. Stockport: Dewi Lewis Publishing.
Foucault, M. (1992). 'What Is an Author?' in C. Harrison and P. Wood, *Art in Theory*. Oxford: Blackwell. First published in 1969, *Bulletin de la Société Française de Philosophie*, No. 63, Paris.

Fox, William L. (2001). *View Finder: Mark Klett, Photography, and the Reinvention of Landscape.* Albuquerque: University of New Mexico Press.
Friedman, Martin, ed. (1982). *The Frozen Image: Scandinavian Photography.* New York: Abbeville Press.
Frizot, Michel, ed. (1998). *A New History of Photography.* Cologne: Könemann. Originally published in French in 1994.
Frohnapfel, Doris (2005). *Border Horizons.* Bergen: National Academy of the Arts.
Galassi, Peter (1981). *Before Photography.* New York: Museum of Modern Art.
Ganis, John (2003). *Consuming the American Landscape.* Stockport: Dewi Lewis Publishing.
Gernsheim, Helmut (1955). *The History of Photograph from the Earliest Use of the Camera Obscura in the Eleventh Century up to 1914.* London and New York: McGraw-Hill.
Gersht, Ori (2005). Interview, in *Great* 63. London: The Photographers Gallery.
Gilroy, Paul (1993). *The Black Atlantic; Modernity and Double Consciousness.* London: Verso.
Godwin, Fay (1985). *Land.* London: Heinemann
——— (1990). *Forbidden Land.* London: Cape.
——— (2001). *Landmarks.* Stockport: Dewi Lewis Publishing.
Gohlke, Frank (1992). *Measure of Emptiness: Grain Elevators in the American Landscape.* Baltimore: Johns Hopkins University Press.
Goin, Peter (1996). *Humanature.* Austin: University of Texas Press.
Goin, Peter and Ellen Manchester (1992). *Arid Waters.* Reno, NV: University of Nevada Press.
Goldberg, Vicki and Robert Silberman (1999). *American Photography: A Century of Images.* San Francisco: Chronicle Books.
Gombrich, E.H. (1978). *The Story of Art.* London: Phaidon, 13th edn. First published in 1950.
Gorman, Stephen (1999). *The American Wilderness; Journeys into Distant and Historic Landscape.* New York: Universe Publishing.
Grants, Andrejs (2002). *Fotogrāfijas.* Riga: Neputns.
Green, Nicholas (1990). *The Spectacle of Nature.* Manchester: Manchester University Press.
Grierson, Su (2001). *Eyeshine.* Exhibition catalogue. Glasgow: Street Level Photoworks.
Grundberg, Andy (1999). *Crisis of the Real; Writings on Photography since 1974.* New York: Aperture.
Grundberg, Andy, ed. (2001). *In Response to Place.* Boston, MA: Bulfinch Press.
Gunnarsson, Torsten (1998). *Nordic Landscape Painting in the Nineteenth Century.* Trans. Nancy Adler. New Haven and London: Yale University Press.
Gupta, Sunil (1990). 'Photography, Sexuality and Cultural Difference', *Camerawork Quarterly* 17 (3).
Hales, Peter Bacon (1988). *William Henry Jackson and the Transformation of the American Landscape, 1843–1942.* Philadelphia: Temple University Press.
Hall, Stuart (1997a). 'The Work of Representation' in S. Hall, ed., *Representation: Cultural Representations and Signifying Practices.* London: Sage and Open University.
——— (1997b). 'The Work of Representation' in S. Hall, ed., *Representation: Cultural Representations and Signifying Practices.* London: Sage and Open University.
Hamilton-Paterson, James (1998). 'The Cultural Impact of Oceans' in Trudy Wilner Stack, ed., *Sea Change, The Seascape in Contemporary Photography.* Tucson: Center for Creative Photography, University of Arizona.
Hammond, Anne (2002). *Ansel Adams, Divine Performance.* New Haven and London: Yale University Press.
Harker, Margaret (1979). *The Linked Ring: The Secession Movement in Photography in Britain 1892–1910.* London: Heinemann.
Haughey, Anthony (2006). *Disputed Territory.* Dublin: Dublin Institute of Technology and Gallery of Photography.
Haworth-Booth, Mark, ed. (1975). *The Land: Twentieth Century Landscape Photographs.* Selected by Bill Brandt. London: Gordon Fraser Gallery.
——— (1992). *Camille Silvy: River Scene, France.* Malibu, CA: J. Paul Getty Foundation.
Hesling, Ingrid (1994). 'Anarchy in Arcady' in Liz Wells, ed. (1994). *Viewfindings; Women Photographers, 'Landscape' and Environment.* Tiverton, Devon: Available Light, pp. 17–24

Hewison, Robert (1987). *The Heritage Industry*. London: Methuen.
Hill, Paul (1990). *White Peak Dark Peak*. Manchester: Cornerhouse Publications.
Hobsbawn, Eric (1962). 'Land' in *The Age of Revolution*. London: Abacus.
——— (1975). 'The Land' in *The Age of Capital*. London: Weidenfeld & Nicolson.
——— (1987). 'An Economy Changes Gear' in *The Age of Empire*. London: Weidenfeld & Nicolson.
Hobson, Stephen (1994). 'Manual: Et in Arcadia Ego', *Perspecktief* 47–48, June, pp. 72–82.
Hockney, David (2001). *Secret Knowledge: Rediscovering the Lost Techniques of the Old Masters*. London: Thames and Hudson.
Holzherr, Andrea and Timothy Persons, eds (2007). *The Helsinki School; New Photography by TaiK*.
Home, Donald (1984). *The Great Museum: The Re-presentation of History*. London: Verso.
Hopkinson, Tom (1993). 'Bill Brandt's Landscapes' in Nigel Warburton, ed., *Bill Brandt, Selected Texts and Bibliography*. Oxford: Clio Press. Originally published in *Photography*, Vol. 9, No. 4 (April 1954), pp. 26–31.
Huddleston, John (2002). *Killing Ground, Photographs of the Civil War and the Changing American Landscape*. Baltimore and London: Johns Hopkins University Press.
Hughes, Robert (1997). *American Vision*. London: Harvill Press.
Irigaray, Luce (1993). *je, tu, nous: Toward a Culture of Difference*. London and New York: Routledge. Originally published in French, 1990.
Jämsä, Martti (2003). *Summertime*. Helsinki: Musta Taide.
Jay, Martin (1998). 'Scopic Regimes of Modernity' in Nicholas Mirzoeff, ed., *The Visual Culture Reader*. London and New York: Routledge, pp. 66–9. Originally published in Hal Foster, ed. (1988), *Vision and Visuality*. Seattle: Bay Press.
Jude, Ron (2004). *Landscapes (for Antoine)*. Syracuse, NY: Everson Museum of Art. Exhibition catalogue.
Kapa (2000). *kapa*. Helsinki: Musta Taide.
Kaufman, Polly Wells (1996). *National Parks and the Woman's Voice*. Albuquerque: University of New Mexico Press.
Kemal, Salim and Ivan Gaskell, eds (1993). *Landscape, Natural Beauty and the Arts*. Cambridge: Cambridge University Press.
Killip, Chris (1988). *In Flagrante*. London: Secker and Warburg.
——— (2001). *Chris Killip*. London: Phaidon Press, series 55.
King, Clarence (1878). *Systematic Geology*, Vol. 1 of *Professional Papers of the Engineer Department U.S. Army*. Washington DC: Government Printing Office.
King, Thomas Starr (1869). *The White Hills; their legends, landscape and poetry*. Boston: Woolworth, Ainsworth and Company; Riverside, Cambridge: H.O. Houghton and Company.
Kippin, John (1995). *Nostalgia for the Future*. London: Photographer's Gallery.
——— (2001). *Cold War Pastoral: Greenham Common*. London: Black Dog Publishing.
——— (2004). *Compton Verney*. Warwickshire: Compton Verney House Trust.
Kippin, John and Chris Wainwright (1989). *Futureland*. Newcastle: Laing Art Gallery.
Klein, Kirsten (1997). *Eau*. Nykøbing Mors, Denmark: Galerie Birthe Laursen.
——— (2000). *Kirsten Klein*. Paris: Galerie Birthe Laursen.
Klett, M. and E. Manchester (1984). *Second View: The Rephotographic Survey Project*. Albuquerque: University of New Mexico Press.
Klett, M. et al. (2004). *Third Views, Second Sights*. Santa Fe: Museum of New Mexico Press.
Knorr, Karen (1994). 'The Virtues and the Delights – Reinventing History', *Portfolio* 19. Edinburgh: Photography Workshop.
Kornhauser, Elizabeth Mankin and Amy Ellis (2003). *Hudson River School, Masterworks from the Wadsworth Atheneum Museum of Art*. New Haven and London: Yale University Press and Hartford: Wadsworth Atheneum Museum of Art.
Kouhia, Harri and Jan-Erik Lundström (1998). *State of Siege, Annika von Hausswolff's Visual World*. Umea, Sweden: Bildmuseet.
Kovalainen, Rivta and Seppo, Sanni (2006) *Tree People*. Helsinki: Hülinielu.
Krauss, Rosalind (1989). 'Photography's Discursive Spaces' in Richard Bolton, ed., *The Contest of Meaning* Cambridge, MA: MIT Press; originally published in *Art Journal* 42, Winter 1982.

Kuhn, Hans (1983). 'The Farmer and the Viking: Forms of Romantic Nationalism in Nineteenth-Century Scandinavia' in J.C. Eade, ed., *Romantic Nationalism in Europe.* Monograph No. 2, Humanities Research Centre. Canberra: Australian National University.

Lange, Susanne (2007). *Bernd and Hilla Becher: Life and Work.* Cambridge, MA: MIT Press.

Langford, Martha (2005). *Image and Imagination.* Montreal: McGill-Queen's University Press.

Levi-Strauss, Claude (1969). *Conversations with Charles Charbonnier.* London: Jonathan Cape. Original French publication, 1961.

Lippard, Lucy R. (1997). *The Lure of the Local.* New York: New Press.

—— (1998). 'Outside (but not necessarily beyond) the Landscape' in *Moments of Grace: Spirit in the American Landscape. Aperture* No. 1150, Winter.

Lister, Martin and Liz Wells (2001). 'Seeing Beyond Belief: Cultural Studies as an Approach to Analysing the Visual' in Theo van Leeuwen and Carey Jewitt, eds, *Handbook of Visual Analysis.* London: Sage.

Lundström, Jan-Erik (2002). *The Politics of Place.* Umea: Umea University BildMuseet.

Mann, Sally (1992). *Immediate Family.* London: Phaidon.

—— (2005). *Deep South.* New York: Bulfinch Press.

MANUAL (2002). *Errant Arcadia.* New York: International Center of Photography and Houston: Houston Artist Fund.

Massey, Doreen (1994). *Space, Place and Gender.* Cambridge: Polity Press.

—— (2005). *For Space.* London: Sage.

Matless, David (1998). *Landscape and Englishness.* London: Reaktion Books.

McGrath, Roberta (1987). 'Re-reading Edward Weston', *Ten/8* No. 27, reproduced in Liz Wells, ed. (2003). *The Photography Reader.* London: Routledge.

Mellor, Kate (1997). *Island.* Stockport: Dewi Lewis Publishing.

Meyer, Robert (1988). *Norsk Landskap.* Oslo: Dreyers Forlag A/S.

—— (1989). *Den Glemte Tradisjonen.* Skrifter 1. Oslo: Kunstforenings.

Misrach, Richard (1990). *Bravo 20: The Bombing of the American West.* Baltimore, MD: Johns Hopkins University Press.

—— (1999). *Desert Cantos, 1979–1999.* Granada: Diputación de Granada.

—— (2005). *Golden Gate.* New York: Aperture, 2nd edn.

Mitchell, W.J.T., ed. (1994). *Landscape and Power.* London and Chicago: University of Chicago Press.

Moi, Toril, ed. (1986). *The Kristeva Reader.* Oxford: Blackwell Publishers.

Morris, Lynda, ed. (2002). *Jeff Wall Landscapes.* Norwich: Norwich Gallery and Birmingham: Article Press.

Morris, Meaghan (1988). 'Two Types of Photography Criticism Located in Relation to Lynn Silverman's Series' in *The Pirate's Fiancée.* London: Verso.

Morris, William (1993). 'The Lesser Arts' in *News from Nowhere and Other Writings.* London: Penguin. Original lecture, 1877.

Morris, Wright (1999). *Time Pieces, Photographs, Writing, and Memory.* New York: Aperture.

Naru, Agu (2004). 'The Invisible Side of the Void', translation courtesy of the artist (Remigijus Treigys). Unpublished.

New Shorter Oxford English Dictionary (1993). Oxford: Oxford University Press.

Newhall, Beaumont (1982). *The History of Photography.* New York: MoMA.

Nipperday, Thomas (1983). 'In Search of Identity: Romantic Nationalism, its Intellectual, Political and Social Background' in J.C. Eade, ed., *Romantic Nationalism in Europe.* Monograph No. 2, Humanities Research Centre. Canberra: Australian National University.

Nochlin, Linda (1978). *Realism.* Harmondsworth: Penguin.

Panofsky, Erwin (1991). *Perspective as Symbolic Form.* New York: Zone Books. Originally published in German in 1927.

Parker, Rozsika and Griselda Pollock, eds (1987). *Framing Feminism, Art and the Women's Movement 1970–1985.* London: Pandora Press.

Pävälainen, Riitta (2003). *Vestige*. Umeå: Galleri Stefan Anderson.
Perry, Gill (1993). 'Primitivism and the "Modern"', in C. Harrison et al., *Primitivim, Cubism, Abstraction: The Early Twentieth Century*. London and New Haven: Yale University Press and Open University.
Persons, Timothy, ed. (2007). *The Helsinki School: New Photography by TaiK*. Ostfildern: Hatje Cantz Verlag.
Pevsner, Nicolaus (1997). *The Englishness of English Art*. Harmondsworth: Penguin Books. Originally published by the Architectural Press, 1956.
Pfahl, John (1997). *Permutations of the Picturesque*. Syracuse, NY: Robert B. Menschel Photography Gallery. Exhibition catalogue.
Phillips, Sandra S. (1996). 'To Subdue the Continent: Photographs of the Developing West' in Sandra S. Phillips et al., *Crossing the Frontier: Photographs of the Developing West, 1849 to the Present*. San Francisco: San Francisco Museum of Modern Art and Chronicle Books.
Pirelä, Marja (2002). *Interior/Exterior*. Helsinki: Musta Taide.
Poggioli, Renato (1968). *The Theory of the Avant-Garde*. Boston: Harvard University Press.
Pollard, Ingrid (1994). *Hidden Histories, Heritage Stories*. London: Lee Valley Park. Exhibition brochure.
—— (2004). *Postcards Home*. London: Autograph and Chris Boot.
—— (2005). 'Lost in the Horizon' in Liz Wells and Simon Standing, eds, *Surface*. Plymouth: University of Plymouth Press.
Power, Mark (2007). *26 Different Endings*. Brighton: Photoworks.
Price, Derrick (2007). 'Bargoed Tip – The History of a Slag Heap' in Liz Wells and Simon Standing, eds, *Change*. Plymouth: University of Plymouth Press.
Pritchard, Janet (2006). *Dwelling: Expressions of Time*. Artist's exhibition statement.
Proust, Marcel (1957). *Remembrance of Things Past*. Uniform illustrated edn. London: Chatto & Windus. Original publication, in 13 volumes, 1912–22.
Pugh, Simon, ed. (1990). *Reading Landscape: Country – City – Capital*. Manchester: Manchester University Press.
Putkonen, Lauri, ed. (1993). *National Landscapes*. Helsinki: Ministry of the Environment, Finland.
Reunala, Aarne (n.d.). 'National Identity in the Forests'. Finnish Forest Research Institute, Helsinki (2006).
Rogoff, Irit (2000). *Terra Informa*. London: Routledge.
Rosenblum, Naomi (1997). *A World History of Photography*. London, New York and Paris: Abbeville Press.
Runólfsson, Halldór Björn (1992). 'Mapping the Infinite' in Jane Alison and Carol Brown, eds, *Border Crossings*. London: Barbican.
Ryan, James (1997). *Picturing Empire*. London: Reaktion Books.
Said, Edward (1993). *Culture and Imperialism*. London: Chatto & Windus.
—— (1995). *Orientalism*. Harmondsworth: Penguin Books. First published London: Routledge and Kegan Paul, 1978.
Sandler, Martin W. (2002). *Against the Odds: Women Pioneers in the First Hundred Years of Photography*. New York: Rizzoli International Publications.
Sandqvist, Gertrude (1992). 'Chaos and God are Neighbours' in Jane Alison and Carol Brown, eds, *Border Crossings*. London: Barbican.
Sandweiss, Martha A. (1987). 'Foreword' in G. Garner, *Reclaiming Paradise: American Women Photograph the Land*. Duluth, MN: Tweed Museum of Art, University of Minnesota.
Sartre, Jean-Paul (1972). *The Psychology of Imagination*. London: Methuen. First published in French in 1940; English trans. 1948. New York: Philosophical Library.
Sarup, Madan (1996). *Identity, Culture and the Postmodern World*. Edinburgh: Edinburgh University Press.
Schama, Simon (1995). *Landscape and Memory*. London: Fontana Press.
Scharf, Aaron (1974). *Art and Photography*. Harmondsworth: Pelican. First published in 1968.

Schreier, Christoph and Eija-Liisa Ahtila (2006). *Breaking the Ice: Contemporary Art from Finland*. Bonn: Kunstmuseum.
Schwander, Lars (1996). *The Danish Landscape*. Copenhagen: Photography Centre.
Searle, A. (2002). 'How many sunsets can you take?', on *American Sublime*, Tate Modern, London, Feb.–May 2002. The *Guardian*, 26 February.
Shabecoff, Philip (2003). *A Fierce Green Fire: The American Environmental Movement*. Washington DC: Island Press, rev. edn.
Snyder, Joel (1994). 'Territorial Photography' in W.J.T. Mitchell, *Landscape and Power*. Chicago: University of Chicago Press.
Society for Photographic Education (2002). *Fact or Fiction: Photography and Mediated Experience*. Annual conference programme.
Sontag, Susan (1979). *On Photography*. Harmondsworth: Penguin.
South Bank Show, ITV, 1986.
Southam, Jem (2000). *Rockfalls, Rivermouths, Ponds: The Shape of Time*. Brighton: Photoworks.
—— (2005). *Landscape Stories*. New York: Princeton Architectural Press.
Spence, Jo (1986). *Putting Myself in the Picture*. London: Camden Press.
Stadtverwaltung Reutlingen (1997). *Reise Nach Reutlingen 1862, Stereoskopbilder des norwegischen Fotografen, Knud Knudsen*. Reutlingen: Heimatmuseum Exhibition Catalogue.
Stathatos, John (1994). 'Susan Trangmar, Dash Gallery, London'. *Portfolio* 19, p. 62.
Sternfield, Joel (1996). *On this Site: Landscape in Memoriam*. San Francisco: Chronicle Books.
Sweetser, Moses Foster (1879). *Views in the White Mountains*. Portland: Chisholm Brothers.
Swingler, Sue (2000). 'Ladies and the Landscape' in Liz Wells, Kate Newton and Catherine Fehily (2000), *Shifting Horizons: Women's Landscape Photography Now*. London: I.B.Tauris.
Szarkowski, John, ed. (1963). *The Photographer and the American Landscape*. New York: Museum of Modern Art.
—— (1966). *The Photographer's Eye*. New York: Museum of Modern Art.
—— (1981). *American Landscapes: Photographs from the Collection of the Museum of Modern Art*. New York: Museum of Modern Art.
Tallinn in your Pocket (2003). Aug./Sept.
Taylor, John (1994). *A Dream of England: Landscape, Photography and the Tourist's Imagination*. Manchester: Manchester University Press.
Thompson, Jon (1999). 'Sublime Moment: The Rise of the 'Critical Watchman' in Arts Council, *The Darkness and the Light*. London: Hayward Gallery.
Thoreau, Henry David (1910). *Walden*. Everyman's Library, London: J.M. Dent and Sons. First published in 1854.
Trangmar, Susan (1992). *Suspended States*. Cardiff: Ffotogallery, Southampton: John Hansard Gallery and Cambridge: Cambridge Darkroom. Exhibition catalogue.
—— (2005). *A Question of Distance*. Newcastle-upon-Tyne: Waygood Gallery.
Tufnell, Ben (2006). *Land Art*. London: Tate Publishing.
Urry, John (1990). *The Tourist Gaze: Leisure and Travel in Contemporary Societies*. London: Sage.
Virilio, Paul (1994). *The Vision Machine*. London: BFI and Bloomingdale, IN: Indiana University Press.
Walker, Joseph, Christopher Ursitti and Paul McGinniss (1991). *Photo Manifesto: Contemporary Photography in the USSR*. New York: Stewart, Tabori and Chang.
Wallace, R. Stuart (1980). 'A Social History of the White Mountains' in Donald D. Keyes, ed., *The White Mountains: Place and Perception*. Durham, NH: University Art Galleries, University of New Hampshire.
Warnke, Martin (1994). *Political Landscape: The Art History of Nature*. London: Reaktion Books.
Watkin, David (1982). *The English Vision*. London: John Murray.

Weaver, Mike (1986). *The Photographic Art*. London: Herbert.
Wells, Liz (2003). 'Icy Prospects' in M. Miles and N. Kirkham, eds, *Cultures and Settlements*. Bristol: Intellect Books.
——— (2006). 'Jorma Puranen' in *Breaking the Ice: Contemporary Art from Finland*. Bonn: Kunstmuseum.
Wells, Liz, ed. (1994). *Viewfindings: Women Photographers, 'Landscape' and Environment*. Tiverton, Devon: Available Light.
——— (2003). *The Photography Reader*. London: Routledge.
——— (2004). *Photography: A Critical Introduction*. London: Routledge, 3rd edn.
Wells, Liz, Kate Newton and Catherine Fehily, eds (2000). *Shifting Horizons: Women's Landscape Photography Now*. London: I.B.Tauris.
Wells, Liz and Simon Standing (2005). *Surface*. Plymouth: University of Plymouth Press.
——— (2007). *Change*. Plymouth: University of Plymouth Press.
——— (2008). *Fictions*. Plymouth: University of Plymouth Press.
Wiener, Martin J. (1981). *English Culture and the Decline of the Industrial Spirit 1850–1980*. Cambridge: Cambridge University Press.
Williams, Raymond (1975). *The Country and the City*. St Alban's, UK: Paladin. First published by Chatto & Windus, 1973.
——— (1983). *Keywords*. London: Fontana Communications Series. First published in 1976.
Williams, Val (1986). *Women Photographers: The Other Observers 1900 to the Present*. London: Virago Press.
Williams, W.E. (1997). *Gettysburg: A Journey in Time*. Philadelphia: Esther M. Klein Art Gallery.
——— (2002). *The Vicksburg Campaign: Photographs of The Civil War Battlefields*, photographed 1997–99. Unpublished presentation.
Williamson, Tom (1995). *Polite Landscapes*. Stroud: Sutton Publishing.
Wolf, Daniel, ed. (1983). *The American Space, Meaning in Nineteenth-century Landscape Photography*. Middletown, CT: Wesleyan University Press. Introductory essay by Robert Adams.
Wollen, Peter (1989). 'Fire and Ice' in John Berger and Olivier Richon, eds, *Other than Itself*. Manchester: Cornerhouse.
Wright, Patrick (1985). *On Living in an Old Country: The National Past in Contemporary Britain*. London: Verso.

WEBSITES

Stimson, Blake, *The Photographic Comportment of Bernd and Hilla Becher*. http://www.tate.org.uk/research/tateresearch/tatepapers/04spring/stimson_paper.htm (accessed 17 August 2010).
http://www.annchwatskyphoto.com (accessed 25 August 2010).
http://www.conundrumonline.org/Issue_3/Renwick.htm (accessed 17 August 2010).
http://www.hamish-fulton.com (accessed 25 August 2010).
http://www.jamesravilious.com (accessed 25 August 2010).
http://www.katemellor.com (accessed 17 August 2010).
http://www.leokamengallery.com/artists/renwickArthur/renwickArthur.html (accessed 17 August 2010).
http://www.markpower.co.uk (accessed 17 August 2010).
http://www.mcachicago.org/ (accessed 25 August 2010).
http://www.nhhistory.org/popresorts.html (accessed 25 August 2010).
http://www.olafureliasson.net (accessed 17 August 2010).
http://www.pilgrimhall.org/museum.htm (accessed 17 August 2010).
http://www.puidenkansa.net/_english/TREE_PEOPLE_PROJECT/TREE_PEOPLE_PROJECT.html (accessed 25 August 2010).
http://www.snac.mb.ca/projects/Indians/arthur_renwick/ (accessed 17 August 2010).
http://thirdview.org (accessed 25 August 2010).
http://www.whitemountainart.com/ (accessed 25 August 2010).

GENERAL INDEX

Aarnes, Sigurd 221
Adams, Ansel 15, 95, 111, 115, 136–40, 142, 155
Adams, Robert 7–8, 47, 128, 129, 136, 142–3, 266–7, 268
Adorno, Theodore 33
Alberti, Leon Batista 6, 24, 36, 37–8
Alison, Jane 217
'All Ireland Walk' (Long) 286–8
Altered Landscapes (Pfahl) 93–5
America 59–63, 116
   and Engish heritage 63–4, 65, 69–71, 72–3
   and environmental photography 98–105
   and landscape 14–15, 59
   and Manifest Destiny 65, 67–8, 69, 72, 90, 110–11, 112, 113, 114, 126
   and Midwest 111–12, 113, 143–6, 263
   and Native Americans 65, 67, 71, 73, 110, 112, 121, 122, 124, 153, 294
   and picturesque 93–7
   and Sioux tribe 121, 123
   and South 74–5, 79–80, 113
   and Southwest 137, 143
   and West 15, 62, 64–5, 81, 107–43, 148–58, 266, 292
      and environmental photography 107–9, 140–3, 148–50
      and landscape photography 111, 115, 124–36, 158
      and settlement 112–14
      and water 151–8
   see also American Civil War; New England; Rocky Mountains; San Francisco; Sierra Nevada Mountains; South Dakota; White Mountains; Yosemite
American Civil War 73–9
   and Black Americans 75, 79
American Indians *see* America: and Native Americans
American Landscapes (Szarkowski) 134, 135
American Sublime (Tate Modern) 67
American West *see* America: and West

'Amidst' (Trangmar) 200
Anarchy in Arcadia (Hesling) 192
Another Country (Killip and Smith) 175, 176
Arcadia Project (MANUAL) 95
Arcadia Revisited (Pfahl) 60
'Arcadian Landscape: the Elegia Tradition' (MANUAL) 97
Arcadian myths 44–5
Arid Waters (Goin) 152
Ass, Marthe 225
Astley, Constance 188–9
'Åtjärnlider' (Klinberg) 230
Atkins, Anna 147, 188, 294
Aulanko Park 242–3
Austen, Jane 161
Australia 41

Bachelard, Gaston 4–5, 44
Back to Nature (Von Hausswolff) 227
Badger, Gerry 175
Baigneurs (Brotherus) 254–5
Balcytis, Vytautas 236
Baltic region 213, 215–16, 235–57, 258–9
Baltz, Lewis 129, 266, 267–8
Barthes, Roland 280, 290
'Battleground Point' (Misrach) 155
Baudrillard, Jean 64
Beauty in Photography (Robert Adams) 8
Becher, Bernd and Hilda 129, 145, 266, 268–9, 271, 281
Bemis, Samuel 87
Benjamin, Walter 11, 13, 32–3, 39, 265, 271
Bentham, Jeremy 46
Bergen 219–20
Berger, John 24, 26, 185
'Les Bergers d'Arcadie' (MANUAL) 96
Bernsten, Per 223
Bierstadt, Albert 66, 125
Bigelow, Jacob 68
'The Birth of Venus' (Botticelli) 25
Black Americans *see* American Civil War
The Black Atlantic (Gilroy) 206
Black Hills (South Dakota) 121

323

Black Kettle (Native American chief) 119
Blake, William 23, 169–70
Bloom, Suzanne 95, 97 *see also* MANUAL
Bogh, Michael 233–4
Bonnell, Sian 193–4
Border Crossings (exhibition) 217
Brady, Matthew 74, 77
Brandt, Bill 166, 185, 187
Brasmane, Mara 238
Bravo 20, The Bombing of the American West (Misrach) 109
Brecht, Bertholt 11, 13, 259, 271
Brennan, Joann 98–9
Breughel the Elder 25
Brewer, John 28–9, 46–7
'The Bridge at Torino' (Canella) 35
Bright, Deborah 13, 16, 21, 28, 62, 69–70, 71–3, 86, 114
Britain 161–2
   and Britishness 163
   and landscape photography 162, 165–81
   and multiculturalism 203–8
   and pastoral landscape 16, 208
   and Roman heritage 163
   see also England
Brotherus, Elina 254–5
Brown, Capability 28, 45
Brown, Carol 217
Brunelleschi, Filippo 6, 24
Burgin, Victor 44
Burke, Edmund 46, 48, 49
Butler, Susan 197, 201–2

Camera Lucinda (Barthes) 290
Cameron, Evelyn 115, 117
Cameron, Julia Margaret 34, 45, 165, 188
'Camp Fire' (Fulton) 285
Canada 81–5, 113
   Newfoundland 82
   Northeast Territories 81
Canella, Giuseppe 35
Cartesianism 5, 37, 39–40, 47, 199–200
Cartier-Bresson, Henri 47–8, 236, 240
Chambers, Eddie 205
Christoffersen, Tom 233
Church, Frederick 31
Chwatsky, Anna 299–301
Clark, Kenneth 25
The Clearing (Gersht) 297–8
'Cloud View from Mt. Washington' (Kilburn Brothers) 91
'Cloud's Rest' (Kilburn Brothers) 127
Cocktails 1990–2007 (Männikkö) 250
Cole, Thomas 31, 65–7

Common Green (Ass) 225
Commonplace Intervention (Lantz) 225
Conisbee, Philip 231–2
Connoisseurs (Knorr) 161
Constable, John 21, 23, 30–1
'Constellation 111' (Trangmar) 202
Consuming the American Landscape (Ganis) 140
Cooper, Thomas Joshua 292–4
Copenhagen (Werner) 232
Cosgrove, Denis 265
Courbet, Gustave 32, 33
The Course of Empire (Cole) 66–7
Crary, Jonathan 40
Creates, Marlene 81–5, 86
Crossing the Frontier: Photographs of the Developing West, 1849 to the Present (San Francisco Museum of Modern Art) 114–15
Cunningham, Imogen 129, 137, 138
Curiosus Naturae Spectator (Puranen) 252

Dahl, Johan Christian 218
'Dancing Home' (Toomik) 214
Daniel-McElroy, Susan 292, 293
Daniels, Stephen 26
The Danish Landscape (Schwander, curator) 232
Danish painting, Golden Age of 231, 233
Dark Days (Darwell) 180–1
Darwell, John 178–81, 192
Davidson, Peter 174
Davies, John 168, 170–2
Dawson, Robert 153
Deal, Joe 267
Deep South (Mann) 79
Delegates: Chiefs of the Earth and Sky (Renwick) 119–21
Democracy in America (de Tocqueville) 64
Denmark 228–35
Dennett, Terry 186
Derges, Susan 294, 296–7
Derrida, Jacques 3, 43, 54, 197
Descartes, René 5
Desert Cantos, 1979–1999 (Misrach) 107–9
Devon 172, 275
Dingus, Rick 132
Disarming the Prairie (Evans) 146
Disen, Andreas 221
Disputed Territory (Haughey) 184
The Distance Between Two Points is Measured in Memories (Creates) 82–4
Distressed Landscapes (Treigys) 238
D-Max (Chambers, curator) 205
Documenta festival 271
Doherty, Willie 181–3, 184

GENERAL INDEX

Dorrian, Mark 21, 22
A Doubtful River (Dawson and Goin) 153
Durer, Albrecht 25
'Düsseldorf School' of photography 281–2
Dutch landscape painting 27–8, 29, 103
Dwelling: Expressions of Time (Pritchard) 85–6

Earle, Edward W. 97
East Anglia 41, 165
'Echo Lake, Franconia Notch' (Kilburn Brothers) 91
Eco, Umberto 64
Ecotopia (International Center of Photography, New York) 143
Eden, image of 64, 65, 90, 113, 114, 122, 137, 140
Edwards, Elizabeth 212
Eliasson, Olafur 234, 279
Ellis, Amy 66–7, 124
Emerson, Peter Henry 41, 165, 178
Engels, Friedrich 163
England 26, 45, 174
 and Englishness 21, 162–5, 205
 and landscape painting 28–9, 30, 165, 170
 and North 170, 174–5, 176, 181
 and Northeast 175–8
 see also Britain; East Anglia; Peak District; Sunderland; Yorkshire moors
Enlightenment 20, 46, 55, 170
environmental photography 44, 51, 190–3, 233, 241–2
 and America 98–105
 and American West 107–9, 140–3, 148–50
Errant Arcadia (MANUAL) 97
Eskildsen, Joakim 228–9
Eskola, Taneli 242–3
Estonia 214, 215, 216, 236, 240, 245
Et in Arcadia Ego (MANUAL) 95–6
'Et in Arcadia Ego' (Poussin) 96
'Et in Arcadia Ego: Observer and Tomb' (MANUAL) 97
Europe 54" 54'– 25" 19' (Narkevicius) 235
European landscape painting *see* landscape: art
European Union 53, 204, 214, 282
Evans, Frederick 166
Evans, Terry 115, 146–8, 151, 154
'Evening in Kew Gardens' (Brandt) 166
Exmoor 172
'Explosion No. 1' (Magnusson) 222
Expressionism 220
Extreme Horticulture (Pfahl) 60
Eyeshine (Grierson) 192

Facos, Michelle 225–6
'Falls of Kaaterskill' (Cole) 67
Faragher, John Mack 112
Farrell, David 183–4
Fenton, Roger 29, 40, 165, 188
Field Museum (Evans) 147–8
'Field Museum, Echinaccea, 1899' (Evans) 148
'Field Museum, Spartina, 1857' (Evans) 148
Finland 211, 213, 214, 215, 216, 226, 234
 landscape and identity of 241–57
'The Fires' (Misrach) 108
'The Flood' (Misrach) 108
Foot and Mouth crisis (Darwell's documentation of in Cumbria) 180–1, 192
The Forest (Gersht) 298
'Fort Collins' (Robert Adams) 144
Foucault, Michel 39–40, 280–1
'Frankfurt School' of Marxist theory 32–3
French Realist painting *see* Realism
French structuralist philosophy 4–5
Freud, Sigmund 49–50, 196
Friedlander, Lee 155, 233
Friedrich, Casper 50, 255
Frith, Francis 40, 165, 188
Frohnapfel, Doris 282–4
'Frontiers of Utopia' (Knorr) 160
Fulton, Hamish 82, 264, 285–6
Futureland (Wainwright and Kippin) 176, 177

Gamdrup, Mads 234–5
Ganis, John 140–1, 142
Gardner, Alexander 115
geography, definition of place through 3, 4, 7–8, 12, 14, 20, 21, 46, 53–4, 56, 111–12, 265
Germany 282
Gernsheim, Helmut 38
Gersht, Ori 297–9
Gettysburg (Williams) 77–8
Gettysburg battle/battlefield 73, 79
'The Geysers Power Plane …' (Pfahl) 62
Ghosting (Kempadoo) 207
Gilpin, Laura 116, 135
Gilroy, Paul 55, 56, 206
Glacial Erratic (Bright) 69, 71, 73
Glover, Gina 194–6
'Glowing Bush' (Rødland) 223
Godwin, Fay 166, 167, 168, 186, 189–90, 191
Gohlke, Frank 145–6
Goin, Peter 115, 148–50, 151, 152, 153
Golden Age of Danish painting *see* Danish painting, Golden Age of
Golden Gate (Misrach) 107

325

Goldsworthy, Andy 8
Gombrich, Ernest 24, 25, 30, 36
Gorman, Stephen 110
Grand Tour 33, 66
Grants, Andrejs 239–40
'Gravel Pit, Kanopolis, Kansas' (Evans) 147
A Green and Pleasant Land (Davis) 170
Greenland 252
Grierson, Su 192
Groundings (Bonnell) 193
Grundberg, Andy 117, 154–7
Gursky, Andreas 281
Guttu, Ane Hjort 225

'Half Dome and Moon' (Ansel Adams) 139
Hall, Stuart 204
Halso, Ilkha 247
Halverson, Karen 155
Hamilton-Patterson, James 23
Hammerbeck, Wanda 151–3
Hange, Jens 223
Hardy, Thomas 21
Harker, Margaret 47
'Hastings from the beach low water' (Frith) 40
Haughey, Anthony 184
Hausswolff, Annika von 227, 255
Hawarden, Lady 188
Haworth-Booth, Mark 33, 193
'The Hay Wain' (Constable) 21
'Haystack' (Morris) 51
'Heaven's Fire' (Pfahl) 93
'Helsinki School' of photography 254, 255
Hemingway, Ernest 65
Hesling, Ingrid 192
Hidden Histories, Heritage Stories (Pollard) 277–9
Highnam, Paul 267
Hill, Ed 95
    see also MANUAL
Hill, Paul 167, 168–9
Hiss, Tony 146
Hobson, Stephen 96
Hockney, David 38
Höfer, Candida 281
Hokusai, Katsushika 102–3
Hopkinson, Tom 166
Huddleston, John 74–6
'Hudson River School' of painting 31, 66–7, 87, 91
Hughes, Robert 31, 63–4, 67
Humanature (Goin) 148–50
Hundred Views of Mount Fuji (Hokusai) 102–3

Ibsen, Henrik 221
Iceland 279–80

Icy Prospects (Puranen) 253–4
I–D Nationale (O'Donnell) 205
The Idea of North (Davidson) 174
identity and place 53–6
Image and Imagination (Langford/Renwick) 121
Imaginary Homecomings (Puranen) 212
Immediate Family (Mann) 80
In Flagrante (Killip) 176
In Response to Place (exhibition) 147, 154, 157
Indians *see* America: and Native Americans
Innocent Landscapes (Farrell) 183
Inside the View (Sear) 199–200
Interior/Exterior (Pirelä) 248–9
Inuit people 84
Ireland 168, 181–4, 286
Irigaray, Luce 185, 193
Isle of Man 175
Italian Renaissance art *see* Renaissance: and art in Italy

Jackson, William Henry 124, 130, 138
James, Henry 65
Jämsä, Martti 250
Jay, Martin 37
Jeffrey, Ian 294
Jenkins, William 267–8
Jensen, Per Bak 233–4, 235
Johnson, Frances Benjamin 116
Johnson, Robert Underwood 136
Jokisalo, Ulla 254
'Journey on the Flight to Egypt' (Ronzoni) 35
Jude, Ron 99–102, 103

Kant, Immanuel 46
Kapa (Kapanen), Martti 247
Keila, Jan 242
Kemp, Martin 297
Kempadoo, Roshini 206–8
Kennard, Peter 21
Kilburn Brothers 90–2, 126
Killing Ground (Huddleston) 75
Killip, Chris 168, 175–6
King, Clarence 34
King, Thomas Starr 86, 88–90
Kippin, John 176, 177–8
Kirsten, Klein 229–31
Klett, Mark 115, 130, 132, 135, 151, 152, 292
Klingberg, Margareta 227
Knorr, Karen 161–2
Knudsen, Knud 219–20, 221
Kornhauser, Elizabeth Mankin 66–7, 124–5
Kovalainen, Ritva 244–6, 292
Krauss, Rosalind 34, 37

GENERAL INDEX

Kristeva, Julia 5, 196–7
Krogh, Anna 235
Kruger, Barbara 185
Kuhn, Hans 217

Labrador 82
Lacan, Jacques 197
The Land (Brandt) 166
Land (Godwin) 190
Landmarks (Godwin) 190
landscape/landscape art/photography
   and aesthetics 35–50
   and American West 111, 115, 124–36, 158
   and art 23–9, 36
   and identity 53–6, 211
   and journey 284–8
   and memory 262–4, 288–302
   and representation 4–9
   and space/place 2–4, 19–20, 53–6
   and time 51–3
   and topography 262, 264, 265–84
Landscape and Memory (Schama) 262
Landscape and Power (Mitchell) 2
Landscapes and Politics (Dorrian and Rose) 21
Landscapes (for Antoine) (Jude) 99–102
Lange, Dorothea 135, 167
Lange, Susanne 268, 271
Langford, Martha 121
Language is a Foreign Country (Puranen) 252
Lantz, Maria 225, 226
Lapland 250–3
Latvia 215, 238, 239
Lemagny, Jean-Claude 169
Lessing, Gotthold 36
Levi-Strauss, Claude 27
Lewis, Dave 205
Liggins, Andrea 198–9, 200
Like a Breath in Light (Pirelä) 249–50
Lindahl, Axel 220
Lippard, Lucy R. 84, 261, 262
Liquid Form (Derges) 297
Liquidation (Gersht) 298
Lithuania 215–16, 235–6
Long, Richard 8, 82, 264, 285, 286–8, 290
'The Long Walk' (Fenton) 40
Lorrain, Claude 27, 28, 30, 45
'Lucky Pennies' (Bright) 72
Lunaatika (Merila) 240
Lundström, Jan-Erik 227

Magnusson, Petter 222–3
Managing Eden (Brennan) 99, 100
Manchester, Ellen 126, 152
Manet, Edouard 32, 255

Manifest (Bright) 72–3
Manifest Destiny *see* America: and Manifest Destiny
Mann, Sally 79
Männikkö, Esko 250
MANUAL 95–7
   see also Bloom, Suzanne; Hill, Ed
Marcuse, Herbert 33
'Marlboro Man' 117–18, 292
Mass Observation 174
Massachusetts Institute of Technology (MIT) 68
Massey, Doreen 12, 19, 289
Mayflower, the 69, 71
McAlinden, Mikkel 225
McGrath, Roberta 185
Mellor, Kate 271–2
'Merced River, Yosemite, Cal.' (Kilburn Brothers) 126
Merila, Herkki-Erich 240
Meyer, Robert 221
Michelangelo 25
Midwest *see* America: and Midwest
Millais, John Everett 32
Misrach, Richard 107–9, 115, 132, 150, 155, 292
MIT *see* Massachusetts Institute of Technology
Mitchell, W.J.T. 2
Modernistic Journey (Guttu) 225
Mois de la Photo (Langford, director) 121
'Moonrise over Pie Pon …' (Pfahl) 95
Moore, Raymond 166, 167, 168, 171, 172
Moran, Thomas 124, 125
Morris, Meaghan 41–3
Morris, William 164
Morris, Wright 51–2, 144–5
'MO-TA-VAH-TO' (Renwick) 119
Mother Land (Mann) 79–80, 86
Muir, John 136
Munch, Edvard 220
Museum of Modern Art (New York) 34, 132, 134, 166
'Music 1' (Pfahl) 94–5
Muybridge, Eadweard 132, 137, 266
My Weather Diary (Silomäki) 255–7
'Myths and Heroes in Nineteenth Century Nation-building in Norway' (Aarnes) 221

Narkevicius, Deimantas 235
National Landscapes (Finnish Environment Ministry) 211
National Romanticism 218, 225–6, 231, 232
Natural Magic (Derges) 294

Naturalistic Photography for Students of the Art (Emerson) 41
'Nature Reserve' (Kippin) 177–8
Nausea (Sartre) 99, 101
The Navigation Series (Wainwright) 176
Neue Sachlichkeit (Bechers) 268
Nevada desert 107, 108
New England 66, 67, 71, 72, 85, 86–7, 92
The New Industrial Parks Near Irvine, California (Baltz) 268
New Topographics: Photographs of a Man-Altered Landscape (exhibition) 129, 142, 145, 266
The New West (Robert Adams) 143
New Zealand 188–9
Newfoundland *see* Canada: Newfoundland
'Niagra' (Church) 31
Niagra Falls 31, 60, 66, 81, 93, 124
'Niagra Falls' (Church) 31
'Niagra Power Project, Niagra Falls, NY' (Pfahl) 61–2
Niagra Sublime (Pfahl) 93
Nipperday, Thomas 216, 217
Nochlin, Linda 32
Nordic region 213–14, 216–35, 252–4, 257
'Norsk Landskap' (Berntsen et al.) 223
North America *see* America; Canada
'North Light' (Kippin) 177
Northanger Abbey (Austen) 46–7
Northeast Territories *see* Canada: Northeast Territories
Northern Ireland 181–4
Norway 213, 214, 216, 217, 218–25, 235
Norwegian Scenarios (Torgnesskar) 224
Nostalgia for the Future (Kippin) 177–8
Nuclear Landscapes (Goin) 150

The Observer and the Observed (Derges) 294
Oceans Apart (Pollard) 206
O'Donnell, Ron 205
'Of Mother Nature and Marlboro Men …' (Bright) 114
On this Site: Landscape in Memorium (Sternfield) 121–2
Organized Freedom (Männikkö) 250
O'Sullivan, Timothy 34, 74, 77, 115, 128, 132, 266
'Over the Sea to Skye' (Brandt) 166

Paine, Thomas 64
Päiväläinen, Riitta 257
Palladio, Andrea 28
Panofsky, Erwin 36, 37, 38
Park City (Baltz) 268
Pastoral Interlude (Pollard) 205
Pathways to Memory (Glover) 195–6

Peak District 168
Perfect Times, Perfect Places (Robert Adams) 143
Permutations on the Picturesque (Pfahl) 60, 92, 93
Perpetual Mirage, Photographic Narratives of the Desert West (exhibition) 125
Perspective of Nudes (Brandt) 185
Pfahl, John 60–2, 73, 92–5
Phillips, Sandra S. 114–15, 119, 138
Photo Manifesto: Contemporary Photography in the USSR (Walker et al.) 236–7
The Photographer and the American Landscape (exhibition) 134
The Photographer's Eye (Szarkowski) 134
photography
  and painting 30–5
  and space/place 56
Picture Windows (Pfahl) 60
Pilgrim Fathers 63–4, 69, 71, 72, 86
Pirelä, Marja 248–50
Plato 37, 49
Plymouth, Massachusetts 63, 71, 86
Plymouth Rock, Massachusetts 69–72
The Poetics of Space (Bachelard) 4
The Politics of Place (exhibiton) 223
Pollard, Ingrid 205, 206, 276–8
Poussin, Nicolas 27, 28, 96, 97
Power, Mark 273–5
Powerplaces (Pfahl) 61–2
Pre-Raphaelites 45, 46
Price, Derrick 170
Primitivists 46
Prince, Richard 117–19
Pritchard, Janet 85–6
Prospects (Torgnesskar) 223–4
Proust, Marcel 291
Puranen, Jorma 212, 252–4
Puritans 64, 88
Putting Hills in Holland (Bonnell) 193
Pyramid Lake, Nevada 153, 155

Ravilious, James 172, 178
Realism 32, 218, 231
'Red Setters in a Red Field' (Pfahl) 93–4
Remembrance of Things Past (Proust) 291
Re-Modelling Photo-History (Spence and Dennett) 186–7
Renaissance 6, 22, 25–6, 27, 37, 45, 95, 252
  and art in Italy 25, 26, 30
Renunciation (Gamdrup) 235
Renwick, Arthur 119–21
Repton, Humphrey 28, 45
Republic of Ireland *see* Ireland
Requiem (Eskildsen) 228–9
Reykjavik 279

GENERAL INDEX

'Ring of White Marble' (Long) 286
Rio Grande River 150
'River Scene, France' (Silvy) 33
'The Road' (Eskildsen) 231
Roberts, Ellen 116
Robinson, H.P. 165
Rocky Mountains 91, 112, 143
Rodger, George 166
Rødland, Tobjørn 223
Rogoff, Irit 49
Romanticism 50, 69, 90, 97, 216, 218, 220, 223, 298
Ronzoni, Pietro 35
Rose, Gillian 21, 22
Rozenfelds, Gatis 240
Ruff, Thomas 281
Runólfsson, Halldór Björn 217–18
Russia 215–16
  see also Soviet Union

'Sacred Ground' (Williams) 79
Said, Edward 206–7
Sami people 212, 213, 250–2, 254
San Francisco 107
Sandberg, Johan 223
Sandler, Martin W. 115, 116
Sandqvist, Gertrud 220
'Sarjasta The New Painting …' (Brotherus) 255
Sartre, Jean-Paul 99–101, 289, 290
Sarup, Madan 53–4
Scandinavia 216–35
Schama, Simon 11, 262–3, 298
Scharf, Aaron 33
Schwander, Lars 232–3
Seaborne, Mike 275
Sea Change (Hamilton-Paterson) 23
Sear, Helen 199–200
Searle, Adrian 67
Seaside Stories (Pollard) 206
Second View (Klett et al.) 130–2, 135
Seppo, Sanni 244–5, 292
Seurat, Georges-Pierre 282
Shabecoff, Philip 67–8
Shaen, Margaret 188
The Shape of Time (Southam) 292
Shifting Focus (Butler, curator) 197, 200
Shipsides, Daniel 181, 184
Shore, Steven 267
Sierra Club 136, 138
Sierra Nevada Mountains 136, 137, 153, 155
'Silent Thunder' (Pfahl) 93
Silomäki, Jari 255–7
Silverman, Lynn 41–3
Silvy, Camille 33
Sioux tribe *see* America: and Native Americans

'Six Oranges, Delaware Park …' (Pfahl) 95
'Skjeggedalsfossen, Hardanger' (Knudsen) 221
Sleeping Places (Creates) 82
Smith, Graham 168, 175
'Snow Storm – Steam-Boat off a Harbour's Mouth' (Turner) 30
Socialist/Soviet Realism 236, 258
Somewhere Else (Doherty) 182–3
Sontag, Susan 292
South Dakota 121, 123
South Uist 175
Southam, Jem 261, 275, 276, 292
Soviet Union 214, 215–16, 236–8
  see also Russia
'Spectral Vapors' (Pfahl) 93
'Speculum Orbus Terrae' (Puranen) 252–3
Speed (Southam) 275
Spence, Jo 186–7
Spender, Humphrey 174
Spotted Tail 119
Stathatos, John 200
Sternfield, Joel 121–2
'Steves Farm, Stevenson' (Wall) 103
Stieglitz, Alfred 108, 138, 292
Stigneev, Valery 237
Stinessen, Siggen 223
Strand, Paul 175
The Streens (Derges) 296
Struth, Thomas 281–2
'A Sudden Gust of Wind' (Wall) 103
Summer Nights (Robert Adams) 143
Summertime (Jämsä) 250
Sunderland 177
Suonpää, Juha 243
Suspended States (Trangmar) 201
Sweden 213, 214, 215, 221, 225–9
Sweetness and Light (Kempadoo) 206–7
Sweetser, Moses Foster 86, 87, 88
A System of Edges (Power) 273
'Systema Naturae' (Puranen) 253
Szarkowski, John 34, 132–5

Tainted Prospects (Pfahl) 60
Talbot, Fox 38
'Terra Incognito' (Puranen) 253
'Tertiary Conglomerates, Weber Valley Utah' (O'Sullivan) 132
'Tertiary Conglomerates (Witches Rocks No. 5)' (Dingus) 132
Third View (Klett et al.) 130
Thoreau, Henry David 64, 65, 68, 69, 87, 99
'Three Mile Island' (Pfahl) 62
The Time of Space (Long) 286
Time Pieces (Morris) 51
Toomik, Jaan 214

Torgnesskar, Per Olav 223–4
Tracing the Line (Goin) 150
'Tracks, Bonneville Salt Flats …' (Pfahl) 95
Trangmar, Susan 200–202
'Travels and Translations' (Puranen) 252
Travels with Canvas (Puranen) 254
Tree People (Kovalainen and Seppo) 245–6, 292
Treigys, Remigijus 238
Truckee River 153
'Truth and Landscape' (Robert Adams) 7–8
The Truth in Painting (Derrida) 43
'Tufa Domes, Pyramid Lake' (O'Sullivan) 34
Tufnell, Ben 286–8
Tunbjörk, Lars 226–7
Tunnels (Glover) 194–5
Turner, J.M.W. 22, 23, 30, 55
Turning Back (Robert Adams) 143

Uelsmann, Jerry 166
United States of America *see* America
Untitled Landscapes (Trangmar) 200
USA *see* America

'Valley of the Connecticut' (Kilburn Brothers) 91–2
Van Eyck, Jan 24
The Vicksburg Campaign: Photographs of the Civil War Battlefields (Williams) 78–9
'View of the White Mountains' (Cole) 66–7
Views in the White Mountains (Sweetser) 86
Vigeland, Gustav 220
Vilnius 235, 236
Virgil 45
Virilio, Paul 40
The Virtues and the Delights (Knorr) 162

Wainwright, Chris 176–7, 178
Walden (Thoreau) 64
Walden Pond, Massachusetts 64
Wales 164, 170
Walker, Joseph 238
Wall, Jeff 102–4

Wallace, R. Stuart 86
'Wanderer above the Sea Fog' (Friedrich) 255
Water (Klein) 229
'Water in the West' (Evans et al.) 151–3, 157–8
Waterfalls (Pfahl) 60
Watkins, Carleton 115, 137, 138, 266
'Wave Theory I–V, Puno Coast, Hawaii' (Pfahl) 95
The Weather Project (Eliasson) 279
Weaver, Mike 45
Webb, John S. 229
Webb, Mary 153
Weekends (Rozenfelds) 240
Wegman, William 155
Werner, Sigvart 232
West *see* America: and West
West from The Columbia (Robert Adams) 143
Weston, Brett 167
Weston, Edward 8–9, 48, 115, 129, 137, 138, 166, 292
What Remains (Mann) 80
WHEN I WAS A GIRL (Chwatsky) 299–301
The White Hills; their legends, landscape and poetry (King) 88–90
White Mountains, New Hampshire 15, 66, 86–92
White Peak, Dark Peak (Hill) 168–9
Williams, Raymond 44–5, 53, 163
Williams, William Earle 76–9
'Witches Rocks, Weber Valley, Utah' (Dingus) 132
Wollen, Peter 263
women and landscape/nature 185–203
Women and Men on the Overland Trail (Faragher) 112
Wright, Patrick 163

Yorkshire moors 175
Yosemite, California 127, 136–40

'ZIN-TAH-GAT-LAT-WAH' (Renwick) 119

INDEX OF ILLUSTRATIONS

'Abandoned Field with Glacial Stone' (Pritchard) 85
Adams, Ansel 139
Adams, Robert 144
After Ski (Kapa) 247
'Alf Pugsley returning a lamb to its mother' 173
'All Ireland Walk' (Long) 287
Altered Landscapes (Pfahl) 94
American Civil War 76, 77, 78
Anarchy in Arcadia (Hesling) 191
Arcadia Project (MANUAL) 8
'Archie Parkhouse in a wood near Dolton' 173
'Artificial Boulders' (Goin) 149
Ashby, Turner 76

Baltz, Lewis 269
'Bargoed Viaduct' (Davies) 171
The Beastly Image of the Beast (Suonpää) 244
Becher, Bernd and Hilda 270
'Benches in a park …' (Frohnapfel) 283
Black Hills (South Dakota) 123
Black Kettle (Native American chief) 120
Bonnell, Sian 194
Border Horizons – Photographs from Europe (Frohnapfel) 283
Brennan, Joann 100
Bright, Deborah 70
'Brighton' (Mellor) 272

Cameron, Evelyn 116
'The Center of the Battlefield' (Huddleston) 77
Chwatsky, Anna 300
'Cloud's Rest' (Kilburn Brothers) 127
'Collapsed sheds during the Great Blizzard' (Ravilious) 173
Compton Verney (Kippin) 179
'Constellation IV' (Trangmar) 201
Consuming the American Landscape (Ganis) 141
Cooper, Thomas Joshua 293
Creates, Marlene 83
'Creek' (Hesling) 191

Dark Days (Darwell) 180
Davies, John 171
Dawson, Robert 154
Deep South (Mann) 80
Delegates: Chiefs of the Earth and Sky (Renwick) 120
Dennett, Terry 187
Derges, Susan 295
Desert Canto I: The Terrain (Misrach) 106
Devon 173
Dingus, Rick 133
Disputed Border (Haughey) 182
The Distance Between Two Points is Measured in Memories (Creates) 83
A Doubtful River (Dawson and Goin) 154
Dwelling: Expressions of Time (Pritchard) 85

'Earthmover' (Ganis) 141
'Echo Lake, Franconia Notch' (Kilburn Brothers) 92
'Electro-shocking for Apache Trout …' (Brennan) 100
Eliasson, Olafur 279
An English Eye (Ravilious) 173
Eskildsen, Joakim 231
'Et in Arcadia Ego: Observer and Tomb' (MANUAL) 98
Evans, Terry 148
'The Evil Cottage' (McAlinden) 226
Exmoor 173
'Explosion No. 1' (Magnusson) 222
Eyeshine (Grierson) 192

Fenton, Roger 29
Finland, landscape and identity of 244, 245, 247, 248, 249, 251, 256, 258
Frohnapfel, Doris 283
Futureland (Wainwright and Kippin) 177

Ganis, John 141
Gersht, Ori 298
Gettysburg (Williams) 78
Ghosting (Kempadoo) 207

331

Glacial Erratic (Bright) 70
Glover, Gina 195
Godwin, Fay 190
Gohlke, Frank 145
Goin, Peter 149
'Great Falls of the Passaic' (Pfahl) 58
A Green and Pleasant Land (Davis) 171
The Green River Series (Eliasson) 279
Grierson, Su 192
Guttu, Ane Hjort 224

'Hadrian's Wall' (Darwell) 180
Halso, Ilkha 248
Halverson, Karen 156
Hammerbeck, Wanda 151
Haughey, Anthony 182
'Haystack' (Morris) 52
Hesling, Ingrid 191
Hidden Histories, Heritage Stories (Pollard) 277
Hill, Paul 169
Horizons (Silverman) 42
'Horizon No. 9' (Silverman) 42
Huddleston, John 77
Humanature (Goin) 149

'In Line' (Gersht) 298
'Industrialisation' (Spence and Dennett) 187
Inside the View (Sear) 199
Interior/Exterior (Pirelä) 249

Jensen, Per Bak 234
Jude, Ron 101

Kapa (Kapanen), Martti 247
'Kaustinen' (Kapa) 247
Kempadoo, Roshini 207
Kennard, Peter 18
Kilburn Brothers 88, 92, 127
Killing Ground (Huddleston) 77
Kippin, John 179
Klein, Kirsten 232
Klett, Mark 131
Klingberg, Margareta 230
Knorr, Karen 160
Knudsen, Knud 219
Kovalainen, Ritva 245

Land (Godwin) 190
Landet utom sig (Tunbjörk) 228
Landscapes (for Antoine) (Jude) 101
'Larch' (Derges) 295
Liggins, Andrea 198
Liquidation (Gersht) 298

'The Long Walk' (Fenton) 29
'Lucky Pennies' (Bright) 70
Lunaatika (Merila) 241
'Lunaatika II' (Merila) 241

Magnusson, Petter 222
MANUAL 98
Mellor, Kate 272
Merila, Herkki-Erich 241
Misrach, Richard 106
Modernistic Journey (Guttu) 224
'MO-TA-VAH-TO' (Renwick) 120
Mother Land (Mann) 80
'Mount Rushmore National Monument' (Sturnfeld) 123
'Mucking Flats' (Mellor) 272
'Music 1' (Pfahl) 94
My Weather Diary (Silomäki) 256

'No. 6' (Mann) 80
'No. 13' (Sear) 199

'Öland' (Tunbjörk) 228
On Land (Hill) 169

Päiväläinen, Riitta 258
'Parti fra Odda I Hardanger' (Knudsen) 219
'Party with Rainbow at Hot Springs' (Dawson) 154
Pathways to Memory (Glover) 195
Pfahl, John 94
Pirelä, Marja 249
'Plain St., Ithaca, NY' (Jude) 101
Pollard, Ingrid 277
Power, Mark 274
Prairie Specimens (Evans) 148
'Pram' (Glover) 195
Prince, Richard 118
Pritchard, Janet 85
'Prospector Village ...' (Baltz) 269
Puranen, Jorma 210
Pyramid Lake, Nevada 154

'Raincloud above Draaby Dove' (Klein) 232
Ravilious, James 173
'Red Mudstone, Sidmouth' (Southam) 276
'Relation' (Päiväläinen) 258
Re-Modelling Photo-History (Spence and Dennett) 187
Renwick, Arthur 120
Rephotographic Survey Project 131
Requiem (Eskildsen) 231
Restoration (Halso) 248
'River Hayle January 2000' (Southam) 260

INDEX OF ILLUSTRATIONS

Rockfalls, Rivermouths and Ponds (Southam) 260, 276
'Rosie Webb, Labrador 1988' (Creates) 83
'RR Trains on Mt. Washington' (Kilburn Brothers) 88
Runnfeldt, Steve 149

'The Santa Fe' (Misrach) 106
'Sarianna' (Pirelä) 249
'Scrub' (Bonnell) 194
'Seamark' (Jensen) 234
Sear, Helen 199
Second View (Klett et al.) 131
Seppo, Sanni 245
'Sheep Crossing on Scott's Ferry' (Cameron) 116
'Shotgun Cartridges' (Haughey) 182
'Signs 2' (Treigys) 239
Silomäki, Jari 256
Silverman, Lynn 42
Southam, Jem 260, 276
Spence, Jo 187
Sternfield, Joel 123
'Steves Farm, Stevenson' (Wall) 104
The Streens (Derges) 295
Summer Nights (Robert Adams) 144
Summertime (Jämsä) 251
Suonpää, Juha 244
Suspended States (Trangmar) 201

'Teesside' (Wainwright) 177
'Tertiary Conglomerates (Witches Rocks No. 5)' (Dingus) 133
'Torness' (Grierson) 192
Trangmar, Susan 201
Tree People (Kovalainen and Seppo) 245
Treigys, Remigijus 239
Tunbjörk, Lars 228

Uncertain Terrain (Liggins) 198
'Unexpected Nightfall …' (Cooper) 293
'Untitled' (Guttu) 224
'Untitled' (Silomäki) 256
'Untitled 6' (Halso) 248
Untitled (cowboys) (Prince) 118

'Valley Oak Tree …' (Halverson) 156
Vestige – Ice (Päiväläinen) 258
The Virtues and the Delights (Knorr) 160
'The Visit' (Kippin) 179

Wainwright, Chris 177
Wall, Jeff 104
'Water Towers' (Bechers) 270
Waterfalls (Pfahl) 58
Webb, Rosie 83
'Westward Ho!' (Mellor) 272
WHEN I WAS A GIRL (Chwatsky) 300
'Wilfred Pengelly setting up stooks' (Ravilious) 173
'Witches Rocks, Weber Valley, Utah' (Dingus) 133

Yosemite, California 127, 139

333